On Divine Foreknowledge

LUIS DE MOLINA

On Divine Foreknowledge
(Part IV of the *Concordia*)

*Translated, with an Introduction
and Notes, by*
ALFRED J. FREDDOSO

Cornell University Press

ITHACA AND LONDON

Copyright © 1988 by Cornell University

All rights reserved. Except for brief quotations in a review, this book, or parts thereof, must not be reproduced in any form without permission in writing from the publisher. For information, address Cornell University Press, 124 Roberts Place, Ithaca, New York 14850.

First published 1988 by Cornell University Press.

International Standard Book Number 0-8014-2131-4
Library of Congress Catalog Card Number 88-3887
Printed in the United States of America
Librarians: Library of Congress cataloging information
appears on the last page of the book.

The paper in this book is acid-free and meets the guidelines for
permanence and durability of the Committee on Production Guidelines
for Book Longevity of the Council on Library Resources.

CONTENTS

PREFACE

Luis de Molina, S.J. (1535–1600), was a leading actor in the remarkable sixteenth-century revival of Scholasticism on the Iberian Peninsula, a revival fueled in large measure by the Protestant Reformation and the subsequent Catholic response at the Council of Trent. Though little known nowadays, Molina played a central role in one of the most tumultuous intramural doctrinal disputes in Catholic intellectual history.

The dispute, revolving around the perennial theological question of how best to reconcile the doctrine of human freedom with the doctrines of grace, providence, foreknowledge, and predestination, pitted the youthful Society of Jesus (founded in 1540) against the more established religious orders, especially Thomas Aquinas's own Dominicans. On the side of the Jesuits, self-proclaimed champions of human freedom, the main protagonists were Molina and the brilliant young luminary Francisco Suarez (1548–1617). On the side of the self-avowed defenders of divine prerogative stood the Mercederian Francisco Zumel (1540–1607) and, above all, the Dominican Domingo Bañez (1528–1604), perhaps best known as the friend and spiritual adviser of the celebrated mystic and Doctor of the Church Teresa of Avila. And as anyone familiar with this turbulent period in Church history might have anticipated, in the wings loomed the imposing figure of Cardinal Robert Bellarmine, S.J. (1542–1621), a distinguished theologian in his own right but, more important in this case, a voice of moderation and reconciliation within the often tempestuous domain of ecclesiastical politics.

The publication in 1588 of the first edition of Molina's *Concordia* ignited a fierce controversy that had already been smoldering for several years and that threatened to cause even deeper divisions in a Church still reeling from the effects of the Reformation. Political and religious leaders in Spain and Portugal finally implored the Vatican to intervene. In 1597 Pope Clement VIII established the Congregatio de Auxiliis (Commission on Grace), thus initiating a ten-year period of intense study and public disputation which rendered the *Concordia* one of the most carefully scrutinized books in Western intellectual history. For a long time things did not go well for the Jesuits; in 1600 Molina died in Madrid amid rumors that his opinions were about to be condemned in Rome. However, largely as a result of the efforts of Bellarmine and Cardinal Jacques du Perron, himself a convert from Calvinism, Molina's views emerged unscathed in the end. In 1607 Pope Paul V issued a decree forbidding the antagonists to call one another's views heretical or even temerarious, in the technical jargon of theological censure. The Holy See would, the pope continued, resolve the issue at an opportune time. It stands as a tribute to the prudence of Paul V and his successors that this "opportune" time has yet to arrive.[1]

Molina's place in the history of theology is thus well established. But this does not explain why a professional philosopher trained mainly in the "analytic tradition" should be resurrecting a relatively esoteric piece of Scholastic theology. The explanation is, in fact, quite simple: Molina's treatment of God's foreknowledge is strikingly creative and yet at the same time more deeply rooted in its proper theological setting than almost anything written on this topic in the last twenty years by analytic philosophers of religion. (This last point is extremely important; I will return to it in Section 1 of the Introduction.)

But if the explanation is simple, the path has been somewhat more circuitous. My interest in temporal modality led me naturally into the debates over freedom and divine foreknowledge. Convinced as I was (and still am) that in philosophical theology one can do no better than begin with Aquinas, in 1981 I decided to offer a graduate seminar on St. Thomas's disputed questions *De Veritate*, a work that contains his most extensive discussion of God's knowledge. The debate between Molinists and Bañezians, as it happens, finds its source at least partly in puzzles generated by the Thomistic texts. I already had been alerted to (or at least reminded of) the debate by Robert Adams's paper "Middle Knowledge and the Problem of Evil"[2] and Anthony Kenny's little book *The God of the Philosophers*.[3] With the aid of John Heitkamp, then a graduate

---

[1] Those who wish to learn more of Molina's life and the *De Auxiliis* controversy should consult Friedrich Stegmüller, "Neue Molinaschriften," *Beiträge zur Geschichte der Philosophie und Theologie des Mittelalters,* band 32 (Münster, 1935), pp. 1*–80*; and Johann Rabeneck, S.J., "De Vita et Scriptis Ludovici Molina," *Archivum Historicum Societatis Iesu* 19 (1950): 75–145. For an engaging historical account in English of the dispute itself and of Bellarmine's role in resolving it, see James Brodrick, S.J., *Robert Bellarmine: Saint and Scholar* (London, 1961), chap. 8.

[2] *American Philosophical Quarterly* 14 (1977): 109–117.

[3] Oxford, 1979.

student in the Medieval Institute at Notre Dame, I began to appreciate the complex philosophical and theological context of the *Concordia*. Because Molina's Latin was difficult for me to read at sight, I decided to make a written translation of various sections of Part IV. As I read and translated, I became more and more convinced that I did not yet have a firm enough grasp of the issues to make an intelligent contribution to the contemporary discussion. So in 1983 I abandoned the project of applying my previously published work on temporal modality to the problem of freedom and foreknowledge and instead plunged headlong into the *Concordia*. The more I conversed with colleagues about the content of the work, the more they encouraged me to translate the whole of Part IV, the section on divine foreknowledge, and make it generally available. Thus the present volume was born.

My hope is that this book as a whole will help to reshape and refocus the current discussion of divine foreknowledge in ways that make it more sensitive to the broader theological context within which questions about God's knowledge have traditionally arisen. What we learn from the history of this debate, it seems to me, are not just strategies for dealing with a problem that is already well understood, but also how to understand the problem itself and the criteria for an adequate resolution of it. There is, I am convinced, a general lesson to be learned here, since all too often the contemporary discussion of an ostensibly "traditional" theological problem turns out to have only a loose connection with the problem that those who established the tradition took themselves to be dealing with.

Now a word about the *Concordia* itself, the complete title of which is *Liberi Arbitrii cum Gratiae Donis, Divina Praescientia, Providentia, Praedestinatione et Reprobatione Concordia* [The Compatibility of Free Choice with the Gifts of Grace, Divine Foreknowledge, Providence, Predestination and Reprobation]. As mentioned above, the first edition (O) was published in 1588, and the second and revised edition (A) appeared in 1595. In addition, most sections of the *Concordia* (including almost all of Part IV) are found in parallel form in another source (C), Molina's *Commentaria in Primam Divi Thomae Partem* [Commentaries on the First Part of St. Thomas's *Summa Theologiae*], published in 1592.

Fortunately, we have an excellent critical edition of the *Concordia*, prepared by Johann Rabeneck, S.J., and published in 1953 at Oña and Madrid. Rabeneck's goal, ably accomplished, was to establish a canonical version of the second edition, correcting typographical errors and other flaws in various copies of A with alternate readings from O and C. In addition, he painstakingly tracked down and verified each of Molina's numerous references to the works of his predecessors and contemporaries. The result is an edition in which the translator can have full confidence.

The actual text of the *Concordia* occupies pages 1–611 of Rabeneck's volume. It opens with a brief two-page commentary on *Summa Theologiae* I, question 14, article 8, "Whether God's Knowledge Is a Cause of Things," and is thereafter divided into seven parts:

    I. On the Power of Free Choice [156 pages]
    II. On God's General Concurrence [64 pages]
    III. On the Assistance of Divine Grace [70 pages]
    IV. On Divine Foreknowledge [113 pages]
    V. On God's Will [24 pages]
    VI. On Divine Providence [22 pages]
    VII. On Predestination and Reprobation [158 pages]

Parts I–IV constitute Molina's strikingly extensive commentary, divided into fifty-three disputations, on a single article from the First Part of St. Thomas's *Summa Theologiae,* namely, question 14, article 13, "Whether God Has Knowledge of Future Contingents." Part IV comprises Disputations 47–52 in the first edition and Disputations 47–53 in the second edition. Disputation 53 contains Molina's long response to some of Zumel's criticisms of the first edition.

Translating Molina's Latin into English has proved to be a difficult challenge. His style has justifiably been described as "lumbering." Whether because of a Renaissance-inspired desire to emulate Cicero or simply because of the tendency toward careful qualification which naturally results when one's work is regularly being sent off by intellectual foes to the relevant ecclesiastical authorities, Molina often resorts to sentences that are twelve, thirteen, or even fourteen lines long in the critical edition. I have resisted the strong temptation to divide these sentences into shorter ones. The reason is that, after several attempts at it, I became convinced that I could not do this without altering the sense of the original. To cite a simple example, when a sentence of such length is of the form 'Since *A, B, C,* and *D,* it follows that *E,*' it is not at all clear that nothing is lost if one changes it to '*A. B. C. D.* So *E.*' I have used lowercase roman numerals and letters to mark subordinate clauses, thus making the structure of these sentences easier to grasp. Anyone who is still annoyed by the length of many of the sentences should keep in mind that the readers of the original had exactly the same complaint; even the sympathetic Bellarmine seems on occasion to have been exasperated by Molina's writing style. So in this regard I have done nothing more than preserve an arguably important feature of the Latin text. Within such constraints I have tried to make the text as readable as possible.

The notes to the translation are of three basic types: (i) explications of technical philosophical concepts with references, where appropriate, to contemporary as well as medieval sources; (ii) references to other sections of the *Concordia* and *Commentaria*; and (iii) references to works of other authors cited by Molina in the text. When a cited author is likely to be unfamiliar to contemporary readers, I have provided a brief biographical sketch. I have relied heavily on Rabeneck for references to the texts cited by Molina, though I have checked Rabeneck's citations for accuracy in cases where this was possible.

A volume of this size owes much to others. There is no better intellectual environment for engaging in philosophical theology than that nurtured by the Philosophy Department at the University of Notre Dame. Indeed, it would be difficult to name a single one of my colleagues who has not in some context or other made a comment or suggestion that led (in many cases without their knowledge) to some substantial improvement in this book. I am deeply grateful in particular to those associated over the past few years, either permanently or as visiting fellows, with Notre Dame's Center for Philosophy of Religion, especially the Reverend David Burrell, C.S.C., Thomas Flint, Laura Zimmerman Garcia, Thomas Morris, Richard Otte, Philip Quinn, and David Widerker, each of whom has had a significant impact on this project.

At various points along the way I have benefited as well from suggestions made by Robert Audi, William Craig, William Hasker, Christopher Menzel, and Robert Sleigh. (Sleigh has encouraged me, perhaps unintentionally, to become, *per impossibile*, even more strident than I was before in insisting that a close study of sixteenth- and early seventeenth-century Scholasticism will contribute immensely to our understanding of pre-Kantian modern philosophy.) In addition, a number of graduate students in both the Philosophy Department and the Medieval Institute at Notre Dame have by their persistence forced me to dig deeper into the issues surrounding divine foreknowledge. They include Stephen Bilynskyj, John Heitkamp, Stephen Julian, Kevin Kolbeck, Thomas Loughran, John Rylander, Jonathan Strand, and Jerry Walls.

Nor could I in good conscience fail to thank my readers, Scott MacDonald and Eleonore Stump, who carefully scrutinized the entire manuscript and made enough incisive criticisms to keep me busy making revisions throughout the summer months of 1987. It is hard to imagine two more astute reader reports than theirs.

Work on this project has been generously supported by a Research Materials Grant from the National Endowment for the Humanities, whose overworked staff has always treated me with exceptional patience and courtesy, and by a summer grant from Notre Dame's Institute for Scholarship in the Liberal Arts, under the able leadership of Michael Loux and Nathan Hatch.

Finally, I wish to single out for special thanks and praise a brilliant philosopher and splendid man whose influence on my thought and, more important, my life has been more profound than either of us can fully appreciate *in statu viatoris*. To Alvin Plantinga I dedicate this book.

ALFRED J. FREDDOSO

Notre Dame, Indiana

On Divine Foreknowledge

INTRODUCTION

This introduction has three main purposes. First, I have tried to provide enough background from Parts I–III of the *Concordia* to put the reader in a position to grasp the modal notions and account of freedom presupposed in Part IV. Second, I have tried to make Molina's own theory and his criticisms of alternative theories more accessible to contemporary readers than an untutored perusal of Part IV might allow. Third, I have indicated ways in which a contemporary Molinist might attempt to respond to the most common objections to Molina's theory of middle knowledge. Thus the last section of the Introduction complements Disputation 53, Part 4, where Molina himself responds to some objections.

1 Foreknowledge and Providence

1.1 *Two Questions about Foreknowledge*

In Part IV of the *Concordia* Molina comes to grips with two distinct questions concerning God's knowledge:

(a) How is it that God knows future contingents with certainty, that is, what is the source of and explanation for the fact that God knows future contingents with certainty?

(b) How is this divine foreknowledge to be reconciled with the contingency of what is known through it?

I will call (a) the *source-question* and (b) the *reconciliation-question*. Both questions stand in need of amplification, but for now I will assume that their import is plain enough for us to broach the key but often neglected issue of how they bear on each other.

[1]

The problem posed by the reconciliation-question cannot be fully comprehended until we grasp clearly the criteria for an adequate answer to the source-question. This assertion is bound to strike some as peculiar. The central philosophical difficulty posed by God's foreknowledge of future contingents, they will contend, is how to reconcile it with the contingency of its objects and, more specifically, with creaturely free choice. But an answer to the source-question is obviously not germane to *that* problem. Perhaps it is just a brute inexplicable fact that God has foreknowledge; perhaps not. But in any case it matters little as far as the reconciliation-question is concerned how God comes by His foreknowledge.

Although this attitude appears to be widespread today, it is nonetheless profoundly misguided. Indeed, its very pervasiveness is symptomatic of the surprising extent to which the lively contemporary discussion of foreknowledge and freedom is detached from the theological context within which perplexities about foreknowledge and contingency have traditionally arisen.[1]

I do not, of course, mean to deny that the reconciliation of freedom and contingency with *any* sort of foreknowledge is extremely problematic. I will call this the problem of *simple* precognition. However, I do mean to affirm that the problem of *divine* precognition runs far deeper than the problem of simple precognition. To understand exactly why, we must begin by recognizing that the belief in divine foreknowledge is not in itself a foundational tenet of classical Western theism. Instead, it derives its lofty theological status from its intimate connection with the absolutely central doctrine that God is perfectly provident. But the doctrine of providence carries with it a causal dimension that virtually guarantees that no solution to the problem of *simple* precognition, even comprehensive and infallible precognition, will constitute a full and adequate solution to the problem of *divine* precognition.

1.2   *The Doctrine of Providence*

Let me elaborate this last point and in so doing set the stage for Molina's treatment of divine foreknowledge. As traditionally expounded,

---

[1] For an excellent overview of the recent literature, see William Hasker, "Foreknowledge and Necessity," *Faith and Philosophy* 2 (1985): 121–157. At one point (p. 125) Hasker explicitly sets aside the question of *how* God knows the contingent future, even though he later (p. 140) acknowledges the connection in traditional theology between divine foreknowledge and the doctrine that God has providentially prearranged things "in view of this knowledge." Notice, too, that the relationship between foreknowledge and providence must be more complex than this last remark suggests. For God's providential act of will must in some way be prior to His knowing the *actual* or *absolute* future. Otherwise, His foreknowledge would present Him with a fait accompli. More on this below.

the doctrine of divine providence involves the thesis that God, the divine artisan, freely and knowingly plans, orders, and provides for all the effects that constitute His artifact, the created universe with its entire history, and executes His chosen plan by playing an active causal role sufficient to ensure its exact realization. Since God is the perfect artisan, not even the most trivial details escape His providential decrees. Thus, whatever occurs is properly said to be *specifically decreed* by God; more precisely, each effect produced in the created universe is either specifically and knowingly *intended* by Him (*providentia approbationis*) or, in concession to creaturely defectiveness, specifically and knowingly *permitted* by Him, only to be then ordered toward some appropriate good (*providentia concessionis*).[2]

So divine providence has both a cognitive and a volitional aspect. By His prevolitional knowledge God knows with certainty which effects would result, directly or indirectly, from any causal contribution He might choose to make to the created sphere.[3] This prevolitional knowledge is potentially practical knowledge. That is, it serves as a principle of action capable of being directed by an appropriate act of the divine will toward the purposeful production of particular created effects—in much the same way that the artisan's prevolitional knowledge is a principle of action capable of being directed by an appropriate intention toward the purposeful production of particular artifacts. This is why medieval theologians were wont to assert that God's prevolitional knowledge is a cause of things.[4] The volitional aspect of divine providence has

[2]See Aquinas, *Summa Theologiae* I, q. 22, a. 1–4, and q. 103, a. 1–8; and *De Veritate*, q. 5, a. 1–10. In *De Veritate*, q. 5, a. 4, St. Thomas attributes the distinction between *providentia approbationis* and *providentia concessionis* to St. John Damascene, *De Fide Orthodoxa* II, chap. 29. Here and in what follows I join Molina in using the term 'intend' to cover whatever God wills either antecedently or consequently. For an explanation of this distinction see Disputation 53, pt. 3, n. 13.

Near the end of Part IV Molina emphasizes against certain unnamed critics that his own theory does indeed entail that *every* effect—evil as well as nonevil—is individually decreed by God. See Disputation 53, pt. 3, secs. 7–8 and 14–18.

[3]By dubbing such knowledge *prevolitional* I mean to point to a *conceptual* or *logical*, rather than *temporal*, ordering within the divine knowledge. Here I follow Molina, who claims repeatedly that such an ordering has a basis in reality. See especially Disputation 53, pt. 1, sec. 20.

[4]See, e.g., Aquinas, *Summa Theologiae* I, q. 14, a. 8. Molina comments on this article at the very beginning of the *Concordia*. See Johann Rabeneck, ed., *Luis de Molina, S.J.: Liberi Arbitrii cum Gratiae Donis, Divina Praescientia, Providentia, Praedestinatione et Reprobatione Concordia* (Oña and Madrid, 1953), pp. 3–4 (hereafter cited as Rabeneck). St. Thomas holds that God's prevolitional knowledge, that is, the knowledge God has independently of any free act of will on His part, is a *remote* cause of created effects, whereas His providential act of will is a *proximate* cause of those effects. Since, as we shall see, God makes a causal contribution to *every* created effect, including those brought about by free created causes, it follows that God's prevolitional knowledge is a (partial) remote cause of free human choices and acts. Hence, Stephen Davis is mistaken in his conjecture that St. Thomas

two distinct but complementary moments. First, God chooses one from among the infinity of total sequences of created effects which are within His power to bring about, where, according to orthodoxy, the choice not to create anything at all is a limiting option always open to Him. Second and concomitantly, He wills to make a causal contribution that He knows with certainty will result in His chosen plan's being effected down to the last detail.

This thumbnail sketch delineates a broad array of assumptions shared by Molina and his Bañezian rivals.[5] Yet it also leaves unresolved an equally wide range of critical issues that spawned rancorous disputes among sixteenth-century Catholic theologians, issues Molina deals with at length in the *Concordia*: What precisely does God know by His prevolitional knowledge and what constraints, if any, does that knowledge impose on the scope of His power? What are the modes of God's causal activity in the created universe? What causal contribution does He make to the sinful or otherwise defective effects that He permits? Exactly how is God's causal involvement to be reconciled with the attribution of genuine causal power to created substances and, in particular, with the attribution of free choice to rational creatures? More fundamentally, what is the nature of contingency and of free choice?

I delve into these difficulties below, but for the moment I will highlight the shared assumptions in order to make clear just how the two questions we began with are related to each other. Molinists and Bañezians agree that it is *because* He is perfectly provident that God has comprehensive knowledge of what will occur in the created order. More precisely, God's speculative postvolitional knowledge of the created world—His so-called knowledge of vision—is to be explained *wholly* by reference to (i) His prevolitional knowledge and (ii) His knowledge of what He Himself has willed to do. Unlike us, God does not have to be acted upon by outside causes in order for His cognitive potentialities to be fully actualized; He

---

means to exempt free human actions from the dictum that God's knowledge is a cause of things. See Davis's *Logic and the Nature of God* (Grand Rapids, Mich., 1983), pp. 64–65. This issue is discussed more fully in Section 2 below.

[5]I do not want to give the impression that Bañezianism and Molinism exhausted the field in sixteenth-century Catholic debates over divine foreknowledge of future contingents. Indeed, in Disputations 49 and 51 Molina criticizes two other positions, positions that in Section 3 below I call the eternalist theory and the concomitance theory. Nonetheless, it is fair to say that Bañezianism and Molinism were the dominant positions in late sixteenth-century Catholic theology.

In what follows I use the terms 'Bañezian' and 'Bañezianism' to designate the position, to be spelled out in some detail below, which Molina saw as his chief rival. This position is very often referred to as 'Thomism' in the Catholic theological literature on divine foreknowledge. I will refrain from calling it such, however, mainly in deference to those who have insisted, rightly or wrongly, that Bañez departed radically from St. Thomas.

does not, as it were, have to look outside Himself in order to find out what His creative act has wrought. (Indeed, as a being who is 'pure actuality', He *cannot* depend causally on any other being for His perfections.) Rather, He knows 'in Himself' what will happen precisely because He knows just what causal role He has freely chosen to play within the created order and because He knows just what will result given this causal contribution on His part.

In short, no contingent truth grasped by the knowledge of vision can be true prior to, even conceptually prior to, God's specifically intending or permitting it to be true or to His specifically willing to make the appropriate causal contribution toward its truth. This explains the spirit behind Aquinas's hard saying that whereas we humans acquire truth by conforming our intellects to the created world, the created world itself is capable of yielding such truth only because it in turn, as a necessary condition for its very existence, conforms to the intellect of the transcendent divine artisan.[6] Accordingly, since it is *divine* foreknowledge of future contingents we are concerned with, and not just *simple* foreknowledge of future contingents, an adequate answer to the source-question must essentially appeal to God's active causal role in the created world and must eschew even the faintest suggestion that God's knowledge of effects produced in the created world is causally dependent on the activity of His creatures.

1.3 *Two Consequences*

This intertwining of the doctrines of divine foreknowledge and divine providence has two important consequences for our understanding of the reconciliation-question, one obvious and the other more subtle. First, the problem posed by the reconciliation-question is more extensive than the problem of simple precognition, since a *complete* answer to the reconciliation-question must include *both* a solution to the problem of simple precognition *and* a solution to the problem of how to reconcile contingency and freedom with the fact that God knows the future, including the contingent future, because He has providential control over its being the way it is.

The second and less obvious consequence is this: Unless we keep the close bond between providence and foreknowledge vividly in mind, we

---

[6]See Aquinas, *De Veritate*, q. 1, a. 2, for an especially clear statement of this point. Notice that God's speculative knowledge, as so conceived, does not correspond to the knowledge that might be had by an ideal observer viewing the world from an 'absolute' or 'purely epistemic' point of view. To the contrary, God's knowledge of vision is the speculative knowledge had by a provident creator who causally contributes to what He knows.

are likely to be tempted by solutions to the problem of divine precognition which are incompatible with the doctrine of divine providence. For instance, certain Ockhamistic solutions seem to entail (i) that free creatures cause God to have (or have had) the beliefs about future contingents He actually has and also (ii) that those same creatures have the power to cause God to have (or have had) beliefs about future contingents contrary to those He in fact has.[7] Similarly, one standard "Thomistic" solution involves the claim that God has something akin to *perceptual* knowledge of future contingents, the main difference between God and us being that His perceptual field has no spatial or temporal limitations.[8] So stated, this solution apparently entails that God acquires His knowledge of vision from created things themselves and thus that true future contingents have their truth conceptually, if not temporally, prior to God's intending or permitting them to be true. (I will return to St. Thomas in a moment.) Still other responses to the reconciliation-question in essence dissolve the problem of divine precognition by limiting the scope of God's knowledge. Some philosophers have argued, for example, that even if God has all the knowledge of the created world anyone could possibly have, this is still not enough for Him to have the certain and comprehensive knowledge of future contingents attributed to Him by traditional philosophical theology—so that in creating the world God freely chooses to keep Himself partially ignorant of the future in order to allow for the possibility of creaturely freedom.[9] Clearly, if the picture of divine providence sketched above is

---

[7]I myself must plead guilty here, since I at least hint at such a position in "Accidental Necessity and Power over the Past," *Pacific Philosophical Quarterly* 63 (1982): 54–68, and "Accidental Necessity and Logical Determinism," *Journal of Philosophy* 80 (1983): 257–278. Whether this position is actually Ockham's is a moot point. His own discussions of future contingency appear in Marilyn McCord Adams and Norman Kretzmann, trans., *William Ockham: Predestination, God's Foreknowledge and Future Contingents*, 2d ed. (Indianapolis, Ind., 1983).

For recent criticisms of Ockhamistic replies to the reconciliation-question, see Hasker, "Foreknowledge and Necessity," sec. IV, pp. 130–137; and John Martin Fischer, "Freedom and Foreknowledge," *Philosophical Review* 92 (1983): 67–79, and "Ockhamism," *Philosophical Review* 94 (1985): 81–100. Some of the relevant issues are treated in Sections 3.4 and 4.5 below.

[8]This position, which may or may not be St. Thomas's, is discussed at some length in Section 3.2 below. Notice that it is not necessary to appeal to God's eternity or timelessness in order to make use of a perceptual model. Stephen Davis employs such a model in *Logic and the Nature of God*, pp. 52–67, though he denies that God is timeless.

[9]This thesis has recently been defended or at least looked upon with kindness by a number of highly influential authors. See, e.g., J. R. Lucas, *The Freedom of the Will* (Oxford, 1970), pp. 75–77; Richard Swinburne, *The Coherence of Theism* (Oxford, 1977), pp. 172–178; Peter Geach, *Providence and Evil* (Cambridge, 1977), pp. 40–66; and Robert Adams, "Middle Knowledge and the Problem of Evil," *American Philosophical Quarterly* 14 (1977): 109–117, and "Alvin Plantinga on the Problem of Evil," pp. 225–255 in James Tomberlin and Peter Van Inwagen, eds., *Alvin Plantinga* (Dordrecht, Holland, 1985).

an important constituent of orthodox belief, then no such responses to the reconciliation-question are acceptable.

Admittedly, many modern theologians and philosophers have jettisoned this strong conception of divine providence, ultimately, it seems, on the ground that it excludes genuine contingency and genuine human freedom. Molina, like St. Thomas before him, would undoubtedly respond in the first place that the theological authority of Scripture and Tradition, along with sound philosophical scrutiny of the notion of a perfect being, militates forcefully against any such move. But Molina's work is especially noteworthy and exciting precisely because he is prepared to meet the modern challenge on its own terms. To wit, he begins with exceptionally strong notions of contingency and freedom and goes on to argue with much ingenuity that these notions mesh perfectly with an equally strong interpretation of the doctrine of divine providence. What's more, as I argue below, the objections to Molina's theory, although not without merit, are by no means decisive. We should be wary, then, of being swept too easily into thinking that the reconciliation-question cannot be given a plausible answer unless the doctrine of divine providence is in effect eviscerated.

1.4   *The Role of St. Thomas*

Having fixed the broad systematic context for the sixteenth-century debate over divine foreknowledge, I will now show briefly how the work of St. Thomas helped shape the concrete dialectical parameters of that debate. As noted in the Preface, Part IV of the *Concordia* constitutes one segment of Molina's remarkably extensive commentary on question 14, article 13 of the First Part of the *Summa Theologiae*. In that place, as well as in question 2, article 12 of the earlier disputed questions *De Veritate* (though not, curiously, in *Summa Contra Gentiles* I, chapter 67), St. Thomas uses perceptual models to explain his contention that all temporal things—past, present, and future—are present to God in eternity and hence that future contingents are known by Him as present rather than as future. This apparently led many commentators to attribute to St. Thomas the view, discussed by Molina in Disputation 49, that the presence of things to God in eternity is by itself a sufficient ground for His knowing future contingents with certainty. Like us, God perceives what is present to Him; unlike us, He has present to Himself all past and future entities. And since perceiving something to be the case does not entail causing it to be the case, God's knowledge of future contingents is compatible with their contingency.

But this cannot be the whole story. As is abundantly evident from the Thomistic corpus taken as a whole, St. Thomas never intends to suggest that God is a passive recipient of information about the created world. To the contrary, in many places he states quite unambiguously that the created world is known by God just as an artifact is known by the artisan who has fashioned it; and in equally many places he explicitly denies that created things are a cause of God's knowledge of them.[10] Why, then, does he resort to perceptual models? Why does he not instead emphasize God's providential designs and His active causal contribution to the future? Does he recognize a tension here? If not, is it because he is uncharacteristically blind to a real problem or instead because he believes upon reflection that there is no problem?

Such questions helped define the particular dialectical context of the sixteenth-century disputes over grace, foreknowledge, divine causation, providence, predestination, and reprobation.[11] In fact, both Bañezianism and Molinism are probably best regarded as alternative attempts to compensate for what many Catholic thinkers, especially in light of the Reformers' influential writings on these very matters, took to be a lacuna or at least a lack of explicitness in St. Thomas's work.

Of course, some commentators, then and now, have wished a plague on both Bañez and Molina, claiming in effect that both sides misinterpret St. Thomas, who himself had long before forged an acceptable *via media* between their extreme positions. Maybe so, though in fairness to Molina and Bañez and perhaps to St. Thomas himself, I should report that I for one do not find the arguments for this claim very convincing.[12]

---

[10]See, e.g., *Summa Theologiae* I, q. 14, a. 5, 8, and 16; *De Veritate*, q. 2, a. 3 and 14; *Summa Contra Gentiles* I, chap. 65, and II, chap. 24.

[11]See the beginning of Disputation 49 (secs. 1–7) for Molina's own convoluted discussion of how St. Thomas ought to be interpreted.

I should acknowledge here that the historical sketch I have given, although accurate as far as it goes, pays scant attention to the lively fourteenth- and fifteenth-century debates over future contingency, debates that very often issued in distinctively non-Thomistic accounts of divine foreknowledge. For the relevant historical background and a philosophically sophisticated discussion of the key issues, see Calvin Normore, "Future Contingents," pp. 358–381 in Norman Kretzmann, Anthony Kenny, and Jan Pinborg, eds., *The Cambridge History of Later Medieval Philosophy* (New York, 1982), and "Divine Omniscience, Omnipotence and Future Contingents: An Overview," pp. 3–22 in T. Rudavsky, ed., *Divine Omniscience and Omnipotence in Medieval Philosophy* (Dordrecht, Holland, 1985). I have included in the Bibliography references to several translations by Norman Kretzmann of fourteenth- and fifteenth-century material, as well as several Kretzmann translations of medieval commentaries on chapter 9 of Aristotle's *De Interpretatione*.

Molina, it should be noted, lumps together the various non-Thomistic positions and deals with them en masse in Disputation 51. See Section 3.4 below.

[12]For some recent attempts to articulate and defend an alternative "Thomistic" position, see Mark Pontifex, *Freedom and Providence* (New York, 1960); Dom M. John Farrelly, O.S.B., *Predestination, Grace and Free Will* (Westminster, Md., 1964); Jacques Maritain, *God and the Permission of Evil* (Milwaukee, 1966); Bernard Lonergan, S.J., *Grace and Freedom* (New York, 1971); and James Ross, "Creation II," pp. 115–141 in Alfred J. Freddoso, ed.,

1.5 An Outline of What Follows

In what follows I discuss the main theses of Part IV of the *Concordia*.
Section 2 is devoted to Molina's account of contingency and freedom,
and I there explicate the causal modalities he makes use of in his discussion of the relation between providence and foreknowledge. Section 3
focuses on his critique of the major alternatives to his own view of how
God foreknows future contingents with certainty. In Section 4 I expound Molina's controversial theory of middle knowledge and examine
his attempt to reconcile freedom and foreknowledge. Finally, in Section
5 I briefly address the most important objections to the theory of middle
knowledge.

2 Contingency and Freedom

2.1 Preliminary Comments

Part IV of the *Concordia* opens with a brief discourse on contingency
and its sources. After making a few remarks about the bearers of modal
attributes and about metaphysical and temporal modality, I sketch an
account of causal modality meant to serve as a backdrop for Molina's
assertions about divine causation, contingent effects, and future contingency. I then turn to his account of creaturely free choice and to his
views on natural, as opposed to free, indeterministic causation.

Part I of the *Concordia* is devoted to free choice and Part II to causation, both divine and creaturely. Since Part IV presupposes a familiarity
with at least the main contours of Parts I and II, this section of the
Introduction furnishes the reader with the metaphysical background
required for a thorough appreciation of Molina's discussion of God's
foreknowledge.

2.2 The Bearers of Modal Attributes

Molina typically ascribes modal attributes such as necessity and contingency to states of affairs (*complexiones*) and propositions (*complexiones*
or *propositiones* or *enuntiationes*), entities that, he assumes throughout,
are eternally and indeed necessarily available as objects of God's intel-

---

The Existence and Nature of God (Notre Dame, Ind., 1983). In Section 3.4 below I discuss in
general some of the problems afflicting any position that tries to mediate between
Bañezianism and Molinism. In addition, I hope to articulate in another place some specific
difficulties I have with the works just alluded to—especially Lonergan's, which is probably
the most subtle and certainly the most influential.

lect, related in some intimate fashion to the divine ideas attributed to
God almost unanimously by medieval theologians.[13]

As just intimated, Molina's use of the Latin term *complexio* oscillates
between the English terms 'proposition' and 'state of affairs'. Accordingly, I will simply assume that there is an exact isomorphism between
propositions and states of affairs. That is, to each proposition there
corresponds just one state of affairs, and vice versa; and a proposition is
true (false) if and only if the corresponding state of affairs obtains (fails
to obtain). In addition, Molina takes propositions and states of affairs to
be tensed, though he reserves a special use of present-tense verbs to
express the *eternal* rather than the *temporal* present.[14] Future contingents are thus properly construed as future-tense propositions or states
of affairs of a certain sort to be specified below.

Three distinct types of modality play a prominent role in Part IV, and
I deal with them one by one. In so doing I speak only of states of affairs,
leaving it to the reader to formulate the matching theses about propositions. Also, I make use of the currently popular notion of a possible
world, taking it for granted that the idea of a total and comprehensive
way things might have been is tolerably clear in itself and intuitively
accessible to the reader.

2.3   *Metaphysical Modality*

The first type of modality is what I call (though Molina does not)
metaphysical modality. Metaphysical necessity and impossibility are the
strongest species of necessity and impossibility. A metaphysically necessary state of affairs is one that obtains no matter what, whereas a metaphysically impossible state of affairs is one that fails to obtain no matter
what. States of affairs corresponding to elementary mathematical and
logical truths are normally taken to be paradigmatic instances of metaphysically necessary states of affairs, whereas their complements (or negations) are paradigmatic instances of metaphysically impossible states
of affairs. Metaphysical contingency, on the other hand, is the weakest
species of contingency. A metaphysically contingent state of affairs is one
that might obtain and that also might fail to obtain, where 'might' is taken
in the widest sense. For instance, Sandra Day O'Connor's having served

---

[13]It may be that abstract entities such as properties, states of affairs, and propositions
should simply be *identified with* various elements (predicates, sentences, nominalizations of
sentences) in the language of the divine mind. For an argument on behalf of this thesis, see
Michael J. Loux, "Towards an Aristotelian Theory of Abstract Objects," *Midwest Studies in
Philosophy* 11 (1986): 495–512.

[14]See Disputation 48, sec. 8.

on the Supreme Court in 1985 is a state of affairs which might never have obtained, even though it in fact obtains and indeed cannot any longer (in 1986) be made not to obtain. Again, even if the water on my stove is now being made to boil by causes that have necessitated its boiling, still the water's boiling at this time is a metaphysically contingent state of affairs. For the water might never have existed, and even given its existence, it might never have been acted upon by causes that would make it boil at the present time.

We can put all this into possible-worlds jargon as follows, where 'S' designates a state of affairs:

S is *metaphysically necessary* if and only if S obtains at every moment in every possible world.

S is *metaphysically impossible* if and only if S does not obtain at any moment in any possible world.

S is *metaphysically contingent* if and only if S is neither metaphysically necessary nor metaphysically impossible.

God's prevolitional knowledge of all the metaphysically necessary states of affairs is called His *natural* knowledge.[15] Molina maintains that God's natural knowledge could not have had objects other than those it in fact has. The reason is that for any state of affairs S, S's having the metaphysical modality it has is itself a metaphysically necessary state of affairs.[16] If S is metaphysically contingent, then the state of affairs of S's being metaphysically contingent is itself metaphysically necessary—and likewise if S is metaphysically necessary or impossible. In short, what is metaphysically necessary or impossible or contingent does not vary from one possible world to another. So God has the same natural knowledge in every possible world in which He exists and has any natural knowledge at all, and, in addition, by His natural knowledge He knows the metaphysical modality of every state of affairs. What's more, if we grant with Molina and his contemporaries that God's existing and being all-knowing are themselves metaphysically necessary, it follows further that God has exactly the same natural knowledge in every possible world. It is, so to speak, part of His nature to know all the metaphysically necessary states of affairs—and this is one reason such knowledge is called *natural*.

---

[15] In calling such knowledge prevolitional I do not, of course, mean to imply that God lacks it after His act of will. I simply mean to contrast it with the sort of knowledge, namely, *free* knowledge, that God has only posterior to, and because of, His act of will. (Once again, the ordering relations invoked here are *conceptual* and not *temporal*.)

[16] See Disputation 50, sec. 6.

According to Molina, metaphysical modality "pertains to the natures" of things.[17] To know a thing's nature is, in technical terms, to *comprehend* it, and to comprehend it is, as Molina puts it, to know "all the possible modes of the thing," that is, to know the exact range of its metaphysical possibilities.[18] But this, it seems, is just to know the metaphysical modality of each state of affairs that involves it. So God's natural knowledge includes a perfect comprehension of the natures of all possible entities—and this is another reason for calling it *natural*.

Notice that God's natural knowledge includes a comprehensive grasp of all the active and passive causal powers creatures might have and exercise, since such causal powers are ultimately rooted in their natures.[19] What's more, by His natural knowledge God knows all the possible spatial and temporal arrangements of creaturely agents and patients and hence knows all the ways in which they might causally interact with one another. And by His natural knowledge He also knows prevolitionally (i) what *would* result from any possible causal interaction in which all the relevant created causes act deterministically and (ii) what *might* result from any possible causal interaction in which some created cause acts indeterministically. This is why, as explained in Section 1, God's natural knowledge is, like that of an artisan, potentially a cause of things.

Still, God does not by His natural knowledge know which, if any, states of affairs *will actually* obtain by virtue of the causal activity of created substances. This He can know only by His postvolitional or *free* knowledge. For all such states of affairs are metaphysically contingent and, in addition, their obtaining at any given time is a function not only (i) of the 'intrinsic' natures of the relevant created causes but also (ii) of the 'extrinsic' arrangement of those causes at the time in question and, even more fundamentally, (iii) of God's free decision to create, conserve, and cooperate with them.

So all states of affairs which obtain because of the causal activity of created substances are metaphysically contingent.[20] Still, as Molina is quick to emphasize, such contingency

---

[17]See Disputation 47, sec. 2, and Disputation 50, sec. 6.

[18]See Disputation 52, sec. 9, and Disputation 53, pt. 1, secs. 18 and 20.

[19]This, at least, is the standard view of medieval Aristotelians. For a recent attempt to articulate and defend some of the central elements of this view, see my "The Necessity of Nature," *Midwest Studies in Philosophy* 11 (1986): 215–242. Among these central elements is the claim that laws of nature are metaphysically necessary propositions linking causal powers, tendencies, and dispositions with natural kinds. See pp. 231–236 of the paper just mentioned.

[20]What I have said does not imply that *all* metaphysically contingent states of affairs known by God are known through His *free* knowledge. This is so only for metaphysically

does not rule out fatalistic necessity. For if all agents acted by a necessity of nature, then, without a doubt, even if nothing pertaining to the natures of the terms were incompatible with things turning out otherwise, everything that occurs would still, in relation to its causes as constituted and arranged in such a universe, occur with a fatalistic and infallible necessity in just the way it in fact occurs.[21]

So if there is to be genuine indeterminism and freedom, then some states of affairs which obtain because of created causes must be not only metaphysically contingent but also contingent in a way that "rules out the fatalistic and extrinsic necessity that results from the arrangement of causes."[22] This is *causal* or *natural* contingency, and I deal with it below, in Section 2.5.

2.4 Temporal Modality

Before that, however, I must introduce another type of modality indispensable to any sophisticated treatment of foreknowledge and free-dom, namely, *temporal* or *accidental* modality.[23] This modality has to do neither with the natures of things nor with the arrangement of causes in the universe, but rather with the mere passage of time. For some meta-physically contingent states of affairs become necessary simply by virtue of being fixed unalterably as part of the history of the world, regardless of their causal ancestry.

Suppose Susannah played baseball at some past time T. Then the metaphysically contingent state of affairs of Susannah's having played baseball at T is now necessary in such a way that it can no longer be caused not to obtain; and its complement is now impossible in such a way that it can no longer be caused to obtain. Any possible world sharing the same history with our world at the present moment (call it T^*) is such that at no time at or after T^* in that world can anyone or anything cause it to be false that Susannah played baseball at T or cause it to be true that she did not play baseball at T. And this is so even if she *freely* played baseball at T.

---

contingent states of affairs whose obtaining constitutes a created *causal effect* in one of the ways to be spelled out below. In fact, Molina's theory of middle knowledge is distinctive precisely because it entails that God has *prevolitional* knowledge of some metaphysically contingent states of affairs, namely, conditional future contingents. More on this in Sections 2.8 and 4.2 below.

[21] Disputation 47, sec. 2.

[22] Ibid.

[23] For some background, see my "Accidental Necessity and Logical Determinism." (As I note in Section 4.5, however, I no longer subscribe to the account of accidental necessity laid out in that paper.)

In Section 4, below, we see that an exact characterization of the accidental modalities cannot be given unless we first take a stand on certain controversial issues, issues with regard to which Molina himself holds a minority view. However, all sides agree at least that a state of affairs is now accidentally contingent if it can still be caused to obtain and still be caused not to obtain. They also concur that this sort of contingency, although stronger than metaphysical contingency, is too weak to rule out that "fatalistic and extrinsic necessity that results from the arrangement of causes." For even if a metaphysically contingent state of affairs is now accidentally contingent as well, its obtaining or not obtaining at some future time might nonetheless be wholly determined by presently operative causes. Real freedom requires an even stronger notion of contingency. To this I now turn.

2.5 Causal Modality

To appreciate Molina's account of causal contingency we must have at least a rough grasp of the metaphysical framework within which the medieval Aristotelians approach questions concerning causal modality and efficient causation. I have elsewhere developed and defended this framework at some length.[24] So my treatment of it here is relatively elementary and informal, even at the risk of oversimplification.

The medieval Aristotelians conceive of the created world as a dynamic system of interacting substances endowed by nature with causal powers, dispositions, and inclinations. Their natures thus delimit the range of causal contributions, both active and passive, which created substances can make toward the production of effects. In typical cases certain substances (agents) act upon other substances (patients) to produce a given effect.[25] So efficient causation is a relation holding between substances (agents and patients) on the one hand and states of affairs on the other.[26] For instance, in a given set of circumstances a gas flame acts

[24]See my "The Necessity of Nature." Also, for a discussion of some of the philosophical and theological issues at stake in the debate between Aristotelian and occasionalist philosophies of nature, see my "Medieval Aristotelianism and the Case Against Secondary Causation in Nature," in Thomas V. Morris, ed., *Divine and Human Action: Essays in the Metaphysics of Theism* (Ithaca, 1988).

[25]An *atypical* case that plays a central role in medieval philosophy and theology is that of creation *ex nihilo*, in which God acts to bring about a created effect but does not act *on* any patient in so doing.

[26]The states of affairs in question ordinarily involve states of the substances that are acted upon. Whether all such states must be thought of as involving accidents inhering in these substances is a moot ontological question that would receive different answers from different medieval Scholastics.

upon a steel kettle filled with water in such a way as to bring about the state of affairs of the water's boiling.

The system is dynamic because the various substances are poised to make characteristic causal contributions in the appropriate circumstances unless they are in some way impeded or prevented from doing so. In the above example the water will boil unless something either stops the action of the gas flame or removes the water from the sphere of its causal influence. So the causal contribution actually made at any given time by a group of potentially interacting substances is a function both of the causal powers they have and of their being in a position to exercise those powers at that time.

Deterministic causation results when the relevant substances are such that given the opportunity to exercise their causal powers, they automatically come together to bring about the unique effect to which they are naturally ordered in the relevant circumstances. When I put the kettle of water over the gas flame at time T^*, I have initiated a deterministic causal chain that, if left unimpeded, will result in the water's boiling at some future time, say T. Of course, one deterministic causal chain of this sort might be impeded by another. If a piece of plaster falls from the ceiling just after T^* and knocks the kettle off the stove, then the water will not boil at T. But suppose that no other chain of deterministic causes is poised to interfere with the one in question. In that case we can reasonably attribute to the world itself an all-things-considered deterministic propensity toward the water's boiling at T. I will call this sort of propensity a *deterministic natural tendency*. And if the water boils at T as a result of this tendency, then the state of affairs of its boiling *obtains by a necessity of nature* at T. So a deterministic natural tendency is an all-things-considered deterministic propensity on the part of the world toward a given state of affairs S at a given time t, a propensity that, if left unimpeded by indeterministic causes, issues forth in S's obtaining at t by a necessity of nature.

In the place cited above I have proposed a detailed analysis of the concept of a deterministic natural tendency. The informal remarks above have been, I trust, sufficient to render this notion passably clear and to motivate the following rough characterization of causal or natural necessity, impossibility and contingency:

S is *naturally necessary* (or *obtains by a necessity of nature*) at t if and only if S obtains at t by virtue of the world's having at t^* (at or before t) a deterministic natural tendency toward S at t.

S is *naturally impossible* (or *fails by a necessity of nature to obtain*) at t if and only if the complement of S obtains at t by virtue of the world's having at t^* (at or before t) a deterministic natural tendency toward it at t.

S is *naturally contingent* at *t* if and only if *S* is (i) metaphysically contingent, and (ii) accidentally contingent at *t*, and (iii) neither naturally necessary nor naturally impossible at *t*.

So a present-tense state of affairs which obtains at a time *t* is naturally contingent at *t* only if it is caused to obtain at *t directly* by an *indeterministic* cause. As we shall see below, natural contingency as thus explicated is too narrow a notion to encompass everything that Molina wants to classify under the rubric of a *contingent effect*. But it is nonetheless true that nothing will count as a contingent effect unless at least *some* states of affairs which actually obtain are naturally contingent at the times they obtain.

Now suppose that all the causal contributions of created agents themselves resulted from deterministic natural tendencies. Then every causal effect of created agents would obtain by a necessity of nature. In short, the world would be thoroughly deterministic. This bears out Molina's claim that "if all agents acted by a necessity of nature, then . . . any cause that . . . was able to [read, had the power to *and* was in a position to] impede another cause would in fact impede it."[27] For the intersection of any two or more deterministic causal chains would itself occur by a necessity of nature.

By contrast, if the world is *not* utterly deterministic, then there are substances whose causal activity is not always determined to a unique effect by the conjunction of their intrinsic natures with the extrinsic arrangement of causes in the universe. Such substances are thus (i) capable of bringing about states of affairs which are naturally contingent at the time they obtain and also (ii) capable, to the extent that their power allows, of interfering with deterministic natural tendencies.

As Molina sees it, God is the paradigmatic indeterministic cause, an all-powerful being capable of freely impeding any and every deterministic natural tendency in the created world. He is the *first* or *primary* cause and His causal activity is absolutely pervasive. He created the original constituents of the universe *ex nihilo*, and no creature can exist or possess causal power through any interval of time unless God conserves it and its powers in being at every instant in that interval. What's more, no creaturely or *secondary* cause is able to exercise its causal power unless God also acts contemporaneously to bring about its effect.[28]

---

[27] Disputation 47, sec. 2.

[28] See, e.g., Aquinas, *Summa Contra Gentiles* III, chaps. 66–70, and *De Potentia*, q. 3, a. 7; and Molina, *Concordia*, Part II, disp. 25–28 (Rabeneck, pp. 159–185). In these places Aquinas and Molina explicitly reject the view that God's causal contribution to ordinary

2.6 *God's General Concurrence*

This last point deserves closer attention. When God brings about a created effect by Himself, He acts as a *particular* cause, since His causal contribution by itself determines the specific nature of the effect. However, the medieval Aristotelians maintain, in opposition to occasionalists, that all *creatures* have genuine causal power, too—though, as just noted, in order for them to exercise this power God must also act to produce the relevant effect. When He thus cooperates with secondary causes, He acts as a *general* or *universal* cause of the effect, and His causal contribution is called His *general concurrence* or *concourse* (*concursus generalis*). The nomenclature is indicative of the fact that in such a case the particular nature of the effect is traceable not to God's causal contribution, necessary though it is in order for any effect to be produced at all, but rather to the natures and causal contributions of the relevant *secondary* causes, which act as *particular* causes of the effect.

Medieval writers frequently appeal to the sun's causal influence on terrestrial events in order to illuminate this point. By providing heat and light the sun causally contributes to animal reproduction on earth. But this causal influence is general, since it has to be channeled or rendered particular by further causes. So, for instance, the sun is a general cause in the production of, say, this calf, since its causal contribution has to be channeled toward the production of a calf (as opposed to, say, a duckling) by further, particular, causes (a cow and a bull). Likewise, God's general causal influence is required in order for secondary causes to bring about any effects whatever anywhere in the created world. But God's causal influence as the primary and maximal universal cause must be particularized and channeled toward given effects by secondary causes. So, for instance, when the gas flame makes the water boil, the fact that the effect is the boiling of water rather than, say, the blossoming of a flower is due not to God's causal contribution (which might just as well have contributed to the water's freezing, had other conditions obtained), but rather to the specific natures of the secondary causes (gas, water, and the like). God's general concurrence is, so to speak, a determinable that has to be particularized by the secondary causes. St. Thomas puts it this way: "The proper effect of the primary agent is being . . . whereas the secondary agents, which, as it were, particularize and deter-

---

natural effects is exhausted by His creating and conserving the causes of those effects. This view is, in fact, regarded as false by virtually all medieval Scholastics, even though it falls far short of the claim that God's causal role in the production of (nonmiraculous) natural effects is limited to His having created secondary causes.

mine the action of the primary agent, produce as their proper effects further perfections that serve to determine being."[29]

To sum up, then, *pace* occasionalism, secondary causes make a unique and unduplicated causal contribution to the effects they produce, and yet they are not capable of producing effects without God's positive and contemporaneous cooperation.

This much is accepted by both Molina and his Bañezian rivals. They part ways, however, on two significant issues. First, Molina insists that God's general concurrence is an action of God's *directly on the effect* and not on the secondary agents themselves, whereas his Thomistic opponents take God's general concurrence to be a divine action *directly on the secondary agents* ("premoving" them) and *through* them on the effect. Molina thus denies what his opponents affirm, namely, that secondary causes must be *moved* by God in order to exercise their causal power. In this way he stresses their autonomy, albeit limited autonomy, in reaction to what he takes to be the excessively occasionalistic tenor of the Thomistic position. This disagreement about whether God's general concurrence constitutes a "premotion" is both deep and deeply puzzling. But since the issues involved do not figure prominently in what follows, I leave a full discussion of them for another time.

The second disputed point has to do with the intrinsic character of God's general concurrence. When secondary causes produce an effect that God intends them to produce, God's general concurrence is said to be *efficacious* with respect to that effect. But when, because of some defect on their part, they fail to produce an effect that God intends them to produce and for the sake of which He grants His cooperation, then His general concurrence is said to be *inefficacious* (though still *sufficient* or *enough*) with respect to the intended effect. If a deficient effect (for example, a sinful action) is instead produced, it is one that God merely permits rather than intends. Against this backdrop, Molinists and Bañezians disagree about whether efficacious and inefficacious concurrence differ from each other *intrinsically*. Bañezians hold that efficacious concurrence is *intrinsically* or *essentially* efficacious with respect to the intended effect and that merely sufficient concurrence is *intrinsically* inefficacious with respect to such an effect. Molina contends to the contrary that God's general concurrence is in itself neither efficacious nor inefficacious, but is instead an intrinsically 'neutral' causal influence that is *rendered* efficacious or inefficacious extrinsically by the relevant second-

---

[29]*Summa Contra Gentiles* III, chap. 66. The analogy with the sun is, as Molina himself points out, defective in one crucial respect, namely, that God's general causation is exactly contemporaneous with the action of the agent, whereas the sun's is not. See *Concordia*, pt. II, disp. 26, secs. 12–13 (Rabeneck, pp. 167–169).

ary causes. As we will see, this disagreement has an immediate and profound impact on the analysis of free choice and of causal indeterminism in general.

2.7 *Contingent Effects*

God is the paradigmatic indeterministic cause. But suppose God were the *only* indeterministic cause. And suppose further that His causal role in the created world were limited to creation, conservation, and general concurrence, and that He never interfered with or impeded any deterministic natural tendency. Then, says Molina, "contingency would be taken away from all the effects of secondary causes and everything would have to happen by a kind of fatalistic necessity."[30]

To grasp the full import of this remark we need to understand more precisely what is to count as a contingent effect. According to our previous characterization of natural contingency, the only naturally contingent states of affairs that actually obtain are brought about directly or immediately by the action of an indeterministic cause. Yet even a state of affairs S that obtains by a necessity of nature at a time t might still be a *contingent effect* in the sense that at some previous (perhaps far distant) time the world did not have a deterministic natural tendency toward S at t. To return to our simple example, even though the water's boiling obtains by a necessity of nature at T, nonetheless, prior to my freely putting the kettle on the fire the world did not have a deterministic natural tendency toward the water's boiling at T—assuming with Molina that human free choice is essentially indeterministic. So the water's boiling at T is a *contingent effect*. Thus, contingency as ascribed to effects is diffusive, having its source in the action (or inaction) of an indeterministic cause and then spreading outward even along causal chains that are themselves wholly deterministic.[31]

We might be tempted at this point to conclude that an effect is contingent just in case it has the action of an indeterministic cause

[30]Disputation 47, sec. 9.

[31]We must include inaction (or failure to act) here, since even if a present effect E does not have the action of an indeterministic secondary cause anywhere in its causal ancestry, it might nonetheless be true that E would not be occurring now if at some earlier time t an indeterministic agent A had not failed to do something that it had the power and the opportunity to do. In such a case, A's inaction is clearly part of E's causal history and, moreover, a part that renders E a contingent effect. Further evidence of E's contingency is the fact that in order for God to have foreknown from eternity that E would occur now, He would have to have foreknown from eternity that A would fail (indeterministically) to act at t.

I should also note that in the following discussion I am drawing from Disputation 47, secs. 10–11; Disputation 52, secs. 18–19; and Disputation 53, pt. 3, secs. 2–4.

somewhere in its causal ancestry. But such an analysis is too crude. For given the orthodox doctrine that God freely creates, conserves, and cooperates with secondary causes, it would follow that *every* effect produced in the created world is contingent, even one with no indeterministic secondary causes in its causal history. Yet, as the passage just quoted demonstrates, Molina sees clearly that if God's action were the *only* actual source of contingency, then the world would for all practical purposes be thoroughly deterministic.

What we need, obviously, is an account of contingent effects which allows us to draw a meaningful distinction between the contingent and noncontingent (or necessary) effects of *secondary* causes, so that an effect produced by secondary causes will be contingent only if its causal ancestry includes the action (or inaction) of some indeterministic *secondary* cause; otherwise it will count as a necessary effect. Speaking more generally, an effect is *contingent* if and only if it either is produced immediately by God alone or has the action (or inaction) of an indeterministic secondary cause somewhere, either immediately or remotely, in its causal history. And an effect is *necessary* if and only if it is produced by secondary causes but does not have the action (or inaction) of any indeterministic secondary cause anywhere in its causal history. So the definition of a necessary effect presupposes the divine activities of creation, conservation, and general concurrence.

If we combine Molina's discussions of contingent effects in Disputations 47, 52, and 53, Part 3, we can distinguish four distinct categories of such effects:

Category A: effects that God freely produces by Himself and that do not in any way presuppose the action (or inaction) of indeterministic secondary causes. Examples are God's creation and conservation of spiritual substances (angels and intellective souls) and of matter as such.

Category B: effects that God freely produces by Himself but that presuppose the action (or inaction) of indeterministic secondary causes to provide the circumstances for His unilateral action. For instance, the man born blind is made to see by God's action alone, but his very existence and many of his properties have resulted from the free actions (or omissions) of his ancestors, parents, friends.

Category C: effects that are naturally contingent at the time they are produced, having been brought about directly by an indeterministic secondary cause. The most obvious examples are free choices themselves.

Category D: effects that occur by natural necessity at the time they are produced, but have the action (or inaction) of indeterministic secondary causes somewhere in their causal ancestry. An example is the boiling of the water at some time after the water is put into proximity to the gas flame by the free action of some human agent.

According to Molina, God is the immediate source of the contingency of effects in categories *A* and *B,* with effects in the latter category also having indeterministic secondary causes as a remote source of their contingency. By contrast, effects in categories *C* and *D* have indeterministic secondary causes as the immediate source of their contingency and God as a remote source of their contingency.

2.8 *Absolute and Conditional Future Contingents*

God knows future *necessary* effects with certainty simply by virtue of (i) His natural knowledge and (ii) His knowledge of the total causal contribution He Himself wills to make to the created world. Moreover, among future *contingent* effects, only those produced by *secondary* causes (effects in categories *C* and *D*) pose a special epistemic problem. Everyone will agree that it is simply by virtue of knowing His own causal intentions that God knows which contingent effects in category *A* will be produced. And once we grant God knowledge of the contingent effects of secondary causes, He can know which effects in category *B* will be produced simply by virtue of knowing, once again, His own causal intentions. Accordingly, in what follows I restrict the term 'future contingent' to the effects of *secondary* causes.

We customarily think of future contingents as categorical future-tense states of affairs which now obtain or, alternatively, as categorical present-tense states of affairs which will obtain.[32] These are what Molina calls *absolute future contingents.* Examples might include the state of affairs of its being the case that Peter will freely sin at *T* (category *C*) and its being the case that this water will boil at *T,* where the boiling of the water will emanate in part from my having freely decided at *T** to place the kettle on the stove (category *D*).

We will better understand Molina's views and the controversies generated by them, however, if we take absolute future contingents to be derivable from conceptually prior conditional states of affairs which we might fittingly call *conditional future contingents.* These conditional states of affairs indicate which effects in categories *C* and *D would in fact be*

---

[32] By 'categorical' I mean states of affairs which are most naturally expressed by simple subject-predicate sentences (including quantified sentences). Excluded are states of affairs most naturally expressed by conjunctions or disjunctions of such sentences or by conditional sentences. This distinction between categorical and compound (or 'hypothetical') propositions is standard in medieval logic.

produced, remotely or immediately, by indeterministic secondary causes under a condition or hypothesis that specifies a possible spatio-temporal arrangement of secondary causes. An example might be the state of affairs of its being the case that Peter would freely sin at T if hypothesis H were to obtain at T, where H includes among other things Peter's having the power and opportunity at T to sin freely. Another example might be the state of affairs of its being the case that the water would boil at T if H were to obtain at T, where H includes among other things my having had the power and opportunity at T^* to put the kettle on the stove.[33] If the condition H will in fact obtain, then the consequent is an *absolute* future contingent; if H will not obtain, then the whole conditional is a mere *conditioned* future contingent.

More formally, let S be a present-tense categorical state of affairs and $F^t(S)$ the state of affairs of its being the case that S will obtain at t, where t designates a time; and let $F^t(S)$ *on* H be the state of affairs of its being the case that S would obtain at t if hypothesis H were to obtain at t. Then:[34]

$F^t(S)$ *on* H is from eternity a *conditional future contingent* if and only if (i) $F^t(S)$ *on* H obtains from eternity; and (ii) S, H, and $F^t(S)$ *on* H are all metaphysically contingent; and (iii) it is true from eternity that if H were to obtain at t, then S would be a contingent effect produced by secondary causes (category C or D).

$F^t(S)$ is from eternity an *absolute future contingent* if and only if for some H, (i) $F^t(S)$ *on* H is from eternity a conditional future contingent and (ii) it is true from eternity that H will obtain at t.

$F^t(S)$ *on* H is from eternity a *conditioned future contingent* if and only if (i) $F^t(S)$ *on* H is from eternity a conditional future contingent and (ii) it is true from eternity that neither H nor S will obtain at t.

---

[33] When contingent effects of category D are involved, the relevant H must include reference to past situations in which secondary causes had the power and opportunity to act indeterministically. Notice that analogous conditionals describing effects whose causal history includes only deterministic secondary causes are metaphysically *necessary* rather than metaphysically contingent. Hence, they are known by God via His *natural* knowledge.

[34] Since our interest is in *God's* knowledge, I will characterize future contingency 'from eternity'. But the fact that God's knowledge of conditional future contingents is from eternity does not by itself settle the question of whether that knowledge is prevolitional or postvolitional. It is precisely here that Molinists diverge from Bañezians, and the account of future contingency given below is meant to be neutral with respect to this disagreement.

Also, for reasons that are discussed in Section 4.3 below, it is probably best to regard a state of affairs as a conditional future contingent only if the relevant H includes a total description of the causal history and contemporaneous causal circumstances of any exercise of indeterministic causation which figures directly in the production of the effect designated by the consequent.

Molina claims that infinitely many conditional future contingents obtained from eternity and that from eternity God had comprehensive knowledge of them. However—and this is very important, though not widely appreciated—neither of these claims distinguishes him from his Bañezian antagonists.[35] What *is* distinctive about Molina is his controversial claim that God's knowledge of conditional future contingents is *prevolitional* rather than, as the Bañezians would have it, *postvolitional*.

To make this clearer, I will present a preview of Molina's explanation of how it is that God has foreknowledge of absolute future contingents. As we have seen, Molina affirms against the Bañezians that God's general concurrence is *intrinsically* neither efficacious nor inefficacious. Thus, if God had only natural knowledge of metaphysically necessary states of affairs plus knowledge of His own total causal contribution to the created world, He would not thereby know any absolute future contingents. His natural knowledge tells Him only what each indeterministic secondary cause *is able to do*, not what it *would in fact do*, in any possible situation in which it is in a position to act; and if God's concurrence is intrinsically 'neutral', then His own causal contribution to contingent effects in categories *C* and *D* does not uniquely determine those effects. So, according to Molina, if there is genuine causal indeterminism in the created world, God can be provident in the way demanded by orthodoxy only if His prevolitional knowledge includes an understanding of which effects *would in fact* result from causal chains involving indeterministic created causes. But this is just for God to have full *prevolitional* knowledge of *conditional future contingents*. Since this knowledge has metaphysically *contingent* states of affairs as its objects, it is not part of God's *natural* knowledge; since it is *prevolitional*, it is not part of God's *free* knowledge. It stands 'midway' between natural knowledge and free knowledge— hence its title, *middle* knowledge.

On Molina's view, then, the source of God's foreknowledge of absolute future contingents is threefold: (i) His prevolitional natural knowledge of metaphysically necessary states of affairs, (ii) His prevolitional middle knowledge of conditional future contingents, and (iii) His free knowledge of the total causal contribution He himself wills to make to the created world. By (i) He knows which spatio-temporal arrangements

---

[35]For an unambiguous admission of the point in question by a Bañezian, see Reginald Garrigou-Lagrange, O.P., *The One God* (St. Louis, 1943), pp. 461–462 (n. 134) and 471. It is hard to overemphasize the importance of this point, given a marked tendency among recent writers to err by simply identifying the Molinist doctrine of middle knowledge with the claim that God has knowledge of conditional future contingents (or so-called counterfactuals of freedom). This claim, to repeat, is not a distinctively Molinist one, and, indeed, it was never in dispute in the rancorous sixteenth-century debates between Molinists and Bañezians.

of secondary causes are possible and which contingent effects *might* emanate from any such arrangement. By (ii) He knows which contingent effects *would in fact* emanate from any possible spatio-temporal arrangement of secondary causes. By (iii) He knows which secondary causes He wills to create and conserve and how He wills to cooperate with them via His intrinsically neutral general concurrence. So given His natural knowledge, His middle knowledge, and His free knowledge of His own causal contribution to the created world, He has free knowledge of all absolute future contingents.[36] That is, He has within Himself the means required for knowing with certainty which contingent effects *will in fact* emanate from the *actual* arrangement of secondary causes.

By contrast, Bañezians deny that any metaphysically contingent state of affairs, even a conditional future contingent, can obtain conceptually prior to God's decreeing (by either intention or permission) that it obtain. Since they must accordingly try to get by with just (i) and (iii) above, they maintain that Molina's account of God's general concurrence is unacceptably weak and that his account of freedom and causal indeterminism is unacceptably strong. The other theories to be explored in Section 3 resemble Bañezianism in appealing to just (i) and (iii), but they resemble Molinism in holding to a strong account of creaturely indeterminism and freedom. By now we should have a glimmer of why the proponents of these other theories must settle for something less than the robust account of divine providence sketched in Section 1. (More on this in Section 3).

2.9 *Freedom*

Molina's conception of freedom is strongly indeterministic; in modern terms he is an unremitting libertarian. We must not conclude forthwith, however, that the dispute between Molinists and Bañezians over the nature of free choice is a precise analog of the contemporary dispute between libertarians and compatibilists, the latter holding that it is possible for a free action to occur by a necessity of nature. For, as we shall soon see, Bañezians as well as Molinists deny this possibility.

In Disputation 2, after distinguishing freedom from coercion, Molina goes on to say:

> But freedom can be understood in another way, insofar as it is opposed to *necessity*. In this sense that agent is called free which, with all the prerequi-

---

[36] It follows from what has been said that there are two distinguishable moments in God's *free* knowledge. First, God knows how He Himself wills to act; second, He knows what will result from this decision. Only the latter of these moments is, strictly speaking, *post*volitional—even though for the sake of convenience I will continue to use the terms 'free knowledge' and 'postvolitional knowledge' interchangeably.

sites for acting posited, is able to act and able not to act [freedom of contradiction], or is able to do one thing in such a way that it is also able to do some contrary thing [freedom of contrariety]. And by virtue of this sort of freedom the faculty by which such an agent is able so to act is called free. . . . It follows from this that free choice (if it is to be conceded anywhere) is nothing other than the will, in which freedom exists formally, guided by a previous judgment of reason.[37]

A few lines later it becomes clear that such "previous judgments of reason" do not necessitate free acts of will:

And so given the same disposition and cognition . . . on the part of the intellect, the will is by its innate freedom able to will or to dissent or to neither will nor dissent.[38]

My concern here is to isolate the sense in which free action is causally indeterministic on Molina's view. So I will merely lump these cognitive prerequisites with the other causal antecedents of free choice, even though a thorough investigation of freedom would single them out for special consideration.

For Molina, then, to be free with respect to a given object (that is, a state of affairs) is to have a faculty, namely, a will or intellective appetite, by virtue of which one is capable of choosing indeterministically with respect to that object. In paradigmatic instances the agent has three options: (i) to elicit an act of willing the object, (ii) to elicit an act of dissenting from or rejecting the object, or (iii) to refrain from either willing or dissenting. So every free action involves a free choice, which then typically issues forth in a 'commanded' (as opposed to 'elicited') act—most often, in free *human* action, a basic bodily movement.

This is not the place to explore or defend the common Scholastic thesis that every free action involves freedom with respect to elicited mental acts of willing or dissenting. I will only remark in passing that I concur with Alan Donagan's judgment that the modern objections to this thesis are not compelling and sometimes are not even to the point.[39]

At any rate, since the task before us is to formulate a necessary

---

[37] Rabeneck, p. 14. I have inserted the phrases 'freedom of contradiction' and 'freedom of contrariety' to aid the reader's understanding of Molina's use of these phrases in Part IV of the *Concordia*. See Disputation 53, pt. 2, sec. 17. For engaging (though, to my mind, unduly unsympathetic) treatments of Molina's conception of freedom, see Gerard Smith, S.J., *Freedom in Molina* (Chicago, 1966); and Anton Pegis, "Molina and Human Liberty," pp. 75–131 in Gerard Smith, S.J., ed., *Jesuit Thinkers of the Renaissance* (Milwaukee, 1939).

[38] Rabeneck, p. 14.

[39] See Donagan's "Thomas Aquinas on Human Action," pp. 642–654 in Kretzmann, Kenny, and Pinborg, eds., *The Cambridge History of Later Medieval Philosophy*. For more on the distinction between elicited and commanded acts, see Disputation 47, n. 14.

condition for freedom that suffices to express the indeterminism ascribed by Molina to free choice and free action, I will put to one side for
now the distinction between elicited and commanded acts. Instead I will
speak simply of a person's freely making a causal contribution at a given
time to a state of affairs, a state of affairs which may or may not involve
an elicited act.

Libertarians often assume that the indeterminism of free actions can
be epitomized by the simple requirement that a free action be one that is
not naturally determined by the causal history of the world, that is, one
that is not naturally necessitated by causes operative at times before it
takes place. Given our previous characterization of the causal modalities, this requirement can be stated more simply as follows, where P
designates an agent, S a state of affairs, and t a time:

> At t P *freely* contributes causally to S only if (i) at t P contributes causally to S
> and (ii) P's contributing causally to S does not obtain at t by a necessity of
> nature.

This condition is one that modern libertarians accept and that modern
compatibilists repudiate. Nonetheless, it is too weak to capture the causal indeterminism that Molina attributes to free action. A sure sign of this
is that Bañezians can avidly endorse it. Their dispute with Molinists has
to do not with the world's causal history or past deterministic natural
tendencies, but rather with the intrinsic character of *God's* general concurrence *at the very moment* the action takes place.

But just how might one go about arguing that the condition in question is insufficient to capture the causal indeterminism endemic to free
action? Consider the following story:[40]

It is 1984. Katie is about to cast her vote in the presidential elections.
Unbeknown to her, a very powerful genius is closely monitoring her

---

[40]The example that follows resembles those used by Harry Frankfurt in "Alternate
Possibilities and Moral Responsibility," *Journal of Philosophy* 66 (1969): 829–839, and is in
fact adapted, with some significant changes, from John Martin Fischer's reply to Frankfurt
in "Responsibility and Control," *Journal of Philosophy* 79 (1982): 24–40. Frankfurt's examples are meant to illustrate his contention that responsibility does not entail the ability to do
otherwise. It is not clear to me just how the discussion that follows in this section is related to
the puzzles about freedom, control, and responsibility posed by Frankfurt-type examples. I
certainly do not claim that the revised necessary condition for freedom proposed below
provides the basis either for a libertarian response to all Frankfurt-type examples or for a
general libertarian account of the relationship between freedom, responsibility, and the
ability to do otherwise. My hesitation stems in part from the fact that the particular example
I am using is carefully tailored to help clarify the differences between Molinists and
Bañezians. Most important, I stipulate that the genius's action is (like God's general
concurrence) contemporaneous with Katie's decision, though this is by no means a general
feature of all Frankfurt-type examples.

voting behavior. If Katie decides on her own to vote for Mondale, he will do nothing. But if she shows an inclination to decide to vote for Reagan, then at the very moment of decision he will act in such a way as to guarantee that she actually decides to vote for Mondale.

There are two cases to consider. Suppose, first, that Katie is on the verge of deciding to vote for Reagan, but that at the very moment of decision the genius intervenes in such a way as to guarantee that she decides to vote for Mondale instead. Is her choice free? Obviously not. Yet the condition stated above is not strong enough to exclude it, since the genius's action is contemporaneous with Katie's decision and hence not part of the causal history of the world at the moment of decision. Assuming that the genius's action is itself free, Katie's decision is not the culmination of any deterministic natural tendency.

Clearly, we need an additional clause that focuses on the activity of causes other than the agent in question at the very moment when the free action takes place. Consider this:

> At t P *freely* contributes causally to S only if (i) at t P contributes causally to S and (ii) P's contributing causally to S does not obtain at t by a necessity of nature and (iii) the total causal activity at t of causes other than P is compossible with P's not causally contributing at t to S.

(Two or more states of affairs are compossible just in case their conjunction is metaphysically possible.)

According to this amended condition, Katie's deciding to vote for Mondale is not free if the genius intervenes in the way described above. For there is no possible world in which he thus intervenes at t and yet in which Katie fails to decide at t in favor of Mondale. The genius's contemporaneous causal activity precludes any other choice in each such world.

But what if she decides to vote for Mondale on her own, without any "assistance" from the genius? Does she then choose freely? My own clear intuition is that the answer is yes, even though in one fairly obvious sense she could not have done (or willed) otherwise. Apparently, however, this is not the sense of "could have done otherwise" which is central to free action—at least not if our revised necessary condition is correct. For here once again this condition yields a result that matches intuitive expectations. If Katie decides on her own to vote for Mondale, the genius does nothing relevant to her decision at the time she decides, and it seems utterly obvious that in at least one possible world (perhaps very remote from ours) in which the genius refrains from intervening at t, Katie decides not to vote for Mondale.

Though the analogy between God and the genius is imperfect in many respects, Katie's story helps make clear how the debates in sixteenth-century Catholic theology over the nature of freedom came to focus on God's general concurrence, a concurrence that constitutes His contemporaneous causal contribution to creaturely free action. Bañezians reject the amended condition because they hold that God's general concurrence with the free actions of creatures is *intrinsically* efficacious when those actions are not morally evil and *intrinsically* inefficacious when they are. Assume that Katie's deciding to vote for Mondale is not a morally evil act. Then, since God's concurrence with her decision is intrinsically efficacious, there is no possible world in which God makes just *that* contemporaneous causal contribution and in which she refrains from deciding to vote for Mondale. Bañezians must thus reject the revised condition in order to affirm that Katie decides freely. (Notice, though, that by substituting "secondary causes" for "causes" in (iii) we arrive at a condition that no sophisticated Bañezian would contest but that no card-carrying contemporary compatibilist would even think of endorsing. This is important, since it shows that Bañezians are, at least by modern standards, far from being the sort of crass determinists that Molina accuses them of being.) Molina, by contrast, can enthusiastically embrace the amended condition as it stands because he holds that God's concurrence is intrinsically compossible both with Katie's deciding to vote for Mondale and with her not so deciding.

2.10 *Indeterminism in Nature*

Molina's official view is that free action is the only type of indeterministic causation actually found in the created world. In fact, in Disputation 2 he distinguishes *natural* causes from *free* causes precisely by claiming that the former always act by a necessity of nature and are always determined to one effect.[41]

Interestingly, however, in Disputation 47 he acknowledges that it is possible for there to be indeterministic causes not endowed with the cognitive capacities required for free action:

> In this discussion we have not included among the sources of contingency those effects in which, when commenting on . . . Aristotle's *Physics*, we claimed to find contingency, of the sort found in the shattering of a vase full of water, by which the water, if it were frozen and there were no external atmosphere, would rush out to fill the vacuum. For in such a case, if the vase were in all its parts uniform and of equal resistance, then since there would be no more reason it should shatter in this part rather than that part—

[41] Rabeneck, p. 14.

though it would necessarily have to shatter, lest there be a vacuum—clearly, the fracture's occurring in a given part will be said to happen by chance or fortune and hence contingently.[42]

Though conceivable, such effects "do not seem to be able to occur in nature,"[43] presumably because the ideal conditions in which they would be produced cannot be realized in our world.

Since Molina's time, of course, indeterminism has cropped up in physics, chemistry, and biology, and although the jury is still out, such indeterminism seems to be genuinely metaphysical and not just a function of our ignorance. *Pace* Einstein, it appears that God does indeed play dice with the universe.

Notice, however, that Molina's theory of divine providence can easily accommodate indeterminism in nature. This point is overlooked in all the discussions of Molinism which I know of, mainly because they focus exclusively on those conditional future contingents that involve free action. Indeed, many writers simply *identify* Molina's theory of middle knowledge with the thesis that God has prevolitional knowledge of so-called *counterfactuals of freedom*, that is, conditional future contingents specifying how creatures endowed with free choice would *freely* act in various hypothetical situations.

This is a mistake that I have tried to avoid above by speaking of indeterministic secondary causes *in general* (and not just of free causes) and of conditional future contingents *in general* (and not just of counter-factuals of freedom). Indeed, if indeterminism in nature is so much as possible, then counterfactuals of freedom make up only a proper fraction of what God knows by His middle knowledge. For He also knows by His middle knowledge how *natural* indeterministic causes would act in all possible situations involving them. So on Molina's view God really can play dice with the universe, and hence there can be genuine causal indeterminism in nature. But, Molina insists, a truly provident God knows by His middle knowledge exactly which numbers will come up on each roll.

3 Alternatives to Molinism

3.1 *Foreknowledge and Orthodoxy*

We are now in a position to investigate the three accounts of divine foreknowledge which Molina deems his most important competitors. All

[42]Disputation 47, sec. 13.
[43]Ibid.

of them presuppose as a theological certitude that God has comprehensive and infallible knowledge of absolute future contingents. Indeed, this presupposition serves as a touchstone of orthodoxy for both Catholic and Reformed thinkers in the sixteenth century—and no wonder, given the extensive support for it in both Scripture and Tradition. Years later the First Vatican Council was to put the matter officially beyond dispute for Roman Catholics in its Dogmatic Constitution on the Catholic Faith: "By His providence God watches over and governs all the things He has created, reaching from end to end with might and disposing all things with gentleness (see Wisdom 8:1). 'All things are exposed and open to His eyes' (Hebrews 4:13), even those things that are going to occur by the free action of creatures."[44] Not surprisingly, then, Molina never seriously entertains the idea that God might lack knowledge of future contingents. That this idea has gained a foothold in some sectors of twentieth-century Christian philosophy and theology would no doubt be a source of consternation not only to him but also to his contemporaries on both sides of the Reformation—and well it should be, in light of the intimate connection between foreknowledge and providence.

Molina takes up the rival accounts in Disputations 48–51 and 53, Parts 1 and 2. Here I provide just a brief commentary.

3.2 Disputations 48 and 49: The View from Eternity

According to the standard interpretation endorsed by all of the most important Thomistic commentators before the late sixteenth century (Cajetan excepted), St. Thomas holds that God knows all future contingents with certainty *solely* because future entities, although they do not yet exist 'outside their causes' in time, nonetheless exist in eternity and so are present to the divine vision. Further, their existence in eternity is *real* and not just *objective*, where objective existence is had by a thing merely insofar as it is an object of thought.

In the idiom of states of affairs, St. Thomas holds that if $F^t(S)$ is from eternity a future contingent and t is still in our future, then S, though it does not yet obtain in time, obtains from eternity and in eternity as an object of God's knowledge of vision. S *really* obtains in eternity; God's knowing it is not merely a matter of His knowing that it *will* obtain at t. Indeed, future contingents *cannot* be known with certainty *as future*. What God knows is that S *now* obtains, where 'now' designates an everpresent eternal duration that admits of no past or future, and the source

---

[44]H. Denzinger and A. Schönmetzer, eds., *Enchiridion Symbolorum*, 32d ed. (Freiburg, 1963), 3003 (new numbering), p. 587.

of God's knowledge, according to the standard interpretation, is just the fact that *S* obtains in eternity.

Let me provide some background here on God's relation to time. The Aristotelian Scholastics generally agree that whereas God's existence is metaphysically necessary, the existence of time or temporal succession is metaphysically contingent, tied directly to change and motion in the created universe. They thus reject the 'temporalist' thesis, popular in some quarters today, that God is an essentially temporal being and that time taken as infinite in both directions is the proper durational measure of God's being.[45] They hold instead that the proper and adequate measure of the divine being is *eternity* and not *everlasting time*. In itself eternity is a duration that admits of neither before nor after, since God has full and perfect being all at once. He alone exists *adequately* or *properly* in eternity. Unlike finite creatures, He is pure actuality and thus does not have potentialities that need time in order to be actualized; nor is He subject to losses of perfection that take place over time. He would still exist and be just as perfect even if there were no such thing as time. Time is the proper and adequate durational measure only of finite beings, which are both perfectible and corruptible.[46]

But although God's eternity is metaphysically independent of time, it necessarily 'embraces' every moment of time that in fact exists. Indeed, it is because of His eternality that God is temporally omnipresent. Medieval philosophers often explicate this temporal omnipresence by analogy with God's spatial omnipresence. God is necessarily present by His being, power, and knowledge to every *spatial* location that He causes to exist. That is, He gives being to whatever exists at any place, and He is able to act or bring about effects at any place, and He has exhaustive knowledge of whatever transpires at any place. No one place is intrinsically more accessible to Him than any other; all are equally accessible (or present) to Him and He is equally present to each. So, too, because of His eternality He is necessarily present by His being, power, and knowl-

---

[45]The most penetrating defense I have seen of the temporalist thesis is found in Nicholas Wolterstorff, "God Everlasting," pp. 77–98 in Steven M. Cahn and David Shatz, eds., *Contemporary Philosophy of Religion* (Oxford, 1982). The best recent defense of the doctrine of eternity and related doctrines is contained in two long papers by Eleonore Stump and Norman Kretzmann: "Eternity," *Journal of Philosophy* 79 (1981): 429–458, and "Absolute Simplicity," *Faith and Philosophy* 2 (1985): 353–382. See also William Hasker, "The Intelligibility of 'God is Timeless,'" *New Scholasticism* 57 (1983): 170–195; and David Burrell, C.S.C., "God's Eternity," *Faith and Philosophy* 1 (1984): 389–406.

[46]Medieval theologians also typically posit a special durational measure for angels, who are not subject to physical generation and corruption or to physical motion. This measure is called *aevum* (aeviternity) and is marked by a succession of discrete cognitional and volitional states. (See Disputation 49, secs. 22–24). In order to keep my presentation as simple as possible, I ignore aeviternity in what follows.

edge to every *temporal* location that He causes to exist. That is, He gives being to whatever exists at any time, and He is able to act or bring about effects at any time, and He has exhaustive knowledge of whatever transpires at any time. No one time is intrinsically more accessible to Him than any other; all times are equally accessible (or present) to Him and He is equally present to each. And it is because of His temporal omnipresence that time-bound entities, which exist *adequately* or *properly* in time, also exist, albeit *nonadequately* or *improperly,* in eternity as well. That is, they are present to God in eternity, but only because of God's temporal omnipresence and not because they have eternity as their proper durational measure.

So creatures exist *adequately* in time and *nonadequately* in eternity. We should not infer, however, that they have two kinds of existence, one temporal and one eternal. Rather, they exist nonadequately in eternity with the very same existence by which they exist adequately in time. To say that they exist in eternity as objects of God's power and knowledge is just to say that God is present by His power and knowledge to all the times at which they exist.

Here, however, there is a parting of ways, at least as Molina sees it. He holds that just as a place cannot be present to God when it does not exist (for co-presence is a dyadic relation requiring the existence of both terms), so too a moment or interval of time cannot be present to God before it exists (for, once again, co-presence is a dyadic relation requiring the existence of both terms). This failure of co-presence is not, Molina emphasizes, due to any defect in God; rather, it is simply due to the nonexistence of the moment or interval in question. Yet, Molina laments, Boethius and St. Thomas seem to hold (i) that a future time can now, in the temporal present, exist in eternity and be present to God in eternity even though it does not yet exist in its own right and, concomitantly, (ii) that a merely future entity can now, in the temporal present, exist in eternity and be present to God in eternity even though it does not yet exist in time. That is, Boethius and St. Thomas seem to hold that for any future time *t,* all the things that will exist at *t* even *now* exist in eternity, and all the states of affairs that will obtain at *t* even *now* obtain in eternity, where 'now' designates the temporal present.

To be sure, Molina cheerfully concedes that the proposition 'All future things exist in eternity' is true, as long as 'exist' expresses the *eternal* present.[47] What he means is simply that there will never be a creature that exists in time without being present to God in eternity, and this by virtue of the fact that God's eternity, as explained above, necessarily

---

[47]See Disputation 48, secs. 9–11, and Disputation 49, secs. 15–16.

'embraces' every moment of time that happens to exist. He vigorously denies, however, that merely future entities, which do not yet exist in time, now exist in eternity, where 'now' designates the *temporal* present:

> It should not be thought that the things that come to be successively in time exist in eternity *before* they exist in time—as though it was because of some sort of anticipation they have in eternity with respect to existence outside their causes that they are known with certainty in eternity while they are still future in time. Yet this is what would have had to be true in order for it to be the case that it was because of the existence of things in eternity that God foreknew them with certainty before they came to be true.
>
> But if *this* was the claim being made by Boethius, St. Thomas, and the others who affirm on this basis that God knows future contingents with certainty, then I frankly confess that I do not understand it, nor do I think that there is any way in which it can be true.[48]

Perhaps Molina simply misunderstands Boethius and St. Thomas here. For it is certainly difficult to imagine either Boethius or St. Thomas assenting to the claim that merely future things exist in eternity *now* (that is, at the present time), even before they come to exist in time. More probably, Molina is charging that this claim is one that Boethius and St. Thomas (on the standard interpretation) are logically committed to, given their account of how God knows future contingents with certainty. The argument runs like this: In order for the presence of things in eternity to be the sole source of God's knowledge of future contingents, it must be the case that the proposition 'All future things exist in eternity' is now true. But this proposition has two readings. If 'exist' expresses the eternal present, then the proposition is true but unhelpful to the defender of the standard interpretation. For, as we saw above, it merely asserts that nothing will ever exist in time without also existing in eternity. What the defender of the standard interpretation needs instead is the stronger claim that all future things (now) exist in eternity even though they do not (now) exist in time—and it is for this reason that God knows with certainty things that are now (in time) future contingents. But this is just to assert the proposition 'All future things exist in eternity' while taking 'exist' to express the *temporal,* and not the *eternal,* present.

I will leave it to others to judge the cogency of this argument. There is, however, a related point worth tarrying over briefly. Molina's strong adherence to the doctrine that God is eternal does not deter him from using tensed language when speaking of God's knowledge of and causal

---

[48]Disputation 49, sec. 16.

influence on temporal creatures. He apparently takes such language to be permissible and, indeed, appropriate as long as it is carefully dissociated from the temporalist thesis that God's act of understanding and act of willing are *properly and adequately* measured by time. So, it seems, according to Molina it is perfectly correct to assert, *pace* St. Thomas, that God knows future contingents with certainty *as future*. At the very least we can say this much: An absolute future contingent $F^t(S)$ is known by God with certainty prior—at least conceptually prior—to S's obtaining in either time or eternity.

So Molina has certain difficulties with the way St. Thomas understands and employs the concept of eternity. Still, this is not his only, or even his most penetrating, objection to the view embodied by the standard interpretation. In fact, the objections that follow have force even if we grant provisionally that future contingents are even now really present in eternity as objects of God's knowledge.

The first objection is that the standard interpretation cannot account for God's knowledge of *all* future contingents. In particular, the presence of things in eternity cannot be a source of certitude regarding *conditioned* future contingents, since the antecedents and consequents of conditioned future contingents never obtain in time and hence do not obtain in eternity either.[49] Yet it is clear from Sacred Scripture that God knows conditioned future contingents. For instance, Christ knew that the inhabitants of Tyre and Sidon would have repented and been converted if the wonders worked in Chorozain and Bethsaida had been worked in their presence (Matt. 11). Similarly, God revealed to David that if he stayed in Keilah, Saul would invade, and, further, if David stayed and Saul invaded, then the men of Keilah would hand David over to Saul (1 Sam. 23). So David fled. Again, Wisdom 4 tells us that God often takes the virtuous from this life prematurely because He knows that they would become corrupted by sin if they were to live longer. (In Section 5.2 I briefly discuss Molina's use of these biblical texts.)

Notice, this objection is one that Bañezians endorse wholeheartedly. They, too, believe that God knows conditioned as well as absolute future contingents, and they, too, hold that this knowledge of conditioned future contingents cannot have as its source the presence of things in eternity.[50] Their problem with Molina has to do instead with his claim

---

[49]See Disputation 49, sec. 9.

[50]Garrigou-Lagrange claims that St. Thomas makes use of the notion of eternity not to explain the *source* of God's foreknowledge of future contingents, but instead to demonstrate that this foreknowledge is *intuitive* rather than *inferential*. See *The One God*, p. 454. According to both Molinists and Bañezians, God's knowledge of absolute future contingents is *based on* His prevolitional knowledge, but is not *inferred from* the latter in any way that involves a process of reasoning. God has *all* His knowledge from eternity, despite the fact that some part of that knowledge is conceptually prior to other parts.

that the knowledge in question is prevolitional rather than the result of God's free act of will.

So the presence of things in eternity cannot be the source of God's knowledge of conditioned future contingents. Nor, Molina argues further, can it be the source even of God's knowledge of *absolute* future contingents. For, as we saw in Section 1, if God is truly provident, then He has perfect knowledge of absolute future contingents simply by virtue of (i) His prevolitional knowledge of what would happen given any possible causal activity on His part, and (ii) His knowledge of the actual causal contribution He freely wills to make to the created world. So if $F^t(S)$ is an absolute future contingent, then S's actual obtaining, whether in time or eternity, is conceptually posterior to God's knowledge of $F^t(S)$. For this reason S's actually obtaining at t adds not a whit of certitude or perfection to God's knowledge. God does not need future things to be present in eternity in order to know them; He knows them 'in' His own act of will. So, Molina concludes, the presence of things in eternity is wholly irrelevant to the question of how a perfectly provident being comes to know absolute future contingents.[51] And this, too, is an objection Bañezians acquiesce in, though they deny with good reason that it counts against what St. Thomas actually said—even if it does count against the view commentators standardly attribute to him.

The third objection also invokes the doctrine of providence. If God is perfectly provident, then His specifically willing or permitting a given contingent effect S cannot be conceptually posterior to His knowing with certainty that S does or will obtain. Otherwise His willing or permitting S would be a *reaction* to something already accomplished and known prior to His specific approbation or permission; His particular knowledge of S would in effect be *prevolitional*. But a perfectly provident being knows each *absolute* future contingent *in, and not before,* His specifically willing or permitting it. It is up to Him to decide which future contingents are absolute and which will remain forever merely conditioned. And His knowledge of absolute future contingents follows upon and cannot precede this choice.

The standard interpretation seems to violate this stricture by using perceptual metaphors that strongly suggest the following conceptual sequence: A future contingent effect is first there to be seen by God; then it is in fact seen and known by God; and only then is it specifically

---

[51] In Disputation 49, sec. 15, Molina says: "The proposition 'From eternity all things coexist with God or are present to God with their own existence outside their causes,' taken in the sense explained in the preceding disputation, contributes nothing, as I see it, either toward establishing the certitude of divine foreknowledge concerning future contingents or toward reconciling the contingency of things with divine foreknowledge."

decreed, that is, willed or permitted by Him, depending on whether or not He approves of what He sees.

This, of course, is just the reverse of what the doctrine of providence requires, at least as Molina sees it. And not only Molina. For St. Thomas himself says the very same thing in many places. That is why Bañezians argue that the standard interpretation is mistaken and that St. Thomas could not have held that the presence of things in eternity is the sole and sufficient source of God's knowledge of future contingents. We now turn to the Bañezian version of Thomism.

3.3 Disputations 50 and 53: Divine Predeterminations

What I have dubbed Bañezianism actually encompasses several distinct theories that agree on primary principles but, as Disputation 53 attests, diverge on various subtleties. I will try to give a clear presentation of the fundamentals here.[52]

Bañezians and Molinists concur that a provident God has *within Himself* the resources to know all future contingents with certainty. Creatures do not cause God to have knowledge of them; rather, by His own act of will God Himself brings it about from eternity that He knows absolute future contingents. The origins of this knowledge lie entirely in (i) His prevolitional knowledge and (ii) His free causal contribution to the created world.

But what exact role is to be attributed to each of these elements? Molina begins with a strong account of freedom and causal indeterminism according to which God's causal contribution to the contingent effects of secondary causes is not by its intrinsic nature efficacious with respect to those effects—even the good ones. So in order for God to have knowledge of *absolute* future contingents, He must know *prevolitionally* exactly which contingent effects would in fact result from His (intrinsically neutral) concurrence with any possible array of secondary causes. It follows that some metaphysically contingent states of affairs, namely, *conditional* future contingents, obtain prior to and hence independently of God's willing or permitting them to obtain.

Whereas Molina starts 'from below' with creaturely freedom, Bañezians begin 'from above' by stressing that God is sovereign and the source

---

[52] Here I follow Garrigou-Lagrange, *The One God*, pp. 449–473. The main parameters of Bañez's theory are contained in his *Scholastica Commentaria in Primam Partem Summae Theologicae S. Thomae Aquinatis*, first published in 1585. A modern edition, edited by Luis Urbano, O.P., appeared in Madrid in 1934. Molina's discussion of this theory is far richer in arguments and details than my presentation here might suggest, so I urge the reader to look carefully at Disputation 50 and the first two parts of Disputation 53.

of all goodness. Because God is sovereign, they claim, no metaphysically contingent state of affairs, not even a conditional future contingent, can obtain without His antecedent approbation or permission. Inasmuch as God is the source of all goodness, no good effect can be produced by creatures without His intrinsically efficacious concurrence. If God's concurrence were intrinsically neutral instead, then His causal contribution in any given case could result in either a good effect or an evil effect—which is both absurd and contrary to the faith. Still, both faith and reason also teach us that some creatures have the power of free choice. So the indeterminism proper to freedom must, *pace* Molina, be defined as nondetermination by *secondary* causes only.

We should note in passing that the dispute over efficacious concurrence is not confined to the natural order. Catholics believe that through Christ's salvific act God beneficently confers supernatural grace on human beings. More pertinent, by His *actual* grace He (i) antecedently empowers and disposes us to elicit free acts that are supernaturally meritorious as well as morally good (*prevenient* actual grace) and (ii) contemporaneously concurs with such acts (*cooperating* actual grace). Predictably, Bañezians contend that cooperating grace is *intrinsically* efficacious when good acts ensue and *intrinsically* inefficacious or merely sufficient when evil acts ensue. Molina counters that although actual grace is a supernatural influence on us that inclines and incites us to act well, it is not *in itself* efficacious or inefficacious, but is instead efficacious or inefficacious only because of our free cooperation with it or freely chosen lack thereof.

So on the Bañezian scheme God foreknows the *good* contingent effects of created agents just because He causally predetermines those effects. The *evil* effects He knows by the very fact that He has *not* efficaciously concurred with their causes to produce the corresponding good effects. I will return to this last point, but first I must fill out the Bañezian picture in a way that highlights its differences with Molinism.

Let us say that God is in a *creation situation* when (as we conceive it) He possesses prevolitional knowledge but has not yet decided what to will or permit.[53] At this stage, Bañezians aver, God has only *natural* knowledge of metaphysically necessary states of affairs. Despite His ultimate control over all contingent states of affairs, He has not yet decided which ones will obtain.

Suppose that $F^t(S)$ *on H* is a metaphysically contingent state of affairs which would be a conditional future contingent if it obtained, and

[53] Once again, despite my use of temporal language, the ordering relations invoked here are meant to be conceptual and not temporal.

suppose further that S would be a *good* effect were it to obtain at t in situation H. Note that if this conditional is indeed contingent, H does not specify the *intrinsic character* of God's concurrence with the causes of S. At most, H can say only that God *does* concur, leaving open the question of whether this concurrence is intrinsically efficacious or intrinsically inefficacious.

Unlike Molina, Bañezians hold that in a creation situation God does not yet know whether $F^t(S)$ *on* H obtains. That is up to Him to decide. Yet by His *natural* knowledge He does know that $F^t(S)$ *on* H would obtain and be a conditional future contingent *if* He were to resolve that in the event that H obtained at t, He would grant intrinsically efficacious concurrence to the causes of S. This is a metaphysically necessary truth. Likewise, by His *natural* knowledge God knows that $F^t(S)$ *on* H would not obtain *if* He resolved that in the event that H should obtain at t, He would grant only inefficacious concurrence to the relevant causes. This, too, is a metaphysically necessary truth.

Now, Molinists and Bañezians all believe that a provident being's creative act of will is absolutely comprehensive; God decides from eternity not only what He will in fact do but also what He would have done in situations that will never obtain but might have obtained. He knows, for instance, whether the Incarnation would have occurred even if Adam had not sinned.

Bañezians may properly hold, then, that what God does first (as we conceive it) in a creation situation is to determine which states of affairs are conditional future contingents.[54] He does this by deciding, for each possible ordering H of created causes capable of producing a good contingent effect, whether or not He will grant intrinsically efficacious concurrence to the relevant indeterministic causes in the event that H should obtain. Given His resultant *free* knowledge of *conditional* future contingents, He then decides which of the antecedents of these conditionals He decrees (that is, wills or permits) to obtain. This gives Him knowledge of all those *absolute* future contingents that He predetermines by His efficacious concurrence.

But what of the evil effects that God only permits and does not causally predetermine? How does He know them?

Bañezians disagree on the fine points here, but all of them hold that the very fact that God does *not* causally predetermine an intended good

[54]The following reconstruction is my own, though it seems to be perfectly consistent with the main Bañezian sources I have consulted and with what Molina says about the Bañezian theory in Disputation 53, pt. 3, secs. 10–18. What's more, the modern Molinist Louis Billot, S.J., attributes the same sequential ordering of divine decrees to his Thomistic opponents in *De Deo Uno et Trino* (Rome, 1926), p. 211.

effect *S* in an actual situation *H* entails that *S* will *not* obtain in *H*. So by antecedently resolving to act by merely sufficient concurrence to produce *S* in *H*, God knows with certainty that *S* will *not* obtain in *H*. If, for example, God does not predetermine, via His intrinsically efficacious grace, the intended effect of Judas's repenting, it follows directly that Judas will not repent—even though God intends that he repent and grants him grace sufficient for, albeit *merely* sufficient for, repentance. And so, too, for every other evil effect.[55]

Molina, needless to say, has grave reservations about this account of God's knowledge of future contingents. Three of the objections I cite below concern God's relation to evil effects, and the last has to do with the Bañezian conception of freedom.

The first charge is that Bañezians lack an explanation of the *detailed* knowledge God has of evil effects. It is not enough simply to show how God knows that a good effect will not obtain; one must also show how God knows *exactly* which evil effects will obtain instead. Take the state of affairs of Peter's remaining loyal to Christ in *H*, where *H* is the situation in which Peter in fact freely denies Christ. Given that God's concurrence with Peter in *H* is in itself merely sufficient to produce the intended effect of Peter's remaining loyal, it follows only that Peter will not remain loyal. But there are any number of ways in which Peter might deny Christ, any number of intentions he might act on, different degrees of cowardice or outright malice his act might evince, different words he might use. How can God know all the relevant details with precision, given only His prior resolution not to causally predetermine Peter's remaining loyal in *H*?

Bañezians are not without resources here. One possible strategy is to argue that many components of evil effects are not themselves intrinsically evil and hence are such that God might causally predetermine them. There is nothing inherently wrong, for instance, with Peter's uttering the words "I have never seen him before in my life." On occasion, his so speaking might be positively virtuous. So even in *H*, the claim goes, God can efficaciously concur in the production of *this* element of Peter's sin. The promise is that if we follow this course to the

---

[55] For Molina's discussion of the Bañezian account of the causal genesis of evil effects, see esp. Disputation 50, secs. 11–14, and Disputation 53, pt. 2, secs. 1–9. Interestingly, this account is meant to apply to *natural* as well as to *moral* evil. That is to say, God sometimes permits natural effects (for example, birth defects) which He does not intend, just as He sometimes permits moral evils that He does not intend. Christians believe that God, as the Lord of history, invariably orders such evils, whether they are natural or moral, toward some further goods. (Notice, however, that it does not follow from this belief that those further goods provide the *reason* for God's permission of the relevant evils. This is a separate matter.) Below I limit my examples to moral evils.

end, we will reach a unique and fully determinate evil state of affairs that is produced in *H* just in case God fails to predetermine the intended effect but does predetermine each of the nonevil components of the evil effect that is instead produced.

Molina retorts that Peter's sin just *consists in* his saying the relevant words in circumstances *H*. The fact that it is not *always* wrong for him to speak in this way is beside the point. What is crucial is that his doing so in *H* constitutes a sin, and so if God *predetermined* rather than just *permitted* Peter to utter these words while in *H*, then God Himself would be to blame.

The strategy in question and Molina's response to it plunge us deep into the murkiest issues in action theory, issues I will not pursue here.[56] Molina reports in any case that neither Bañez nor Zumel himself relies on this strategy. Yet what positive alternative do they have to offer? How exactly will they explain God's detailed knowledge of evil without appealing either to middle knowledge or to divine predetermination of evil effects? They surely want to avoid claiming that when God does not predetermine a free agent to a good effect, the agent is led by a necessity of nature into a unique sinful action. This is just the error that Catholics accuse the Reformers of making, as Molina is only too happy to point out.

Molina's second objection aims to discredit what Bañezians consider a chief virtue of their account, namely, the radical asymmetry they posit in God's causal contribution to good and evil effects. Molina points out that a sinful act might possibly differ from a virtuous counterpart only in, say, some historical circumstance. For instance, it could be that the very same act of sexual intercourse, with all its physical and psychological components, is virtuous if the agents are married but sinful if they are not. Suppose further that the history of the couple's relationship in the two cases is exactly similar except for a brief visit to a priest. Is it not silly, Molina asks, to think that God's intrinsically efficacious concurrence is required in the one case but not in the other? After all, if the agents are capable of performing the act without intrinsically efficacious concurrence when it is sinful, why should they not likewise be capable of performing the same act without intrinsically efficacious concurrence when it is virtuous?

[56]How, for instance, are actions individuated? Is Peter's uttering the relevant words at *T* a distinct action from his uttering those words at *T while in circumstances H*? If so, does it follow that these two actions might have distinct causal histories, so that God could efficaciously concur in the production of the one but not of the other? Or is there, rather, just one action here with several components? If so, what is the relationship between an action and its components? How is the causal history of the various components related to the causal history of the action itself?

Third, how can Bañezians affirm that God truly intends the good effects He chooses not to predetermine by His intrinsically efficacious concurrence? If God really intends for Judas to repent and if He can bring this about simply by granting Judas intrinsically efficacious grace, then why does He refrain from doing so? More generally, why fault *creatures* for their sinful actions if those actions invariably result from the mere absence of *God's* intrinsically efficacious concurrence?

This leads us directly to Molina's fundamental philosophical problem with Bañezianism, its conception of creaturely freedom. As we saw above, Bañezians are not compatibilists in any standard sense. They deny that free acts can result from deterministic natural tendencies; they even go so far as to accept the condition that an act occurring at a time *t* is free only if some contrary act is compossible with the activity at *t* of all secondary causes other than the agent of the act in question. They thus reject what the modern Bañezian Reginald Garrigou-Lagrange labels "determinism of the circumstances."[57]

Yet Molina insists repeatedly that this is not enough. He argues in effect that the intrinsic nature of God's concurrence just *is* one of the circumstances of human action. So if that concurrence is intrinsically efficacious or inefficacious and not intrinsically neutral, then putatively free creatures are little more than puppets in the hands of God, and God alone is free.

In the same vein, Molina accuses his opponents of distorting what Christ says in Matthew 11. For if the Bañezians are right, then the Tyronians and Sidonians would not be converted by Christ's miracles unless God *in addition* concurred with their acts of faith by His intrinsically efficacious grace. Yet such grace would have likewise effected the conversion of the people of Chorozain and Bethsaida if it had been granted to them. How, then, can we resist concluding that any differences between the two groups are traceable not to *their own* actual or potential use of free choice but rather *solely* to *God's* prior resolution to confer intrinsically efficacious concurrence in the one case but not in the other? But then it seems utterly unjust of Jesus to reproach the residents of Chorozain and Bethsaida for their lack of faith and to compare them unfavorably with their neighbors.

Bañezians respond that their account of freedom is both philosophically sound and, unlike Molina's, fully consistent with the doctrine that God is the ultimate source of all goodness. Moreover, God's transcendence makes it perfectly appropriate to hold that His concurrence is *not* one of the circumstances of the free actions of creatures. As St. Thomas

[57] Garrigou-Lagrange, *The One God*, pp. 461 and 465.

makes clear, God stands *wholly outside* the order of created causes; He determines not only the good effects themselves but even the *modality* with which they are produced. Thus, God can *causally predetermine* that a good effect should be brought about *freely* by secondary causes.[58] What's more, God's efficacious grace necessarily acts in harmony with free choice. Suppose that Peter has just performed a good action under the influence of God's efficacious grace. Bañezians can still consistently hold that if Peter had chosen to perform an evil action instead, God would not have conferred intrinsically efficacious grace on him. So even though Peter's action necessarily results from God's intrinsically efficacious grace, that grace is efficacious only in cooperation with creaturely free choice.

Though Bañezians fail to qualify as modern compatibilists, the above exchange is nonetheless redolent of the familiar debate between libertarians and compatibilists. My own sympathies lie with Molina, but I realize that the prospects for a conclusive victory are dim at best. Still, as I noted in Section 2.9, there are sound intuitive grounds for accepting the strong necessary condition on freedom which separates Molinists from Bañezians. In fact, if St. Thomas is right in holding that a transcendent being alone can contemporaneously move a created will directly and from within, then only God can actually assume the role played by the genius in Katie's story. But in the case of Katie many of us had clear intuitions confirming the Molinist contention that when the genius intervenes efficaciously, Katie's decision is not free—and this despite the fact that the genius acts only 'through' her will. So even if Molina is rash in claiming that Bañezianism *obviously* annihilates human freedom, Molinist freedom is surely undeserving of the epithet "I know not what freedom" hurled at it, Molina reports, by one of his more ardent antagonists.[59]

3.4 Disputation 51: Concomitant Decrees

Molina and Bañez agree (i) that God's decreeing (willing or permitting) that a contingent effect S will obtain is prior, in our way of conceiving it, to His knowing from eternity that S will obtain and (ii) that this eternal knowledge that S will obtain is in turn prior to S's actually obtaining in time. To be sure, Molina denies, where S is good, that S is *causally* predetermined by God and, where S is evil, that S results from the mere absence of God's intrinsically efficacious concurrence. Still, on

---

[58]See, e.g., Aquinas, *Summa Theologiae* I, q. 19, a. 8. For a sustained defense of this claim, see Garrigou-Lagrange, *God: His Existence and Nature* (St. Louis, 1936), pp. 71–91.

[59]Disputation 53, pt. 2, sec. 20.

the Molinist scheme good contingent effects are *predetermined* in that by His middle knowledge God plans for them in detail and knows that they will ensue given the total causal contribution He has willed to make to the created world. Likewise, evil effects are *antecedently permitted* in that by His middle knowledge God allows for them in detail and knows that they will ensue given that same causal contribution. So despite their quarrels, Molina and Bañez agree that by His act of will God brings it about that He knows each absolute future contingent $F^i(S)$ from eternity, prior to and independently of S's obtaining in time. This knowledge simply flows from His having antecedently ordered all of creation as the Lord of history.

In Disputation 51 Molina examines a position whose leading principles are shared by any attempt to find a viable alternative to Bañezianism and Molinism. All sides hold that God's decreeing and knowing a contingent effect cannot be *posterior* to its obtaining. Otherwise, God would not be truly provident. But, the claim goes, the causal indeterminism involved in contingent effects also rules out the idea that God's decreeing and knowing them is *prior*, in our way of conceiving it, to their obtaining. It follows that, for any future contingent $F(S)$, (i) God's decreeing $F(S)$, (ii) His knowing $F(S)$, and (iii) S's obtaining are all *simultaneous* or *concomitant*.

This argument for the 'concomitance theory' rests upon two presuppositions. The first is that a contingent effect S has *metaphysical determinacy* or *certitude* only when, and not before, S is produced by its causes. This principle, endorsed by Molina, rests on a strong account of indeterminism which directly excludes causal predeterminations of the Bañezian ilk.[60] The second presupposition is that until a contingent effect S has *metaphysical certitude*, no one, not even God, can have *epistemic certitude* with respect to $F(S)$. This premise, accepted by Bañezians, cuts against Molinism. For a key Molinist tenet is that middle knowledge gives God *epistemic certitude* with respect to each absolute future contingent $F(S)$ prior to S's having *metaphysical certitude*. As Molina puts it, God knows with (epistemic) certainty what is in itself (metaphysically) uncertain.[61]

The two presuppositions together entail the seeming paradox that God can foreknow with certainty that a contingent effect S *will* obtain at

---

[60]More precisely, a contingent state of affairs S has metaphysical certitude only after each of the indeterministic causes in its causal ancestry has acted. After that time S either actually obtains (category C effect) or is *completely* present in its deterministic causes (category D effect). So, strictly speaking, a contingent effect of category D will have metaphysical certitude before it obtains. I will, however, ignore this complication below.

[61]See, e.g., Disputation 52, secs. 33 and 35.

a time *t* only if He already knows with certainty that *S does* obtain at *t*. So it is no surprise that writers like William James and Peter Geach should appeal to such premises in rejecting the classical doctrine that God has comprehensive knowledge of the contingent future.[62] Concomitance theorists, however, shy away from this radical move. They contend instead that when a contingent effect *S* comes to obtain at a time *t*, then *at t itself* God concomitantly causes it to be the case that He has always known $F^t(S)$. Likewise, *at t itself* He concomitantly causes it to be the case that he has always decreed $F^t(S)$. This is the 'temporalist' version of the theory. According to the 'eternalist' version, God's knowing and willing are properly measured by eternity, and so it is better to say that *as* (and *not before*) contingent effects occur in time, God concomitantly causes it to be the case that He *eternally knows and decrees* them.

Although concomitance theorists thus allow for comprehensive divine knowledge of the contingent future, their clear intent is to deny, à la James and Geach, that God antecedently plots out in detail the whole history of the world, complete with all its contingent effects. The most that God can do antecedently is to decide how He will accommodate each possible eventuality, so that as history unfolds He can keep integrating the way things in fact turn out into a unified eternal plan. If Peter freely sins at *T*, then at *T* God concomitantly causes it to be the case that He eternally permits Peter to sin at *T* and eternally knows that he will sin at *T*. If Peter instead acts virtuously at *T*, then at *T* God concomitantly causes it to be the case that it is Peter's acting well at *T*, and not his sinning, that is eternally part of the divine scheme. But at times *before T* neither Peter's sinning at *T* nor his acting well at *T* is as yet fixed unalterably as part of God's eternal plan. So God's foreknowledge of future contingents is in no way a function of antecedent providential decrees.

Temporalist proponents of the theory must attribute to God at least limited power over the past. They typically claim along Ockhamist lines that even though the 'hard' causal history of the world is now accidentally necessary and so unalterable by any human or divine power, many 'soft' facts about the past, including facts about God's past knowledge of absolute future contingents, are accidentally contingent and still subject to human or at least divine power.[63] For instance, even if it was true ten

---

[62]See James, "The Dilemma of Determinism," pp. 145–183 in *The Will to Believe and Other Essays in Popular Philosophy* (New York, 1897, 1956); and Geach, *Providence and Evil*, pp. 40–66.

[63]For more on the distinction between hard and soft facts, see Marilyn Adams, "Is the Existence of God a 'Hard' Fact?" *Philosophical Review* 76 (1967): 492–503; Joshua Hoffman and Gary Rosenkrantz, "Hard Facts and Soft Facts," *Philosophical Review* 93 (1984): 419–

years ago that Peter would sin at T, where T is in our future, this soft fact about the past is now accidentally contingent and still within Peter's power to render false. Peter, of course, will not *exercise* the power in question at T, but this does not mean that he *lacks* it. Likewise, even if God knew ten years ago that Peter would sin at T, where T is in our future, this soft fact about God's past knowledge is now accidentally contingent. God will still have the power at T to cause it to be the case that He has always known that Peter would *not* sin at T. Given that Peter in fact sins at T, it follows only that God does not *exercise* this power at T, not that He *lacks* it. Prior to T, then, God's eternal plan is still flexible enough to accommodate whatever free choice Peter makes.

We can easily anticipate two of Molina's objections to the concomitance theory. First, though this theory pays lip service to God's knowledge of future contingents, its advocates hold both that God's prevolitional knowledge is merely *natural* and that His contribution to contingent effects is neither intrinsically efficacious nor intrinsically inefficacious. They are thus forced to deny, against the doctrine of providence, that God's knowledge of the contingent future arises solely from the conjunction of His prevolitional knowledge with His knowledge of His own causal contribution to the world. Far from God's *providing for* future contingents, He literally *reacts to* them as to effects brought about independently of His *specific* approval or permission.

Second, the concomitance theory does not explain the source of, and perhaps does not even allow for, God's knowledge of *conditional* future contingents, since it invokes neither middle knowledge nor predetermining decrees. In this regard it resembles the standard interpretation of St. Thomas.

But Molina breaks new ground by claiming, third, that *any* version of the concomitance theory must attribute to God not only power over soft facts about the past but also power over the hard causal history of the world. The most engaging argument for this claim occurs in section 19 of Disputation 51 and concerns Christ's prophecy of Peter's denial.

At T Jesus utters the Aramaic for "You will deny me three times." Concomitance theorists hold that before T^*, the time of the denial, Peter's sin is not yet a fixed part of God's plan. But in that case, argues Molina, neither is Christ's utterance. For suppose Peter refrains from sinning at T^*. Then, on the concomitance theory, at T^* God will cause it to be true that He has always known (or eternally knows) that Peter will

434; and John Martin Fischer, "Freedom and Foreknowledge" and "Hard-Type Soft Facts," *Philosophical Review* 95 (1986): 591–601. In "Accidental Necessity and Logical Determinism" I attempted to draw a similar distinction between two senses of the expression 'the history of the world'.

not deny Christ at T^*. But what of Christ's previous utterance? At T^* the fact that Christ has already made this utterance is clearly part of the world's causal history. It is a hard fact about the past by anyone's reckoning. Now if this fact cannot be altered at T^*, then the alleged prophecy will have been false. But this is absurd, since the God-man cannot err in this manner. The only way out for concomitance theorists is to claim that if Peter does not sin at T^*, then at T^* God will cause it to be the case that Christ did not utter the words in question at T. But this is to attribute to God power over a hard fact about the past—which even concomitance theorists admit is absurd.

I will return to the problem of prophecy in Section 4. Note for now that Molina rejects the Ockhamist distinction between the hard and the soft past, at least insofar as this distinction is meant to undergird the thesis that there is power (albeit limited power) over the past. To the contrary, he holds that the schema

Agent P has the power at t to contribute causally to S's obtaining before t

never expresses a truth. Nonetheless, Molina insists (i) that Peter has at T^* the power to refrain from sinning and (ii) that if he were to exercise this power, then Christ would never have uttered the dire prophetic words. That is, the corresponding schema

Agent P has the power at t to contribute causally to S^*'s obtaining at or after t; and if S^* were going to obtain at or after t, then S would never have obtained before t

may express a truth even if S is past-tense and already at t part of the causal history of the world. Below I will show how Molina reaches these conclusions and argue that his solution to the problem of prophecy far outstrips its competitors.

4 The Theory of Middle Knowledge

4.1 *Preliminary Remarks*

Like Molina, I have laid out the essentials of the theory of middle knowledge while treating the alternative accounts of God's knowledge of future contingents, especially Bañezianism. Following the contours of Disputation 52, I will now first fill in the more significant details of the theory and then show how Molina reconciles divine foreknowledge with creaturely freedom.

4.2 *Divine Knowledge: Natural, Middle, and Free*

As noted above, middle knowledge derives its name from the fact that it stands 'midway' between natural knowledge and free knowledge. Like natural knowledge but unlike free knowledge, middle knowledge is prevolitional, with the result that God has no more control over the states of affairs He knows through His middle knowledge than He does over the states of affairs He knows through His natural knowledge. Like free knowledge but unlike natural knowledge, middle knowledge is such that the states of affairs known through it might have failed to obtain, with the result that what God knows through His middle knowledge may vary from one possible world to another just as what He knows through His free knowledge may vary from one possible world to another. So God has middle knowledge only if He knows some metaphysically contingent states of affairs over which He has no control.

There is another way in which middle knowledge lies between natural and free knowledge. Natural knowledge has among its objects all the *possible* future contingents, whereas free knowledge has among its objects all *actual* or *absolute* future contingents. By contrast, middle knowledge has as its objects *conditional* or *subjunctive* future contingents that stand 'between' the actual and the merely possible. By His natural knowledge God knows that it is metaphysically possible but not metaphysically necessary that Adam will sin if placed in the garden; by His free knowledge He knows that Adam will in fact be placed in the garden and will in fact sin. What He knows by His middle knowledge, on the other hand, is something stronger than the former but weaker than the latter, namely, that Adam will sin *on the condition* that he be placed in the garden. So God has middle knowledge only if He knows all the conditional future contingents.

As stressed above, however, this necessary condition is not sufficient. For even Bañezians, who vehemently repudiate middle knowledge, cheerfully concede that God knows conditional future contingents. So we must combine the two conditions and say that God has middle knowledge if and only if He has comprehensive *prevolitional* knowledge of *conditional future contingents*.

4.3 *Creation Situations and Divine Power*

As characterized in Section 3, a creation situation reflects the extent of God's prevolitional knowledge. In fact, we might simply define the creation situation for a world w ($CS(w)$) as the set that has as members all and only those states of affairs which God knows prevolitionally in w;

and we can say that a creation situation *obtains* just in case each of its members obtains. If we grant that God exists and is all-knowing in every possible world, it follows that each world contains a creation situation.

Creation situations mark the range of the divine power or, better, the range of effects that may issue, directly or via secondary causes, from exercises of that power. In other words, creation situations constitute the antecedently fixed frameworks within which God operates as a cause. So, as intimated above, God has no control over the states of affairs that belong to the creation situation He finds Himself in. What He *does* have control over is each state of affairs that is such that neither it nor its complement is a member of that creation situation.

Bañezians hold that the only prevolitional knowledge God has or can have is *natural* knowledge, and that He has this knowledge in every possible world. So for any worlds w and w^*, $CS(w)$ is the same as $CS(w^*)$. That is, there is just one possible creation situation, namely, the set, call it N, which has as members all and only the metaphysically *necessary* states of affairs. On the Bañezian view, then, it is a necessary truth that God has control over every metaphysically *contingent* state of affairs.

Molina, to be sure, believes that any creation situation contains N as a subset. He also agrees that any creation situation obtains in, and hence is shared by, many distinct possible worlds. For this is just to say that in any creation situation God has alternative courses of action to choose from, each culminating in the actualization of a distinct possible world. In contrast to Bañezianism, however, Molinism entails that there are many—indeed, uncountably many—distinct creation situations, each containing, in addition to N, a full complement of mutually compossible conditional future contingents known by God through His middle knowledge. More formally,

> $CS(w)$ is a *Molinist creation situation* if and only if $CS(w)$ is a set of states of affairs such that (i) every member of N is a member of $CS(w)$ and (ii) for any pair of potential conditional future contingents of the form $F^t(S)$ *on H* and $F^t(not\text{-}S)$ *on H*, the one that obtains in w is a member of $CS(w)$ and (iii) every metaphysically contingent state of affairs included (or entailed) by the conjunction of two or more members of $CS(w)$ is itself a member of $CS(w)$.[64]

Each creation situation $CS(w)$ defines a set of possible worlds which has as members all and only those worlds in which $CS(w)$ obtains.

---

[64]The last condition ensures that truth-functional compounds of conditional future contingents belonging to $CS(w)$ will themselves belong to $CS(w)$. It also ensures that the complement of a conditional future contingent S belongs to $CS(w)$ just in case S does not itself belong to $CS(w)$.

Following Thomas Flint, I will call this set the *galaxy* for $CS(w)$.[65] Thus a world w^* is a member of the galaxy for $CS(w)$ if and only if $CS(w^*)$ is the same as $CS(w)$. Since distinct creation situations are mutually incompatible, each possible world belongs to at most one galaxy. What's more, it follows from what was said above that each possible world belongs to at least one galaxy. So creation situations divide the field of possible worlds into groups, namely, the galaxies, which are mutually exclusive and jointly exhaustive.

Intuitively, the galaxy for $CS(w)$ has as members the only worlds that God can antecedently arrange to be actualized, by His own power and that of secondary causes, should He find himself in $CS(w)$. For instance, if He knows prevolitionally in $CS(w)$ that Adam will sin if placed in H, then He cannot arrange things in such a way that Adam will be in H and yet not sin. For no world that includes this absolute future contingent is a member of the galaxy for $CS(w)$. Of course, even if God in fact puts Adam into H, He still *intends* that Adam *not* sin. And it may even be true in $CS(w)$ that there is a situation very much like H in which Adam would not freely sin. Nonetheless, H itself is such that if God antecedently wills or permits it to obtain, then Adam will sin by his own free choice. Over this fact God has no control, since He has no control over which creation situation actually obtains. In general, if God finds Himself in $CS(w)$, then He is able to decree that a world w^* be actualized if and only if $CS(w^*)$ is the same as $CS(w)$, that is, if and only if w^* is a member of the galaxy for $CS(w)$ and hence accessible to God's providential decrees. And unlike Bañezianism, Molinism entails that for any creation situation $CS(w)$ there will be possible worlds that God cannot antecedently decree to be actualized should He find Himself in $CS(w)$.[66]

Though a Molinist creation situation puts more restrictions on the exercise of God's power than does its Bañezian analog, ample room is left for the execution of divine providence—or so, at least, Molina claims. First, it is still entirely up to God whether or not to create anything at all.[67] Second, it is still true that no creature can produce even the most trifling effect unless God cooperates with it by His general concurrence. Third, any good act effected by a free creature requires, in addition to divine general concurrence, the particular though nondeter-

[65] See Thomas P. Flint, "The Problem of Divine Freedom," *American Philosophical Quarterly* 20 (1983): 255–264.

[66] This is the thrust of Alvin Plantinga's argument against 'Leibniz's Lapse' in *The Nature of Necessity* (Oxford, 1974), pp. 169–184. For an attempt to accommodate this argument in constructing an account of omnipotence, see Thomas P. Flint and Alfred J. Freddoso, "Maximal Power," pp. 81–113 in Alfred J. Freddoso, ed., *The Existence and Nature of God.*

[67] This first thesis, although consistent with Molinism, is not entailed by it. Molina accepts on faith the notion that each galaxy contains a world in which no creatures exist.

mining causal influence of various sorts of natural and supernatural divine assistance. Supernaturally meritorious acts, for example, require the causal influence of prevenient and cooperating actual grace. Fourth, no evil effect can be brought about by a creature if God does not antecedently and specifically permit it. So even though God has no control over which creation situation obtains or hence over which galaxy He must choose from, He nonetheless does have total control over which effects, if any, are *actually* produced in the created universe. Finally, Molina can still consistently hold that God's providential act of will is absolutely comprehensive. That is, in $CS(w)$ God not only decides which world in the galaxy for $CS(w)$ will be actualized, but He also decides, for any creation situation $CS(w^*)$ distinct from $CS(w)$, what He *would have* decreed had He been in $CS(w^*)$ instead. All these elements taken together, Molina asserts, constitute the strongest account of divine providence consistent with a correct understanding of the doctrine that some creatures are endowed with the power of free choice.

Let me return briefly to the characterization of a Molinist creation situation. Many philosophers stand ready to dispute Molina's assumption that necessarily, for any pair of potential conditional future contingents of the form $F^i(S)$ *on H* and $F^i(not\text{-}S)$ *on H*, exactly one obtains and one does not. I believe that this assumption, known as the law of conditional excluded middle, is plausible, but I acknowledge that a full defense of it must be set within a general theory of subjunctive conditionals at odds in certain respects with currently popular theories.[68] Still, two points are worth immediate mention. First, some might object to the assumption in question on the grounds that the antecedent H is not always 'informative' enough to 'sustain' either $F^i(S)$ or $F^i(not\text{-}S)$ as a consequent. Even though I do not endorse the conception of the relation between antecedent and consequent which underlies this objection, I should nonetheless point out that Molina can and ought to endorse the added stipulation that $F^i(S)$ *on H* is a potential conditional future contingent only if H includes a *total* description of the causal history and contemporaneous causal circumstances of any exercise of indeterministic causation which figures directly in the consequent. Alternatively, a Molinist can consistently hold that the obtaining of a potential conditional future contingent is always relative to a total causal context of this sort, in much the same way that the obtaining of, say, a past-tense state

---

[68]For some relevant background, see Robert Adams, "Middle Knowledge and the Problem of Evil," p. 110; David Lewis, *Counterfactuals* (Oxford, 1973), pp. 79ff.; and Robert Stalnaker, "A Theory of Conditionals," pp. 98–112 in Nicholas Rescher, ed., *Studies in Logical Theory* (Oxford, 1968), pp. 106ff. I discuss this complicated issue more in Section 5.6 below. I hope to address the relevant questions at length elsewhere.

of affairs is always relative to a time. Second, Thomas Flint has shown in effect that as long as we grant that conditional future contingents can in principle provide God with 'positive' information about the activity of indeterministic secondary causes in various hypothetical situations, the Molinist can get by just as well with the weaker and hence more digestible assumption that, necessarily, any potential conditional future contingent is such that either it or its complement obtains.[69] As we shall see in Section 5, some philosophers reject even this assumption. But it is important to separate their more general objection from the 'informativeness' objection cited above.

4.4 Comprehension and Supercomprehension

Even if there are 'positive' conditional future contingents, how might they be known? Bañezians have no special problem here: God knows conditional future contingents in the same way He knows absolute future contingents, namely, in and through His decreeing that they obtain. But such an approach is obviously not available to Molina. In the end he appeals simply to God's cognitive perfection and to the depth of His prevolitional grasp of all possible creatures.

In Section 2 we saw that, according to Molina, comprehending an entity involves grasping the metaphysical modality of every state of affairs involving it. So it is by His *natural* knowledge that God comprehends each possible entity, including Himself. But comprehension so characterized plainly does not include any knowledge of conditional future contingents. If I comprehend Adam, I know that both his sinning in the garden and his not sinning in the garden are metaphysically possible. But I do not thereby know whether or not Adam will in fact sin if placed in the garden. Middle knowledge demands a cognition that penetrates far deeper than comprehension as just defined, a cognition that came to be known in Molinist literature as 'supercomprehension'.

Though this term is not Molina's own, he clearly believes that God alone can supercomprehend and that creatures alone can be supercomprehended. For the cognitive power of one who supercomprehends

---

[69]See Flint, "The Problem of Divine Freedom." That is, for any state of affairs of the form $F^t(S)$ *on H*, either it or its complement, that is, *not-*$[F^t(S)$ *on H*$]$, obtains. So the claim is that the law of bivalence will do just as well as the law of conditional excluded middle, provided that some affirmative states of affairs of the form in question obtain. This qualification is necessary, since Molinism would be undermined if no such affirmative state of affairs could obtain. For in that case there would be just one possible creation situation: the union of N with the set of all the negations of potential conditional future contingents. Moreover, in such a creation situation God would have no positive knowledge of how created indeterministic causes would act.

an entity must, Molina claims, "surpass in perfection by an infinite distance" the entity in question.[70] More precisely, one who super-comprehends must be able to have epistemic certitude regarding states of affairs that do not (at least as yet) have metaphysical certitude. As Molina rather misleadingly puts it, by His middle knowledge God knows creatures "in a more eminent way than that in which they are knowable in themselves."[71]

We must be careful not to misinterpret Molina here. He is not making the absurd claim that by His middle knowledge God knows something that is not there 'objectively' to be known. To the contrary, the states of affairs which God knows by His middle knowledge really obtain from eternity and the corresponding propositions are really true from eternity. Nor is Molina asserting that conditional future contingents are completely inaccessible epistemically to anyone other than God. He would gladly concede that even human beings can have well-grounded beliefs about how they themselves or others would freely act in various hypothetical situations.[72] (I return to this point in Section 5.8.)

Molina is claiming instead that what is 'there' to be known prevolitionally about future contingents can be known *infallibly* and *with certitude* only by a cognitively perfect being, where a subject P has infallible cognition of a state of affairs S in an epistemic context C only if it is metaphysically impossible that P be mistaken in C about whether or not S obtains. Only God can have such cognition of conditional future contingents, and this by virtue of the fact that only the divine cognitive power exceeds what is required for the mere comprehension of creatures.

This way of putting it helps explain Molina's contention that God does not know *prevolitionally* what *He Himself* would choose to do in any creation situation, including the actual one. For His cognitive power does not surpass *His own* nature in the way that it surpasses creaturely natures. So it is only in and by His act of will that He knows what He Himself in fact decrees and what He would decree in other creation situations. This is part of His *free* knowledge and not of His middle knowledge.

The foregoing account of how God has middle knowledge is arguably

---

[70]Disputation 52, sec. 13.

[71]Ibid., secs. 11 and 35. The discussion that follows is meant as a reply to Robert Adams's (as well as Suarez's) objection that the words quoted here commit Molina to the incoherent claim that God knows something it is metaphysically impossible for anyone to know. See Adams's "Middle Knowledge and the Problem of Evil," p. 111.

[72]Suarez makes much of this point in *De Scientia Quam Deus Habet de Futuris Contingentibus*, bk. 2, chap. 5, pp. 198–200 in Suarez, *Opera Omnia* (Venice, 1741), vol. 10.

the weakest link in the Molinist chain. Yet it is not for that reason obviously untenable. Some Molinists have retreated at this point to the simple assertion that because God is essentially omniscient, one has only to establish that conditional future contingents obtain in order to show that God has comprehensive and infallible prevolitional knowledge of them. Supercomprehension is thus rendered superfluous—or at least swept under the rug.

This claim, although promising in some respects, is weaker than Molina's own, mainly because it can supply no rationale for the thesis that God has no prevolitional knowledge of what He Himself will do. Perhaps this point is not important, but, then again, perhaps it is. For Molina argues at some length that God's own freedom of choice would be obliterated if He had infallible knowledge of His own free decisions conceptually prior to His making them.[73] I will not rehearse the argument here, but will only point out that if it is sound, Molinists are burdened with the task of finding some way to explain the fact that God has prevolitional cognition of the free actions of creatures but lacks prevolitional cognition of His own free actions.

4.5 *Foreknowledge and Freedom*

Now for Molina's reconciliation of divine foreknowledge with creaturely freedom. He first argues that his theory coheres with and is corroborated by the traditional maxim according to which it is not the case that a contingent effect S will obtain because God foreknows that S will obtain, but rather God foreknows that S will obtain because S will in fact obtain.[74]

The first half of this maxim is easy enough to establish within the Molinist scheme. God's knowing that, say, Peter will deny Christ is a piece of *free* knowledge and is thus conceptually posterior to the act of will by which God decrees Peter's being so situated that he will freely deny Christ. So unlike God's prevolitional knowledge, which in Molina's own words is a *partial* and *remote* cause of created effects, God's free knowledge that Peter will sin comes too late, conceptually speaking, to cause anything at all and is in fact itself an *effect* of God's act of will. In technical terms, God's free knowledge is a speculative knowledge of

---

[73]See Disputation 52, secs. 11–15, and Disputation 53, pt. 1, secs. 17 and 19. Since the argument found in these places, if successful, rules out only *infallible* knowledge of one's own future free choices, it applies to God alone and cannot be turned into a general argument for the claim that no agents can have justified true beliefs regarding their own future free choices.

[74]For Molina's discussion of this point, see Disputation 52, secs. 10 and 19.

vision and, unlike His prevolitional knowledge, not a potentially practical knowledge ordered toward the production of effects. Thus it is not because of God's knowledge of Peter's sin that Peter will sin.

But what of the second half of the maxim? What of the claim that God foreknows that Peter will deny Christ *because* Peter will in fact deny Christ. Molina, as emphasized above, dismisses the notion that Peter causally contributes to God's free and eternal knowledge of the act in question. After all, God had this knowledge long before Peter existed and, Molina insists repeatedly, there is no power of any sort over the past. Nor, as far as I can tell, does (or should) Molina subscribe to the idea that Peter causally contributes to God's foreknowing that Peter would deny Christ if placed in the relevant circumstances. For, once again, God had this piece of middle knowledge long before Peter existed.

How, then, can it be true that God knows that an effect S will obtain *because S* will obtain? As I understand it, Molina's answer is a general one holding for *all* the effects of secondary causes, both necessary and contingent. It goes like this: God's *knowing* that S will obtain follows upon His *decreeing* (either approvingly or merely permissively) that S will obtain. But this divine decree, which is a *partial* and *proximate* cause of its object, is guided by infallible prevolitional knowledge of how any possible secondary cause would act in any possible set of circumstances involving it. Thus God's decreeing that S will obtain guarantees, and so renders it true from eternity, that S will be produced with God's concurrence by the relevant secondary causes. In short, God knows postvolitionally that S will obtain because His own decree has already guaranteed that the future-tense state of affairs $F(S)$ obtains from eternity.

The prevolitional knowledge pertinent to necessary effects is purely natural, whereas with contingent effects middle knowledge comes into play as well. What God knows through His middle knowledge is, to be sure, metaphysically contingent. It need not have been the case that, say, Peter would deny Christ if placed in the relevant circumstances. Still, given that God knows infallibly by His middle knowledge that Peter would in fact freely deny Christ if placed in those circumstances, it follows that by decreeing that Peter will be in those circumstances God ensures that it is true from eternity that Peter will freely sin—long before Peter actually brings about the effect in question. So God freely knows that Peter will sin because it is already true by divine decree that Peter will sin, just as God freely knows that a given necessary effect will obtain because it is already true by divine decree that it will obtain. And it is in this sense—and this sense alone—that God knows by His free knowledge that S will obtain *because S* will in fact obtain.

I will now briefly examine Molina's response to what is generally acknowledged to be the most powerful argument for the thesis that divine foreknowledge is incompatible with creaturely freedom. My presentation of the argument will be more detailed than his, so that I can show clearly how his response differs from all the others. (I follow Molina in shifting here to the language of propositions.)

Four principles serve as presuppositions of this argument. All deal with temporal or accidental necessity. The first is simply an intuitively appealing account of what it is for a proposition to be accidentally necessary at a given time:

(A) p is accidentally necessary at t if and only if (i) p is metaphysically contingent and (ii) p is true at t and at every moment after t in every possible world that shares the same history with our world at t.

From (A) it follows directly that this necessity is closed under entailment for metaphysically contingent propositions:

(B) If (i) p entails q and (ii) q is metaphysically contingent and (iii) p is accidentally necessary at t, then q is accidentally necessary at t.

If a proposition is now such that it can no longer be false, then obviously any proposition it entails is likewise such that it can no longer be false.

The third principle relates accidental necessity to causal power and, once again, appears to follow directly from (A):

(C) If p is accidentally necessary at t, then no agent has the power at or after t to contribute causally to p's not being true.

If a proposition is such that it can no longer be false, then it seems clear that no agent can cause it to be false.

The fourth principle, finally, gives a sufficient condition for a proposition's being accidentally necessary. Here P represents the past-tense propositional operator:

(D) If p is true at t, then the proposition Pp is accidentally necessary at every moment after t.

That is, once a proposition has been true at a given time, its having been true at that time is from then on necessary and hence, by (C), not subject to any future causal influence.

These principles all have considerable intuitive appeal. At the very least, each has been deemed nonnegotiable by one or another of the many eminent thinkers who have wrestled with the problem of divine foreknowledge.

Now take a future act that is allegedly both free and foreknown, for example, Peter's sinful denial of Christ at T, where T, we will assume, is in our distant future. The following argument purports to show that if this action of Peter's has ever been foreknown by God, then it cannot be free, because *no* agent (Peter, God, Katie's genius) could have the power at or before T to make it false that Peter is sinning at T:[75]

(1)   The proposition *God foreknows, infallibly and with certainty, that Peter will sin at T* is now true. [assumption]

(2)   So at every future moment the proposition *God foreknew, infallibly and with certainty, that Peter would sin at T* will be accidentally necessary. [(1) and (D)]

(3)   But the proposition *God foreknew, infallibly and with certainty, that Peter would sin at T* entails the metaphysically contingent proposition *If T is present, Peter is sinning*. [assumption]

(4)   So at every future moment the proposition *If T is present, Peter is sinning* will be accidentally necessary. [(2), (3) and (B)]

Therefore, no agent will have the power at any future moment to contribute causally to its being the case that the proposition *If T is present, Peter is sinning* is not true. That is, no agent (Peter, God) will have the power at any future moment to make it true that Peter is not sinning when T is present. [(4) and (C)]

There are three standard responses to this argument. In summarizing them below, I also briefly note Molina's objections to them.

Aristotelian responses in effect concede the point of the argument by denying (1) on the ground that since the proposition *Peter will sin at T* is about the contingent future, it cannot be known infallibly and with certainty prior to T. Some who favor this response explicitly reject the doctrine that God knows or can know the contingent future. Others, following St. Thomas, admit that the contingent future cannot be known with certainty *as future* but insist that God can nonetheless know the contingent future *as (eternally) present* in a way that does not jeopardize

---

[75]The argument presented here is a reconstruction of the second objection (sec. 3) in Disputation 52. Molina replies to it in secs. 32–34. In "Accidental Necessity and Logical Determinism," I laid out and discussed an exactly similar argument for logical determinism, though I did not in that place cite Molina's position as one of the possible replies.

creaturely freedom. Molina rejects this Thomistic response, in part, it seems, because he believes that future contingent propositions are true from eternity by divine decree and hence can be known from eternity by God *as future*. There is another reason as well for having doubts about this Thomistic response. Consider the proposition *Now (before T) it is true to say that God knows eternally that Peter sins at T*. If Thomists accept this proposition, as it seems they should, it can serve as the first premise of another argument that is both exactly like the one laid out above and ostensibly insoluble by appeals to God's eternity. On the other hand, suppose that they reject this proposition. What possible justification might they offer for this rejection? If they claim, following Aristotle, that it is not true before *T* that Peter will sin at *T*, then how can God reveal future contingents to time-bound creatures through His prophets? At the very least, some further explanation is called for here.

What I will dub the Geachian response denies (3) by claiming that the proposition *God foreknew, infallibly and with certainty, that Peter will sin at T* entails only that the world was at one time tending toward Peter's sinning at *T*.[76] Since such a tendency may be impeded or even reversed before *T*, it does not follow from this proposition that if *T* is now present, then Peter is sinning. This response, unlike its Aristotelian counterpart, allows future contingent propositions to be known by God with certainty, but it also clearly entails that the resulting divine knowledge falls far short of comprehensive knowledge of the contingent future. At best, God can have only comprehensive knowledge of present tendencies toward the contingent future.

The Ockhamistic response, on the other hand, rejects the inference from (1) to (2) on the ground that (D), despite its intuitive attractiveness, does not distinguish the 'real' history of the world from the 'soft' past, which is still under God's control.[77] God, the Ockhamists maintain, still has the power before *T* to cause it to have been true that He foreknew with certainty that Peter would *not* sin at *T*. To be sure, He will never exercise this power, but this does not mean that He lacks it. As we saw in Section 3.4, Molina rejects this response by insisting that no proposition at all, even one that does not, strictly speaking, concern the *causal* history of the world, can now be caused to have been true or caused to have been false by any agent, God included.

At this point it might seem that Molina has closed off every viable avenue of escape. And, indeed, I can attest from personal experience

---

[76]See Geach, *Providence and Evil*, pp. 40–66.

[77]This is analogous to the position I defended in "Accidental Necessity and Logical Determinism," as a response to the argument for logical determinism. The reader might wish to consult that paper for a more extensive discussion of Ockhamism.

that at first glance his response to the argument is apt to strike one as astonishing. In a word, he rejects the inference from (2) and (3) to (4) by denying (B), the thesis that accidental necessity is closed under entailment:

> Even if (i) the conditional is necessary (because . . . these two things cannot both obtain, namely, that God foreknows something to be future and that the thing does not turn out that way), and even if (ii) the antecedent is necessary in the sense in question (because it is past-tense and because no shadow of alteration can befall God), nonetheless the consequent can be purely contingent.[78]

But how so? After all, (B) follows directly and obviously from (A). Molina is not very explicit here, but it is clear that he must reject (A) as well as (B). Consider this line of reasoning: God's foreknowledge is not a cause of Peter's sinning. To the contrary, it is evident that Peter's sinful act satisfies the necessary condition for indeterministic freedom presented in Section 2.9. There is, after all, no reason to think that God's foreknowledge makes the sin occur by a necessity of nature or that it is in any way a contemporaneous cause of the sin. Yet it is also true that there is absolutely no power over the past. If God knew from eternity that Peter would deny Christ at T, then no agent can now cause it to be true that God never knew this. But if God's past foreknowledge is thus accidentally necessary and entails that Peter will sin at T, and if, in addition, Peter's action will satisfy the causal conditions necessary for it to be free, then accidental necessity must not be closed under entailment. Since this conclusion conflicts with (A), it must be the case that (A) does not correctly capture the necessity of the past.

Notice in passing that this chain of reasoning presupposes the falsity of a principle that libertarians might naturally be inclined to endorse, namely, that an agent P freely performs an action A at a time t only if there is a possible world w such that (i) w shares all and only the same *accidentally necessary propositions* with our world at t and (ii) at t in w P refrains from performing A. In opposition to the Ockhamists, Molina holds that God's past beliefs are just as necessary in the sense in question as are any other truths about the past. And, of course, there is no possible world in which God once believed that Peter would sin at T and in which Peter does not in fact sin at T. Yet if this alleged condition on freedom is meant to capture the sense in which free action is indeterministic, then Molina himself has what seems to be a wholly adequate alternative condition. For he can distinguish what is accidentally neces-

[78]Disputation 52, sec. 34.

sary at a given time from what belongs, strictly speaking, to the causal history of the world at that time, where the world's causal history includes only past exercises of causal power.[79] And consonant with what was said about freedom in Section 2.9, he can distinguish the principle just rejected from the benign principle that an agent *P* freely performs an action *A* at a time *t* only if *P*'s performing *A* does not obtain at *t* by a necessity of nature, where what occurs at a given time by a necessity of nature is a function of the *causal history* of the world at that time. Since Molina holds that God's foreknowledge of absolute future contingents is not a cause of anything, he can consistently hold that Peter's sin satisfies this principle.

But what can a Molinist substitute for (A)? The best I have been able to come up with is this:

(A*)   *p* is accidentally necessary at *t* if and only if (i) *p* is metaphysically contingent and (ii) *p* is true at *t* and (iii) for any possible world *w* such that *w* shares the same causal history with our world at *t*, no agent has the power at or after *t* in *w* to contribute causally to *p*'s not being true.

Because Molina brooks no power of any sort over the past, every truth about the past is equally impervious to any present or future causal activity.[80] So no agent can now cause it to have been true that God never

---

[79]The notion of the causal history of the world may well be equivalent to the conjunction of what Ockhamists are wont to call 'hard' facts about the past. In this sense, Molina is not rejecting the claim that there is some distinction to be drawn between 'hard' and 'soft' facts about the past. What he rejects is instead the claim that agents can have causal power over the soft facts about the past.

[80]As I emphasize in Section 5.7 below, we must draw a sharp distinction between an agent's *causally contributing* to a state of affairs *S*, on the one hand, and *S*'s obtaining being (merely) *counterfactually dependent* on something an agent does. I have no exact account of this distinction to offer, but I have tried to flesh it out more precisely in Section 3 of "Medieval Aristotelianism and the Case against Secondary Causation in Nature." At any rate, a Molinist will insist that genuine causal contribution is always future-oriented, whereas mere counterfactual dependence may, given the model provided by the theory of middle knowledge, be past-oriented or backtracking.

Also, a Molinist can consistently accept the claim that there may be different degrees of counterfactual dependence. God's middle knowledge seems *directly* or *strongly* counterfactually dependent on how indeterministic secondary causes would act, whereas other past-tense states of affairs may be only *indirectly* or *weakly* dependent on such actions, since the dependence in question is metaphysically contingent and has to be mediated by God's middle knowledge. Suppose, for instance, that I will not in fact sin in *H*, but that if God had known from eternity that I would sin if placed in *H*, then He would have decided to actualize a possible world other than the one He has in fact actualized—a world in which, say, Abraham never exists. In that case, Abraham's having existed would be *weakly* counterfactually dependent on how I act in *H*. Alvin Plantinga discusses cases like this in "On Ockham's Way Out," *Faith and Philosophy* 3 (1986): 235–269. On Plantinga's own account of accidental necessity (see p. 261), those past-tense states of affairs which are directly counterfactually dependent on future indeterministic causes are *not* accidentally

foreknew that Peter would sin at *T*. In short, this is false at every moment prior to *T*:

> Peter now has the power to contribute causally to its being false that God foreknew that Peter will sin at *T*.

But, of course, Peter's sin will be free. So this is true at some time prior to *T*:

> Peter now has the power to contribute causally to its being false that he sins when *T* is present.

It follows that accidental necessity as characterized by (A*) is not closed under entailment. Now suppose further that Peter were going to exercise the power in question and refrain from sinning at *T*. Then from eternity God would have known infallibly by His middle knowledge that Peter would not deny Christ if placed in the relevant circumstances. That is, the following is true:

> If Peter were going to contribute causally to its being false that he sins when *T* is present, then God would never have believed that Peter would sin at *T*.

So even though Peter cannot now cause it to be true that God never believed that he would sin at *T*, he nonetheless can now cause something, namely, his not sinning at *T*, such that had it been true from eternity that he would cause it if placed in the relevant circumstances, God would never have believed that he would sin at *T*. And, significantly, the theory of middle knowledge provides an intuitively accessible model on which both parts of this claim come out true.

Notice that Molina can apply exactly the same solution to the problem of prophecy. Once Christ prophesies at *T** (before *T*) that Peter will

---

necessary. So his account differs from the Molinist account embodied in (A*). I am inclined, however, to believe that this difference is merely verbal. A Molinist may agree that there are several sorts of temporal necessity, one of which is captured by (A*) and another of which is captured by Plantinga's formula, as long as it is not claimed that any agent has *causal power* over the past. A more interesting historical question is whether Ockham or his followers would have accepted Plantinga's account. For on this account it seems to follow *straightforwardly* that the past-tense proposition *Jesus uttered the prophecy that Peter would deny him at T*, even if true, is not accidentally necessary at any time before *T*; and although Ockhamists would welcome this result, they might nonetheless worry that the victory had been won too easily. For most of them struggle with the intuition that the past physical utterance of a given string of words is a paradigmatic instance of a 'hard' fact about the past. For a discussion of various Ockhamist attempts to solve the problem of prophecy, see Aron Edidin and Calvin Normore, "Ockham on Prophecy," *International Journal for the Philosophy of Religion* 13 (1982): 179–189.

deny him at T, then no agent (Peter, God) can any longer cause it to be false that Christ uttered the words in question. And Christ's uttering these words at T^* clearly entails that Peter will deny him at T.[81] Yet his uttering of the words does not make Peter's denial occur at T by a necessity of nature; nor is it a contemporaneous cause of Peter's sin. So despite the fact that before T it is accidentally necessary that Christ uttered the prophetic words, Peter's denial satisfies the causal preconditions for free action. What's more, if Peter were going to refrain from denying Christ in the relevant circumstances, then God would have known this from eternity by His middle knowledge and would have ensured from eternity that Christ would not utter the words in question at T^*.

I know of no other even remotely plausible solution to the problem of prophecy. Aristotelianism and Geachianism do not so much as allow for the possibility that future contingents might be prophesied infallibly. Thomism, if it does allow for this possibility, is subject to the problem noted above. Ockhamism commits one to having to choose between the Scylla of claiming that God can undo the causal history of the world and the Charybdis of claiming that divine prophecies might be deceptive or mistaken.[82] On a personal note, my own conversion from Ockhamism to Molinism is a direct result of my having finally and reluctantly reached the conclusion that Ockhamism simply cannot deal adequately with genuine prophecy of future contingents.

But what of (A*) itself? Is it an adequate substitute for (A)? Since the right-hand side of (A*) is obviously a necessary condition for accidental necessity, the issue boils down to whether it is a sufficient condition as well. Our preanalytic intuitions are not, I believe, subtle enough to yield a clear and definitive answer. So the choice between (A) and (A*) in the final analysis must be made on systemic grounds. But that puts Molinism in a relatively favorable position, since the theory of middle knowledge is a tool of immense philosophical and theological power. Beyond what we have already seen, a moment's thought suggests applications to theological issues that go far beyond the immediate concerns of the *Concordia*: the inspiration of Sacred Scripture, the infallibility of Church teachings on faith and morals, the efficacy of petitionary prayer. (Notice that

---

[81]Some Ockhamists have resisted this claim, but to my mind unsuccessfully. For a concurring opinion, see Edidin and Normore, "Ockham on Prophecy."

[82]Normore suggests that Ockhamists have been unduly reluctant to concede that God might deceive. See his "Divine Omniscience, Omnipotence and Future Contingents: An Overview," p. 19. As Normore himself is aware, however, such a concession would have profound theological consequences in a tradition built upon the thesis that divine revelation is trustworthy because God "can neither deceive nor be deceived," to quote the act of faith once memorized by every Catholic schoolchild.

even though Molina must deny that God literally reacts to prayers, as though prayers had causal influence over Him, he can still hold that God decrees certain future states of affairs in part because He knows that His creatures will in the relevant circumstances pray that those states of affairs obtain.)

I do not, of course, mean to imply that Molinism is immune to criticism. Indeed, in the next section we will look at objections that have led some to think that accepting the theory of middle knowledge is too high a price to pay for any supposed benefit. But I hope to have succeeded in at least intimating just how great the benefits in fact are, especially for one striving to remain faithful to traditional Christian doctrine.

5   Objections and Replies

5.1   *Preliminary Remarks*

In considering the most important objections to Molinism, I make no pretense that my responses are exhaustive. (This is especially true for the objection considered in Section 5.6 below.) I do, however, hope to show at least that none of the objections is decisive as it stands and to indicate promising lines of defense which might fruitfully be pursued in more depth. I will begin with four theological objections and then move on to three philosophical ones. The sources for these objections include the modern Bañezian Reginald Garrigou-Lagrange and the philosophers Robert Adams, Anthony Kenny, and William Hasker.

5.2   *The Use of Sacred Scripture*

The first objection, aimed at Bañezianism as well as Molinism, raises doubts about the strength of the scriptural underpinnings for the claim that God knows conditional future contingents. Kenny's terse argument goes as follows:

> It would commonly be thought nowadays by theologians that the biblical texts quoted by Molina do not prove his case. The passage about Tyre and Sidon is clearly rhetorical. The knowledge of what people would have done if they had not died, as attributed to God by the Wisdom of Solomon, is no more than a knowledge of their characters and dispositions when alive. The oracle consulted by David, the ephod, had only two sides to it, probably marked 'yes' and 'no'. Such an apparatus would be incapable of marking the difference between knowledge of counterfactuals and knowledge of the truth-value of material implications. Since the antecedent of David's ques-

tions was false, the same answers would have been appropriate in each case.[83]

Among those contemporary theologians who accept the doctrine of divine providence, many lean toward some version or other of the concomitance theory. So it is hardly surprising that they should feel a need to cast aspersions on the conclusions drawn by Molinists and Bañezians from these biblical texts. But Kenny's arguments, at least, are far from compelling.

Jesus' words concerning Tyre and Sidon are indeed clearly rhetorical; but, as Kenny himself would undoubtedly admit, it hardly follows that they are *merely* rhetorical. Often enough, the plain truth has far greater rhetorical force than an obvious exaggeration. So Molinists and Bañezians may justifiably insist that the burden of proof is on those who claim that the words in question are not to be taken in the most natural way. Remember, too, that a few lines later (Matt. 11:22–24) Jesus "solemnly assures" his listeners that on the day of judgment it will go easier for Tyre, Sidon, and even Sodom than for Chorozain, Bethsaida, and Capernaum. The clear message is that those he has favored with miracles are less receptive to his demand for repentance than their heathen neighbors would have been had they been likewise favored.

Second, the passage from Wisdom says explicitly that those to be taken prematurely by death are *now* upright and pleasing to God, that is, *now* have *good* characters and *virtuous* dispositions. What's more, even if these people now have certain tendencies toward evil, such present tendencies are able to be impeded and hence cannot serve as a basis for infallible knowledge of the future. So the knowledge ascribed to God by the text in question must be more than just "knowledge of their characters and dispositions when alive." What God knows with certitude is that those whose characters and dispositions are now righteous *would* acquire corrupt characters and vicious dispositions if they were allowed to live longer.

Third, David consulted the ephod to get advice about how he should act, and we may safely assume that even if *God* knows of the distinction between counterfactual and material implication, *David* did not. But in that case God's affirmative answers were deceptive if His advice presupposed that David's questions involved material implication. At the very least, David would have every right to feel betrayed upon learning that yes was likewise an "appropriate" answer to the alternative question, "If I stay in Keilah, will Saul refrain from invading?"

---

[83] Kenny, *The God of the Philosophers* (Oxford, 1979), p. 64.

There is more to be said here, but even this much shows that Kenny's arguments are hardly irresistible as they stand.

5.3 *The Asymmetry Thesis*

According to Bañezians, the Molinist thesis that God's concurrence and actual grace are intrinsically neutral entails that God is related in exactly the same way to both good and evil free actions. As Garrigou-Lagrange puts it: "God would be no more the author of good than of bad acts, at least as regards their intrinsic and free determination, because neither good nor bad acts would come from Him, at least as regards the [exercise] of these acts. He would be the cause of the good determination only by proposing the desirable object. And this even men can do."[84]

That is, on Molina's theory God's internal and direct aids of grace do not causally determine free creatures to elicit morally good acts of will. And although God can try to move the wills of such creatures extrinsically and indirectly by making what is truly good seem desirable to them as an end to be sought, this sort of causal influence, all agree, is nondetermining. (This, in fact, is the type of causal influence we ourselves can exercise over one another's free actions through argument, commandment, threat, prohibition, and counsel.) So Molinists must admit that God's *total* causal contribution to free actions is nondetermining and hence that the very same causal influence on God's part may result indifferently in either a good act or an evil act. It follows that any Molinist who holds that God is a cause of good must likewise hold that God is a cause of evil in exactly the same sense. By the same token, it follows that any Molinist who denies that God is a cause of evil must likewise deny that God is a cause of good. But this violates the asymmetry thesis according to which God is a cause of the goodness of good effects but not of the evil of evil effects.

As should be obvious, however, what is here claimed to follow does not follow at all. According to Molina, actual grace is a *particular* rather than a *general* cause. Unlike God's general concurrence, this grace endows a free agent with a causal tendency, more specifically, a tendency toward choosing the good. Thus, actual grace is "intrinsically neutral" only in the sense that it is not deterministic, that is, only in the sense that its presence is compatible with the agent's making an evil choice. It is *not* "intrinsically neutral" in the stronger sense of not inclining the agent in one direction or the other.

[84]*The One God*, p. 466.

So God's causal relation to good and evil effects is indeed asymmetric on the Molinist scheme. If a good act of will is elicited, then the grace in question is a particular (though partial) efficient cause of the act and hence partially determines the specific moral character of the act; if an evil act of will is elicited, then this act has been elicited *despite* and *in opposition to* the inclination toward the good engendered by the grace. So when a good act is elicited, it is perfectly proper to say that it was elicited *because of* God's grace acting as a cause that inclined the agent internally toward such an act. When an evil act is elicited, it is perfectly proper to say that God's particular causal influence on the subject has been impeded, so that His only *effective* causal contribution to the act has been His general concurrence, which is intrinsically neutral in the strong sense and hence does not determine in any way the specific moral character of the act.

5.4 *The Principle of Predilection*

The next objection concerns God's role in determining the goodness of created agents relative to one another. Bañezians claim that Christian doctrine entails what Garrigou-Lagrange calls the 'principle of predilection', according to which "no one would be better than another unless he were loved more and helped more by God."[85] But Molina argues that God's concurrence and actual grace are intrinsically nondetermining and so he must hold that it is possible for two persons, say, Peter and Judas, to be situated in exactly similar circumstances and to receive equal actual grace and yet for the one (Peter) to act well and the other (Judas) to sin. This violates the principle of predilection. For in such a case it would not be God's grace that singles Peter out from Judas, "since what two persons equally have is not a reason for singling out one from the other"; instead, Peter's being better than Judas would stem entirely from "that which of himself he adds to [God's grace], namely, . . . his consent to and use of the grace."[86]

Molinists might be tempted here to deny the principle of predilection. But this would be a very risky move, since, as Bañezians are wont to point out, something very much like this principle finds frequent expression in St. Paul's epistles and is reaffirmed against the Pelagian heresy by theologians of the stature of St. Augustine and St. Thomas. So Molinists have little to gain and much to lose by conceding that on their theory Peter singles himself out from Judas in a way contrary to the

[85] Ibid., p. 463.
[86] Ibid.

Pauline dictum that "God has mercy on whom He wishes, and whom He wishes He makes obdurate."[87]

A more promising and indeed perfectly defensible strategy is simply to deny that Molinism breaches the principle. It is God, after all, who grants the grace that by His middle knowledge He knows with certainty will be efficacious for Peter's acting virtuously. So it is God who gratuitously singles Peter out by arranging things in such a way that Peter will freely act well. By the same token, God permits Judas to sin by allowing him to be so situated that, as God knows via middle knowledge, he will freely sin. That God should so favor Peter over Judas is just as much a mystery on the Molinist scheme as on the Bañezian. And although this is a mystery many feel deeply disturbed by (the doctrine of predestination lurks in the background, of course), it is nonetheless one that is deeply rooted in Sacred Scripture and in the teachings and theological tradition of the Church.

5.5 *Divine Passivity*

Molina denies that creatures cause God to have knowledge of either absolute or conditional future contingents. Nonetheless, Bañezians charge, Molinism entails that God is in some sense or other dependent on creatures for His middle knowledge. Garrigou-Lagrange poses a dilemma:

> God's knowledge cannot be determined by anything which is extrinsic to Him, and which would not be caused by Him. But such is the *scientia media* [middle knowledge], which depends on the determination of the free conditioned future; for this determination does not come from God but from the human liberty, granted that it is placed in such particular circumstances. . . .
> Thus God would be dependent on another, would be passive in His knowledge, and would no longer be Pure Act. The dilemma is unsolvable: Either God is the first determining Being, or else He is determined by another; there is no other alternative. In other words, the *scientia media* involves an imperfection, which cannot exist in God. Hence there is a certain tinge of anthropomorphism in this theory.[88]

---

[87]Rom. 10:18. I should note in passing that Molinism as defined here does not uniquely determine all the important questions concerning predestination and reprobation. Does God, for example, decide to predestine, say, Peter independently of His middle knowledge and only then use His middle knowledge to ensure that Peter will be saved? Or does He rather, as Molina himself holds, predestine Peter concomitantly with His decision to actualize a possible world in which, as He knows by His middle knowledge, Peter would respond well to supernatural grace?

[88]*The One God*, pp. 465–466.

According to Molina, what God knows by His middle knowledge is, to be sure, dependent on what His creatures would do in various situations. From eternity God knew that Peter would deny Christ if placed in such-and-such circumstances. But if Peter had not been going to deny Christ in those circumstances, then God would not have believed what He in fact believed. So we may properly say that God's middle knowledge is from eternity 'counterfactually dependent' on what creatures will do if placed in various circumstances. But this does not distinguish middle knowledge from any other sort of knowledge God has about creatures. Obviously, *all* God's knowledge of created effects—of necessary effects as well as contingent effects, of absolute future contingents as well as conditional future contingents—is counterfactually dependent on what secondary causes would do in various circumstances. In general, for any created effect S such that S will or would obtain in circumstances H, if the relevant secondary agents were not going to cause S to obtain in H, then God would never have believed that S would obtain in H. Even Bañezians must admit this. So the mere fact that God's middle knowledge is counterfactually dependent on what creatures would do is not at all problematic, but is rather a simple consequence of God's being necessarily omniscient.

What, then, is the source of the Bañezian complaint? It can only be the Molinist claim that God does not and cannot determine which conditional future contingents obtain and which do not. Since God does not actively determine what He knows by His middle knowledge, He must be passively determined by the objects of that knowledge. But in that case God suffers from an imperfection.

Bañezians, I trust, have a plausible argument to show that God's status as the sovereign "first determining Being" is not compromised by the fact that He has no control at all over the metaphysically necessary states of affairs He knows by His natural knowledge. (He is not, presumably, 'passively determined' by such states of affairs.) Whatever the argument might look like, the conclusion will be that a first determining Being has control in a world w over every state of affairs which is such that neither it nor its complement is a member of the creation situation for w. But, of course, this conclusion is perfectly acceptable to Molina. So the present objection must in the final analysis be aimed at the contention that creation situations contain metaphysically contingent states of affairs.

In that case, however, this objection seems to have no independent status, but is instead reducible to one or the other of two more basic objections. On the one hand, since Molina's claim that creation situations contain metaphysically contingent states of affairs is based mainly on his analysis of causal indeterminism, the objection might simply be construed as an attack on that analysis. I have already discussed this issue in some detail. On the other hand, perhaps the worry is that a meta-physically contingent state of affairs would have no grounds for obtaining, and so would not and could not obtain, unless it was causally determined to obtain. To this matter I now turn.

5.6   *The Ground for Conditional Future Contingents*

Bañezians object that conditional future contingents cannot obtain before God's act of will or hence be objects of God's prevolitional knowledge. Thus Garrigou-Lagrange:

> Before the divine decree, there is no object for the *scientia media,* because the conditionally free act of the future is not determined either in itself or in another. . . . The *scientia media* does not precede the divine decree, because there is no cause in which this conditioned future is determined; for it is not determined in the divine cause or in human liberty or in the circumstances; and if it is said that God knows infallibly this conditioned future by explor-ing the circumstances, then this theory would end in determinism of the circumstances. Thus the *scientia media,* which is devised to save human liberty, would destroy it.[89]

Bañezians go on to infer that since God does indeed know conditional future contingents, He must be able, in a way that does not threaten human freedom, to decree that they obtain.

Robert Adams disagrees with this inference, but is in full sympathy with the charge that Molinism does not provide adequate grounding for conditional future contingents. Since his presentation of the argument is the most sophisticated I know of, I will quote it at length. After citing the biblical passage concerning David and Saul, Adams writes:

> This passage was a favorite proof text for the Jesuit theologians. They took it to prove that God knew the following two propositions to be true:
>
> (1) If David stayed in Keilah, Saul would besiege the city.
> (2) If David stayed in Keilah and Saul besieged the city, the men of Keilah would surrender David to Saul. . . .
>
> I do not understand what it would be for [these] propositions to be true, given that the actions in question would have been free, and that David did not stay in Keilah. I will explain my incomprehension.
>
> First we must note that middle knowledge is not simple *fore*knowledge. . . . For there never was nor will be an actual besieging of Keilah by Saul, nor an actual betrayal of David to Saul by the men of Keilah, to which those propositions might correspond.

[89]Ibid., p. 465.

Some other grounds that might be suggested for the truth of (1) and (2) are ruled out by the assumption that the actions of Saul and the men of Keilah are and would be free in the relevant sense. The suggestion that Saul's besieging Keilah follows by *logical* necessity from David's staying there is implausible in any case. It would be more plausible to suggest that Saul's besieging Keilah follows by *causal* necessity from David's staying there. . . . But both of these suggestions are inconsistent with the assumption that Saul's action would have been free.

Since necessitation is incompatible with the relevant sort of free will, we might seek non-necessitating grounds for the truth of (1) and (2) in the actual intentions, desires and character of Saul and the Keilahites. . . .

But the basis thus offered for the truth of (1) and (2) is inadequate precisely because it is not necessitating. A free agent may act out of character, or change his intentions, or fail to act on them. Therefore the propositions which may be true by virtue of correspondence with the intentions, desires and character of Saul and the men of Keilah are not (1) and (2) but

(5) If David stayed in Keilah, Saul would *probably* besiege the city.

(6) If David stayed in Keilah and Saul besieged the city, the men of Keilah would *probably* surrender David to Saul.

(5) and (6) . . . will not satisfy the partisans of middle knowledge. It is part of their theory that God knows infallibly what definitely would happen, and not just what would probably happen or what free creatures would be likely to do.[90]

I will join Adams here in speaking of propositions rather than states of affairs. The leading principle of his objection is that a proposition *p* is true only if there are what we might call *adequate metaphysical grounds* for the truth of *p*. He then argues inductively that there are not and indeed cannot be adequate metaphysical grounds for the truth of the alleged objects of middle knowledge—at least not if a strong libertarian account of freedom and causal indeterminism is correct. It follows that there are not and cannot be true conditional future contingents. In keeping with contemporary parlance, we might thus aptly say that Adams espouses *antirealism* with respect to conditional future contingents.

As Alvin Plantinga has pointed out, the notion of adequate metaphysical grounds appealed to here is far from pellucid.[91] Still, the objection to Molinism posed by Adams and (albeit less precisely) by Garrigou-

[90]Adams, "Middle Knowledge and the Problem of Evil," pp. 110–111.

[91]See "Replies to My Colleagues," in Tomberlin and Van Inwagen, eds., *Alvin Plantinga*, pp. 374–375. Plantinga suggests that counterfactuals of freedom relating to *God's* free action are routinely accepted as true by Christians. At the very least, one such conditional proposition, *Even if Adam and Eve had not sinned, God would have become incarnate*, became the focus of a famous theological debate, with some (for example, Duns Scotus) holding it to be true and others (for example, St. Thomas) arguing that the contrary counterfactual of freedom, *If Adam and Eve had not sinned, God would not have become incarnate*, is true instead.

Lagrange seems to have considerable intuitive appeal. So I will assume that the fundamental notion underlying the objection has at least some validity and attempt to flesh it out sympathetically.

We must, it is clear, draw a basic distinction between the grounds for the truth of metaphysically necessary propositions and the grounds for the truth of metaphysically contingent propositions. The former will presumably involve just the constant and necessary relations of natures or properties to each other. (Of course, it need not be that all of these relations are self-evident to us or even so much as conceivable by us.) But, the claim goes, such grounds are inadequate to underwrite the truth of metaphysically contingent propositions. These require *causal* grounding in order to be true. That is, they must be *caused to be true* by some agent or agents, since it is not of their nature to be true.

The idea of metaphysical grounding is commonly invoked in similar fashion by those who espouse antirealism with respect to *absolute* future contingents, that is, by those who deny that there are or can be contingent truths about the absolute, as contrasted with the conditional, future. They typically claim that there are at present no adequate metaphysical grounds for, say, Peter's freely denying Christ at some future time *T*, and that the proposition *Peter will freely sin at T* thus cannot now be true—even if it turns out that when *T* is present Peter freely denies Christ. And they support their antirealism regarding *absolute* future contingents with arguments exactly like the one Adams produces for the case of *conditional* future contingents. Specifically, they note that the causal history of the world up to the present does not logically entail Peter's sinning at *T*; nor does the world now have a deterministic natural tendency toward this state of affairs. Perhaps, because of Peter's character and the present likelihood of a test of his virtue occurring at *T*, it is now true that the world is tending, albeit nondeterministically, toward his sinning at *T*. That is, perhaps the proposition *Peter will probably sin at T* is now true, where the probability in question is metaphysical rather than epistemic. But, of course, this proposition might now be true even if the proposition *Peter is sinning* turns out to be false when *T* is present. So there are not and cannot be adequate metaphysical grounds at present for the truth of the absolute future contingent *Peter will sin at T*.

Sophisticated Molinists will not only welcome but insist on this parallel between antirealism regarding conditional future contingents and antirealism regarding absolute future contingents. Indeed, they will go so far as to claim that the former entails the latter. For on the Molinist view the absolute future is conceptually posterior to, and emerges by divine decree from, the many conditional futures that define the creation situation God finds Himself in. To be sure, concomitance theorists will deny that this entailment holds, since on their view God knows absolute future contingents without knowing conditional future contingents. But the close parallel between the arguments for the two sorts of antirealism undeniably engenders an inclination in those who espouse one of them to embrace the other as well.

The most promising Molinist strategy for dealing with the 'grounding' objection is, I believe, to build upon the arguments against antirealism regarding the absolute future. I cannot do this exhaustively here but will instead concentrate on just one such argument, an argument having to do with prediction viewed both retrospectively and prospectively.

Suppose that John has ruefully predicted beforehand that Peter will deny Christ at time T. Then, after Peter's denial at T, John can reasonably maintain that his prediction was true and thus that he spoke the truth before T when he asserted the proposition *Peter will deny Jesus*. So it is reasonable to hold that this proposition was true before T.

The same point can be made more starkly in the case of random events. Suppose I predict that on the next toss the coin in your hand will come up heads. And suppose for the sake of argument that the coin's coming up one way or the other is wholly indeterminate, so that prior to the toss the world is not tending, even nondeterministically, either toward the coin's coming up heads or toward its coming up tails. In that case

(P)   The coin will probably come up heads

and

(Q)   The coin will probably come up tails

are both false, where the probability in question is objective or metaphysical. Suppose, finally, that when you toss the coin, it in fact comes up heads. In that case it is perfectly reasonable for me to claim that my prediction was true, that is, that I spoke the truth in asserting beforehand the proposition *The coin will come up heads*. So it is reasonable for me to maintain that this proposition was true before you tossed the coin, even though neither (P) nor (Q) were true at that time.

So much for the retrospective argument. The prospective argument appeals to common intuitions about what we are asserting when we make predictions about the future. If I know that you have promised to meet me for dinner at 6:00 P.M. and know further that you are a very reliable person, then I am highly justified in asserting that you will in fact meet me at 6:00 P.M. To be sure, my *evidence* for this assertion consists in my beliefs about your character and in other beliefs about the world's present tendencies. But *what* I assert is the nonmodal proposition

   (R)   You will meet me at 6:00 P.M.

and not the 'probabilistic' proposition

   (S)   You will probably meet me at 6:00 P.M.,

where the probability is, once again, objective or metaphysical. This is so even if, when challenged, I hedge my prediction by saying something like "She will *probably* meet me at 6:00 P.M." For normally the probability so expressed is *epistemic* rather than *metaphysical*. That is, the hedging is indicative of my wavering confidence in the truth of (R) rather than of my firm belief in (S). Or so, at least, many of us would be prone to claim.

But if there are true absolute future contingents, what are the metaphysical grounds for their truth? Notice, exactly the same question can be raised about past-tense propositions that are true in the present. What are the grounds for the present truth of, say, the proposition *Socrates drank hemlock*? Let p stand for present-tense propositions and P for the past-tense propositional operator. The proper response, I think, is that there are *now* adequate metaphysical grounds for the truth of a past-tense proposition Pp just in case there *were* at some past time adequate metaphysical grounds for the truth of its present-tense counterpart p. Likewise, a realist about the absolute future will claim that there are *now* adequate metaphysical grounds for the truth of a future-tense proposition Fp just in case there *will* be at some future time adequate metaphysical grounds for the truth of its present-tense counterpart p. So in order for propositions about the past or the future to be true now, it is not required that any agent *now* be causing them to be true. Rather, it is sufficient that some agent has caused or will cause the corresponding present-tense propositions to be true.

But if this is so, then it seems reasonable to claim that there are now adequate metaphysical grounds for the truth of a conditional future contingent $F^t(p)$ on H just in case there *would* be adequate metaphysical grounds at t for the truth of the present-tense proposition p on the condition that H should obtain at t. At any rate, the argument leading up to this claim is exactly the same as before. Take the case of Peter and John. John might just as easily make his prediction by asserting the conditional proposition *If Peter were tempted anytime soon to deny Jesus, he would succumb*. And after Peter's denial John may reasonably maintain that what he had asserted was true. Indeed, even if Peter had luckily been spared any such temptation, John could still reasonably maintain that what he had asserted was true—and he might even be able to convince Peter of this.

Again, in the coin tossing example, I could just as easily have said, "If you tossed the coin, it would come up heads." As before, both

(T)   If you tossed the coin, it would probably come up heads

and

(U)   If you tossed the coin, it would probably come up tails

would be false. But after the toss is completed and the coin comes up heads, it seems perfectly reasonable for me to claim that I spoke the truth when I asserted beforehand the proposition *If you tossed the coin, it would come up heads,* even though both (T) and (U) were then false. What's more, unless conditional future contingents are unlike all other conditional propositions, they can be true even if their antecedents are false. So given that the proposition in question was true when I made the prediction, I may reasonably claim that it would still have been true even if the coin had never been tossed. Of course, in that case we would never have found out whether or not the proposition was true, but that is another matter.

The prospective argument likewise goes as before. Knowing you well, I might say with confidence, "If you promised to meet me at 6:00 P.M., you would do so." To be sure, my *evidence* for this assertion consists in my beliefs about your character and about tendencies the world would have if you were to make the promise in question. Still, *what* I assert is the proposition

(V)   If you promised to meet me at 6:00 P.M., you would meet me at 6:00 P.M.,

and not the probabilistic proposition

(W)   If you promised to meet me at 6:00 P.M., you would probably meet me at 6:00 P.M.,

where the probability in question is metaphysical. Once again, of course, a third party might challenge my prediction and even induce me to qualify it by saying, "Well, she would *probably* meet me." But the probability thus invoked would at least normally be epistemic, reflecting my

wavering confidence in (V) rather than my unflinching confidence in the
weaker (W).

The position I am urging has some far-reaching consequences for the
semantics of subjunctive conditionals. I am suggesting, in effect, that
when such conditional propositions are not probabilistic, the connection
between antecedent and consequent is not reducible to any logical or,
more important, causal connection. This suggestion cuts against the
spirit, if not the letter, of the standard possible-worlds semantics for
subjunctive conditionals. For it is usually assumed that the similarities
among possible worlds invoked in such semantics are conceptually prior
to the acquisition of truth-values by the subjunctive conditionals themselves. The intuitive idea seems to be that the truth-value of a subjunctive conditional p depends asymmetrically on the categorical (including
causal) facts about the world at which p is being evaluated, so that until
the full range of such categorical facts is in place, the truth-value of p is
still indeterminate. On this view, then, the determination of the true
conditional future contingents is posterior to the determination of
which possible world is actual. This is the source of one of Kenny's
complaints about middle knowledge:

> Prior to God's decision to actualize a particular world those counterfactuals
> [about the behavior of free humans] cannot yet be known: for their truth-
> value depends . . . on which world is actual. . . . The problem is that what
> makes the counterfactuals true is not yet there at any stage at which it is
> undecided which world is the actual world. The very truth-conditions which
> the possible-world semantics were introduced to supply are absent under
> the hypothesis that it is undetermined which world the actual world is.[92]

I will not tarry over the moot question of whether the standard
possible-worlds semantics for subjunctive conditionals in fact implies or
presupposes that the acquisition of truth-values by such conditionals is
conceptually posterior to and dependent on the determination of which
world is actual. It is clear, however, that on the Molinist view the dependence runs in just the opposite direction when the conditionals in question are conditional future contingents. For Molinists hold that conditional future contingents delimit prevolitionally the range of worlds God
is able to actualize. If the standard possible-worlds semantics for subjunctive conditionals presupposes otherwise, then Molinists will have to
modify it or propose an alternative capable of sustaining realism with

---

[92]*The God of the Philosophers*, p. 70. For more on the possible-worlds semantics for
subjunctive conditionals, see Lewis, *Counterfactuals*; and Stalnaker, "A Theory of Conditionals."

respect to conditional future contingents. There are, in any case, independent grounds for having doubts about the standard semantics, for example, its inability to accommodate the intuitively plausible belief that subjunctive conditionals with impossible antecedents may differ from one another in truth-value.[93]

My aim here has merely been the negative one of showing that the grounding objection is not conclusive. I believe I have succeeded in this. But, as Michael Dummett has suggested, the doctrine of middle knowledge is the most vivid and perhaps the most extreme example of philosophical realism in the history of thought.[94] And I freely admit that the positive task of elaborating a metaphysical and semantic foundation for this doctrine is enormous and has hardly yet begun.

5.7 *Conditional Future Contingents and Freedom*

The last two objections try to show that Molinism suffers from irremediable defects even if it is granted that there are true conditional future contingent propositions. The first of these objections is raised by William Hasker, who argues in "A Refutation of Middle Knowledge" that the truth of such future contingents is incompatible with creaturely freedom.[95]

Hasker's paper is divided into two parts. He first tries to establish that created agents do not and cannot bring about the truth of those conditional future contingent propositions that involve their own free actions. Although I believe that Hasker's argument for this conclusion is seriously flawed, I have already conceded, and indeed insisted, that Molinism does not entail that created agents *cause* conditional future contingents to be true or to have been true from eternity.[96] So if Hasker is

---

[93] For a brief discussion of this point, see my "Human Nature, Potency and the Incarnation," *Faith and Philosophy* 3 (1986): 27–53, esp. pp. 43–45.

[94] See Dummett's *Truth and Other Enigmas* (Cambridge, Mass., 1978), p. 362.

[95] *Nous* 20 (1986): 545–557.

[96] The basic flaw in Hasker's argument in the first part is his claim that the proponents of middle knowledge hold, or should hold, that the truth of a counterfactual of freedom is as fixed in the worlds closest to the actual world as is the truth of a law of nature. (See n. 7, in which Hasker appeals to the argument of Kenny's quoted in Section 5.6 above.) On this basis he argues roughly as follows: Suppose that the proposition (P) *If Elizabeth were offered a research grant, she would accept it* is true. Then (P) would still be true even if Elizabeth did not accept the grant. The reason is that the true counterfactuals of freedom, including (P), remain fixed in those closest possible worlds in which Elizabeth does not accept the grant. So if Elizabeth were not to accept the grant, it would be because the grant was never offered to her and not because (P) was false. Thus (P) remains true whether or not Elizabeth accepts the grant, and so it is reasonable to deny that she can bring it about that (P) is true.

As a matter of fact, however, Molina is in no way committed to holding that because God

using the term 'bring about' in a straightforward causal sense, Molinists should have no problem accepting the conclusion of this part of his paper.

He then goes on to argue, however, that if creatures cannot cause conditional future contingents to be true, then they lack a power that is absolutely essential for their acting freely. A somewhat simplified version of the argument goes like this:

Suppose that the proposition

(X)   If Peter were in *H,* he would deny Christ

has always been true and that its contrary,

(Y)   If Peter were in *H,* he would not deny Christ,

has always been false. Within the present dialectical context, all agree that Peter does not and cannot cause either (X) or (Y) to be true or to have been true. Suppose now that Peter is in *H.* Molinists contend that even though, given the truth of (X), Peter in fact denies Christ in *H,* he nonetheless has the power to refrain from denying Christ. But, counters Hasker, this cannot be so, since "a little thought" will show the following principle to be true:

(Z)   If (i) agent *A* has the power to bring it about that *p* is true and (ii) *p* entails *q* and (iii) *q* is false, then *A* has the power to bring it about that *q* is true.

Let *p* be the proposition *In H Peter does not deny Christ.* According to Molinists, Peter has the power at the relevant time to bring it about that *p* is true. But *p* entails (Y), which by hypothesis is false. So given principle

---

cannot decide which counterfactuals of freedom are true, the truth of these counterfactuals is just as fixed in nearby worlds as is the truth of laws of nature, over which God does have control. To the contrary, Molina holds that even though the truth of counterfactuals of freedom is in no way dependent on what *God* decides, it is dependent (though not *causally* dependent) on what *creatures* would freely do. For a more rigorous presentation of the Molinist defense against this argument, see Thomas Flint, "Hasker's 'Refutation' of Middle Knowledge" (unpublished paper).

Note, by the way, that if Hasker takes the argument of the first part of the paper to show not only that free creatures cannot *cause* counterfactuals of freedom to be true, but also that there is nothing they can do such that were they to do it, contrary counterfactuals of freedom would have been true, then it is essential for the Molinist to refute the argument of the first part of the paper as well as that of the second part. I assume in the text that Hasker means to cast aspersions only on the stronger causal thesis when he denies that creatures can "bring about" the truth of counterfactuals of freedom. But in conversation David Widerker has shaken my confidence in this assumption.

(Z), Peter has the power to refrain from denying Christ in *H* only if he has the power to bring it about that (Y) is true. But as we have just seen, Molinists concede that Peter does not have the power to bring it about that (Y) is true. Therefore, concludes Hasker, they are likewise forced to concede that he does not have the power to bring it about that *p* is true. It follows that Peter does not have the power to refrain from denying Christ in *H*. But the same argument applies to all creaturely actions. So, Hasker concludes, Molinism implies that no creature can refrain from acting as it in fact does act.

To begin with, I reiterate my assumption that Hasker is taking the phrase 'bring it about that *p* is true' to be equivalent to 'cause *p* to be true' or, better, 'causally contribute to *p*'s being true,' where *A*'s having the power to contribute causally to *p*'s being true entails something stronger than *A*'s merely having the power to do something such that, were *A* to do it, *p* would be or would have been true. For, as we saw above, if 'bring about' is taken (improperly, I would argue) in this weak sense of mere counterfactual dependence, then Molinists can consistently claim that created agents do in fact have the power to bring about the truth of conditional future contingents. So if the argument just presented is to pose a serious threat to Molinism, 'bring about' must be taken in a stronger sense.

It is worth noting immediately that (Z) will be rejected by those who accept either compatibilism or Bañezianism and yet deny that anyone has power over the past. Suppose once again that Peter in fact sins in *H*. Then, a typical compatibilist will claim that even if the conjunction of the actual causal history of the world (*C*) with the laws of nature (*L*) entails that Peter will sin in *H*, it is nonetheless true that Peter has the power to refrain from sinning in *H*—and this despite the fact that he lacks the power to cause the proposition *not-*(*C and L*), which is in fact false, to be true. Likewise, a Bañezian will claim that even though God's having decided from eternity not to confer intrinsically efficacious grace on Peter in *H* entails that Peter will sin in *H*, Peter nonetheless has the power not to sin in *H*—and this despite the fact that he lacks the power to cause the proposition *God decided from eternity to confer intrinsically efficacious grace on Peter in H*, which is in fact false, to be true. So these thinkers will deny that (Z) as it stands is true.

But perhaps it is unseemly for Molinists to make common cause in this way with compatibilists and Bañezians. Consider, then, that (Z) will also be rejected by all those libertarians who believe that there are contingent truths about the absolute future and yet deny that there is any sort of causal power over the past. They will hold that even though the proposition *In H Peter does not deny Christ* entails the proposition *It has never been*

the case that Peter will deny Christ in H, still Peter has the power to refrain
from sinning in *H*—and this despite the fact that he does not have the
power to cause the proposition *It has never been the case that Peter will deny
Christ in H,* which is false, to be true. All that is required, they will
contend, is that Peter have the power to do something such that were he
to do it, the proposition *It has never been the case that Peter will deny Christ in
H* would be true. And, like Molina, they will insist that Peter's having
such power in *H* is fully consonant with a strong libertarian account of
the causal indeterminacy involved in free action.

So Molinists are not alone in rejecting (Z), even though they can
consistently concede the possibility that some close relative of (Z), suita-
bly qualified to circumvent their proposed counterexamples, might be
true. To be sure, their position would be stronger if they could produce
some *uncontroversial* counterexample to (Z), one that would convince
even the friends of (Z) that some modification is called for. But even in
the absence of such a counterexample, Molinists can appeal to strong
intuitive grounding for their opposition to (Z), since both the belief that
there is no power over the past and the belief that there are true absolute
future contingents are intuitively appealing. Moreover, the evident systemic virtues of Molinism, both philosophical and theological, provide
yet another reason for rejecting any competing theory that includes (Z).

5.8 *Knowledge of Conditional Future Contingents*

According to the final objection, even if conditional future contingent
propositions are, as Molinism insists, true prior to any act of the divine
will, these propositions are nonetheless by nature such that it is impossible that anyone should know them. After all, by Molina's own lights
conditional future contingents lack "metaphysical certitude" prior to
God's act of will; indeed, those that remain forever merely *conditioned*
future contingents never attain metaphysical certitude. So even if we
grant that their *being true* does not require their having metaphysical
certitude, it hardly follows that their *being known* does not require their
having such certitude. Compare what Aquinas says about *absolute* future
contingents. He seems to admit that there are true absolute future
contingents even while insisting that, because of their lack of metaphysical determination, they cannot be known by anyone "as future." So the
Molinist must show not only how conditional future contingents can be
true, but also—and this is a separate task—how they can be *known.*

Those who pose this objection will not be appeased by Suarez's retort
that since whatever is true is thereby in itself intelligible and hence
knowable, Molinists need only show how conditional future contingents

might be true in order to establish that an omniscient being can have middle knowledge.[97] They will counter that just as any plausible account of omnipotence must distinguish what *can* obtain from what *can be caused* to obtain by even the most powerful conceivable agent, so too it may well be that a plausible account of omniscience will have to draw a distinction between what is *true* and what is *knowable* by even the most powerful conceivable intellect. The Suarezian gambit thus fails to convince.

How, then, might Molinists respond more effectively? My suspicion is that the gulf separating the objector from the Molinist is in this case so deep and fundamental that no convincing reply is possible. Nonetheless, something can be said. First of all, if we think of knowledge merely as justified true belief, then it seems fairly obvious that even we finite subjects have knowledge of at least some conditional future contingents. At the very least, we have true justified beliefs about how we would freely act under specified conditions. For instance, I have a highly justified belief that were I offered a no-strings-attached grant to do research for five years and to do just as much teaching as I cared to do, I would freely accept it. So if this conditional is true, then I know it. Likewise, I have highly justified beliefs about how my wife and children and close friends would freely act in various hypothetical situations. And contrary to what Adams claims, it seems clear to me that the propositions I believe in such cases are nonprobabilistic conditional future contingents. It may be appropriate to call my knowledge 'probable', but the probability in question is epistemic, reflecting the fact that my justification falls short of rendering the relevant propositions certain. The upshot is that if even *we* can have some limited knowledge of conditional future contingents, it is hardly surprising that *God* can know them.

This line of response is not without merit. Nonetheless, it obviously has limited usefulness. After all, God's middle knowledge is absolutely certain and infallible and is not inferred from an antecedent knowledge of the characters of free creatures. And it would surely be foolhardy to claim that *our* knowledge of conditional future contingents enjoys this high epistemic status.

At this point, I think, the best the Molinist can do is to provide a model to aid our thinking. Molina speaks here of supercomprehension, whereas Suarez relies on talk about God's comprehensive grasp of individual essences. Can we flesh out these notions in a way more appealing to the imagination?

The best attempt to do this that I know of is Calvin Normore's. Since I cannot improve on Normore's own words, I will quote them in full:

[97]See Suarez, *De Divina Gratia*, prologue 2, chap. 7, no. 1, p. 24 in *Opera Omnia*, vol. 7.

Imagine that God's mind contains a perfect model of each possible thing—a complete divine idea of a particular or, if you like, an individual concept. Imagine that God simulates possible histories by thinking about how the being which is A would behave under circumstances C—i.e., he simulates C and 'sees' how A behaves. Now *if* there is a way in which A *would* behave in C, a perfect model should reflect it, so if conditional excluded middle is valid such a model is possible and God knows the history of the world by knowing that model, i.e., by knowing his own intellect and his creative intentions.

But would the belief 'state' which God would be in on the basis of such a model be a state of knowledge? Would it not rather bear to knowledge much the same relation which veridical hallucination bears to perception? Here we have a particularly striking form of another problem of divine omniscience. How can God be transcendent on the one hand and, on the other, know what transpires in the world? It seems to me that anyone who claims that a *transcendent* God knows contingent facts will have to admit significant disanalogies between divine and human knowledge. It also seems to me that supposing God's knowledge of the world to be like veridical hallucination locates these disanalogies in the right place. First it goes some way toward accounting for the intuitive (as contrasted with discursive) character of divine knowledge; God knows contingent facts intuitively because he 'sees' rather than infers that they obtain. Second by admitting counterfactual connections (however mysterious) between divine belief and its mundane objects, such an account preserves at least some of the intuition that God *knows* and is infallible. Third by making these connections indirect it suggests a way one might also admit divine impassibility. Moreover almost any mediaeval writer would have considered the counterfactual connections suggested weaker than true (Aristotelian) causal connections.[98]

Normore here brings together nicely many of the themes discussed above. God's knowledge of the world is providential and hence only counterfactually (and not causally) dependent on contingent effects. The fact that God's middle knowledge varies from one creation situation to another does not entail that creatures *cause* God to have such knowledge. (Of course, there remains the philosophical task of delineating more precisely the difference between 'true' causal dependence and mere counterfactual dependence.) So God knows but does not 'find out' how His creatures freely act. Moreover, the suggested model is consonant with, though it goes beyond, what Molina seems to be aiming at in his brief remarks about supercomprehension.

None of this will suffice to silence Molina's philosophical and theological critics. But in the end it is crucial to ask exactly what the alternatives

---

[98]Normore, "Divine Omniscience, Omnipotence and Future Contingents: An Overview," pp. 15–16.

are. Those unsympathetic with Molina's wider theological project may of course simply reject the notion of providence which underlies it, either by denying God's existence altogether or, more insidiously, by replacing the conception of a perfectly provident being with that of a limited God more like us. But those who—correctly, to my mind—resist the temptation to remake God in our own image have to contend with Molina's trenchant criticisms of Bañezianism and the concomitance theory. When the alternatives are posed starkly in this way, it is clear to me for one that Molinism is at least as good as its competitors—and, indeed, arguably better.

Luis de Molina, S.J.

Liberi Arbitrii cum Gratiae Donis, Divina Praescientia,
Providentia, Praedestinatione et Reprobatione
Concordia

Part IV
Question 14, Article 13, Disputations 47–53

DISPUTATION 47

On the Source of Contingency

1. Thus far we have subjected our freedom of choice to intellectual scrutiny, reconciled it to the extent our weakness allows with God's general concurrence and with divine grace, and shown with the clarity permitted us that there is contingency both in the works of nature and in those of grace.

In order that we might return to the explication of St. Thomas and to the issues that pertain to this article,[1] we must now, first of all, investigate the source of contingency, so that the contingency of future things might thereby be fully and more clearly established. What's more, we will explain the way in which God knows future contingents, and, finally, we will reconcile divine foreknowledge with our freedom of choice[2] and with the contingency of things.

2. To understand the source or origin of contingency, we must note that there are two senses relevant to the present undertaking in which a state of affairs may be said to be contingent.[3]

---

[1] Molina refers here to Part I, question 14, article 13, of St. Thomas Aquinas's *Summa Theologiae*, "Whether God Has Knowledge of Future Contingents." The first four parts of the *Concordia*, which occupy pp. 5–405 of the critical edition prepared by Johann Rabeneck, S.J. (see Introduction, n. 4, above), constitute an extended commentary on this article, consisting of 53 disputations. Unless otherwise indicated, the disputations cited below from the *Concordia* are part of the commentary on Part I, q. 14, a. 13.

[2] Literally, the freedom of our choice (*nostri arbitrii libertas*). In Disputation 2, where Molina discusses the nature of free choice, he claims that free choice is a power that has the will as its subject, though the exercise of this power has intellective or cognitive prerequisites as well. See Rabeneck, pp. 13–19, and Section 2.9 of the Introduction.

[3] Molina here and elsewhere uses the Latin term *complexio* in a way that sometimes suggests the translation 'proposition' and at other times suggests the translation 'state of affairs'. For instance, in the next paragraph he speaks of the subject and predicate of a *complexio*, whereas two paragraphs after that he talks about a *complexio* being indifferent as to whether it is going to occur or obtain (*evenire*). I have chosen the translation 'state of

A state of affairs is contingent in the *first* sense when, if you think just of the natures of the terms, the subject no more lays claim to the predicate that is affirmed of it than to the opposite of that predicate. For instance, that Socrates is sitting is contingent, since Socrates as such no more lays claim to sitting than to standing or to lying down.

Contingency taken in this sense does not rule out fatalistic necessity. For if all agents acted by a necessity of nature, then, without a doubt, even if nothing pertaining to the natures of the terms were incompatible with things turning out otherwise, everything that occurs would still, in relation to its causes as constituted and arranged in such a universe, occur with a fatalistic and infallible necessity in just the way that it in fact occurs.[4] For any cause that, given the constitution and arrangement of the universe in question, was able to impede another cause would in fact impede it. Thus, given this hypothesis, anyone who knew all the causes in such a universe would thereby know infallibly and with certainty all the things that were going to be.

By contrast, a given future state of affairs is called contingent in a *second* sense, because it rules out not only the necessity that has its source in the natures of the terms, but also the fatalistic and extrinsic necessity that results from the arrangement of causes. So given this universe of things which we see around us and given that all the causes are arranged in just the way they are now in fact arranged, such a state of affairs is still

---

affairs' for two reasons. First, later in Part IV Molina uses the image of a *complexio* as a combination of simple *things* (*simplicia*) rather than of linguistic items. Indeed, the Latin word *extremum*, translated here as 'term', is often used by medieval writers to stand not for linguistic entities but for the things they apply to. Second, Molina commonly uses the terms *propositio* and *enuntiatio* when he wants to speak unambiguously of propositions. Notice that Molina apparently thinks of a proposition as an interpreted sentence— whether spoken, written, or mental—rather than as a nonlinguistic abstract entity. This is a standard, though by no means the only, Scholastic view of propositions. See Norman Kretzmann, "Medieval Logicians on the Meaning of 'Propositio,'" *Journal of Philosophy* 67 (1970): 767–787.

[4]Molina construes the notion of an agent in a broad Aristotelian sense to include both free and nonfree (or 'natural') sources of causal activity. So individual substances are thought of as agents endowed with causal powers, tendencies, and dispositions; and (efficient) causation is treated as a relation between an agent and an event (or state of affairs) rather than, in keeping with standard Humean accounts, as a relation between events (or states of affairs). For an excellent thumbnail sketch of the resulting Aristotelian view of nature, see Peter Geach's essay on Aquinas in P. T. Geach and G.E.M. Anscombe, *Three Philosophers* (Ithaca, 1961), esp. pp. 101–109. I have tried to provide a systematic account of natural necessity within such a framework in "The Necessity of Nature," *Midwest Studies in Philosophy* 11 (1986): 215–242.

This philosophical conception of nature is—deservedly in my opinion—undergoing a revival in contemporary philosophy of science. See esp. R. Harré and E. Madden, *Causal Powers* (Totowa, N.J., 1975). For an excellent discussion of the effect of this and other philosophical conceptions of nature on Christian theology and, specifically, on the theology of miracles, see Stephen Bilynskyj, "God, Nature and the Concept of Miracle" (Ph.D. diss., University of Notre Dame, 1982).

indifferent as to whether it is or is not going to obtain by virtue of the same causes through which it ordinarily obtains.

It is in this second sense that we will be speaking of contingency in the present context, as we inquire into its source. For the very natures of the terms of a state of affairs are the source of contingency taken in the first sense.

3. In Disputation 35 we considered the position of Scotus, who asserts that the divine will is by itself the total source of contingency.[5] There we argued against this position and rejected it as dangerous and as not sufficiently in accord with the Catholic faith.

Therefore, in order that it might be clear which causes are the source or origin giving rise to the contingency of various things, it should be noted that there are some things (for example, angels, the heavens, the human soul, and primary matter) whose production and conservation depends solely on God in such a manner that they cannot in any way be destroyed by the power of natural agents, whereas there are other things whose conservation does not depend on God alone. Again, there are some things that belong to the order of nature, whereas there are other things that pertain to the order of grace and everlasting happiness (for example, the supernatural means whereby we are disposed toward and prepared for everlasting beatitude).[6]

---

[5] Rabeneck, pp. 218–222. In Disputation 35 Molina cites the following texts from Duns Scotus's *Ordinatio*: I, dist. 2, q. 2; I, dist. 8, q. 5; I, dist. 39; and II, dist. 1, q. 3. He goes on to attack the thesis, which he attributes to Scotus, that if God were to exercise exactly the same causal influence He now exercises on the created universe, but by a *necessity of nature* rather than *freely*, then no effects would be contingent. Molina contends to the contrary that even if *per impossibile* the antecedent of the foregoing conditional were true, there would still be genuine causal contingency as long as some creatures had freedom of choice or at least a 'trace' of freedom, as in the case, to be discussed shortly, of certain brute animals.

[6] On Molina's view, explained more clearly in Disputation 53, pt. 2, sec. 25, God gratuitously wills for human beings not only a supernatural *end*, namely, the everlasting beatific vision of God Himself, but also the supernatural *means* by which we are to attain that end within the order of salvation contingently established by God. More specifically, through the life, death, and resurrection of Jesus Christ human beings are gratuitously furnished with supernatural aids and graces that empower us and dispose us to act righteously and thus to *merit* eternal life within the framework of the order of salvation freely ordained by God. So, on the one hand, the fundamentally gratuitous nature of salvation is preserved, along with the doctrine that it is only by God's *special supernatural* assistance that any of us is empowered to merit salvation or is even so much as moved toward exercising that power; whereas, on the other hand, the emphasis on merit is meant to highlight the fact that God does not force salvation on us, but leaves us free instead to refuse His gracious offer and to condemn ourselves by our own sins. One crucial difference between Molina and his Bañezian opponents centers about the question of whether God's assistance, when efficacious, is, as the Bañezians claim, *intrinsically* or *essentially* efficacious or whether it is not instead efficacious only *contingently* or by 'extrinsic denomination', to use the relevant Scholastic term. This question is addressed directly and at length in Disputation 53. See Sections 2.6–2.9 of the Introduction.

4. Let this, then, be the *first conclusion*: Since, as was proved in Part I, q. 3, a. 4, disp. 1,[7] no created thing is necessary in relation to the first cause, but rather all were produced by Him in such a way that they were able not to exist, it follows that God's free will should be regarded as the sole source of all the contingency discerned (i) in the fact that there were things that were first produced by God alone (as, for instance, in the original establishment of this universe with respect to all its parts and embellishments), and also (ii) in the fact that those things whose conservation depends on God alone are conserved and continue in existence.

In relation to effects of this sort, however, God should be called a *free* cause rather than a *contingent* cause. Even though the effects themselves were produced freely by Him and hence are not *contingent* effects in the sense of having been produced accidentally or fortuitously by the concurrence of two diverse causes and unintentionally on the part of both, but are instead *free* effects, still, because they were able to be produced and also able not to be produced by their cause, and because they are able to be conserved in the future and also able not to be conserved by that same cause, it can be said with absolute propriety that these effects did and will exist *contingently*. From here on we will join the other Doctors in speaking in this way, and it is in this sense that we are here investigating the contingency of those things.[8]

The proposed conclusion is perfectly obvious. For the fact that all effects of the sort in question are such that they are able to exist and able not to exist derives from God's free will alone, and so God's will must be called the sole source of and total explanation for their contingency.[9]

5. Before we propose the remaining conclusions, it should be noted that although we must not countenance in brute animals even the

---

[7]The disputation referred to here is titled "Whether in God Essence and Existence Are the Same." As explained in the Preface, in 1592 Molina published his massive *Commentaria in Primam Divae Thomae Partem* (hereafter cited as *Commentaria*), a commentary on Part I of Aquinas's *Summa Theologiae*, specifically on questions 1–64 and 106–113. Page references (with "a" and "b" indicating left and right column, respectively) will be to the printed edition I have access to, that published in Lyons in 1622. The present reference, accordingly, is to *Commentaria*, p. 48a–b.

[8]As will become clear below, Molina numbers among the contingent effects of secondary (or created) causes not only those effects that result directly from the activity of indeterministic secondary causes (for example, free choice) but also those effects that, though they occur at a given time by a necessity of nature, have the activity of indeterministic secondary causes somewhere in their causal ancestry. This point is discussed more fully in Section 2.7 of the Introduction.

[9]Molina is a bit careless here. As is clear from other places in Part IV (see, e.g., Disputation 50, sec. 6), he does not mean to suggest that God freely decides which things are *able* to exist and which things are not *able* to exist. Rather, to put it somewhat loosely, of the things that are able to exist, He freely decides which ones will *in fact* exist and which ones will *in fact* not exist.

freedom that, in Disputation 2,[10] we claimed to exist in insane people and in children before they have attained that use of reason which suffices for blame and merit, nonetheless it seems highly likely that in brute animals there is a certain trace of freedom with regard to some of their movements, so that it is within their power to move in one direction or another. For when a beast, wearied by sitting for a long time, desires to take a walk and is not attracted to any special place by a cognition of and desire for some object located in that place, then it seems plainly to be within its power to move in one direction or another. I would not, however, attribute so great a trace of freedom to beasts that it might be within their power not to move toward a certain object even if they were aroused by a desire for the object preceded by a cognition of it, and even if there were no cause, for example, fear of the stick or of some other thing, holding them back. Still, anyone who does not wish to concede even this trace of freedom to beasts should in no way regard the appetitive faculty of brute animals as the proximate source of any contingency.

6.   Perhaps you will object that although freedom or its trace (if such is to be posited) is in the *appetitive* faculty formally and in the way that a thing is in its *subject,* nonetheless, in the way that a thing is in its *source,* freedom is in the indifferent cognition and understanding that has to precede a free act.[11] But this sort of cognition cannot exist in animals,

---

[10]Rabeneck, pp. 13–19, esp. p. 14, sec. 4, and pp. 17–19, sec. 12.

[11]This objection derives from Francisco Zumel, *In Primam Divae Thomae Partem Commentaria,* q. 14, a. 13, disp. 2, appendix (Salamanca, 1590), pp. 411b–416a (hereafter cited as Zumel, *Commentaria*). Zumel (1540–1607), the thirty-second general of the Order of Our Lady of Mercy (Mercederians), was professor of moral philosophy at Salamanca in the last two decades of the sixteenth century. He was one of Molina's two main theological antagonists (the other being the Dominican Domingo Bañez) and a key figure in the ecclesiastical investigations into Molina's theological opinions. Not to be outdone, Molina launched his own counterattack against Zumel's views. Disputation 53 below is, in fact, an extended critique of Zumel's account of divine predetermination and efficacious concurrence. Also, in 1594 Molina authored a shorter response to the charges leveled by Zumel against the *Concordia.* This response to Zumel is found in Friedrich Stegmüller, "Neue Molinaschriften," *Beiträge zur Geschichte der Philosophie und Theologie des Mittelalters,* band 32 (Münster, 1935), pp. 451–473 (hereafter cited as Stegmüller).
    The philosophical question at issue here is an interesting one that has not been widely discussed in recent action theory: Is free choice an appetitive power common to human beings and higher animals, with the main difference between them being that humans are capable of entertaining and thus of willing or dissenting from or simply not willing cognitively more sophisticated objects? (These objects are, I think, best taken to be states of affairs.) Or is free choice instead a fundamentally cognitive power, namely, the power to decide in favor of one or another contrary state of affairs entertained 'indifferently', and then to mobilize, as it were, one's appetitive apparatus in accordance with that decision. One who takes the first view is likely not to balk at Molina's ascription of a "trace" of freedom to brute animals. Such creatures are on his view free to will or not to will (though *not* to dissent from) very simple objects. On the other hand, one who takes the second view is automatically committed, it would seem, to denying animals any sort of freedom, since

since it has to be a cognition that collates and compares one object with another and distinguishes one object from another; but there can be no such cognition in animals. Indeed, in order for a brute animal to be able to direct its movement indifferently in one direction or another, it would have to understand the end toward which it is striving *as an end,* and it would have to comprehend each sort of appropriateness or inappropriateness involved in directing its movement in one direction rather than another, and it would have to compare these sorts of appropriateness with one another, and it would have to infer and deduce from this comparison which sorts outweigh and overrule the others. Likewise, in order for an animal to be truly indifferent as to getting up or holding back for a while and remaining on the ground, or in order for it to be truly indifferent as to taking a step or holding its foot back, it would have to understand its acts *and* their negations, along with the sorts of fittingness and appropriateness which they have, and it would have to compare these with one another. But all this is completely alien to brute animals.

7. The proper response, however, is that in order for someone to be said to be endowed with that freedom of choice which suffices for merit and mortal guilt, and for works of art and of human prudence, or for works that must be done with moderation, it is by no means necessary that he think of and deliberate about all the things mentioned in the proposed objection every time he acts freely in any way whatsoever; rather, what is necessary is that he *be able* to think of and deliberate about all those things—more or less, since he might have been endowed with more native insight and natural prudence, and he might have been more versed in the tasks to be accomplished, and he might have acquired more experiential knowledge and proficiency in the relevant matters. In any case, it is not necessary that all those thoughts and deliberations occur beforehand whenever human beings do something freely, with respect to either the exercise or the species of the act.[12]

---

they are incapable of entertaining the negations of—or, in general, contraries of—the objects presented to them cognitively. Zumel appears to hold a variant of the second view. He concedes that free choice is an appetitive power, that is, that it has the will as its subject, but contends that it is present in the will only because it "flows from" what he calls "indifferent cognition." That is, free choice is present in the will only if the sophisticated cognitive abilities characteristic of human beings are present in the intellect.

[12]This distinction between the exercise and the species of an act is important for Molina's discussion below of the freedom enjoyed by brute animals as well as for the theory of action in general. Suppose that I am free with respect to both the exercise and species of an act of willing an object *A*. Then, first of all, I may either positively will *A* or negatively not will *A*. In the latter case there is no exercise of an act of willing and hence I need not

Take those utterly dissolute people who care nothing for, nor even think about, their own salvation or the law of God, but who are drawn like brute animals to the pleasures of taste and touch. Surely, when they consent immediately to some shameful object presented to them as pleasurable, they do so without any comparisons or deliberations of the sort in question. And yet as long as they *could have* thought of and deliberated about those things and neglected to do so, this is enough for them to be said to have willed the act freely (with respect to both its exercise and species) and for mortal guilt to be imputed to them.[13]

Again, when experienced or inexperienced people are headed somewhere, and proceed more or less rapidly, and travel along one or another part of a road or rough terrain, and stop for a while or keep on going farther, clearly, they do all of these things freely. And yet, as experience itself testifies, they do not reflect on or deliberate about the things mentioned in the above objection; instead, in order for them to be acting freely it suffices that they have an awareness of the general area through which they are passing, along with the innate freedom to walk in one manner or another or to stop.

In the same way, when a brute animal arises from sleep and either goes for a casual walk or sets off to look for food wherever it may appear, it might walk along this or that path from among the infinitely many forward paths it is able to walk along; it might move more or less quickly; it might take the first step now or a little later; it might stop for a while or keep on going. In order for all this to be the case, it seems sufficient that the animal have an awareness of the general area it is able to traverse, along with the innate trace of freedom which resides in its appetitive faculty or (what is the same thing) along with its innate trace of domin-

---

conceive of or entertain as an object the negation of *A*, namely, not-*A*. Rather, I entertain *A*, but simply do not exercise an act of willing with respect to it. Suppose, on the other hand, that I do in fact exercise an act of willing. Then if I am free with respect to the *species* of the act, I may either will *A* or will not-*A*. So we can distinguish freedom with respect to the *exercise* of an act of willing (that is, freedom to will or not will *A*) from freedom with respect to the *species* of the act (that is, freedom to will *A* or will not-*A*). Notice that the former does *not* entail the latter, since freedom with respect to the species of the act, but not freedom with respect to its exercise alone, requires an 'indifferent' cognition of both *A* and not-*A* as potential objects of a positive act of willing. Molina will accordingly insist below that animals may have freedom with respect to the exercise of an act, for example, willing or not willing to take a step in a given direction, even if they have no conception of the negation or, in general, any contrary of the bodily movement that is the object of that act of willing.

[13] Molina does not mean to suggest here that the ability to deliberate about these things is *by itself* a sufficient condition for the agent's freely willing a given act. Obviously, there are other necessary conditions as well. His point is simply that the cognitive prerequisites for free action can, sometimes at least, be satisfied by the mere *ability* to deliberate about such things.

ion over the acts in question. So it is up to the animal whether it takes one path or another, or whether it traverses it more slowly or more quickly, or whether it sets off now or a little later, or, last, whether it stops for a while or keeps on going.

For when freedom or a trace of freedom is present in the appetitive faculty, and when the object is not so strongly attractive that it necessitates this faculty by its character, then freedom or a trace of freedom is by itself sufficient for the appetitive faculty's not commanding a movement it is able to command—and thus a cognition of the *negation* of a movement is not required in order for the faculty not to command the movement.[14] Nor is it necessary, in order for a human being or an animal not to command a movement, that he *will* or *desire* not to command it—this latter *would* require a cognition of the negation of the movement; rather, it is enough that he be related merely negatively to the movement by virtue of his not commanding it, as is possible.[15] This point has not been sufficiently attended to by some writers.

In the same way, when freedom or a trace of freedom is present, it is because of that freedom or trace of freedom *alone* that, given one and the same awareness of the object and of the path, a more or less rapid movement may be commanded.

Moreover, each of the things which has thus far been claimed to depend on the trace of freedom is more than sufficient for establishing that the proximate source of some contingency lies in the appetitive faculty of brute animals. This is manifestly obvious.

8. So in response to the objection it should be said, first of all, that we, unlike Durandus, do not locate freedom in cognition rather than in appetite;[16] nor, again, do we posit as many judgments and commands in

[14]Scholastic theories of action typically distinguish between *elicited* acts, that is, acts of intellect and will which are not themselves "undertaken" (to use Roderick Chisholm's apt term), and *commanded* acts, which are the objects of elicited acts. The simplest examples of commanded acts are elementary bodily movements. So, for instance, my willing to raise my hand is, typically at least, an *elicited* act, whereas my raising my hand is a *commanded* act. A complete human action would characteristically include acts of both sorts. For a lucid explanation of this distinction and others within the context of St. Thomas's action theory, see Alan Donagan, "Thomas Aquinas on Human Action," pp. 642–654 in N. Kretzmann, A. Kenny, and J. Pinborg, *The Cambridge History of Later Medieval Philosophy* (New York, 1982).

[15]See n. 12 above. Being "related merely negatively" to the movement is *not to will* the movement rather than to *will the opposite* of the movement.

[16]The allusion here is to William Durand de Saint-Pourcain (c. 1270–1332), a French Dominican who was bishop of Limoux, Puy, and Meaux at various times during the early decades of the fourteenth century. In the *Concordia* Molina often refers to Durandus's commentary on Peter Lombard's *Sentences*—though not, interestingly enough, given the present citation, in Disputation 2, where he discusses the question of whether freedom should be located in the will or the intellect.

the cognitive faculty as others do. Instead, we believe that a simple cognition of the object as pleasurable or as desirable in some other way suffices by itself for an appetitive act, not only in the sentient appetite of animals but also in the human and angelic wills.[17] (We will say something about this below, in the material on the sin of the angels; and we have discussed it at greater length in Part I–II, q. 9, a. 1, where we explained Aristotle's view on this matter.)[18] Finally, it should be said that in order for animals to have a trace of freedom, it suffices that they have a cognition of the general area through which they are able to travel by walking or flying or swimming; likewise, it suffices that the cognition of the object whose image attracts them not move them so strongly that by its character the animal's desire necessitates the exercise of the act—as has been explained. Nor is it necessary that there be cognitions, comparisons, and deliberations of the sort mentioned in the objection. This, too, has been explained.

9.   With these points thus established, let this be the *second conclusion*: If you excluded the free choice of both human beings and angels, as well as the sentient appetite of brute animals with respect to those acts wherein there is found a trace of freedom, and if you posited the universe with its present constitution and assumed that God did nothing over and beyond the common course and order imposed on things, then contingency would be taken away from all the effects of secondary causes, and everything would have to happen by a kind of fatalistic necessity.[19]

[17]The Scholastics commonly refer to the human will as an "intellective" or "rational" appetite, in contrast to the merely "sentient" appetite found in animals. There are, of course, competing accounts of the differences between the two sorts of appetite, and some of these accounts conflict directly with Molina's claim that animals have a trace of freedom. For instance, in one place St. Thomas claims that a necessary feature of sentient appetite is that the animal does *not* have dominion over its own appetitive inclinations, but is instead intrinsically determined to act. See *De Veritate*, q. 22, a. 5, resp.

[18]Molina's discussion of the sin of the angels is found in *Commentaria*, q. 63, a. 2 and 3, disp. unica, part 5, concl. 1, p. 620a; and his lectures on Part I–II of the *Summa Theologiae* survive in manuscript form in the National Library at Lisbon (F.G. 2804). By the way, this is just one of several references by Molina to Aquinas's *Summa Theologiae* in which he does not mention the work by name, but instead just mentions the relevant part of the *Summa*. This is standard late Scholastic procedure.

In the place cited from the *Commentaria* Molina argues that one need not, in order to sin, erroneously judge that the bad object willed is morally good or good *simpliciter*; rather, it is sufficient merely that *some* sort of goodness, even if only usefulness or pleasure, be perceived in the object or believed to be in it.

[19]Molina holds that God continuously conserves all secondary (that is, created) agents and concurs or cooperates with all their causal activity. And he further holds that God's conserving and concurring activity is in every instance a metaphysically necessary condition for the secondary agent's bringing about any effect at all. (See n. 22 below.) This is why

This conclusion is proved by the fact that, given the above assumptions, every secondary cause will act by a necessity of nature, and any cause which, given the constitution of this universe, is able to impede another cause will in fact impede it. Therefore, whatever is going to occur will occur in such a way that it is not able to issue from its causes in any other way, and thus whatever is going to occur will occur by the fatalistic and extrinsic necessity of its causes.

10. The *third conclusion* is this: Given the same constitution of the universe and given that God does nothing over and beyond the common course and order of things, the *primary, though remote,* source of contingency for the effects of all the secondary causes belonging to the natural order is God's will, which created the free choice of human beings and angels and the sentient appetite of those beasts that seem to be endowed with some sort of trace of freedom with respect to certain acts;[20] on the other hand, the *proximate and immediate* source is the free choice of human beings and angels, along with the sentient appetite of beasts with respect to those acts in which beasts seem to have a trace of freedom.

The first part, namely, that the divine will is the primary source, is perfectly obvious, since if anything else is to count as a source of contingency, then it is necessary that it, in turn, have its existence from the divine will, so that it is by all means necessary as well always to designate the divine will as the primary source.

The second part is proved from the fact that since (i) the other secondary causes act by a necessity of nature, and each of them is such that, given that it is not impeded and given the circumstances that in fact obtain, it is determined with respect to what it does or to that which follows from it under those same circumstances, whereas (ii) only angelic

---

he adds the condition that God does "nothing over and beyond the common course and order imposed on things."

Notice, however, that since God's conservation and concurrence are *free* acts on His part, it might seem to follow that *every* future effect of secondary causes is a contingent effect. For given the exact arrangement of causes that now obtains, God still has the power and freedom not to concur with the secondary causes that will in fact bring about any given future effect E at any given future time T. So for any such E and T, E's occurring at T is now a contingent effect even if all the secondary causes of E acting between now and T will act by a necessity of nature. Such a result seems to undermine the sharp distinction between necessary and contingent effects that Molina is trying to draw.

Molina's response, I believe, is that since God's *general* (as opposed to *particular*) causal influence does not by itself determine the nature of the effect, this influence should be presupposed in an explication of what is to count as a necessary effect. This point is discussed in Section 2.7 of the Introduction.

[20]Molina does not mean to imply here that all the effects of secondary causes are contingent effects, but only that God is the primary source of whatever contingency is found in such effects.

and human free choice, along with the sentient appetite of beasts (which has a trace of freedom with respect to some acts), have it within their power to do this or that in one or another way or to refrain entirely from the activity that characteristically emanates from them, it follows that the contingency of any effect that proceeds from secondary causes has one of these three causes as its proximate source.

11. At this point it should be noted that it is one thing to say that every contingent effect of secondary causes emanates proximately from one of these three causes, and quite another thing to say that the proximate source of the contingency of each such effect is one of these three causes; for the first of these claims is false, and the second is true. The reason is that most contingent effects emanate immediately from natural causes, and yet the immediate source of their *contingency* is not the natural cause itself, from which the effects proceed by a necessity of nature, but is instead one of the three causes in question. For example, the fact that this lamp by which I am writing is now emitting light from itself is a contingent effect that was able not to exist; and even though this effect proceeds by a necessity of nature from the lamp itself as from a natural cause, the source of its contingency was not the lamp, but rather the person who by his free choice lit the lamp, along with all the free causes that cooperated in the production of this oil and of the other things required for lighting the lamp. Hence, it is not only those effects that result *immediately* from the three causes in question which are contingent; rather, the innumerable effects of natural causes resulting from a combination of those three causes and the natural causes in this universe are also contingent. Nor is contingency in the effects of natural causes brought about only by variations arising in the effects of natural causes because of the *immediate* influence of one of the three causes in question; rather, contingency in these effects is also brought about by any other variation that later arises from the immediate effects of these three causes in any of the other effects of natural causes which are easily altered when some circumstance is changed.[21]

12. The proposed conclusion contained the qualification: ". . . given that God does nothing beyond the common course and order imposed

---

[21] What Molina has in mind here is well illustrated by his description, spelled out in Disputation 53, pt. 2, sec. 15, of the changes in the history of the world wrought by Adam's sin, as well as by the sins of his descendants. So there are future effects that (i) are contingent with respect to the secondary causes now operative, since their causal history involves free acts that are still future at the present moment, but which (ii) will occur by a necessity of nature at some time after the last free act in their causal ancestry has occurred. For more on this, see Section 2.7 of the Introduction.

on things." The reason is that if God were either to do something of this sort or to withhold the concurrence owed in some sense to natural causes, then the contingency of the effects of natural causes would also be traceable to the divine will as its *immediate* source.[22] Hence, the fact that the Babylonian fire did not consume the three young men, whom it would have consumed had it been left to its own nature, has to be attributed to the divine will, which freely withheld its general concurrence.[23] To be sure, since God is not wont to do such things except because of the order of grace, that is, so that He might in this way draw people to the faith or confirm them more completely in the faith or something similar, effects of this sort can properly be numbered among those that pertain to the order of grace.

13. In this discussion we have not included among the sources of contingency those effects in which, when commenting on Part I–II, q. 13, a. 2, and on Book IV of Aristotle's *Physics*, we claimed to find contingency, of the sort found in the shattering of a vase full of water, by which the water, if it were frozen and there were no external atmosphere, would rush out to fill the vacuum.[24] For in such a case, if the vase were in all its parts uniform and of entirely equal resistance, then since there would be no more reason it should shatter in this part rather than that part—though it would necessarily have to shatter, lest there be a vacuum—clearly, the fracture's occurring in a given part will be said to happen by chance or fortune and hence contingently. Now, someone might contend that it is not correct to infer from the exact and total uniformity of each of the vase's parts that there is no more reason why in such an event the vase should break in this part rather than that part. So let us suppose that God by a special influence gives equal power of resistance to the part or parts you claim the fracture should occur in; from this it will now indeed follow that there is no more reason the vase should break in this part rather than that part—since each part will have received from God the same power of resistance. The same thing will be

[22] This is the first explicit mention of God's general concurrence (*concursus*) in Part IV of the *Concordia*. The standard Scholastic position is that God's causal concurrence is, in addition to creation and conservation, a necessary condition for any secondary cause's being able to produce any effect at all. There are, however, disagreements about the exact nature of this causal concurrence. On Molina's view God's general concurrence is a causal influence *along with* the secondary cause *on* the effect, whereas according to the Thomistic account it is a causal influence *on* the secondary cause which moves it to bring about the effect. See *Concordia*, Disputations 26–28 (Rabeneck, pp. 164–185), as well as Section 2.6 of the Introduction.

[23] See the third chapter of the Book of Daniel.

[24] No commentary on Aristotle's *Physics* is found among the extant writings of Molina's listed in Stegmüller, pp. 10*–21*.

true of the snapping of a cord that is very slender and equally resistant in each part, if its ends should be pulled apart in opposite directions with an application of maximal force. Likewise, if a beast were presented with two objects so well suited to and in keeping with its appetite that it was equally attracted to both of them, then there would likewise be no more reason it should be moved in one direction rather than the other by the combined force of the desire, of the objects and of the other attendant circumstances. In all these instances we claimed that effects would emanate from the causes in question, since in the proposed cases it would be ridiculous to assert that the vase and the cord would not break, or that the beast would not move. But since there is no more reason why the fracture should occur at one point in the vase or cord rather than another, or why the motion of the beast should follow the one path rather than the other, we claimed that these effects would occur contingently in such a way that chance would prevail. Now because these and other similar events do not seem to be able to occur naturally—except perhaps in the case of the beast, which, since it seems to have a trace of freedom of the sentient appetite, would thereby be able to move in the direction it wanted to in such an event—we have not bothered to include them with the other immediate sources of contingency.[25]

14. *The fourth conclusion*: The contingency of effects that pertain to the order of grace must be traced in part to the human and angelic wills and in part to the divine will as its proximate and immediate source. For such an effect emanates freely either from the divine will alone, as with the incarnation of the Son of God and the infusion of certain habits and gifts, or from a created will that the divine will is cooperating with and helping by means of some special assistance.[26]

This conclusion is obvious and requires no proof.

[25] It is interesting to note here that Molina's account of divine providence can easily accommodate the prevalent contemporary scientific view that there is *genuine* causal indeterminism in nature. He creates the conceptual space for indeterministic natural effects by holding that (i) they, like free actions, are not infallibly predetermined by God, but also that (ii) God need not causally predetermine them in order to foreknow them with certainty, since He can know them with certainty through something very much like the middle knowledge that Molina attributes to Him regarding free actions. These points will become clearer below in Disputations 49, 52, and 53. See Section 2.10 of the Introduction.

[26] By *special* assistance Molina means the supernatural grace that empowers human beings to bring about meritorious supernatural effects.

Whether All the Things That Exist, Have Existed,
and Will Exist in Time Are Present to God
from Eternity with Their Own Proper Existence

1. Now that the contingency of things has been confirmed, it has to be explained how future contingents are known by God and how the foreknowledge He has of them coheres with their contingency.

But before we resolve the question posed in this place by St. Thomas,[1] we will examine in the three disputations following this one the various positions of the Doctors on these same issues. And in order that we might be able to discuss St. Thomas's position more expeditiously in the next disputation, we must first of all examine the problem posed in the title of this disputation.

2. As is patently evident both from the article in question and from the many other places cited by Capreolus in book I, dist. 36, q. 1, and dist. 38, q. 1,[2] St. Thomas held that all the things that exist, have existed, and will exist in the course of time are from eternity present to God in His eternity with that very same actual existence that they have, have had, and will have outside their causes in the course of time—so that the things that come to exist successively in time exist all at once in eternity with the existence by which they come to exist successively in time.[3]

---

[1] *Summa Theologiae* I, q. 14, a. 13. See Disputation 47, n. 1. The "question posed" is whether future contingents are known with certainty.

[2] Johannes Capreolus (c. 1380–1444) was the first of the three great Dominican commentators on Aquinas in the fifteenth and sixteenth centuries, the other two being Tommaso de Vio Caietanus (Cajetan) and Francisco Sylvestri Ferrariensis. (See n. 6 below.) Known as "the soul of St. Thomas," Capreolus wrote the *Libri Defensiorum Theologiae Divi Thomae Aquinatis*, three books of philosophical and theological comments on St. Thomas's commentary on Peter Lombard's *Sentences*.

[3] Here and in what follows I have translated the Latin *esse existentiae* by 'actual existence'. Two paragraphs hence, *esse existentiae* is contrasted with *esse objectivum* (or *cognitum*), that is, to put it somewhat loosely, the sort of being a thing has as an object of thought.

For, as was shown in Part I, q. 10, a. 1, disp. 1, 2, and 4,[4] eternity is in itself a certain indivisible duration, a simultaneous whole having as a unit an infinite durational latitude by virtue of which it coexists and corresponds as a whole with the whole of time and as a whole with each interval and point of time—not unlike the way in which the human soul is wholly in the whole human body and wholly in each of its parts, and the way in which the divine essence is wholly in the whole universe (and, indeed, in the infinite space that we imagine as spreading out in all directions beyond the universe) and wholly in each part and point of that universe.[5] It follows that the whole of time and whatever exists or successively comes to exist in it coexists with and exists in the indivisible now of eternity, before which there is nothing and after which there is nothing, and in which there is found no before or after and no past or future, but only an indivisible, simultaneously whole duration—as was shown in Disputation 2, cited just above.

It is under this interpretation that St. Thomas's position is defended by Cajetan (in his commentary on this article), Capreolus (in the places cited above) and Ferrariensis (in his commentary on *Contra Gentes* I, chap. 66 and 67) and attacked by Scotus, Durandus, and others.[6] For

---

[4]*Commentaria,* pp. 73b–76b and 78a–79b.

[5]The Scholastics distinguish two ways in which something can be in a place: *circumspectively* and *definitively*. A thing *x* is *circumspectively* in a place *P* only if (i) the whole of *x* is in the whole of *P* and (ii) each proper part of *P* is such that a proper part of *x* is in it. Thus, the cup on my desk is circumspectively in the place it occupies, and the same holds in general for ordinary physical objects and the places they occupy. By contrast, *x* is *definitively* in *P* only if (i) the whole of *x* is in the whole of *P* and (ii) each proper part of *P* is such that the whole of *x* is in it. The Scholastics generally hold, for instance, that the rational soul is definitively in its human body, that the body of Christ is definitively in the sacrament of the altar, and that angels are able to be present to spatial locations definitively, though not circumspectively. See, e.g., Ockham, *Quodlibeta Septem* IV, q. 21, pp. 400–403 in Joseph Wey, C.S.B., ed., *Ockham: Opera Theologica,* vol. 9 (St. Bonaventure, N.Y., 1980).

[6]As pointed out in n. 2 above, Capreolus, Cajetan, and Ferrariensis were the three outstanding Dominican commentators on Aquinas in the fifteenth and sixteenth centuries. So it is natural for Molina to cite them here and in Disputation 49 when questions arise about the proper interpretation of St. Thomas. Capreolus has already been introduced. Tommaso de Vio Caietanus (1469–1534) is generally recognized as the most distinguished commentator on St. Thomas. Master general of the Dominicans from 1508 to 1518, Cajetan was an important Catholic figure in the ecclesiastical turmoil at the very beginning of the Reformation. He is most famous for his work on analogy as a metaphysical notion and for his insightful and at times highly speculative commentary on Aquinas's *Summa Theologiae.* In fact, he was influential in the movement to replace Lombard's *Sentences* with the *Summa Theologiae* as the standard text that theology students had to comment on in order to obtain their advanced degrees. Francisco Sylvestri Ferrariensis (c. 1474–1528) taught at various Dominican houses of study before ending up at Bologna in 1520. A leader, along with Cajetan, in the early sixteenth-century revival of Scholasticism, he was master general of the Dominicans from 1525 until his death. He is best known for his commentary on Aquinas's *Summa Contra Gentiles* (hereafter cited as Ferrariensis, *Contra Gentes*).

this reason we have to repudiate Sylvester (in the *Conflatus*), Hervaeus (in book I, dist. 38), and Hispalensis (in the same distinction, q. 1), who maintain that St. Thomas should be interpreted as speaking not about an *actual existence* that the things that come to exist successively in time are supposed to have from eternity in eternity, but rather about an *objective* or *cognitive existence* through which they are known in light of that same actual existence that they will have in the course of time.[7]

3.   This position of St. Thomas's is attacked by Scotus (in book I, dist. 39), Durandus (in book I, dist. 38, q. 3), Gregory and Gabriel (in the same distinction), Aureoli (in the place cited by Capreolus), and several others.[8]

First objection. That which does not exist is not able to coexist with anything, since coexistence requires the existence of both terms. But future things do not yet exist, nor have they existed. Therefore, they do not coexist from eternity with either God or eternity, and hence they are not present to God from eternity with their actual existence.

4.   *Second objection.* Just as in God eternity embraces every time, so too the immensity of the divine essence embraces or touches every place. But God is not present to, nor does He coexist with, any place before that place exists, as was explained in Part I, q. 8 and 10.[9] Therefore, neither will eternity be present to or coexist with any time before that time exists;

---

[7]Molina refers here to three lesser commentators on St. Thomas. Sylvestro Mazzolini Prieras (1456–1523) was, like Cajetan, a Dominican deeply involved in Church affairs at the beginning of the Reformation. His *Conflatus ex Sancto Thomae*, referred to here by Molina, is a commentary on Part I of the *Summa Theologiae*. Hervaeus Natalis (c. 1250–1323), also a Dominican, was the leader of the French Thomist movement at the beginning of the fourteenth century. Molina here refers to Hervaeus's commentary on the *Sentences*. "Hispalensis" is a name used for the Spanish Dominican Didacus de Deza (1444–1523), since he served as archbishop of Hispali (Seveille) from 1504 to 1523. He was the author of *Novarum Defensionum Doctrinae Angelici Doctoris Beati Thomae de Aquino super Primum Librum Sententiarum*, a defense of St. Thomas's commentary on book I of the *Sentences*.

[8]Durandus was introduced in Disputation 47, n. 16. Gregory à Rimini was born toward the end of the thirteenth century and died in 1358. In 1357 he became superior general of the Hermits of St. Augustine, having taught before that at Paris, Bologna, Padua, and Perugia. Molina refers here to Gregory's commentary on the *Sentences*. Gabriel Biel (c. 1410–1495) was a German Scholastic, the most prominent of the fifteenth-century nominalist theologians. Molina refers here to Gabriel's *Sentence* commentary, titled *Epithoma Pariter et Collectorium Circa Quattuor Libros Sententiarum*. Peter Aureoli (c. 1280–1322) was a French theologian who won fame for his defense of the doctrine of the Immaculate Conception. The archbishop of Aix-en-Provence from 1321 until his death, he is best known for his *Sentence* commentary, referred to here, and for his commentary on the literal sense of Sacred Scripture.

[9]*Commentaria*, pp. 66a–70a and 73b–89a.

it follows from this that a future time that does not yet exist neither coexists with nor is present to eternity, either now or from eternity.

5. *Third objection.* Things that are not able to coexist with each other will not be able to coexist with some third thing, either. But past time and future time are not able to coexist together with one other. Therefore, they are not able to be present to God from eternity with their actual existence, nor are they able to coexist with eternity.

6. *Fourth objection.* If the things that exist successively in time existed together from eternity in eternity itself, then, since contradictories may be true successively in time—for instance, the proposition 'Adam exists' was once true, and the proposition 'Adam does not exist' is now true—contradictories would be true simultaneously in eternity. But that is absurd.

7. *Fifth objection.* If the things that exist successively in time existed together from eternity in eternity itself, then it would follow that the nonexistence of a thing that is generated is not prior to the existence of that same thing. Further, it would follow that the existence of one and the same thing is produced before it is produced in time; and so it would follow either that the thing is produced twice or else that it cannot be produced in time—both of which are utterly absurd.

8. In order to understand the interpretation under which this doctrine of St. Thomas's can be defended, it should be noted that the verbs that we use as copulas in propositions signify, in addition to their principal significatum, a certain duration as the measure of the truth of those propositions.[10] For if the verb is present-tense, it consignifies present duration; if past-tense, past duration; and if future-tense, future duration.

Furthermore, present duration, which is the sort relevant to what we are talking about here, can be of two types, namely, (i) the present time or present moment of time, or (ii) eternity, which is always present. Indeed, eternity cannot be a past or future duration, since of course there cannot be any past or future in eternity taken in itself.

From this it follows that past-tense and future-tense verbs neither signify nor are able to signify eternity as the measure of the truth of

---

[10]The notion of signification is being used here in an extended sense. When he refers to the 'principal significatum' of the copula, Molina seems to have in mind not an entity of any sort but simply the joining together of the subject and predicate.

propositions. Instead, they can signify only time, in which there can be such a thing as the past and the future. Hence, the sense of the propositions 'Adam existed' and 'The Antichrist will exist' is this: 'Adam existed in past time' and 'The Antichrist will exist in future time.' By contrast, present-tense verbs can signify as the measure of the truth of propositions both (i) time or the moment of present time and (ii) the present eternity. There can thus be two readings of the proposition 'Adam exists.' One is this: 'Adam exists in the duration of present time or of the moment of present time'—and the proposition is false on this reading. The other reading is this: 'Adam exists in the present duration that is eternity.' The proposition is true on this reading, since he exists in the indivisible, to be sure, but infinite now of eternity, which embraces all of time and in which there exists whatever exists in time—though he exists in eternity *because of* the existence that he had at the time at which he existed. For if we imagine that in the indivisible now of His eternity, which is beyond all time and embraces the whole of time, God Himself forms the proposition 'Adam exists in this, my now of eternity,' we understand clearly that this proposition is true.

And so, even though in ordinary usage we take present-tense propositions to signify present time as opposed to past or future time, nonetheless such propositions can be understood in both senses, especially when the subject of discourse is, as it is for us now, the existence of things in eternity.

9. Having laid this foundation, Cajetan (in his commentary on this article) and Capreolus and Ferrariensis (in the places already cited) claim that the following propositions can have two readings: 'All things coexist with God,' 'All things exist in eternity,' 'All things coexist simultaneously with God or with eternity.'

On one reading the verbs 'coexist' and 'exist' signify present time, as opposed to past or future time, and the propositions have this sense: 'In the present time (or, at the moment of present time) all things coexist with God, exist in eternity, coexist simultaneously with God or with eternity.' And they contend that on this reading the propositions are false, since in order for one thing to be correctly said to coexist with another or to exist in another, it is required that both exist in the interval consignified by the copula of the proposition in which this is affirmed; therefore, since future things do not exist either in the present time or at the moment of present time, it follows that they do not at that time coexist with God or with eternity, nor do they at that time exist in eternity—as is quite clear from what we said in q. 10, a. 1, disp. 2.[11] If

---

[11]*Commentaria*, pp. 74a–76b.

you wish, you might also look at the arguments that Cajetan uses in this place to reach the same conclusion. Those who attack St. Thomas's teaching seem to have interpreted the above propositions in the way just explained.

10.   But said propositions can have another sense, such that the verbs in question consignify not the present time but an always present eternity. Here is the other sense: 'In the now of eternity all things coexist with God'; 'In the now of eternity all things exist in eternity'; 'In the now of eternity all things coexist simultaneously with God or with eternity'— that is, they exist neither before nor after (since there is no such thing as before eternity or after eternity), but rather they exist in that indivisible and infinite now of eternity that embraces the whole of time. On this reading the propositions are true, and it is in this way that they are understood by St. Thomas and by Boethius in *De Consolatione* V, last prose;[12] and it is as so understood that they appear frequently in the writings of the saints, especially Augustine and Anselm.

11.   It is in this same sense that the holy Fathers sometimes deny that in God there is foreknowledge, properly speaking. For in the indivisible now of eternity, which is the duration proper to the divine knowledge, all things are present and coexist; and in this eternal now there is no before or after, as though in some now of eternity it might be possible to know things before they exist. So it follows that in God there is no foreknowledge with regard to the existence of things in eternity—though in relation to time there is, altogether properly speaking, foreknowledge in God, since He knows things an infinitely long time before they exist. Nor does the fact that things are produced afterward give rise to any alteration in the divine knowledge. It is in this way that Augustine is to be understood in *De Quaestionibus ad Simplicianum* II, q. 2, when he says that God's knowledge with respect to things that are future in time does not, properly speaking, have the character of foreknowledge.[13] And it is in this same way that Anselm is to be understood in *De Casu Diaboli*, chap. 21, when he says, "God's foreknowledge is not properly called foreknowledge; for someone to whom all things are always present does not have foreknowledge of future things, but rather has knowledge of present things."[14] The same goes for Boethius in *De Consolatione* V, last prose,

---

[12]Molina refers here, of course, to Boethius's *De Consolatione Philosophiae.*

[13]*PL* 40, 138. (Throughout I use the standard abbreviations *PG* and *PL* for Migne's *Patrologia Graeca* and *Patrologia Latina*, followed by volume and column numbers.)

[14]*PL* 158, 353C. Here and in what follows I have made my own translations of passages that Molina quotes from the Fathers, the saints, and the theologians. I have also, somewhat more hesitantly, made my own translations of the scattered biblical passages quoted from the Latin Vulgate.

when he claims that what can be properly said to be in God is not foreknowledge, but rather providence.

12.   I am surprised that Cajetan, in his commentary on this article, credits himself with being the first to discover this way of defending St. Thomas's doctrine, since Capreolus before him (in the places already cited) had defended it in the same way, and since the very same distinction was hinted at by Richard (in *Quodlibeta* III, q. 1) and by others among Cajetan's predecessors.[15]

13.   Still, I should caution that the following propositions must not, it seems, be conceded: 'All things have existed from eternity in eternity,' or 'All things have coexisted from eternity simultaneously with God or with eternity.' For since the copulas of these propositions are past-tense, they cannot signify, as the measure of the truth of these propositions, the duration of eternity, in which there is no past; rather, they are able to signify only the duration of past time. The following propositions, on the other hand, can be conceded: 'All things coexist from eternity with God,' 'All things are from eternity present to God with their own actual existence,' 'All things coexist from eternity simultaneously with God or with eternity.' For it is indeed the case that from eternity itself all things coexist in the now of eternity and are present to God and to eternity. What's more, it is these latter propositions—and not those others above—which St. Thomas uses in this place. The following proposition can also be conceded: 'From eternity it has always been true to say, "All things are present to God or coexist with God."' For its sense is this: 'At any past time when the proposition "All things coexist with God" was put forth, it was true, as long as the verb "coexist" consignified the now of eternity.'

14.   *Response to the first objection.* As for the first argument by the opponents,[16] given that the major premise is conceded, the minor premise may be conceded as well if its meaning is that future things do not yet exist in the present time and have not existed in the past. But then the consequence should be denied, if its consequent is understood as saying that future things do not coexist from eternity with either God or eternity *in the very now of eternity* which is consignified by the verb 'coexist.' For even though future things neither exist at the present time

[15]Richardus de Mediavilla (Richard of Middleton) (c. 1249–1302) was a Franciscan who taught at Paris from about 1284 to 1286. He endorsed the condemnations of Aristotelianism promulgated at Paris in 1277, but nonetheless proved to be a highly sympathetic critic of Aquinas. Dubbed the "Solid Doctor" (*Doctor Solidus*), Richard is best known for his commentary on the *Sentences* and for three series of *Quodlibeta*.

[16]See sec. 3 above.

nor have existed in the past, they nonetheless exist in the indivisible now of eternity which embraces the future time in which they will exist. On the other hand, if in the consequent the verb 'coexist' signifies an *interval of time*, so that its meaning is that future things coexist with neither God nor eternity in real time or in the imaginary time that has elapsed from eternity up until the present moment of time, then the consequence should be conceded. For since those things did not exist in that interval of time, they could not have coexisted in that interval with either God or eternity. And it is in this sense that the conclusion seems to be understood by the objectors, even though St. Thomas did not teach the contrary.

15. *Response to the second objection.* As for the second argument,[17] given that the major and minor premises are conceded, the first consequence should also be conceded. For since, in order for two things to coexist, the existence of both of them is required, it certainly does involve a contradiction for eternity to be present to or coexist with a time, or for a time to be present to or coexist with eternity, *before* the time exists *either in itself* (given that whatever is in time should be said to coexist with eternity) *or in eternity* (given that whatever is in the now of eternity, which embraces all of time, may be said to coexist with or be present to eternity). Thus, as far as that which is further inferred is concerned,[18] if in the consequent the verb 'coexist' signifies a *present time*—as opposed to past or future time—in which a future time might coexist with eternity, then the second consequence should also be conceded. Nor does St. Thomas claim the contrary. If, however, the verb signifies eternity itself, in which a time that is future in relation to the moment of present time might coexist with and be present to that very same eternity, then the second consequence should be denied—and this whether the consequent in question is asserted now or at any other time, real or imaginary, with respect to eternity. For in eternity consignified in this way by the copula, since it embraces future time, that future time coexists with and is present to that same eternity.

16. *Response to the third objection.* As for the third argument,[19] the major premise should be conceded if its sense is this: 'Things that are not

---

[17]See sec. 4 above.

[18]The consequent of the first consequence is, 'Neither will eternity be present to or coexist with any time before that time exists.' Molina apparently takes this proposition to be the *antecedent* of a second consequence, one whose consequent is what he refers to here as "that which is further inferred," namely, 'a future time that does not yet exist neither coexists with nor is present to eternity, either now or in eternity.'

[19]See sec. 5 above.

able to coexist with each other in their own proper durations are not able to coexist together with any third thing in those same durations, if those durations are signified by the copula of the proposition in which the things in question are said to coexist with that third thing.' For, as has been explained, past time and future time cannot coexist together with God or eternity in any interval of time in which they cannot coexist with each other. The major premise should be denied, however, if its sense is this: 'Things that are not able to coexist with each other in their own proper durations are not able to coexist together with some third thing in the duration of that third thing, even if that duration embraces the durations of both of them and is signified by the copula of the proposition in which they are said to coexist together with that third thing.' For past time and future time, which cannot coexist with each other at any time, can coexist in eternity, which embraces both, together with God—whose eternity is His proper duration—or also together with eternity itself.

17. *Response to the fourth objection.* In response to the fourth argument,[20] and also in order to understand which propositions with opposed predicates are true and which are false when the copulas signify the now of eternity, the following should be noted: Some propositions with contradictory predicates are such that both are affirmative, for example, 'Socrates is sitting' and 'Socrates is nonsitting'; whereas others are contradictories in the most proper sense, the one being affirmative and the other negative, for example, 'Socrates is sitting' and 'Socrates is not sitting.'[21] Now in both cases—as well as in any others in which opposed predicates are attributed to the same thing—in order for there to be an opposition when the copula consignifies a temporal now, it is necessary that it consignify the *same* temporal now in both propositions.

---

[20]See sec. 6 above.

[21]Molina here draws upon the standard medieval distinction between negative propositions and negative (or 'infinite') terms. Though it has an infinite predicate, a proposition of the form '*S* is non-*P*' is affirmative and hence is true only if there is something that its subject term refers to, or in technical terminology, *supposits for*. So if there is nothing that the subject term supposits for, then corresponding propositions of the forms '*S* is *P*' and '*S* is non-*P*' will *both* be false; it follows that they are not contradictories. On the other hand, a proposition of the form '*S* is not *P*' (or 'It is not the case that *S* is *P*') is a negative proposition and thus is true if there is nothing its subject term supposits for. So corresponding propositions of the forms '*S* is *P*' and '*S* is not *P*' *are* contradictories. That is, it has to be the case that exactly one of them is true and exactly one of them is false. For more on the important distinction between propositional and terminal negation, see my "Ockham's Theory of Truth Conditions," pp. 1–76 in A. J. Freddoso and H. Schuurman, trans., *Ockham's Theory of Propositions: Part II of the Summa Logicae* (Notre Dame, Ind., 1980), esp. pp. 63–64. Also, see the passage from Aristotle referred to in n. 23 below.

For opposition has to do with the same thing, in the same respect and at the same time. These points are obvious from the *Dialectica*.[22]

18. With these points thus established, it should now be noted that when propositions containing opposed predicates are both affirmative, there is a distinction to be drawn. If the copulas consignify the same temporal now, then the propositions cannot both be true; but if they consignify the now of eternity, then the propositions can be true together. The reason is that since (i) all the attributes that belong to a thing at different times belong to it all at once in the now of eternity, and since (ii) being a sitter and being a nonsitter can belong to Socrates at different times, as can being sighted and being blind, and being cold and being hot, it follows that all these things can be truly attributed to him all at once if the copulas of the relevant propositions consignify the same now of eternity. Thus, when the copulas consignify the now of eternity, then affirmative propositions containing opposed predicates have no opposition to each other. On the other hand, when propositions with the same subject and predicate are such that the one is affirmative and the other negative, then an opposition is found between them, regardless of whether their copulas signify the same temporal now or the same now of eternity. Hence, the propositions 'Socrates is sitting' and 'Socrates is not sitting' are contradictories, regardless of whether the copulas signify the same temporal now or the same eternal now. The explanation for this is that a negation has the force of distributing what it negates, and so to say 'Socrates is not sitting in eternity' is the same as saying 'Socrates is not sitting in eternity *in any respect,* whether insofar as eternity corresponds to this time or insofar as it corresponds to that time or to any other time.' Therefore, as long as Socrates is sitting at some moment of time, 'Socrates is sitting in eternity' is true, whereas 'Socrates is not sitting in eternity' is false. And so the following consequence is invalid: 'Socrates is not sitting at such-and-such a time; therefore he is not sitting in eternity.'

19. From what has been said you can easily see that the rule enunciated by Aristotle in *De Interpretatione* II, chap. 1, namely, that a consequence by which a finite negative is inferred from an infinite affirmative is valid, does not hold for propositions whose copulas consignify the now of eternity, though it *does* hold for propositions that signify the temporal

---

[22]Molina is apparently referring here to his own introduction to Aristotelian dialectics, part of an early series of lectures on the whole of Aristotle's *Organon* which he gave to a group of religious and secular students from 1563 to 1567. The lectures are found in manuscript form in the library of Evora, cod. 118-1-6, with the *Dialectica* coming just after the opening notes on Porphyry's *Isagogue* and just before the lectures on the *Categories*.

now—and it is the latter propositions that Aristotle was speaking of in that place.[23] The reason for this is as follows: The rule in question derives its validity from the fact that contradictory predicates, for example, 'sitting' and 'nonsitting', cannot belong to the same subject at the same instant of time, so that if 'nonsitting' is truly affirmed of Socrates at some moment of time, then 'sitting' will be truly denied of him at that same moment. But because contradictory predicates can be affirmed of Socrates in the same now of eternity, since eternity corresponds to different parts of time, the following consequence is invalid: 'Socrates is nonsitting in eternity; therefore he is not sitting in eternity.'[24]

20. Now that these matters have been explicated, we should say in response to the proposed argument that the two propositions in question,[25] which are true successively in time, are not contradictories, since their copulas do not consignify the same temporal now, but instead consignify different temporal nows—whereas in order for there to be a contradiction it is necessary that they consignify the same time. On the other hand, if they did consignify the same instant of time, then the propositions would indeed be contradictories, but in that case they could

[23] Aristotle, *De Interpretatione*, chap. 10, 19b 23ff. In contrast to us moderns, the medievals divide the *De Interpretatione* into two books, the first consisting of chapters 1–9 and the second of chapters 10–14. Here the description 'finite negative' refers to a negative proposition with a positive or finite predicate (for example, 'Socrates is not sitting in eternity'), whereas the description 'infinite affirmative' refers to an affirmative proposition with a negative or infinite predicate (for example, 'Socrates is nonsitting in eternity'). See n. 21 above.

[24] From what Molina says here and just below we can reasonably infer that he accepts the following principle: 'If "S is P" is true at some time and "S is not P" is true at some other time, then both "S is P" and "S is non-P" are true in eternity.' It is interesting to apply this principle to the predicate 'being' ('exists'). On Molina's view, 'Socrates is a nonbeing,' where the copula signifies the now of eternity, is true if Socrates exists at some times but not at others. But one might object that this proposition is not only false but impossible. For it obviously implies that Socrates is *not* a being and also implies, since it is affirmative, that Socrates *is* a being. Molina's response is that although 'Socrates is a nonbeing' is, for the reasons given, impossible if its copula signifies the *temporal* now, things are otherwise if its copula signifies the *eternal* now. For in that case 'Socrates is a nonbeing' does *not* imply that Socrates is not a being, and hence is not an impossible proposition. We can understand this as follows: As an affirmative proposition, 'Socrates is a nonbeing' implies that Socrates exists at the moment signified by the copula, namely, the now of eternity. To be sure, it also signifies that he is a nonbeing at that moment. But, as we have already seen, Molina holds, apparently without inconsistency, that contrary predicates can be true of the same substance at the same eternal moment (though not, of course, at the same temporal moment).

My comments here should not be construed as a defense of Molina's position; in fact, I would freely admit that there are further complications that arise from these comments and that thus remain to be dealt with. I only mean to suggest that the position is less vulnerable to obvious objections than it might at first appear to be.

[25] As is clear from sec. 4, the two propositions referred to here are 'Adam exists' and 'Adam does not exist.'

not both be true. So if the proposed argument has to do with propositions that consignify different moments of time and so are not contradictories, and if it is being claimed that the truth of both of them is simultaneous in the now of eternity insofar as it embraces the different times at which they are found to be successively true, then the whole argument should be conceded and it does not contain anything absurd. And it is in this sense alone that what Cajetan asserts in this place can be true, namely, that there is nothing incongruous about two propositions that contradict each other with respect to the temporal now both being true in the same now of eternity; still, this is an improper way of putting the point.[26] On the other hand, if it were being claimed instead that even if the copulas of the two propositions consignified the same now of eternity, in which case they would be contradictories, the propositions could still be true simultaneously in eternity, then the validity of the argument would have to be denied. For the negative proposition would be false in that case, since its meaning would be that Adam *in no way* exists in eternity, even insofar as eternity corresponds to a time at which he did exist; and this is patently false.

21. *Response to the fifth objection.* As for the fifth argument,[27] it should be said that there is nothing absurd about the nonexistence of a thing that is generated not being prior to the existence of that same thing in the indivisible now of eternity in the way in which it *is* prior to its existence in time. For eternity lacks a before and an after, and it is a simultaneous whole. Still, the nonexistence of a thing that is generated exists in eternity nonadequately[28] and only because eternity corresponds to a

---

[26]Cajetan's way of putting the point is "improper" because it suggests that the law of noncontradiction does not apply in eternity. Molina insists that the two propositions are *not* contradictories in time, but are instead related as 'Adam exists at time T' and 'Adam does not exist at time T^*,' where T is distinct from T^*. Thus, the propositions true in eternity are 'Adam exists' ['Adam is a being'] and 'Adam nonexists' ['Adam is a nonbeing']; and these propositions, as explained above in n. 24, are not contradictories.

[27]See sec. 7 above.

[28]I have simply transposed the technical term *non adequate* into the English 'nonadequately'. A thing x exists *adequately* in eternity only if x has eternity as its own *primary* and *proper* duration, with the result that (i) x would still exist in eternity even if time did not exist, and (ii) if time does exist, then x is present to every moment of it. Recall that for the Christian Aristotelians time is a contingent being, because creation itself is contingent and the existence of time depends on the existence of physical motion and hence of created physical objects. According to the Scholastics, only God Himself exists *adequately* in eternity. (A Platonist would presumably hold that necessarily existing abstract entities also exist adequately in eternity.) By contrast, things that are essentially time-bound exist *nonadequately* in eternity, even if they are sempiternal or everlasting in time. For eternity is not their *proper* duration, and thus they would not exist in eternity if they did not exist in time. In short, their existence in eternity is asymmetrically dependent on their existence in time. See Section 3.2 of the Introduction for further discussion of this point.

time that exists before the thing is generated, whereas the existence of a thing that has already been generated exists in that same eternity, once again, nonadequately and only because eternity corresponds to a time at which the thing is already said to have been generated. The response to the second part of this argument is that the inference should be denied. For the existence of a thing that is generated does not exist in eternity prior to its existing in time, but rather exists in eternity simultaneously with its existing in time. For just as the thing is not produced in the duration of eternity by a production or by causes other than those by which it is produced in time, so too neither does it exist in eternity with an existence other than that with which it exists in time—nor does it exist in eternity prior to its existing in time. Rather, by the very fact that it is produced and exists in time, it coexists in the eternity with which time coexists. Therefore, such a thing does not exist adequately in eternity, but exists in eternity only because eternity corresponds to a time at which the thing exists and only because eternity embraces the time in question with its indivisible, to be sure, but infinite and simultaneously whole durational latitude.

DISPUTATION 49

*Whether Future Contingent Things Are Known by God
with Certainty because They Are Present to Him with Their
Own Existence, and Whether the Contingency of These Things
Might Thereby Be Reconciled with Divine Foreknowledge*

1. In this place St. Thomas, following in the footsteps of Boethius, *De Consolatione* V, last prose, embraces an affirmative answer to the questions posed in the title. This answer is supported by the following principles that he proposes, though not in the same order.

The *first principle* is this: Since eternity, being an indivisible and infinite duration, exists as a simultaneous whole and encompasses the whole of time, all the things that come into existence and exist successively in time are present to God from eternity with that very same existence outside their causes which they acquire successively in time. Therefore, since divine cognition, like divine being, is measured by eternity, it follows that from eternity God's cognition extends simultaneously to all contingent things insofar as they are already present to Him in the duration of eternity with that very same existence outside their causes which they are going to have in the course of time.

2. The *second principle* is this: A contingent thing can be considered in two ways. On the one hand, it can be considered insofar as it already exists in itself outside its causes, in which case it is considered not as future or as contingent with respect to either part, but as present and as determined to one part.[1] And so considered, the thing can be the subject of a certain and infallible cognition. For as long as Socrates is already actually sitting, I visually perceive with certainty that he is sitting. Alternatively, a contingent thing can be considered insofar as it still exists in

---

[1] Throughout Part IV of the *Concordia* Molina refers to contradictory propositions or states of affairs as "parts of a contradiction" or simply as "parts." Accordingly, free choice is said to be "contingent with respect to both parts"; and when the will chooses, it is said to determine itself "to one part."

its cause, in which case it is considered as future and contingent, not yet determined to one part, since of course a contingent cause is indifferent to opposites. Considered in this way, a contingent thing is not the subject of any cognition that is certain and unable to be mistaken, and thus anyone who knows a contingent effect merely in its cause has only *conjectural,* and not *certain,* cognition of it.[2]

3.   From these two principles St. Thomas infers that since, as is clear from the first principle, the divine intellect knows all future contingents, not only as they exist in their causes but also as each of them is actually present in itself to the divine gaze with its own actual existence outside its causes, God knows all contingent things with a cognition that is certain, even though each of them is a future contingent in time if thought of in relation to its causes. And this is why he claims that the contingency of things in time in relation to their causes is compatible with God's infallible and certain foreknowledge. He teaches the same thing in *De Veritate,* q. 2, a. 12, and in *Contra Gentes* I, chap. 67.

4.   Still, there is some doubt about whether it was on this ground alone that St. Thomas claimed that in God there is certain and immutable knowledge of future contingents, or whether he based this claim *also* on the ground that in God there are *ideas* by means of which He would know future things with certainty (at least after the free determination of His will) even if they were not present to Him with their own existence—a ground we will have to examine in more detail in the next disputation and in the penultimate disputation.[3]

5.   Cajetan (in commenting on this article) and certain others among St. Thomas's disciples affirm the second opinion. St. Thomas lends them support when he says in this article, "Hence, all the things that exist in time are eternally present to God, not only because He has the natures of things present to Himself, as some claim, but because His gaze extends eternally to all things as they exist in their presentness."[4] For by the

---

[2]A 'conjectural cognition' (*coniecturalis cognitio*) is one that lacks certitude. More specifically, a subject *S*'s cognition of a proposition *p* in circumstances *C* is *conjectural* only if *S* is able in *C* to be mistaken about whether or not *p* is true. It does not follow from this, however, as the English term 'conjectural' might suggest, that such a cognition is a mere guess. To the contrary, *S*'s believing *p* in *C*, even if conjectural, might be more reasonable than his not believing *p* in *C* or at least more reasonable than his believing the negation of *p* in *C*.

[3]Molina refers here to Disputations 50 and 52 below.

[4]*Summa Theologiae* I, q. 14, a. 13, resp. Here I have translated *rationes rerum* as 'the natures of things'. Below I translate *rationes idearum* as 'ideal natures'.

expression "the natures of things [that God has] present to Himself" St. Thomas seems to mean the ideas of things, as Cajetan (in this place) and certain others maintain; and he seems to be asserting that the future things that exist in time are indeed present to God as objects known with certainty because He has the natures of things present to Himself—yet not for this reason alone, but because His gaze extends to all of them as present to Him with actual existence.

6.   Nonetheless, there seem to be persuasive reasons for thinking that St. Thomas held the contrary view.[5] First of all, in the second principle he distinguishes two states of a future contingent, the one insofar as it already actually exists outside its causes, the other insofar as it still exists in its cause; and he says that in the former state a future contingent can be the subject of a cognition that is certain, but not so in the latter state. Moreover, in *De Veritate*, q. 2, a. 12, corpus and ad 6, he seems clearly to assert that even if the cognition in question is divine, a contingent thing considered in the second state cannot be the subject of a cognition that is certain. This is why he adds in this place, "Hence, anyone who knows a contingent effect merely in its cause has only conjectural, and not certain, cognition of it." Second, if St. Thomas believed that the ideal natures alone sufficed for God's knowing future things with certainty before they exist outside their causes in either time or eternity, then (i) he would have explicated this at more length, and (ii) he would have gone on to explain how God, by means of the ideal natures, could know with certainty things that are within the power of created free choice, and (iii) he would have made clear how freedom of choice might then be reconciled with divine foreknowledge viewed in this way, and (iv) he would not have taken such great pains (a) in explaining the certitude of divine foreknowledge only on the basis of the presence of things with their existence in eternity, and (b) in reconciling the contingency of things with the certitude of foreknowledge just on this basis alone. Third, if in the passage quoted a short time ago St. Thomas had meant to assert that God has certain knowledge of future contingents on *both* sorts of grounds, then he would have said, "Hence, all the things that exist in time are eternally present to God, not only because He has the natures of things present to Himself, as some claim, but *also* because His gaze extends, etc." For that would be a more plausible indication that St. Thomas had intended to say that *either* sort of ground is sufficient. Yet consider the following: (i) the assertion that

the ideal natures are a sufficient ground for knowing future contingents with certainty is incompatible with the doctrine he propounded in the second principle; and (ii) he did not say "but *also* because, etc.," but instead simply said "but because, etc."; and, furthermore, (iii) there is a legitimate explanation for the fact that in this passage he did not totally exclude the ideal natures, namely, (a) in this passage he was speaking not about the presence of just future contingent things but about the presence of *all* the things that exist in time, many of which are necessary and many of which have causes determined to produce them, though these causes are able to be impeded, and (b) the ideal natures *would* suffice for it to be the case that all the things that are necessary or have determined causes are present with certainty to God with objective existence, especially if all of them acted from a necessity of nature. Indeed, it was for this reason not permissible to exclude the ideal natures, and this is why St. Thomas said, "Hence all the things that exist in time are eternally present to God, not only because He has the natures of things present to Himself" (as if to say, "for this explanation by itself would not suffice for it to be the case that *all* things are present to Him even with objective existence in such a way that He knows them with certainty"), "but because His gaze, etc." (as if to say, "this is a *general* explanation of how *all* things are present to Him in such a way that He knows *all* of them, even future contingents, with certainty"). Since, I say, all these things are so, it is likely that St. Thomas in this place did not mean to claim that it is also because of the ideal natures that God knows future contingents with certainty.

7.   But let me say what I think about this whole matter. First of all, despite the arguments just adduced, I would not dare to claim that St. Thomas, whom in all things I sincerely desire to have as a patron instead of an adversary, believed that God knows future contingents with certainty solely on the basis of the presence of things with actual existence. Rather, if he were asked about this issue, he would, I believe, affirm the contrary position.

I am moved to say this, first, because in *Contra Gentes* I, chap. 67, argument 3, he proves that God knows future contingents from the fact that just as a necessary effect is known with certainty from a necessary cause, so too a contingent effect is known with certainty from a complete contingent cause, if the latter is unimpeded.[6] Therefore, since God knows

---

[6]The claim here is that if one knows all the secondary causes that, if unimpeded, will contribute to a possible future effect E and also knows what all the possible impeding causes are, then one knows with certainty whether or not E will occur.

Molina finds himself in an uncomfortable position here. On the one hand, he believes

not only the causes of contingent effects, but also the things by which those causes are able to be impeded, it follows, says St. Thomas, that He knows future contingents with certainty from their causes. It is true, however, that Ferrariensis (in commenting on this passage) interprets the argument as not applying to future contingents whose cause is free choice, since obviously free choice, even when unimpeded, has it within its power to produce or not to produce its effect or to produce this effect rather than some alternative contrary effect; rather, he says, the argument applies to future contingents which emanate from natural causes that are determined by their very nature to produce given effects but are contingent in the sense that they can be prevented from producing those effects.[7]

Second, I am moved by the fact that the position in question would detract from the dignity of the divine knowledge—indeed, would be dangerous from the point of view of the faith, to say no more. Yet I cannot persuade myself that St. Thomas came to any conclusion that would in any degree detract from the dignity of the divine knowledge or that would not be fully in accord with the Catholic faith—especially since (i) there is nothing that absolutely forces this judgment on me, and since (ii) there are some not insignificant indications to the contrary, and since (iii) so many learned men maintain that it was also on the basis of the ideal natures that St. Thomas asserted that God has certain knowledge of future contingents.

8.   Therefore, let this be the *first conclusion* of the present disputation: It is not simply because things exist outside their causes in eternity that God knows future contingents with certainty; rather, before (in our way

---

the above claim to be false, since it fails in the case of future effects brought about with the causal influence of freely acting secondary causes. For one may know that free choice is a possible impeding cause with respect to E without knowing whether or not it will in fact impede E in the relevant circumstances. The reason is that a freely acting agent, unlike an agent acting by a necessity of nature, is both able to act and able not to act in those very circumstances. So, like Ferrariensis, Molina is reluctant to attribute the above claim in all its generality to St. Thomas. At best, it is true only in the case of an effect whose causal history involves no created agents that act indeterministically. On the other hand, Molina is also reluctant to attribute to St. Thomas the mistaken (in his eyes) alternative view that God's certitude regarding future contingents has its source merely in the fact that such things are eternally present to God with their actual existence. This tension comes to a head in the next paragraph.

[7]Ferrariensis, *Contra Gentes* I, chap. 67, tertio. It is perhaps worth noting that given the distinction between necessary and contingent effects presupposed in Disputation 47, natural effects whose causal history involves no indeterministic created causes are *necessary* rather than *contingent* effects. Here, however, Ferrariensis is treating them as a species of contingent effects. See Section 2.7 of the Introduction for more on contingent effects.

of conceiving it, but with a basis in reality)[8] He creates anything at all, He comprehends in Himself—because of the depth of His knowledge—all the things which, as a result of all the secondary causes possible by virtue of His omnipotence, would contingently or simply freely come to be on the hypothesis that He should will to establish these or those orders of things with these or those circumstances; and by the very fact that through His free will He established in being that order of things and causes which He in fact established, He comprehended in His very self and in that decree of His all the things that were in fact freely or contingently going to be or not going to be as a result of secondary causes—and He comprehended this not only prior to anything's existing in time, but even prior (in our way of conceiving it, with a basis in reality) to any created thing's existing in the duration of eternity.[9]

9. This conclusion, as regards its first part (and, indeed, as regards the other parts as well), is so certain that I would not hesitate to say that its negation is dangerous from the point of view of the faith.

The first proof: It is clear from Sacred Scripture that the supreme God has certain cognition of some future contingents that depend on human free choice, but that neither have existed nor ever will exist in reality and that hence do not exist in eternity either; therefore, it is not simply because future contingents exist outside their causes in eternity that God knows them with certainty.

The consequence is obvious, while the antecedent is proved as follows: God knows that there would have been repentance in sackcloth and ashes among the Tyronians and Sidonians on the hypothesis that the wonders that were worked in Chorozain and Bethsaida should have

---

[8]Molina holds that even though there is no real succession among God's cognitive and volitional acts in eternity, still there is a basis in reality for our distinguishing and ordering various acts of intellect and will on God's part. See Disputation 53, pt. 1, sec. 20, last paragraph, for Molina's own explication of the phrase 'in our way of conceiving it, but with a basis in reality'.

[9]Molina's most thorough discussion in Part IV of the notion of *comprehension* occurs in Disputation 53, pt. 1, sec. 20. (See Section 2.3 of the Introduction for further discussion.) Notice the contrast he draws here and later on between comprehending a thing *in oneself* or *in one's free volition* or *from oneself*, on the one hand, and comprehending a thing in a way that depends on that thing's existing or being actual, on the other hand.

Also, Molina often speaks of something's being the case on the hypothesis that God should will to establish or create this or that *order* (*ordo*) of things (or *order* of things and circumstances). What he has in mind is a set of created things partially ordered with respect to time—or, to put it less technically, a succession of things, each of which bears temporal relations to all of the others. God's *establishing* an order of things does not, of course, entail His *producing by Himself* each of the things that is a member of that order. Recall that in Disputation 47 Molina distinguishes those things whose existence God causes by Himself from those whose existence He causes together with secondary causes, both secondary causes acting by a necessity of nature and secondary causes acting freely.

been worked in Tyre and Sidon. This is clear from Matthew 11:21, "If the wonders that have been worked among you had been worked in Tyre and Sidon, they would long ago have repented in sackcloth and ashes."[10] But because the hypothesis on which it was going to occur was not in fact actualized, this repentance never did and never will exist in reality—and yet it was a future contingent dependent on the free choice of human beings.[11] Likewise, in 1 Kings 23:10–12 David consulted the Lord about whether Saul was going to descend upon Keilah, and the Lord responded, "He will descend."[12] He consulted again, about whether the men of Keilah, who had received nothing but kindness from David, were going to hand him and the men with him over into the hands of Saul. And the Lord responded, "They will hand you over." Notice, God knew these two future contingents, which depended on human choice, and He revealed them to David. Yet they never have existed and never will exist in reality, and thus they do not exist in eternity either. The antecedent is further confirmed by the fact that God, foreseeing the sins into which the just would fall if they remained

[10]I assume throughout that the reader is or can easily become acquainted with the context of the scriptural passages cited by Molina.

[11]Here and in sec. 11 below we have the first intimation in Part IV of the doctrine of middle knowledge. (Molina does not actually use the term 'middle knowledge' until Disputation 52, sec. 9; in sec. 13 below he characterizes the knowledge in question merely as "a certain sort of natural knowledge." See n. 16 below.)

Molina argues that the presence of things to God in eternity cannot be the sole basis for God's certitude regarding future contingents. For numbered among the future contingents are not only things that *will in fact be* but also things that *would have been* had certain conditions obtained. The latter are called "conditioned future contingents." (In Section 2.8 of the Introduction I treat condition*ed* future contingents as a species of condition*al* future contingents, namely, the ones that have both false antecedents and false consequents.) Since conditioned future contingents have never existed and will never exist in time, they do not exist in eternity either—and yet God knows them.

Two points of clarification are in order. First, we must distinguish conditioned future contingents from things that are merely possible. Let *S* be the state of affairs of the Tyronians' and Sidonians' repentance and conversion, and let *H* be the counterfactual circumstance consisting in the wonders worked in Chorozain and Bethsaida being worked in Tyre and Sidon. *S on H* and *not-S on H* are equally, Molina would insist, *metaphysically possible*; but, in addition, *S*, but not *not-S*, would have obtained if *H* had obtained. So *S* is a conditioned future contingent, whereas *not-S* is a mere possible relative to *H*.

Second, those who harbor ontological misgivings about merely possible beings or about future beings should be assured that talk of mere possibles and of conditioned future contingents can easily be transposed into more familiar talk about substances, properties, propositions, and states of affairs. In fact, Molina's own manner of speaking should be taken to be neutral among various competing ontological accounts of the temporal and alethic modalities.

[12]1 Sam. 23:10–12. Molina, of course, uses the Vulgate rather than Hebrew titles for the historical books of the Hebrew Scriptures. The Hebrew 1 and 2 Samuel correspond to the Vulgate 1 and 2 Kings; the Hebrew 1 and 2 Kings correspond to the Vulgate 3 and 4 Kings; and the Hebrew 1 and 2 Chronicles correspond to the Vulgate 1 and 2 Paralipomenon.

in this life for a long time, in His mercy often takes them from this world—this according to Wisdom 4:11, "He was snatched away, lest wickedness pervert his mind or deceit beguile his soul," and a bit later at 4:14, "His soul was pleasing to God; because of this He hastened to lead him out of the midst of iniquities." Since, therefore, those sins were numbered among the future contingents and were foreseen by God and yet were never going to have existence in reality, it follows that it is not simply because things exist in eternity that God knows future contingents with certainty.

10. I realize that Cornelius Jansen, along with Ambrose, reads this last text as having to do with the translation of Enoch.[13] But the common interpretation—following Cyprian in *De Immortalitate* (near the end) as well as in book IV of *Ad Quirinum* and Augustine in Letters 105 and 107 and in *De Praedestinatione Sanctorum,* chap. 14—is that it has to do with the translation of the just by death.[14] See Lyranus and Dionysius Carthusianus on the same text.[15] Moreover, this interpretation comports with what precedes and what follows in that chapter, and indeed with the preceding chapter and the following chapter. Whoever wanted to weaken the force of this evidence would have to expound "lest wicked-

---

[13]For the biblical allusion to Enoch's bodily transference to heaven, see Gen. 5:21–24. Molina refers here to Cornelius (Gandavensis) Jansen (1510–1576), bishop of Ghent from 1568 until his death. One of the most influential Catholic exegetes of the sixteenth century, he is especially noted for his commentaries on the Gospels. The reference here is to Jansen's *Annotationes in Librum Sapientia.* (Cornelius Gandavensis Jansen is not to be confused with Cornelius Otto Jansen [1585–1638], whose writings provided a good part of the inspiration for the Jansenist movement in western Europe in the seventeenth and eighteenth centuries.)

St. Ambrose (d. 397) was, of course, the bishop of Milan at the time of St. Augustine's conversion. The references here are to Ambrose's *De Excessu Fratris Satyri* I, n. 30 (*PL* 16, 1300A), to his commentary on the Psalms (*PL* 14, 1080C and 1138D), and to Letter 38 (*PL* 16, 1097B).

[14]St. Cyprian (d. 258), bishop of Carthage and martyr, was a highly educated scholar who converted to Christianity some twelve years before his death. Molina's first reference here is evidently intended to be to Cyprian's *De Mortalitate* (rather than *De Immortalitate*), chap. 23 (*PL* 4, 599). This tract was written during a plague in Carthage, and in it Cyprian urges his flock on toward self-sacrifice in the service of both Christians and non-Christians. The second reference is to Cyprian's *Ad Quirinum* (*Testimoniorum*) III, chap. 58 (*PL* 4, 765). The references to Augustine are found in *PL* 33, 889 and 984, and in *PL* 44, 979.

[15]Nicholas of Lyra (Lyranus; c. 1270–1349) was a Franciscan Scripture scholar who drew upon his mastery of Hebrew and intimate knowledge of the Jewish commentators on the Old Testament in authoring a much used commentary on the whole Bible, titled *Postillae Perpetuae, sive Brevia Commentaria in Universa Biblica.* In fact, this was the first such commentary to find its way into print (Rome, 1471–72). Molina refers here to the commentary on the Book of Wisdom contained in that work.

Dionysius Carthusianus (1402/3–1471) was a German Carthusian monk renowned for both his scholarship and his mystic piety. His collected works fill forty-two volumes. Molina refers here to Dionysius's *Ennaratio in Librum Sapientia,* chap. 4.

ness . . ." as "lest *perhaps* wickedness pervert his mind" and "lest deceit . . ." as "lest *perhaps* deceit beguile his soul"—as if both these things were dubious and uncertain to God. Is there anyone who would not recognize that such a reading of the text is forced, exotic, and absurd, and who would not see that the legitimate reading is the one proposed in common by Augustine (Letter 105, cited above) and the Doctors, namely, ". . . in order that wickedness not pervert his mind and in order that deceit not beguile his soul, as God foresaw would happen . . . and so God hastened to lead him out of the midst of iniquity, because his soul was pleasing to Him"? What's more, even if this passage *is* about the translation of Enoch, the text still has to be explicated in the same way and so corroborates our position.

11. *The second proof*: Through His natural knowledge God comprehends Himself, and in Himself He comprehends all the things that exist eminently in Him and thus the free choice of any creature whom He is able to make through His omnipotence.[16] Therefore, before any free determination of His will, by virtue of the depth of His natural knowledge, by which He infinitely surpasses each of the things He contains eminently in Himself, He discerns what the free choice of any creature would do by its own innate freedom, given the hypothesis that He should create it in this or that order of things with these or those circumstances or aids—even though the creature could, if it so willed, refrain from acting or do the opposite, and even though if it was going to do so, as it is able to freely, God would foresee *that* very act and *not* the one that He *in fact* foresees would be performed by that creature. For it would be insulting to the depth and perfection of the divine knowledge—and indeed impious and not at all compatible with so great a comprehension of the free choice of each creature—to assert that God is

---

[16]First, anything that God is able to create is thereby said to exist "eminently" in God. Second, as pointed out in n. 11 above, Molina does not use the term 'middle knowledge' in Disputation 49. Instead, he employs the term 'natural knowledge' for any divine knowledge that *precedes* (in our way of conceiving it) God's free decision or free volition with respect to which, if any, order of created things to establish. Given this usage, what distinguishes God's knowledge of conditional future contingents from the rest of His natural knowledge is that it is metaphysically possible that He should have known truths other than the ones He in fact knows about conditional future contingents. In other words, truths about conditional future contingents are not metaphysically necessary truths, even though God knows them *prior* to His act of will and thus has no control over them. So, at least, claims Molina. The Bañezians, by contrast, while also attributing to God knowledge of conditional future contingents, insist that this knowledge, far from being *natural* in the above sense, *follows upon* God's act of will and hence is *free* knowledge. All of this is explored more deeply and with ever increasing sophistication as we proceed through Part IV of the *Concordia*. Also, see Sections 2.8, 3.3, and 4.1–4.3 of the Introduction.

ignorant of what I would have done by my freedom of choice (i) if He had created me in some other order of things, or (ii) if, in this very order of things in which He has created me, He had decided to confer on me more or fewer aids than He in fact decided to give me, or (iii) if He had granted me a longer life or handed me over to more serious temptations. So it follows that even before He created anything by His free will, He knew all future contingents with certainty through natural knowledge. That is, through His natural knowledge He knew whether or not they were going to be, *not absolutely speaking* but rather *on the hypothesis* that He Himself should decide to create this or that order of things with these or those circumstances; and from this it follows that by the very fact that He freely chose the order of things which He in fact chose, He knew absolutely and with certainty which contingent things were going to be or not going to be; and He knew this in that very choice and decree of His will, before (at least in our way of conceiving it, with a basis in reality) anything emanated from that decree with its real existence in either time or eternity. Therefore, God does not need the existence of those things in His eternity in order to know them with certainty.

We have been forced to touch upon the whole foundation on the basis of which we believe that God knows all future contingents with certainty, and on the basis of which, if we do not fail, we will in the penultimate disputation perspicuously reconcile freedom of choice and the contingency of things with divine foreknowledge.[17]

12. *The third proof*: God does not get His knowledge from things, but knows all things *in* Himself and *from* Himself; therefore, the existence of things, whether in time or eternity, contributes nothing to God's knowing with certainty what is going to be or not going to be. For prior to any existence on the part of the objects, God has within Himself the means whereby He knows all things fully and perfectly; and this is why the existence of created things contributes no perfection to the cognition He has of them and does not cause any change in that cognition. In God, then, *intuitive* cognition and *abstractive* cognition (or better, cognition of *simple intelligence*) do not differ in any way.[18] Rather, depending only on

---

[17]The reference here is to Disputation 52 below.

[18]Molina here invokes a distinction elaborated in very different ways by Scotus and Ockham. See Scotus, *Quaestiones Quodlibetales* VI and XIII, pp. 135–137 and 290–296 in F. Alluntis, O.F.M., and A. B. Wolter, O.F.M., trans., *John Duns Scotus: God and Creatures* (Princeton, N.J., 1975); and Ockham, *Ordinatio* I, prol., q. 1, pp. 30–38, 44–51, and 60–64 in G. Gál, O.F.M., and S. Brown, eds., *Ockham: Opera Theologica*, vol. 1 (St. Bonaventure, N.Y., 1967). For present purposes it is sufficient to note that most Scholastics would insist, *pace* Ockham, that *intuitive cognition* is a perfect or privileged sort of cognition which can only have as its object something that is *existent* and *present* and which for this reason

whether or not its object exists, one and the same cognition, equally evident and equally perfect in its own right, is called either an intuitive cognition or else a cognition of simple intelligence, as was shown in article 9.[19] By contrast, since in us and in angels the evident cognition of future contingents depends on their existence and on the experience by which we cognitively apprehend that they exist in reality with their real existence, it follows that experiential and intuitive cognition in angels and in us is distinct *in species* from abstractive cognition and is much more perfect than abstractive cognition. And thus it is that the existence of the objects contributes to the perfection of a cognition fashioned by angels and human beings, as was explained in that same article and elsewhere.

13. *The fourth proof*: In God there is providence and predestination with regard to future contingents. Therefore, there is a precognition by which He foreknows with certainty, before anything exists, what is or is not going to be on the hypothesis and condition that He should grant this or that assistance or means, or arrange things in this way or some other way. If this is not so, then how did He preordain and arrange things by His providence, intending good contingent effects via both natural and free causes while permitting evil contingent effects in order that He might draw forth from them greater goods? Likewise, in what sense was there a predestining of various freely acting causes in order that they might achieve contingent effects and goals by these or those means? If the craftsman did not know beforehand what shape the artifact would later have to have, given that his hands and artistic tools were to be applied in one or another way during its construction, then he would not know how to use those means so that the artifact might turn out the way he wanted it to. So, too, if, before God decided by the free decree of His will to furnish the means and to arrange the things in the way in which they have in fact been ordered, He did not foresee what would happen given such an arrangement and order, then He would most assuredly not know how to order things by that decree in the way

---

depends on the existence of its object; whereas *abstractive cognition* is further removed from its object and can have as its object something that is not present or is even nonexistent. Molina argues here that since God's knowledge is perfect and yet not at all dependent on the existence or presence of its objects, the distinction between these two types of cognition or knowledge effectively collapses in God. What we have instead is a distinction between God's knowledge of existent things (knowledge of *vision*) and His knowledge of possibles (knowledge of *simple intelligence*). But this distinction is not based on any *intrinsic* difference between the two types of knowledge or cognition; rather, it is based simply on the act of will by which God decides to create some things and not others.

[19]*Commentaria*, q. 14, a. 9, pp. 158a–159a.

required for the ends. Instead, things would in their actual existence be just as prone to turn out in one way as another, as though by chance and beyond the scope of God's antecedent knowledge, while God would find out from their existence how they had turned out; but this is plainly the height of absurdity and impiety, and should be so judged. Thus it follows that before anything exists, God foreknows future contingents with certainty. Indeed, *before* the free decree of His will He knows them through a sort of natural knowledge and on the hypothesis that He should will to create and arrange things in this or that way, whereas *in* that free decree, which as a cause precedes the existence of future contingents both in eternity and in time, He knows them absolutely and without any hypothesis or condition.[20]

14. The preceding argument can be confirmed by the fact that God permits sins. Now someone is said to permit that which he (i) foresees as going to be unless he prevents it, (ii) is able to prevent, and yet (iii) does not will to prevent. Since, therefore, sins are numbered among the future contingents, it follows that prior (at least in nature or, better, in our way of conceiving it, with a basis in reality) to their existing either in time or in eternity, future contingents are known by God with certainty on the hypothesis that He not will to prevent them. The proposed conclusion will be corroborated still further by what we are about to say in our discussion of the next conclusion.

15. *The second conclusion*: In the sense explained in the preceding disputation, we can, to be sure, easily defend the claim that the proposition 'All the things that exist, have existed, or will exist in any interval of time coexist with God or are present to God with their own actual existence outside their causes' is true at any time it is uttered vis-à-vis eternity, as long as the copulas 'coexist' and 'are' consignify not the temporal now at which they are uttered but the now of eternity, where the now of eternity is taken *not inadequately* (that is, not insofar as it corresponds just to this or that moment or interval of time) but *adequately* (that is, insofar as it is an infinite duration embracing all of time, the past as well as the future even now apprehended by thought); nonetheless, I do not believe, nor is it to be conceded, that (i) the things that come to be in time exist in eternity *before* they exist in time, or that (ii) they are present to God in eternity with their own existence *before* they are actually present in time, or that (iii) it is *because* things exist in eternity

[20]See nn. 11 and 16 above on Molina's use of the term 'natural knowledge' in this disputation.

that God foreknows future contingents with certainty before they exist in time. This is why the proposition 'From eternity all things coexist with God or are present to God with their own existence outside their causes,' taken in the sense explained in the preceding disputation, contributes nothing, as I see it, either toward establishing the certitude of the divine foreknowledge concerning future contingents or toward reconciling the contingency of things with divine foreknowledge.

16. I am moved to assert this for three reasons.[21] First, apart from the fact that, as was explained a little while ago, the existence of created things contributes nothing at all to the knowledge God has of them, and that God's knowledge does not depend on their existence or acquire any perfection or hence any certitude from their existence, it should not be thought that the things that come to be successively in time exist in eternity *before* they exist in time—as though it was because of some sort of anticipation they have in eternity with respect to existence outside their causes that they are known with certainty in eternity while they are still future in time. Yet this is what would have had to be true in order for it to be the case that it was because of the existence of things in eternity that God foreknew them with certainty before they came to be in time.

But if *this* was the claim being made by Boethius, St. Thomas, and the others who affirm on this basis that God knows future contingents with certainty,[22] then I frankly confess that I do not understand it, nor do I think that there is any way in which it can be true. For given this view, it would have to be conceded that when the copula 'exist' consignifies the instant of present time, the following proposition is true: 'The things that will exist in the entire course of time already exist with their own actual existence in eternity.' For even though at the moment of time when this proposition is uttered the things that are still future would not yet exist in time, nonetheless at that very moment of time they would exist in eternity by virtue of an anticipated existence by which things exist in eternity before they come to exist in time. Yet, though many seem to concede this and are accustomed to using this manner of speaking, I did not concede it in the preceding disputation, nor do I believe it to be true. For the things that are produced successively in time have no other causes by which they are produced with their actual existence in

---

[21] The elaboration of these three reasons is spread out over the next four sections. The first reason is discussed in secs. 16 and 17, the second reason in sec. 18, and the third reason in sec. 19.

[22] Molina here considers one way of interpreting the claim that God's certitude with respect to future contingents has its source in the presence of those things with their actual existence in eternity. In n. 25 below I call it the "anticipation" thesis.

eternity than those very same causes by which they are produced in time; nor do these causes produce them in eternity by a different production or with a different existence than that very production by which, and that very existence with which, they produce them in time. Likewise, they do not produce them in eternity in the sense of conferring actual existence on them *within* eternity, that is, within God Himself, who is His eternity (for this claim would be stupid and impious). Rather, they produce them in eternity in the sense that while they are producing them in the duration of time, they are simultaneously bringing it about that they exist in the duration of eternity. For since eternity is indivisible and infinite, and hence coexists as a whole with the whole of time in such a way as to coexist as a whole with each of its parts and points, it cannot come about that a thing exists in time without also existing in the duration of eternity. Since, I say, all these things are so, it follows that no one should think that the infinite duration of eternity, which embraces all of time, is a simultaneous whole in a sense that implies and renders it true that future things exist in it outside their causes *before* they are caused to exist in time. For that would be altogether unbelievable, and it would be concocted without any need, and, as I will presently show, it would obliterate freedom of choice and the contingency of things. Rather, eternity is a simultaneous whole in the sense that it coexists as a whole with the whole of time and with each part of it, but *only when and not before* each of those parts exists in itself—not, of course, because of any defect on the side of eternity, but because such a part of time does not yet exist in its own right and absolutely.

17. Now, it is easy to show that our freedom of choice and the contingency of things are completely destroyed if one asserts that because eternity is a simultaneous whole, things exist in it before they exist in time in such a way that (i) all the things that are future in time already at the present moment exist in eternity—indeed, that from eternity they exist in eternity outside their causes with their real existence—and that (ii) they exist with so great a degree of constancy that this is the source of God's knowing with certainty the things that are contingently future in time. For neither free choice nor any other cause would be able to bring about a future effect without its being the case that the very same causes were, in the very same way and by the very same action, going to bring about at a future time what they had already brought about beforehand in eternity; or else, if they *were* able to bring about some other effect, then surely the effect that they will in fact bring about would not now already exist in eternity with so great a degree of constancy that it would not be able not to exist, and thus the certitude of God's knowledge with

respect to the things that will come to be contingently in time would not be able to derive from their having this sort of existence in eternity.

18. My second reason (and perhaps it amounts to the same thing) is that the things that will exist contingently in time after today are up until today indifferent with regard to whether or not they exist in time as well as in eternity. For instance, an act of my free choice which will exist tomorrow is still able not to exist in time; otherwise, it would not be contingently future in time. But since it does not exist in eternity except by virtue of the existence that it is going to have in time, it is likewise really able not to exist in eternity—or else it would not be contingently future in time. Therefore, it is not because of the existence of this act in eternity that the knowledge by which God knows that the act will exist tomorrow has up until today a certitude containing absolutely no doubt; the act, after all, is able not to exist in eternity. Therefore, it is not the existence of things in eternity that is the source of God's knowing with certainty the things that are still contingently future in time.

For, assuming that the copulas consignify the now of eternity, when we say that all things in time—present as well as past and future—have existence simultaneously in eternity, this must be understood of eternity taken *adequately*, that is, insofar as it corresponds to the whole of time. For even though eternity exists and has existed up until the present day insofar as it corresponds to the present instant and to all of past time, nonetheless it does not yet exist as corresponding to future time. This is not, of course, because eternity is lacking something that would make it correspond to future time; instead, it is because the future time to which it would correspond is not yet present.

An appropriate model is the center point of a circle in relation to the circle drawn around it, which indivisible eternity and the time that moves or runs its course around it are said to resemble.[23] For while the circle is being drawn, the center point does not yet correspond to the part still to be drawn, but corresponds only to the part already drawn. And this is not because the center point is lacking something that is required in order for it to correspond to the part still to be drawn; rather, it is because what is lacking is that very part to which the center point, in itself already existing as a whole, would correspond. But once the entire circle has been drawn, the center corresponds to the whole circumference and to each of its parts. In the same way, as long as the whole of time has not yet elapsed, indivisible eternity corresponds not to the whole of time, but to the part that has elapsed. Therefore, just as the

[23] Scotus uses this same model in *Ordinatio* I, d. 39, q. 1–5.

center point is able never to correspond to a part of the circle that has not yet been drawn, since that part might not be drawn in the future, so too eternity is able not to correspond to the parts of real time that are still future or to the things that will exist contingently in those future parts of time, since real time might cease or, even if it endures, the things in question might not exist in it, as indeed they are able not to exist.

From this it is clear that even though, when the copulas consignify the now of eternity and eternity is taken adequately (that is, insofar as it will correspond to the whole of time even now apprehended in thought), the proposition 'Whatever is future in time is present to God or exists in eternity' is absolutely true (for whatever exists in time, be it more things or fewer, thereby necessarily exists in eternity, which embraces the whole of time), nonetheless, if we are speaking of some particular thing that is still contingently future in time, for example, a sin of Peter's that will exist tomorrow, then the proposition 'This sin is present to God or exists in eternity' is not absolutely true, but true only on the supposition that the sin is going to exist in time.[24] For just as it is still able not to exist in time, it is likewise able not to exist in eternity taken adequately.

19.   Last, I am moved by the fact that if all the things that are future in time were from eternity present to God outside their causes with their own existence—and this because of some sort of anticipation in eternity, an anticipation from which the divine foreknowledge might acquire certitude about things that are still contingently future in time—then it would follow that in our temporal present an actual infinity of things exist outside their causes. They would not, to be sure, exist in the present moment as in a measure of their real existence, but would instead exist in that way in the now of eternity. Still, they would exist in our temporal present as in a measure of their existing in that way in eternity; but it seems altogether absurd to concede that in our temporal present there is an actual infinity of things in eternity, and it seems to involve a contradiction.[25]

---

[24]By an 'absolute' truth Molina seems to mean a truth that is now unpreventable by secondary causes and that hence (as he sees it) can provide the basis for an infallible cognition on God's part in eternity. A 'conditional' truth, on the other hand, is one that is (still) preventable by secondary causes and that hence (as Molina sees it) cannot be the foundation for an infallible cognition.

[25]This argument is at first sight a puzzling one. How, exactly, does it follow from the "anticipation" thesis that there is an actual infinity of things even in the whole course of time, to say nothing of a particular moment of time? The following passage from *Commentaria*, q. 14, a. 12, provides a clue:

"Second conclusion. The divine knowledge extends to infinitely many things not only when it is considered according to its whole [possible] breadth but also insofar as it has the character of a knowledge of vision. St. Thomas proves this from the fact that even though

20.   The foregoing renders clear what we asserted at the end of q. 14, a. 9, namely, that God's knowledge of things that are still contingently future in time does not, properly speaking, have the character of a knowledge of *vision* until those things actually exist in time; rather, in the meantime it has the character of a knowledge of *simple intelligence*, because the things that are its objects do not yet exist.[26] But since the proper duration of that knowledge is eternity, and because in eternity, since it coexists with future time, those things will in the end be present, God's knowledge may simply be called a knowledge of vision in relation to all the things that will exist in any interval of time; and in keeping with the common opinion of the Doctors, we will occasionally refer to it as such.

21.   I want to bring to your attention this further point: In the early commentaries on Ephesians 1:4, "As He chose us in [Christ] . . . ," Jerome says, "He declared us the elect, so that we were saints before the world was made. This has to do with the foreknowledge of God, for whom all future things have already been accomplished and to whom all things are known before they come to be."[27] When he says this, and even when in the later commentaries on the same text he says, "For nothing is new to Him in whose presence all things existed before they came to be," these words are to be understood as meaning not that things preexist with their real existence, but rather that they preexist in objective existence as clearly known.[28] For things that do not exist are said to exist after a fashion in relation to the divine *power*, which calls into existence, or makes to exist, the things that do not exist as well as the things that do

---

there are not going to be infinitely many *substances* (since nothing will be generated after the Judgment Day), still the mental acts of the blessed and of the damned will be multiplied unto infinity; but God actually knows all of these acts simultaneously through the knowledge of vision" (pp. 159b–160a).

So according to Molina and St. Thomas, an actual infinity of things—if not of substances, then at least of mental accidents—will exist in the infinite stretch of future time, and thus an actual infinity of things exists in eternity. Thus far there is no problem. But Molina seems to reason further that if the "anticipation" thesis is true, then that very same actual infinity of things exists at the *present temporal* moment, at least in a derivative sense. For the friends of the anticipation thesis hold that all the things that ever have or ever will exist in time *now* exist in eternity. But this, of course, conflicts with the standard Aristotelian principle that it is impossible for an actual infinity of substances and/or accidents to exist at any one moment of time.

[26]*Commentaria*, p. 141a–b. For more on the distinction between God's knowledge of vision and His knowledge of simple intelligence, see n. 18 above.

[27]*PL* 26, 446. St. Jerome (c. 345–419/20) was, of course, a great Doctor of the Church and the learned translator of the Bible into Latin.

[28]The passage quoted here is actually from the late fourth- and early fifth-century heretic Pelagius (c. 354–c. 418), *Expositiones in XIII Epistolas Sancti Pauli* (*PL* 30, 823D).

exist; in the same way, since things that do not exist are not hidden from God, but rather are known clearly by Him just as if they existed, they are said by Jerome to preexist in the divine *knowledge*. This is why he adds to the second of the above passages, "Not that, as certain heretics imagine, separated souls preexisted in heaven . . ." And commenting on Ecclesiastes 1:10, "Is the word . . . ?" he says, "It should be said that because of God's foreknowledge and predestination all things that are going to be have already been accomplished."[29] Cyril affirms the same thing in *Thesaurus*, book V, last chapter.[30]

22.   Beyond this, Scotus proposes the following argument against this same position of St. Thomas's: Just as eternity is a simultaneous whole and coexists with past and future time, so too the aeviternity of an angel is a simultaneous whole and coexists with past and future time.[31] Therefore, just as it is because of the existence in eternity of those things that are still contingently future in time that God knows future things with certainty before they exist in time, so too because of the existence of those same things in aeviternity an angel will foreknow them with certainty before they exist in time.[32]

23.   To this argument the disciples of St. Thomas have been wont to reply that the two cases are not on a par, since the cognition of an angel is not measured by aeviternity but rather by an instant of discrete time, whereas God's cognition is measured by eternity, in which the things that are contingently future in time actually exist.[33] But since an angel

---

[29]The first of these passages is, again, from Pelagius (see n. 28 above), and the second is indeed from Jerome, *PL* 23, 1020A.

[30]St. Cyril of Alexandria (d. 444), Father and Doctor of the Church, is best known for his staunch opposition to Nestorianism. The present reference is to his *Thesaurus*, assertio 15, *PG* 75, 292ff. (Molina's allusion to book V is based on the way the book is divided in the edition printed at Paris in 1572.)

[31]I here translate *aevum* by the English 'aeviternity'. Many Scholastics hold that just as eternity is God's proper duration and time is the proper duration of physical objects, so too aeviternity is the proper duration of angels. Unlike eternity, aeviternity involves an ordered series of 'moments', specifically a succession of discrete cognitive and volitional acts on the part of an angel; unlike time, aeviternity is a *discrete,* as opposed to *continuous,* series and does not depend for its existence on the motion of material substances.

[32]This argument is formulated very compactly here. It is meant to be a *reductio ad absurdum,* with the absurd conclusion being that an angel can (without divine revelation) foreknow future contingents with certainty. The standard Scholastic view is that angels by nature know temporal things with certainty when and only when those things become present in time.

[33]The Thomists' point here is that a single angelic cognition lasts not for the whole of aeviternity, but only for one discrete moment within it, and so no discrete moment of this sort is such that it coexists with all past and future time. Molina counters that it is at least possible for an angel to have a single everlasting cognition. And besides, he continues, if

could have a simultaneously whole cognition that coexisted as a whole with aeviternity or that in relation to our time lasted as long as aeviternity lasts, this does not seem to be the proper way for them to respond to the argument—especially since if future things always coexist with aeviternity with their actual existence outside their causes in the way that they coexist with eternity, then an angel, once its cognition is posited, will indeed apprehend those things outside their causes already in aeviternity, and he will thus know them with certainty before they exist in time, even if he knows them through a cognition whose duration is not aeviternity, but the now of discrete time.

24. They could better respond as follows, however: Aeviternity has durational breadth not *from itself,* but only by virtue of the fact that an angel is conserved by God for a greater or lesser time; and thus whether an angel coexists with future time depends not only on the future existence of time but also on God's conferring existence on that angel or conserving him in future time. Eternity, on the other hand, has infinite duration *from itself.* (Both these points were explained in q. 10.)[34] And so it follows that the two cases are not on a par, since things that are still future in time do not at this temporal moment coexist with aeviternity in the way that they coexist with eternity. This response has a place only if we claim that eternity is of such a nature that it *makes* those things that are future in time to preexist in itself—as must be claimed if the position of Boethius and St. Thomas is to be defended in some way. For even if such a nature were attributed to *eternity,* it would still be the case that it should not be attributed to *aeviternity* in any way, for the reason we have just given.

---

the Thomistic position on the existence of things in eternity is correct and can be extended to aeviternity as well, then perhaps angels do not have to wait for future contingents to become present in time in order to know them with certainty in aeviternity. Perhaps instead they are able to survey all of aeviternity (and, derivatively, all of time) in just one discrete cognition that does not last for all aeviternity.

[34]*Commentaria,* q. 10, a. 5, disp. 1, pp. 81a–85b.

DISPUTATION 50

Whether It Is through the Ideas That God Knows Future Contingents with Certainty, and at the Same Time the Views of Scotus and Durandus Are Examined

1.   In book I, dist. 39, a. 2, q. 3,[1] St. Bonaventure maintains that God knows future contingents with certainty because He has in Himself ideas of all things through which He knows all future things with certainty, just as if He had those things present with their own existence. Cajetan (in this place) and certain others among St. Thomas's disciples ascribe this same position to St. Thomas on the basis of the passage from this article which we presented and considered in the preceding disputation.[2] Cajetan even asserts that Scotus interpreted St. Thomas in the same way; but in the place that will presently be cited Scotus meant perhaps to argue only against St. Bonaventure and those others whom St. Thomas in this article, without giving any names, claims to have held the position in question.

2.   Scotus argues against this position in book I, dist. 39, a. 1.[3] *First argument.* The ideas in God do not represent the *conjoining* of the predicate with the subject of a contingent state of affairs, which, by the very fact that it is contingent, is indifferent as to whether it obtains or not; instead, they represent only the *terms* of such a state of affairs.[4] But from knowledge, however perfect, of the terms of a future contingent state of affairs it is impossible to know with certainty which part of a contradiction is going to be true, since the terms are neither tied to nor opposed to each other in such a way that it is possible to tell from their natures

---

[1]St. Bonaventure, *Commentaria in Quattuor Libros Sententiarum* I, d. 39, q. 3, a. 2.
[2]Disputation 49, sec. 5.
[3]Duns Scotus, *Ordinatio* I, d. 39, a. 1.
[4]As before (see Disputation 47, n. 2), I translate the Latin *complexio* by the English 'state of affairs', and I further assume that states of affairs can coherently be thought of as having components (terms) and as bearing logical relations (for example, being the contradictory of, being the contrary of, entailing, being entailed by) to other states of affairs.

whether the predicate agrees with the subject—as it *is* possible to tell when a state of affairs is necessary. Therefore, the divine ideas by themselves cannot be a sufficient explanation for God's knowing future contingents with certainty.

3. *Second argument.* The ideas exist and represent things to God *prior to* any free act of the divine will; therefore, whatever they represent, they represent merely *naturally*. But contingent states of affairs are known by God *freely* and *not naturally*, since obviously if He had decided by His free will not to create anything, then He would not have known as future any of those contingent states of affairs which are in fact going to obtain. Therefore, the ideas by themselves cannot be an explanation for knowing future contingents with certainty.

4. *Third argument.* The ideas represent in the same way both future contingent possibles that will never exist and future things that will exist in some interval of time, since the fact that some contingent things are going to be while others are not going to be has its source not in the divine ideas but in God's free will, which freely prearranged the causes by which the things that *are* going to exist contingently were to be produced, but which did not prearrange causes for other things that could have existed and yet are *not* going to exist. Therefore, the divine ideas by themselves cannot be a sufficient explanation for the fact that future contingents are known by God with certainty.

5. *Fourth argument.* The fact that future contingents are going to exist at one time rather than another stems not from the ideas but from God's free will, which decided to create things at one time rather than another and to order them in this way rather than in some other way. Therefore, the divine ideas by themselves cannot be a sufficient explanation for the fact that God knows future contingents.

6. Scotus agrees that the ideas (or, the divine essence known as the primary object)[5] are a sufficient explanation for the fact that through His natural knowledge God knows (i) all the *simples* that can exist by virtue of the divine omnipotence and (ii) all *states of affairs*, not just the necessary ones but also the contingent ones—to be sure, He knows not that the latter *are going to obtain*, but rather that they are *able to obtain*, so

---

[5] Scholastic theologians hold that the divine essence is the *first* or *primary* object of God's act of understanding, and that God knows other things by understanding Himself perfectly as the cause of being for whatever else might exist. See, e.g., St. Thomas Aquinas, *Summa Contra Gentiles* I, chap. 47–49.

that through His natural knowledge He knows each state of affairs which is indifferent to obtaining or not obtaining and hence He knows that each such state of affairs is able to obtain and able not to obtain.[6] For from the natures of the terms it is understood that the one term *is able to* agree with the other, but not that it *in fact* agrees or fails to agree with the other. Besides, even if a state of affairs is contingent, the fact that it is contingent (and is thus both able to obtain and able not to obtain) is nonetheless something necessary; but God knows all necessary truths through His natural knowledge.[7]

7. Even though Scotus agrees with the others on the points just mentioned, still, influenced by the arguments proposed above, he claims that it is solely in the determination of His will that God knows which part of each contradiction is going to turn out to be contingently true in the future, and thus that it is solely in the free determination of His will that He knows future contingents with certainty. And, indeed, there would be no problem with Scotus's position if future contingents included only (i) the things that are *immediately* caused by God, as are all the things that were produced by God alone in the original establishment of the world, and (ii) the things that are brought about by secondary causes acting from a necessity of nature. But future contingents *also* include the things that emanate from created free choice, as well as the subsequent things that proximately or remotely emanate from or depend on those three sources of contingency in the effects of secondary causes that we explained in Disputation 47.[8] Now if (i) Scotus were claiming only that all future contingents of this latter sort depend on the free determination of the divine will to the extent that no such thing would be a positive future contingent if God had not freely decided to create this world with the order of things with which it has in fact been created, and if, further, (ii) he were claiming for this reason that in order for any of these future contingents to be known by God as *absolutely* future, God has to fore-

---

[6]Molina clearly thinks of states of affairs (*complexiones*) as built up out of simples (*simplicia*) along with, presumably, logical operations such as composition of subject and predicate, negation, and conjunction. Thus, to say that God "knows all the states of affairs" is to say at least that God knows what all the various combinations are, and also that He knows with respect to each such combination whether it is metaphysically necessary, metaphysically impossible, or metaphysically contingent. See Section 2.3 of the Introduction.

[7]Molina and Scotus hold with many others that a state of affairs has its metaphysical modality by nature or necessarily. In the present context they maintain that any state of affairs which is in fact metaphysically contingent (that is, able to obtain and able not to obtain) is *necessarily* contingent. For more on God's natural knowledge, see Section 4.2 of the Introduction.

[8]Disputation 47, sec. 8.

know the free determination of His own will, "in" which—as "in a part of" the explanation for His knowledge of it—He would know that thing, then, once again, I would not feel that there is anything in Scotus's position which requires refutation. He wants to claim, however, that even after we have posited the establishment of the whole world and posited the presently existing order of things and causes, the determination of angelic and human free choice to one or the other part of any contradiction at any moment of time (for example, willing or not willing this, or willing the contrary) results from the free determination of the divine will, through which, as through a first cause, God decided from eternity to concur with created free choice, whether by general or by special concurrence, and to determine it in this or that way—as if it depended *solely* on God's free determination and on His mode of acting in cooperation with secondary causes whether free choice and any other secondary cause would act in this or that way or not act at all.[9] This is the position that we discussed at length and attacked in Disputation 35.[10] Thus, just as he located the whole source of contingency in God's free will alone and not at all in angelic and human free choice, even though the latter is the proximate and immediate cause of contingency in relation to some effects (as was explained in Disputation 47),[11] so too he claimed that the free determination of the divine will is the whole explanation and basis for the fact that God knows with certainty which things are contingently future *absolutely* and *in an unqualified way*. But from what was said in Disputations 35 and 47 among others, I take it to be sufficiently obvious that this position of Scotus's is more than dangerous from the point of view of the faith. For it destroys the freedom of choice which in Disputation 23 we demonstrated from Sacred Scripture and from experience itself, and it makes God the cause by which our free choice is turned toward and determined to those sinful acts by which we offend Him and break His law—all of which is incompatible with the Catholic faith.[12]

[9]Molina holds with other Scholastics that when God acts as a *general* cause concurring with the acts of secondary (created) causes, His causal contribution does not determine the exact nature of the effect produced. Rather, the nature of the effect is a function of the natures of the secondary causes involved in the production of the effect. On the other hand, when God acts as a *particular* cause, His causal contribution by itself determines the nature of the effect. See Section 2.6 of the Introduction.

[10]Rabeneck, pp. 218–222. For a brief account of the argument of Disputation 35, see Disputation 47, n. 5.

[11]Disputation 47, sec. 9.

[12]Rabeneck, pp. 134–154. In Disputation 23, which is divided into four parts, Molina proposes a lengthy defense of the claim that human beings have free choice. He makes use of all his resources, appealing to Sacred Scripture, to all the various elements of Tradition (the Fathers, Doctors, conciliar decrees), and to arguments from reason and experience as well.

8. A certain disciple of St. Thomas's, differing only verbally from Scotus, attributes this same position to St. Thomas.[13] For he claims that all the secondary causes of future contingents, causes among which he includes even angelic and human free choice, are subject to the determination and disposition of the divine will, which is the first cause and confers on other causes not only being and power, but also the determination to their particular effects. Because, therefore, contingent effects are known with certainty in their complete and determinate and unimpeded causes no less than necessary effects are known with certainty in their necessary causes, it follows, he claims, that in His essence, given the free determination of His will by which He determines all contingent causes to their effects, God knows all future contingents with certainty, even if they emanate immediately from free choice—indeed, He thereby knows not only the determination of all causes but also which of those causes are or are not, by that very same determination, going to impede the effects of other causes.

Now, he says, the term 'idea', taken in the full and complete sense, does not refer to the divine essence by itself, that is, insofar as it is a *potential* exemplar in imitation of which things *are able to be* produced— in this latter sense there is an idea even of things that are able to exist by the divine power and yet will never in fact exist. Rather, 'idea', taken in the full and complete sense, refers to the divine essence insofar as it is an *actual* exemplar in imitation of which something is *in fact* going to exist; but the essence has this character because of the determination of the divine will that is adjoined to it, a determination by which God from eternity ordained the effects that were going to be produced in time, and so it has this character only in relation to those effects that exist, have existed, or will exist in some interval of time. Thus it is, he says, that here by the phrase "natures of things," that is, the ideas—which, according to St. Thomas, God has before Himself from eternity and in which, he claimed, God knows future contingents with certainty—St. Thomas did not mean the divine essence by itself, that is, insofar as it is an exemplar in imitation of which God *is able to* produce things if He should so will. Rather, he meant the essence *along with the free determination of the will*, a determination by virtue of which the essence is an *actual* exemplar and a complete idea in relation to all the things that are *in fact* going to exist.

[13]This oblique reference is to Molina's chief theological nemesis, the Dominican Domingo Bañez (1528–1604), who taught at Salamanca from 1577 to 1600 and was active in the official ecclesiastical inquiry into Molina's writings. The arguments given here in secs. 8 and 9 are close paraphrases of Bañez's *Commentaria in Primam Partem Summae Theologicae Sancti Thomae Aquinatis*, q. 14, a. 13, pp. 351–352 (hereafter cited as Bañez, *Commentaria*). (The page numbers are taken from the edition prepared by Luis Urbano, O.P. (Madrid, 1934).) For a discussion of the Bañezian position, see Section 3.3 of the Introduction.

9. But since, as we demonstrated at length against Scotus in the places cited above, this determining of the human and angelic will and of other secondary causes by the free determination and influence of the divine will manifestly destroys freedom of choice with respect to their acts in both angels and human beings, the author in question seeks refuge in the distinction between the composed and divided senses.[14] That is to say, he claims that even if contingent causes, as subject to the determination of the first cause, are determined and complete with respect to their operation and are thus unable in the composed sense not to produce those of their effects to which they have been determined by the divine will, nonetheless those causes are unqualifiedly and in the divided sense contingent, indeterminate, and incomplete—and hence their effects should without qualification be called contingent.

But I do not understand this very well. For if, having no idea of what created free choice was going to do in its freedom, God by the free eternal determination of His will and by His influence determines it to whatever He wills, and if, as long as that determination and divine influence remain, free choice is able to do nothing other than that to which it is so determined, then I do not at all see in what sense it remains

---

[14]The distinction invoked here is a crucial one in modal logic and metaphysics. For a standard medieval explication of it, see William of Ockham, *Summa Logicae* II, chap. 9–10, pp. 108–115 in A. J. Freddoso and H. Schuurman, trans., *Ockham's Theory of Propositions* (Notre Dame, Ind., 1980).

A grasp of the distinction sufficient for present purposes can be had by considering the proposition (P) 'This white thing is able to be nonwhite,' where, let us suppose the white thing in question is a simple piece of wood painted white all over. (P) is *false* in the *composed* sense, since so understood it is equivalent to (Q) 'This proposition is possible: "This white thing is nonwhite,"' which is obviously false. That is, when a proposition is taken in the composed sense, its mode (in this case 'possible' or 'able to be') has as its scope the *exact and entire nonmodal counterpart* of the original proposition. By contrast, if (P) is taken in the *divided* sense, then it is equivalent to (R) 'This proposition is possible: "A is nonwhite,"' where 'A' is a proper name of the white piece of wood in question. And (R) is true, since A can become nonwhite or, indeed, could have been nonwhite in the first place. So on this reading the modal term has as its scope not the entire nonmodal counterpart of the original proposition but only the predicate of that proposition.

In the case that Bañez is discussing, the disputed proposition is something like (S) 'Causes $C_1 \ldots C_n$, which have been determined by God to produce effect E, are able not to produce E.' (S) is false in the composed sense, since so taken it is equivalent to (T) 'This is possible: "$C_1 \ldots C_n$, which have been determined by God to produce E, have not and will not produce E."' But (T) is obviously false, since God's determination entails that E is produced by the causes in question. Nonetheless, $C_1 \ldots C_n$ could have existed, we assume, without being so determined by God to produce E, just as A above could have existed without being white. So (U) 'This is possible: "$C_1 \ldots C_n$ have not and will not produce E"' is true, and so (S) is true in the divided sense.

Molina, however, while admitting that (U) is true, denies here and elsewhere in Part IV (see, e.g., Disputation 53, pt. 2, secs. 6 and 19) that its truth is sufficient to establish the claim that the causes in question are contingent in a sense strong enough to preserve free choice. See nn. 15 and 16 below.

genuinely free to strive after what it wills, or by what standard of blame or merit that which it brings about while so influenced and determined by God can be imputed to it. For the fact that it would have been able to do the opposite if by His free will God had willed the opposite and had by His influence determined and turned it to the opposite—this fact does not mean that *our* choice is free, but only that *God* has the freedom to *use our choice* by moving it indifferently to contrary effects, as we showed at length in Disputation 40 when discussing another similar proposition.[15] Therefore, if the author of this position is asserting only the fact just mentioned, while at the same time maintaining that in the divided sense our choice remains a contingent, indeterminate, and incomplete cause with respect to its own effects, then plainly, even if he preserves in this choice a sort of spontaneity not unlike that which is found in a mule being led by a halter in one or another direction, he nonetheless destroys the choice's freedom and without a doubt effects in it a fatalistic necessity (once we posit foreknowledge and the determination of the divine will, both of which exist from eternity).[16]

10.   The same author next considers the following objection against himself: "The divine will does not determine a created will to sin; indeed, it leaves it indifferent and free. But infallible cognition of a future effect cannot be had on the basis of an indifferent and undetermined cause. Therefore, God does not foreknow future sins with certainty."[17]

[15]Rabeneck, pp. 244–257, esp. pp. 254–255. In the place cited Molina is arguing against the claim made by some Thomists that even if God's grace is intrinsically efficacious for the conversion of an adult S, S is still able in the divided sense to resist that grace and not to be converted. Molina counters that on this Thomist position S is able not to be converted only in the sense in which a rock that I move is able not to be moved. In the latter case, I am free not to move the rock, and so the rock is able in the divided sense not to be moved; but there is not the least temptation to claim that the rock is free not to move or that it has any active power to resist my moving it. So, too, Molina argues, S is able in the divided sense not to be converted only because *God* is free not to grant him the efficacious grace in question. But it no more follows from this that S is free to resist God's grace than it followed in the other example that the rock is free to resist my moving it. So, Molina concludes, the Thomists' account of efficacious grace (and of efficacious concurrence generally) has not been shown to be compatible with the thesis that human beings have free choice. For a similar discussion of this issue in Part IV, see Disputation 53, pt. 1, sec. 7.
[16]Molina here makes use of the common philosophical distinction between spontaneity and freedom—or, as it is sometimes characterized, between the liberty of spontaneity and the liberty of indifference. An agent S's acting in a given way at a time t is *spontaneous* if S wants to or wills to act in that way at t. (A similar conditional holds for omissions.) Thus, a well-trained mule might *want* to move in the direction in which it is led; again, a voraciously hungry mule might *want* to walk in the direction of the hay that will appease its overwhelming desire for food. In both cases the mule acts *willingly* or *spontaneously*, but in neither case, it seems, is it *free*. For more on the prerequisites for freedom, see Section 2.9 of the Introduction.
[17]Bañez, *Commentaria*, pp. 352–353.

Now he thinks that he has an adequate response to this objection because, as he puts it, "a created will is inevitably going to fall short with regard to any of the material elements of a virtue unless it is efficaciously determined by the divine will to act well. Therefore, by the very fact that God knows that His will has not determined a given created will to act well with respect to the material element of, say, temperance, He knows evidently that the created will in question is going to sin and to fall short with respect to the material element of that virtue. And so other future contingents God knows in their causes in the sense that those causes have been determined by the first cause; but a culpable future evil He knows in its cause in the sense that the cause *has not been determined* by the first cause *to act well*."[18] These are his words.

11. But there are many things that are dissatisfying in this response.

First of all, he admits that free choice can exercise the actions by which it sins without being determined beforehand by the divine will and influence. Therefore, since these are natural actions and real effects, why isn't free choice likewise able to exercise other merely natural free actions (such as willing to sit or to rise, or willing to walk in this or that direction) without the previous determination and influence of the divine will? For because God is not wont to take away or restrict the innate freedom of secondary causes or to furnish more assistance and influence for natural actions than is necessary for them, it follows that free choice *determines itself* when it is not antecedently determined by the divine will

---

[18] Ibid., p. 353. The "material" element of an action consists of the physical and psychological movements or acts involved in that action. The material element does not by itself completely determine the *species* or *form* of the action, that is, what type of action it is. Indeed, it is possible for a sin and a virtuous action to have exactly similar material elements. For instance, my consenting to and engaging in the bodily movements involved in uttering the word *no* might, given appropriately diverse circumstances, constitute a lie, on the one hand, or an act of truth telling, on the other. (My intention, just insofar as it is a mental act, may also be exactly similar in the two cases, though the object of that mental act of intending will obviously be different in the two cases.) In Disputation 53, pt. 2, secs. 12 and 13, Molina makes the same point by citing the examples of materially identical acts of sexual intercourse (the one extramarital, the other within marriage) and of materially identical acts of engaging an enemy in combat (the one in an unjust war, the other in a just war).

The implied distinction between the formal and the material elements of an action must, however, be handled very carefully and is potentially misleading. Some Bañezians (though not, apparently, Bañez) claimed, for instance, that in a sinful action God concurs with and thus determines the *material* element but not the *formal* element, and that since it is the formal element that makes the act sinful, God does not determine sinful actions. Molina responds in effect that the material and formal elements of an action are not separable in such a facile way. If I do not control the material elements of my actions, he insists, then I am not free not to sin when I do sin. For I sin precisely by freely determining myself to a given material element in the appropriate circumstances.

but is instead left free to elicit or not to elicit an act or to act with respect to one object rather than some other. Thus, it is not the case that God knows the determination of future contingents of *this* sort in a determination of His will by which He determines created free choice to its effects.

This particular author will not, I believe, claim that God determines created free choice to the action by which it sins, and yet that He does not determine it to the *formal* element of a sin.[19] For his words do not suggest such a claim. Nor, again, does free choice determine itself to the formal element of a sin in any way other than by freely determining itself to an action that is a sin—it might, to be sure, will that the action in question not have the character of a sin, if that should be possible. Finally, and most important, the claim in question would be an error from the point of view of the faith, as I believe I showed satisfactorily in Disputation 31.[20]

12.   Second, he does not seem to admit that our will has the freedom to refrain from exercising or the freedom not to exercise the *virtuous* acts that it exercises, in the sense in which he *does* admit that it is free to exercise or not to exercise a *sinful* act when it sins. Thus, he destroys our merit and freedom with respect to a virtuous act, even as far as its exercise is concerned.[21]

13.   Third, his principal thesis is extremely dissatisfying. For even if we graciously conceded it in the case of human beings living after the fall of the first parents (since from adolescence their senses are inclined toward evil), what reason would we have to concede it in the case of angels and in the case of human beings in the state of innocence, who were able without difficulty to refrain from every sin and yet were also able to sin by their innate freedom?[22] For if they had happened to sin of

[19]See n. 18 above for a brief characterization of the distinction between the formal and material elements of a sinful act.

[20]Rabeneck, pp. 193–197. In Disputation 31 Molina cites evidence from Scripture and Tradition for the claim that God does not cause sins.

[21]According to Molina, the very fact that Bañez must tell a special causal story about sinful acts in order to ensure that God is not morally responsible for them presupposes that God, and not the human agent, is totally responsible for the both the species and exercise of the virtuous actions performed by human beings.

[22]According to Catholic doctrine, our first parents were, prior to their sin, endowed with preternatural gifts that rendered them strongly disposed toward virtuous action and thus made it very easy for them not to sin. An interesting philosophical question that arises here is: How *could* they have sinned, given all these gifts? The medievals devoted a good deal of effort to answering this question as well as the even more perplexing question of how the fallen angels could have sinned, given the intellectual and moral excellences of the angelic

their own accord, then, given the position of this Doctor, God would not have known about it; but what could be more absurd than this? Further, even if from the fact that God did not determine a created will to act well it followed with certainty that it would sin, God would still not be certain about whether it was going to sin by a sin of omission or of commission, or about whether it was going to use this means rather than that means in the act of sinning, or about whether it was going to sin with more or less intensity and effort, or about whether it was going to continue in the act of sinning for a longer or shorter time, and so on for the other circumstances that are relevant to the seriousness of the fault and that depend on free choice and thus with respect to which God did not determine free choice. Hence, God would be ignorant of all these future contingents.

14. Last, if created free choice, by the very fact that it is not efficaciously determined by the divine will to act well, necessarily sins in such a way that it is altogether certain and evident to God that it is going to sin, and if from His eternity God decided, as He pleased, to determine or not to determine free choice to act, then I ask: What freedom was there in the angels when they sinned, or in us when we sin, such that if we did not will to sin, then we would not sin? Likewise, in what sense is it true that God has placed us in the hand of our own counsel, so that we might strive after what we will?[23] Again, what grievance will God have on Judgment Day against the wicked, since they were unable not to sin as long as God did not efficaciously incline and determine them to the good, but rather solely by His own free will decided from eternity not so to determine them? Most assuredly, if this position is accepted, then our freedom of choice is altogether destroyed, and God's justice with respect to the wicked vanishes, and a manifest cruelty and wickedness is discerned in God. That is why I regard this position as extremely dangerous from the point of view of the faith—just as we claimed above about Scotus's position as well.

15. Therefore, besides those things that we explicated in the first conclusion of the preceding disputation,[24] we should also affirm that through the divine ideas (or, through the divine essence known as the primary object) all contingent states of affairs are represented with

---

nature. See, e.g., St. Thomas Aquinas, *De Malo*, q. 14, a. 1–5, and q. 16, a. 1–6. Secular analogs of these questions continue to exercise philosophers, as is evidenced by the ample contemporary philosophical literature on so-called 'weakness of will'.

[23]This manner of expression is taken from Ecclus. 15:14–17.

[24]See Disputation 49, sec. 8.

certainty to God, who comprehends in the deepest and most eminent way both His own essence and all things, each of which is contained in that essence infinitely more perfectly than it is contained in itself. All contingent states of affairs are, I repeat, represented to God *naturally, before* any act or free determination of the divine will; and they are represented not only as being *possible* but also as being *future*—not *absolutely future,* but *future under the condition and on the hypothesis* that God should decide to create this or that order of things and causes with these or those circumstances.[25] Once the determination of the divine will is added, however—not a determination by which God determines created free choice to one or the other part of a contradiction (as Scotus and the others maintain), but a determination by which, while leaving created choice free and altogether indifferent to strive after what it will, He decides to create this or that order of things and of causes and of circumstances, an order in which there exist these or those *free* causes— once that determination is made, God knows all the contingent states of affairs with certainty as being future *simply and absolutely,* and now *without any hypothesis or condition.*[26]

And so we disagree with Scotus, because we hold that the explanation for God's knowing with certainty which part of any contradiction among those contingent states of affairs dependent on created free choice is going to obtain is not a determination of the divine will by which God inclines and determines created free choice to one or the other part, but is instead a free determination by which God decides to create free choice in this or that order of things and circumstances. Nor do we believe that this determination is *by itself* a sufficient explanation for God's knowing with certainty which part of each contradiction among those states of affairs is going to obtain; rather, the sufficient explanation is the determination of the divine will along with God's *comprehension* in His essence of each created faculty of free choice through His natural knowledge, a comprehension by means of which He knows with certainty, before the determination of His will, what such-and-such a faculty of free choice would do in its freedom on the hypothesis and condition that God should create it and situate it in this particular order of things—even though it could, if it so willed, do the opposite, and even

---

[25] Here, again, Molina characterizes the knowledge of conditional future contingents as *natural* knowledge. See Disputation 49, nn. 11 and 16.

[26] Molina is careless here. Since the states of affairs in question come in pairs of contradictories, God cannot know *all* of them in the usual sense in which knowing a state of affairs entails its actually obtaining. Clearly, the point Molina wants to make is that after the free determination of His will, God knows with certainty all the unconditional (or 'absolute') future contingents that will in fact obtain.

though if it was going to do the opposite, as it is able to, then God would have known *this* in His essence through that very same knowledge and comprehension, and *not* what He *in fact* knows is going to be done by that faculty of free choice.[27]

And so, since positive contingent states of affairs which depend on free choice cannot obtain in reality unless free choice is created, the fact that God knows absolutely and unconditionally that they are going to obtain depends, to be sure, on the free determination of His will, by which He decides to create free choice at such-and-such a time with such-and-such an order of things and circumstances.[28] But since the faculty of choice thus created and situated in this order of things remains free to turn itself toward one part or the other, God would most assuredly not know determinately which part of a contradiction among contingent states of affairs of this sort was going to obtain unless by the depth, excellence, and perfection of His natural knowledge, through which He comprehends all things in His essence in a certain most eminent manner, He penetrated created free choice in such a way that in it He perceived which part it would turn itself toward by its own innate freedom—even though it could, if it so willed, incline itself toward the opposite part, and even though if it was going to do so, as it is able to, then God would discern this. Therefore, both of the elements just mentioned[29] are required in order for God to know this sort of thing with certainty, and both elements belong to Him by virtue of the perfection by which He is God and which is not only infinite and immense, but also unlimited in every aspect. It is by reason of this perfection that just as it falls under God's *omnipotence* to be able to bring into existence creatures who are endowed with free choice and who have control over their acts (as we discern by experience in our very own selves), so too it falls under His immense and altogether unlimited *knowledge,* by which He comprehends in the deepest and most eminent way whatever falls under His omnipotence, *to penetrate created free choice* in such a way as to discern and intuit with certainty which part it is going to turn itself to by its own innate freedom.

And this is the foreknowledge of future contingents that the Fathers and the light of nature itself teach us belongs to God. For God is such

[27] The "comprehension" spoken of here is what I call *supercomprehension* in Section 4.4 of the Introduction.

[28] By a "positive" state of affairs Molina seems to mean simply a state of affairs which entails the existence of its subject. If there were no creatures, then the negative counterparts of such states of affairs would nonetheless obtain—even though there would be no such thing as created free choice.

[29] The two elements are God's (middle) knowledge of conditional future contingents and the free determination of His will.

that if this foreknowledge did not belong to Him, He would not be God. Thus, in *Dialogus Adversus Pelagianos* III, Jerome says fittingly in the person of Critus, "If you deny someone foreknowledge, you deny him divinity as well."[30] And in *De Civitate Dei* V, chap. 9, Augustine says, "To confess that there is a God and yet deny that He foreknows future things is the most patent foolishness."[31]

16.   In the sense just explained it is absolutely true that the ideas (or, the divine essence known as the primary object) are the firm and certain explanation for the fact that God, who comprehends in the deepest way both Himself and the things that He contains eminently, knows future contingents. Thus, besides St. Thomas in this place (if he in fact held this position), it is also the case that St. Bonaventure and, in general, as many as adopted this way of speaking held this very position, even if they did not explicate the matter satisfactorily. Durandus affirms this same position explicitly in book I, dist. 38, q. 3,[32] where he claims that God knows all future contingents with certainty *in His essence* as in the primary object and cause of all things (though he does not think that the essence has the character of an idea), since by the depth and perfection of His knowledge and of its object He intuits in that essence all the causes of future contingents and the determination of those causes to the production of their effects—the determination not only of the causes that are determined by their very natures, as are those that act from a necessity of nature, but also of the causes, such as angelic and human free choice, which are indifferent and which turn themselves freely toward whichever part they will. What's more, God knows which of those causes are, and which are not, going to impede one another. (Though Durandus does not say so explicitly, all these things should be understood on the hypothesis that God wills to create this or that order of things and causes.)

Moreover, in and from the causes known in this way, future contingents are known with as much certainty as that with which necessary effects are known from necessary causes. It follows that God knows all future contingents with certainty in Himself as in a primary object, and He also knows them with certainty in their own proper secondary causes as in a secondary object.[33]

[30]*PL* 23, 575B.

[31]*PL* 41, 149.

[32]Durandus, *In Sententias Theologicas Petri Lombardi Commentariorum Libri Quattuor* I, d. 38, q. 3.

[33]That is, God knows future contingents primarily by knowing Himself as the *first* and *primary* object. For He knows them as conditional future contingents *in Himself* and without

17. *Response to the first argument.* So in response to Scotus's first argument,[34] the major premise should be denied. For on the hypothesis and under the condition that God should will to create this or that order of things, the divine ideas represent to God *naturally,* before any free determination of His will, every future contingent state of affairs *under that hypothesis and condition.* And this is so by virtue of the depth and excellence of the divine intellect and the divine knowledge, and because of the depth and excellence of the primary object over all the secondary objects that are eminently contained in it.

18. *Response to the second argument.* As for the second argument,[35] assuming that the antecedent has been conceded, the first consequence should also be conceded. However, in response to the minor premise that is then added, we should reply that although it is *not naturally* but *freely* that God knows contingent states of affairs as being future *absolutely and without any condition or hypothesis,* it is nonetheless *not freely,* but rather by a knowledge that *precedes* any free act of the divine will, that God knows these states of affairs as future *on the hypothesis* that He should will to create this or that order of things and causes.

19. *Response to the third argument.* As for the third argument,[36] assuming that the antecedent has been conceded, the consequence should be conceded as well, provided that its consequent is taken to mean that the divine ideas by themselves cannot be a sufficient explanation for the fact that future contingents are known by God with certainty as *absolutely* future. This latter sort of knowledge requires, in addition, a divine precognition of the free volition by which God decides to create this or that order of things. If the consequent is taken to mean, however, that the ideas are an insufficient explanation for God's knowing future con-

---

any dependence on their actual existence, and He knows *in Himself* that determination of His will by which He creates such-and-such an order of things in such-and-such circumstances. Still, given God's knowledge of conditional future contingents, He also understands completely the secondary causes that He has created, so that He also knows contingent effects in and from their contingent causes in the same way that He knows necessary effects in and from their necessary causes.

[34]See sec. 2 above. The major premise is that the ideas do not represent the conjoining of the terms of contingent states of affairs, but only the terms themselves.

[35]See sec. 3 above. The first consequence is that if the ideas represent things to God prior to the determination of His will, then they represent things merely naturally. The minor premise is that God knows contingent states of affairs freely and not naturally.

[36]See sec. 4 above. The consequence is that if the ideas represent indifferently both future contingent possibles that will be actual and other future contingent possibles that will never be actual, then the ideas by themselves cannot be a sufficient explanation for God's knowing the actual future with certainty.

tingents with certainty not only as *absolutely* future but even as future *on the hypothesis and condition* that He should will to create this or that order of things, then the consequence should be denied. Nor in this regard is there any difference between those future contingents that will exist in some interval of time and those that were able to exist but never will exist. For God knows of each of them in the same way that it was or was not going to exist on the hypothesis and condition that He should have decided to create one or another order of things different from the one that He in fact created.

20. *Response to the fourth argument.* The fourth argument[37] proves conclusively that (i) the ideas by themselves are not a sufficient explanation for the fact that future contingents are known by God as being such that they are going to exist at such-and-such a time *absolutely* and *without any condition,* and that (ii) for foreknowledge of this latter sort it is also required that there be knowledge of the determination of the divine will to create the order of things which He has created in the interval of time in which He created it—all of which we willingly concede.

[37]See sec. 5 above.

DISPUTATION 51

Whether Freedom of Choice and the Contingency of Things Are Correctly Reconciled with Divine Foreknowledge by the Thesis That Whatever Is Going to Occur because of Innate Freedom of Choice Is Such That God Will Bring It About That from Eternity He Knew None Other than That Thing

1. We must now examine the thesis by means of which a good many thinkers reconcile our freedom of choice with divine foreknowledge and predestination, and by virtue of which they think that these things cohere well with one another. For they maintain that if, for instance, Peter, who, let us assume, is going to sin at some moment of time, did not sin at that time (which he is capable of because of his freedom), then God would bring it about that He had never known that Peter was going to sin, but that instead He had always known from eternity that Peter was not going to sin. For, they say, since God knows each thing that is going to be in the very mode in which it is going to occur, He will surely know with *necessary* knowledge those things that are going to emanate from their causes necessarily, whereas He will know with *contingent* or, better, with *free* knowledge those things that are going to happen contingently. And since in the case of future contingent events that depend on created free choice, the fact that one part of a contradiction rather than the other is going to obtain does not depend on the divine knowledge—as though it was going to obtain because God foreknows that it will obtain—but instead depends on the freedom of choice by which the faculty of choice turns itself to the one part or the other as it chooses, there is without a doubt as much contingency in God's knowledge, inasmuch as it is knowledge of the one part of the contradiction rather than the other, as there is in the event during the time in which it still exists in its cause. Therefore, they say, even though it is necessary that whatever is going to occur is such that God foreknows it and that whatever God foreknows as future occurs accordingly, and even though because of this the propositions 'Everything foreknown by God will occur' and 'Whatever is going to occur is such that God foreknows that it will occur in that way' are

necessary in the composed sense, nevertheless, they say, just as it is not necessary but altogether contingent that Peter is going to sin in the future (for he is really able not to sin), so too neither is it in any way necessary up until today that God foreknows that Peter is going to sin; rather, this is altogether contingent and free, so that just as Peter is really able not to sin, so too God is able, *now and in the future*, to bring it about that He never foreknew that Peter was going to sin. Hence, they maintain that the necessity of the above propositions in the composed sense is founded *solely* on the necessity of the mutual entailment between the two propositions 'Something is foreknown by God to be such that it is going to occur; therefore it is going to occur,' and conversely; and it is *not* as if up until today there is any necessity, even a necessity of immutability, in the second term, namely, in the divine foreknowledge. For if Peter does not sin, then without any change in His knowledge God will bring it about that He foreknew nothing other than that Peter was not going to sin. Thus, they maintain that the proposition 'Peter's sin, which is foreknown by God, is able not to occur' is true in the divided sense, *not only* because (i) if Peter were in fact not going to sin, as is entirely possible, then God would never have foreknown his sin, *but also* because (ii) if he does not sin, as is possible, God will *at that moment* bring it about that from eternity He foreknew nothing other than that Peter was not going to sin.[1] They use as an analog the proposition 'Whatever is going to run is necessarily going to move.' In the composed sense this proposition is true solely because of the necessity of the consequence 'Something is going to run; therefore it is going to move'—even though there is no necessity in either of the terms, and even though for this reason whatever is going to run is able in the divided sense not to move. For that which is going to run is able not to run as well as not to move in the future.

2.   They reconcile free choice with predestination and reprobation in the same way.[2] For if someone who is reprobate does by his freedom, as

---

[1] Molina is perfectly willing to accept (i); indeed, he will insist on it. So if Peter, who is going to sin tomorrow, were not going to sin tomorrow, then God would have known from eternity that Peter was not going to sin tomorrow. What Molina objects to is the attempt to explain the truth of (i) by the further claim (ii) that if Peter were not going to sin tomorrow, God would *at that time* bring it about that He had known from eternity that Peter would not sin tomorrow. On Molina's own account, God's *free* knowledge would be different in the two cases because His *middle* knowledge would, *antecedently* to His act of will (in our way of conceiving it), have been different from eternity in a way not dependent on His will. So (ii) cannot on Molina's view be a correct explanation for the fact that (i) is true. See Section 3.4 of the Introduction for further discussion.

[2] Since a person's being predestinate (or reprobate) involves divine foreknowledge of that person's final state, predestination and reprobation pose as great a *prima facie* threat to

he is really able to, the things necessary to attain eternal life, then God will bring it about that from eternity he was predestinate and not reprobate. And, conversely, if someone who is predestinate wills, as is possible, not to do the things necessary to obtain eternal happiness, then God will bring it about that from eternity he was reprobate and not predestinate. Therefore, they say, the propositions 'Whoever is predestinate will necessarily be saved' and 'Whoever is reprobate will necessarily be damned' are likewise true in the *composed* sense. But the propositions 'Whoever is predestinate is able to be damned' and 'Whoever is reprobate is able to be saved' are true in the *divided* sense, *not only* because (i) if someone who is predestinate were by his freedom going to do things by which he would incur eternal damnation (as he is really able to, predestination notwithstanding), and if someone who is reprobate were going to do things by which he would attain eternal life, then God from His eternity would have neither predestined the first nor reprobated the second, *but also* because (ii) God will *at that time* bring it about that the first was never predestinate but was reprobate instead, and that the second was never reprobate but was predestinate instead.

3. I am surprised at how many Doctors have embraced this position. Among them are, in the first place, as many as insist that in God there is power over the past even with respect to effects that have already emanated in time from their causes. Included in this group are Altissiodorensis, Gilbert Porritanus, and certain Englishmen, as reported in book I, dist. 42, q. 1, a. 2 by Gregory, who also leans toward their view.[3]

---

human freedom as does divine foreknowledge. Some might even be tempted to claim that the threat is greater, since while predestination and reprobation presuppose deliberate actions or omissions on the part of God's will (for example, His electing some for eternal life and His not electing others), the same is not true of foreknowledge as such. But as we have begun to see and will continue to see, the predominant Scholastic view is that God's will is in some sense or other a cause of *all* His free knowledge of the future. Disagreements typically center on the question of what exactly that sense is.

For interestingly diverse accounts of predestination and reprobation from the thirteenth and fourteenth centuries, see Aquinas, *De Veritate*, q. 6, a. 1–6; Scotus, *Ordinatio* I, d. 41, q. unica; and Ockham, *Ordinatio* I, d. 41, q. unica.

[3]William of Auxerre (Altissiodorensis) (c. 1150–1231) was a renowned master of theology at the University of Paris at the end of the twelfth century and the beginning of the thirteenth century. Deeply involved in the academic and ecclesiastical politics surrounding the introduction of the Aristotelian corpus at Paris, he was best known for his commentary on the *Sentences*, titled *Summa Aurea in Quattuor Libros Sententiarum*. Molina is apparently referring here to *Summa Aurea* I, chap. 12, q. 6.

Gilbert de la Porrée (c. 1075–1154) was a prominent twelfth-century theologian who became bishop of Poitiers in 1142. Here Molina has in mind Gilbert's commentary on Boethius's *De Trinitate* (see *PL* 64, 1287).

The third reference here is to Gregory à Rimini's commentary on the *Sentences* I, a. 2, ad 4. (For more on Gregory, see Disputation 48, n. 8.)

But we will be arguing against these people in q. 25, a. 4.[4] The position in question is also embraced by St. Bonaventure (book I, dist. 40, pt. 2, a. 1, q. 1), by Richard (dist. 38, q. 6), by Scotus (dist. 40, q. unica), by Ockham and Gabriel (dist. 38, q. 1), by Gregory (book I, dist. 42, q. 2, concl. 4) and the rest of the nominalists in general, by Sylvester (*Conflatus*, q. 22, a. 5), by Driedo (*De Concordia Liberi Arbitrii et Praedestinationis* II, chaps. 2 and 3), by Albertus Pighius (*De Libero Arbitrio* VIII, chap. 1), by Andreas à Vega (*Concilium Tridentinum* II, chap. 17, response to the third objection, and XII, chap. 22), and by Antonius Cordubensis (*Quaestiones Theologicae* I, q. 55, dubia 11 and 12).[5]

4. Certain of the Doctors just mentioned defend this position by positing in God a power over the past even with respect to effects that have already issued forth from their causes in time. However, Ockham, Gabriel, Antonius Cordubensis, and some other nominalist Doctors defend it by countenancing in God's eternal act, that is, in the divine knowledge and volition, a power over the past that is indeed not a power by virtue of which the divine knowledge and volition are *absolute* or extend to effects that have already issued from their causes, but is rather a power by virtue of which the divine knowledge and volition (i) are

---

[4]*Commentaria*, pp. 354a–355b. It is important for dialectical reasons to keep in mind that Molina is here dividing his opponents into two broad camps: (a) those just mentioned, who hold that God has absolute power over *all* past effects, and (b) those to be mentioned presently, who attribute to God the more limited power to bring it about that He has *always* (or, has *from eternity*) had correct beliefs about future contingents. For more on the importance of this dialectical point, see n. 12 below.

[5]Unless otherwise indicated, all the books referred to here are commentaries on Lombard's *Sentences*. Most of the authors cited here either need no introduction or have been introduced in the notes to earlier disputations. The last four mentioned are in all likelihood wholly unfamiliar to most readers. Each was in fact a prominent sixteenth-century Catholic theologian who played a significant role in the Counter-Reformation and had at least some influence at the Council of Trent.

Johannes Driedo (c. 1480–1535) was a Dutch theologian who taught at Louvain and who was often cited in late sixteenth-century debates concerning grace and predestination.

Albertus Pigge (Pighius; c. 1490–1542) was a Dutch theologian and humanist whose theological ideas were widely discussed at Trent and in part officially repudiated. In fact, the work cited here by Molina was placed on the Index of Forbidden Books. Nonetheless, Albertus was an able and acerbic defender of a very strong version of the doctrine of papal infallibility, and his historical and systemic work on this topic had a great influence on many Catholic theologians of the time, most notably Robert Bellarmine.

Andreas à Vega (1498–1549) was a Spanish Franciscan theologian who studied and taught at Salamanca. At Trent he debated with the Dominican Dominic Soto over the dogma of justification. The work Molina refers to here is a defense of Trent's teaching on justification, the long title of which is *Tridentini Decreti de Justificatione Expositio et Defensio Libris XV Distincta*.

Antonius Cordubensis (1485–1578) was a Spanish Franciscan theologian who took part in the Council of Trent.

related just to *future contingents* as to objects that are known and either willed or permitted, and (ii) are dependent on future contingents for relations of this sort (which are relations of reason in the divine knowledge and volition).[6] For it is not because God foresees these things as future that they are going to be; rather, it is because they are going to be, by virtue of created free choice, that they are foreseen as future by God.

5.   However, St. Bonaventure, Scotus, and others among the cited Doctors defend this position with a far different line of reasoning and one that has the appearance of being more plausible. For they maintain that the free act of the divine will and, for the same reason, God's free knowledge concerning future contingents do not in themselves cross over into the past, but are instead always issuing forth in that indivisible now of eternity, which in itself never crosses over into the past or is anticipated as future, but is an always present whole and as a whole corresponds to present, past, and future time. Thus, they say, God's free act of will with respect to creatures and His free knowledge concerning contingent things, even though they are conceived of and signified *by us* as past by way of comparison with the time at which *we* exist, are nonetheless *in themselves* present and issuing forth, and in God they are emanating freely, and for this reason, while they are issuing forth, they are able to correspond to this or to that part of a contradiction in light of free choice. From this it follows that if a human being in time chooses this particular part of a contradiction, then God in His eternity determines the act of His will and knowledge in such a way that from eternity His knowledge is of that very same part of the contradiction, so that it was *never* of the other part, and vice versa. And this is so without any change or variation in God's knowledge, and without its being the case that God *begins* to know anything. Instead, it involves His always foreknowing from eternity whatever is going to exist in time, a foreknowledge that (i) accords with how human choice by its innate freedom wills

---

[6]Since the common Scholastic position is that God would not be absolutely perfect if contingent real relations inhered in Him, He is said to be related to the created objects of His willing and understanding only by *relations of reason* or *intentional relations*. This way of putting it has the advantage of highlighting the fact that God's willing and knowing are in no way rendered more perfect by the actual existence of anything outside Himself. More specifically, the mere fact that certain free creatures actually exist does not by itself give God's love for them a clearer focus or greater intensity than it otherwise would have, nor does their mere existence by itself give God any greater insight into how those creatures will use their freedom in the situations in which they will find themselves. Unlike us, God does not have to love anything other than Himself in order to be perfect; instead, His act of creating contingent beings is completely gratuitous. Again unlike us, God does not derive His knowledge of created things from those things themselves, that is, by being causally acted upon by them; instead, He knows them *in* and *from* Himself.

to determine itself and that (ii) depends on this sort of determination. From this it follows that, without any power over the past, there is now in the divine knowledge as much contingency or, better, as much freedom to be from eternity a knowledge indifferently of one or the other part of a contradictory pair of future contingents as there is freedom in created free choice with respect to whether such a part of the contradiction is or is not going to obtain.

6.   *First argument.* Now, this position can be argued for on the basis of St. Augustine's famous remark, "If you are not predestinate, then make yourself predestinate."[7]

7.   *Second argument.* In Jeremiah 18:8 and 10 we read, "If that nation repents from its evil, then I will also repent of the evil that I have threatened to do it. . . . If it does evil in my eyes, so that it does not listen to my voice, then I will repent of the good that I have promised to do it." But since in God there is no repenting that involves a change of will, it follows that in this passage all that is being signified is God's freedom in eternity, a freedom by virtue of which, when a human being freely turns his choice to one or the other part of a contradiction as he chooses, then God likewise freely wills for him a reward or punishment in light of that choice.

8.   *Third argument.* Given the contrary position, it would follow that God did not freely create the world when He created it—which is impious. The inference is proved from the fact that when the divine volition to create the world at a certain time has been posited and the time in question arrives, the world follows necessarily from that volition, as long as the will remains so determined. Therefore, since God willed from eternity to create the world at that point of time at which He created it, it follows that if, when that point of time arrived, He was no longer able to bring it about that He did not will from eternity to create the world at that time, then at that time He created it necessarily and not freely.

9.   *Fourth argument.* Future contingents are really able not to be; otherwise, they would not really be future contingents. Thus, they are really able not to be such that God knows that they are going to occur. In fact, it involves a contradiction for them to be so known by God and yet

---

[7] As Molina points out below in sec. 21, this remark is not as such found in Augustine's writings.

to turn out otherwise in reality;[8] for in that case God would be mistaken and the cognition in question would not be knowledge, since it is, of course, part of the nature of knowledge that it be true and certain. Therefore, if a human being does, as he is able to, the opposite of what he is in fact going to do, God will not in that case know what He now knows the person is going to do, but instead He will know the opposite. But this will be so without any change or variation in the divine knowledge, since in God there is absolutely no change or shadow of alteration.[9] Hence, if a human being does, as he is able to, the opposite of that which he is going to do, then God will bring it about that from eternity He knew not what He now knows, but the opposite.

10. *Fifth argument.* At the point of time at which he wills something, a human being is able not to will that thing, as was shown in Disputation 24.[10] Therefore, in the indivisible now of eternity, which is always present, God is able not to will what He wills and not to know what He in fact freely knows.

11. Although this position sustains itself in the judgment of so many Doctors, it can in no way be commended, since it is not sufficiently in accord either with Sacred Scripture or with the depth, certitude, and perfection of the divine knowledge. And many of the same Doctors who accept it judge it to be quite troublesome; nor do these same Doctors, if read attentively, seem to hold to it very firmly. I believe that so many have adopted this position for no other reason than that no alternative way of reconciling free choice with foreknowledge and predestination occurred to them, even though this position seems clearly to detract from the certitude and perfection of the divine knowledge.

12. Therefore, with St. Thomas in this article (in the response to the first objection, as well as in the other parts) we should say that it is now

---

[8]I have interpolated the Latin term for 'contradiction' here, since it has been omitted from the text through a rather obvious oversight.

[9]This manner of expression is taken from James 1:17.

[10]Rabeneck, pp. 155–158. In Disputation 24 Molina defends the Scotistic view that a human being S is, *at the very moment t* at which he wills something O, able not to will O. In the second proof below (sec. 15) Molina draws a distinction between what is *earlier in nature* and *later in nature* at one and the same moment of time. He then claims in effect that S is able *earlier in nature at t* not to will O, whereas *later in nature, but at the same moment of time,* S has already determined his will to O—and it is only "then" that S is no longer able at t not to will O. The argument of Disputation 24 is aimed against Ockham's thesis that if S wills O at t, then S is not able at t not to will O; the most that can be said is that S is able at t to bring it about that *immediately after t* he does not will O. In general, Molina holds that a correct account of divine or human action must be able to accommodate relations of *natural* (or, equivalently, *conceptual* or *logical*) priority and posteriority *within* one and the same moment of time or of eternity.

already so necessary that God knew from eternity each of the future contingents which from eternity He knew was going to exist that He is now no longer in any way able to bring it about that He did not know it, since obviously there is no such thing as power over the past and since no change or shadow of alteration can befall God. This same position was held by Richard of St. Victor.[11]

13.   Nor did St. Thomas teach the contrary in the response to the last objection in *De Veritate,* q. 6, art. 3.

For he had produced the following argument of the sort in question against the certitude of predestination, a certitude he defends in the body of the article: "That which is able to be and able not to be does not have any certitude. But God's predestination with regard to someone's salvation is able to be and able not to be. For just as He was from eternity able to predestine and able not to predestine, so He is even now able to predestine and able not to predestine, since in eternity there is no difference among present, past, and future. Therefore, predestination does not have certitude."

He responds as follows: "It should be said that, speaking absolutely, God is able to predestine and able not to predestine (or, able to have predestined and able not to have predestined) any given person, since the act of predestination, because it is measured by eternity, never fades into the past, just as it is never future; hence, it is always considered as issuing forth freely from the will. Nevertheless, the thing in question is rendered impossible *on a supposition.* For He is not able not to predestine *on the supposition* that He has predestined, and conversely. For He cannot be mutable. And so it does not follow that predestination can change." These are St. Thomas's words.

From these words it is manifestly clear that all he is teaching is that if God is viewed in the now of eternity, then naturally prior to His determining His will to one part of the contradiction, He is able to predestine and able not to predestine Peter, and for this reason it is true to say, absolutely speaking, that He is able to predestine and able not to predestine Peter (or, able to have predestined and able not to have predestined Peter), since the act of predestination in eternity does not cross over into the past; however, on the supposition—which is not merely imagined to hold, but really does hold—that *later in nature* in that same now of eternity God determines His will to predestine him, so that He

[11]Richard of St. Victor (d. 1173) was a Scottish theologian who in the middle of the twelfth century served as prior of the famous Augustinian abbey of St. Victor in Paris. He is best known for his mystical theology, which profoundly influenced Bonaventure and many others, and for his less influential but highly original theology of the Trinity.

has already determined His will in eternity insofar as eternity corresponds to the whole of past time, it cannot come to be that He has not predestined him, since no change can befall God.[12] There is plainly no alternative interpretation of St. Thomas's response which squares with the words themselves and also with the rest of the teaching of that article.

14. *The first proof*: This position of ours and of St. Thomas's is proved by the fact that if the free act of the divine will in eternity, insofar as eternity corresponds to every moment of time, were freely issuing forth in such a way that God is now able to bring it about that from eternity He willed and knew none of those things that He freely willed and freely knew, then it would follow that there is power over the past even with respect to effects that already exist in time outside their causes. But those opponents with whom we are now arguing do not accept this consequent, and below in q. 25 it will be shown to be false.[13] Therefore, the antecedent is also false.

The inference is proved as follows: Given the antecedent, the volition by which God from eternity willed to create the world at the point of time at which He created it would today be issuing forth freely in such a way that God would be able to determine it to the opposite part and to bring it about today that from eternity He willed never to create the world. But if this is granted, it obviously follows that there is power over the past with respect to effects that already exist in time outside their causes. For since the free determination of the divine will to create the world at that point of time at which He created it is the immediate and total cause of its creation at that time, if God is able *today* to bring it about that His free will was never from eternity determined to create the world but was instead always determined *not* to create it, then He is able today to bring it about that the creation of the world has never previously occurred. For anyone who is able to bring it about that the total and immediate cause of some effect never existed is also able to bring it about that the effect itself never existed. For if a prior cause is removed in such a way that it never existed, then straightaway it is also denied that there existed a later effect that depends entirely on that cause and follows

---

[12]As mentioned above in n. 10, Molina believes that a correct account of divine and human action must be able to accommodate relations such as *being naturally prior to* and *being naturally posterior to* within the same eternal or temporal moment.

[13]*Commentaria*, q. 25, a. 4, pp. 354a–355b. Recall that Molina is here attacking only those proponents of the position under discussion who explicitly disavow the thesis that God has unlimited power over the past. (See n. 4 above.) So if he can show that their arguments in defense of that position entail that there *is* such absolute power over past effects, then he will have made an objection that they themselves will have to acknowledge as damaging.

from it. Nor will it be satisfactory to respond that in eternity, insofar as it corresponds to every moment of time, the divine will is indeed free to determine its act to the opposite part *as long as* no effect has yet issued forth from it in time. This response, I repeat, is not satisfactory. In the first place, what is prior does not depend upon what is posterior. Therefore, if, given the hypothesis that no effect has as yet issued forth from it, the divine will in itself remained free to determine its act to the opposite part and to bring it about that from that same eternity it had never been determined to create the world, then it would likewise be able to bring about that same thing even if its effect *had* already issued forth—and so it would now be able to bring it about that the world has never existed. Second, once its effect has issued forth, the divine will in the now of eternity either is or is not more determined in itself to will to create the world at the point of time at which it created it. If you say that it is *not* more determined, then just as the divine will was able, *before* the occurrence of the effect, to freely determine its act in such a way that there would be a volition not to create the world, so too it will be able to do this *after* the occurrence of the effect. On the other hand, if you say that it *is* more determined, then it changes in itself because of the occurrence of the effect, and it is subject to a shadow of alteration—which is absurd. Moreover, contrary to what you said before, the volition will no longer always be issuing forth freely with respect to both parts in eternity insofar as eternity corresponds to each point and interval of time.

15. *The second proof*: From here we might argue as follows: As was shown in Disputation 24 with regard to *our* will, (i) even though *earlier in nature* at the same moment of time it is free and indifferent to turn and determine itself toward either part, nonetheless *later in nature* at that very same moment of time it has been freely determined to one of the two parts, and (ii) after it has been so determined later in nature, then it is unable, not only at later times but even at *that* very moment of time, to bring it about that it turned itself toward the other part—for after it has been determined to one part, it is not able not to be determined.[14] This very same thing should be said about the *divine* will in the now of *eternity*. Even though *earlier in nature* in that now of eternity which embraces all of time (or better, earlier in our way of conceiving it, with a basis in reality) the divine will is free to determine its act to either part with regard to those things that it freely decides, and even though for this reason that act issues forth as free in eternity, nonetheless *later* in that very eternity (that is, later in our way of conceiving it, but likewise with a

---

[14]Rabeneck, pp. 155–158. See n. 10 above.

basis in reality) that free act *has* issued forth as determined to one part of the contradiction in accordance with God's choice. But once the determined act has thus issued forth (*later* in our way of conceiving it, but *simultaneously* in that indivisible duration of eternity), it is not able not thus to issue forth, since otherwise the possibility would be countenanced that a thing already brought about in a certain way has not been brought about in that way, after it has once and for all been so brought about—which manifestly involves a contradiction. And this is what St. Thomas taught in *De Veritate*, q. 6, art. 3, in the response cited above to the last objection, when he said that on the supposition, which is not merely imagined, that in the now of eternity God has in fact determined His free act in such a way that there is a predestination of Peter (as He has in fact determined it), He is not able not to have predestined him, since this involves a contradiction and could not now happen without some change in God or shadow of alteration.

Let us, then, put the argument this way: In the case of those things that are done freely in indivisible durations, their *being done* and their *having been done* are simultaneous, as are the act's freely *issuing forth* toward either part of the contradiction and its *having issued forth* as determined to one of the two parts. Clearly, then, even though in our way of conceiving it, with a basis in reality, it was first the case that the act of the divine will or knowledge regarding a particular contingent thing that will exist tomorrow issued forth freely in such a way that God was able to determine that act to either part, still this was simultaneous with the act's *having issued* forth as determined to one part—especially in view of the fact that it could not issue forth otherwise than as determined to one part, though in accord with the choice of Him who elicited the act. Therefore, in eternity, insofar as it corresponds to yesterday and to the infinite stretch of time that preceded yesterday, the act of the divine will and knowledge has been determined to that part that is going to obtain tomorrow; and a contingent thing of this sort which is going to exist tomorrow was already then[15] related to the divine knowledge as something actually known, and the knowledge was already then actual knowledge with a special relation of reason to that object. Therefore, if, when created free choice determined itself, the divine will and intellect were able to determine the volition and knowledge to the opposite part and to bring it about that the first part of the contradiction was never willed or known, then there would be power over the past, namely, the power to eliminate the determination of the volition and knowledge which had

---

[15]The "then" refers, of course, to the now of eternity insofar as it corresponds to past time.

already existed before, and the power to eliminate the relation to such
an object, a relation that had also existed previously. This, however,
involves a contradiction, as will be shown in q. 25.[16]

16. This same argument can be confirmed as follows: Since the
world has already issued forth from the divine will as from its proper
cause, and since it would not have been able to issue forth from it if the
will had not already been determined to the production of the world, it
clearly follows that the divine will was determined at least at that point in
time at which the world was established. Therefore, since it was not at
that point determined for the first time (because God was not able to
begin to will anything in time), it follows that it was determined in that
way *from eternity*. But after God has once freely determined His will to
one part of a contradiction, He is no longer able to bring it about that He
did not so determine it; otherwise, He would be able to bring it about
that a given thing has not been effected after it has already been effected. Therefore, at no point of time before the creation of the world
was God able to bring it about that He did not decide from eternity to
create the world at the point of time at which He created it. And for the
same reason He was not able to bring it about that He did not know that
the world was going to exist at that point in time. Since, then, the same
argument applies to every other future contingent, it follows that at no
point of time is God able to bring it about that from eternity He knew the
contrary of what he now in fact knows about any future contingent.

17. *The third proof*: In eternity, insofar as it corresponds to this present time or to any past moment of time, either God sees with certainty,
because of the depth and perfection of His knowledge, which part
Peter's free choice is going to turn itself toward tomorrow, or He does
not see this with certainty. The second answer cannot be given, since
then God would not foreknow future contingents—which is heretical,
contrary to the absolutely clear testimony of Scripture that we will cite in
the next disputation.[17] But if the first answer is given, then it is toward
that part and not toward the opposite part that Peter's free choice will
turn itself; otherwise, God did not see with certainty that Peter was by his
freedom going to turn himself toward that part. Therefore, it is *never*
going to be the case that he turns himself toward the opposite part, even
though he could do it if he so willed; and, consequently, God will never
bring it about on this account that from eternity He never knew what He
now knows.

[16]*Commentaria*, pp. 354–355b. See n. 13 above.
[17]See Disputation 52, sec. 8.

18.   I will now indicate briefly in what way we differ from the authors of the contrary position.

All of us agree that even after the positing of that free determination of the divine will by which God resolved to create this order among the things He decided to create, it is not the case that created free choice was going to do this rather than the opposite because God foreknew it, but, to the contrary, God foreknew it because free choice was going to do it by its innate freedom—even though it was really able to do the opposite if it so willed. Nonetheless, there is disagreement because, as was explained in the two preceding disputations, we maintain that on account of the depth and perfection of His intellect and of His essence as its primary object, God knows with absolute certainty, in His own self and in the secondary causes, what is going to happen contingently by virtue of the freedom of those causes; yet He knows this in such a way that (i) the opposite is able to occur, and that (ii) if it were going to occur, as it is really able to, then from eternity God would have known *this* with absolute certainty and not what He in fact knows. Thus, while the full force of created free choice is preserved and while the contingency of things remains altogether intact in the same way as if there were no foreknowledge in God, God knows future contingents with absolute certainty—not, to be sure, with a certainty that stems from the object, which is in itself contingent and really able to turn out otherwise, but rather with a certainty that flows from the depth and from the infinite and unlimited perfection of the knower, who *in Himself* knows with certainty an object that *in its own right* is uncertain and deceptive.[18] It follows that the contingency of things and freedom of choice with respect to the future are perfectly consistent with God's certain knowledge and will, a knowledge and will that are not only altogether unchangeable, but also fixed and stable to such a degree that it now already involves a contradiction for God to have willed the contrary from eternity or to have known from eternity that the contrary was going to occur.

Our opponents, on the other hand, hold that freedom of choice and the contingency of things accord with and are correctly reconciled with

---

[18]Here and elsewhere Molina claims that God knows with certainty things, namely, future contingents, which are *in their own right (secundum se)* or *in themselves (in se)* uncertain. Clearly, Molina does not mean to imply that these objects are such that it is metaphysically impossible that they should be known with certainty. But then the question arises: What can it mean to say that the objects are uncertain *secundum se* or *in se*? His point seems to be that future contingents are still *metaphysically* or *ontologically* indeterminate, since at present they have existence only in causes that are not yet determined to produce them. This does not, however, impede God's having *epistemic* certitude about them by virtue of His (middle) knowledge and of the determination of His will. So God has epistemic certitude about things that are metaphysically uncertain or indeterminate. See Section 4.4 of the Introduction.

divine foreknowledge by virtue of the fact that if a thing is going to turn out otherwise, then when it actually occurs, God Himself will bring it about that from all eternity He foreknew none other than that very thing that has occurred. But this is as if (i) God acquired knowledge of future contingents from the very occurrence of the things, and as if (ii) before the event there was no more certitude in the divine knowledge than there is in an object that is still contingently future, and as if (iii) God's knowledge did not from eternity have in itself a fixed determination to one part of a contradictory pair of future contingents *before* the thing itself received that same determination in time when it was posited outside its causes. Is there anyone who would not see, were he to weigh the matter the least bit carefully in his mind, that all these things are plainly and overtly incompatible with the altogether absolute perfection of God's knowledge, and that they manifestly destroy the certitude of the divine knowledge and render God uncertain and perplexed about the occurrence of things?

19. *The fourth proof*: Hence we can argue as follows: If the contingency of things had to be reconciled with divine foreknowledge by the thesis that if (i) free choice does the one thing, God will bring it about that He has never foreknown anything other than that very thing, and if (ii), as is possible, free choice does the opposite, God will bring it about that He never knew the first thing, then it would follow that God was not able to foretell with certainty, through the prophets or the man Christ, which things were going to occur contingently because of human free choice, for example, the sin by which Peter was going to deny Christ three times, and many others. But this is heretical, unless perhaps one countenances power over the past even after an effect has already existed in time outside its causes, and claims that if Peter, as was possible, had not sinned, then God would have brought it about that the revelation in question, which had already been previously made, had not occurred.

But it manifestly involves a contradiction for there to be power over the past, especially after an effect has already existed in time outside its causes. Almost all the authors against whom we are now arguing agree with this point themselves, and the very same thing will be demonstrated in q. 25.[19] What's more, if such power over the past were posited, then the certitude of the divine knowledge as well as of the revelations we have about future things would be lost. For what certitude can there be in any knowledge or revelation about which we can truly say that (i) God

---

[19]*Commentaria*, pp. 354a–355b. See n. 13 above.

is able to bring it about that no such thing has ever been known or revealed, and that (ii) whether or not He is going to bring this about depends on a future contingent event that is equally able to be and able not to be, and hence that (iii) whether God will bring this about is now as uncertain and contingent as it is contingent in reality as to whether created free choice is by its freedom going to turn itself toward the one or the other part? Indeed, if this opinion (or, better, this error) is accepted, then Peter and the other Apostles, after having received Christ's revelation about the future denial, were no more certain prior to the time of St. Peter's sin that such a thing was going to occur than they would have been had such a revelation never been made beforehand. For whether God was going to bring it about in the future that this revelation had not been made beforehand depended on the free and uncertain determination of St. Peter's will with respect to both parts.

20.   Finally, if the way proposed by these Doctors for reconciling free choice and the contingency of things with divine foreknowledge is accepted, I do not see how there might be providence in God with respect to future contingents that depend on free choice—if, that is to say, depending on whether this or that part of a contradiction turns out to obtain because of innate freedom of choice, God will bring it about that from eternity He knew that this or that was going to occur. Hence, I do not see how God has provided for this part of the contradiction from eternity as one who foreknew this determinate part on the hypothesis that He Himself should furnish these or those means or aids. As a result, there is no room left for divine predestination or reprobation, if all things still to come in the future are so uncertain to God that it is in light of the part of the contradiction that is going to be actualized by free choice that He is even now going to bring it about that from eternity He foreknew that this or that human being would do this or that, and on this basis bring it about that this or that person was predestinate or reprobate. In addition, the number at this very time of the predestinate and of the reprobate will also be uncertain, since it is in light of future events that God is even now going to bring it about that from eternity He predestined these people or those, more or fewer. But if this is so, then why, when he came to the section on predestination and to the election of some, given that others had not been so elected, did Paul exclaim in Romans 11:33, "O, the depth of the riches and wisdom and knowledge of God; how incomprehensible are His judgments and inscrutable His ways!" Last, given the position under discussion, I do not see how God would have foreknown the repentance of the Tyronians and Sidonians rather than its opposite on the hypothesis that the wonders performed

in Bethsaida and Chorozain should have been performed in Tyre and Sidon, since both parts depended on the free choice of the Tyronians and Sidonians; rather, depending on whether free choice willed to turn itself toward one or the other part, God was going to bring it about that He had foreknown the one or the other from eternity.

Scripture certainly speaks far differently about the certitude and determination of the divine foreknowledge and predestination. For in 2 Timothy 2:19 Paul says, "God's solid foundation stone stands firm, and it bears this inscription: 'The Lord knew those who are His own.'" We will skip over the other passages from Scripture for now. Thus, too, Augustine says in *De Libero Arbitrio* III, chap. 3, "Since God foreknows our will, that which He foreknows is going to be. Therefore, our will is going to be, because He foreknows the will. Nor can the will be if it does not have power; therefore, He foreknows its power, too. Hence, it is not the case that because of His foreknowledge my power is taken away; my power is more certainly present because of it, since He whose foreknowledge does not err foreknew that my power was going to be with me."[20] And in *De Correptione et Gratia*, chap. 7, he says, "As has often been said, they are the elect who are called by design, who are also predestined and foreknown. If any of them perishes, then God is mistaken. But none of them perishes, since God does not err. If any of them falls to human vice, then God is conquered. But none of them falls, since God is in no way conquered."[21] And in *De Fide ad Petrum*, chap. 33, Fulgentius says, "Hold on most firmly, and in no way doubt that all those whom God by His gracious goodness made into vessels of mercy were predestined by God before the creation of the world for adoption as sons of God. And do not doubt that none of those whom God has predestined for the kingdom of heaven is able to perish, and that no one whom He has not predestined is in any way able to be saved."[22] I will skip over the other testimony from St. Augustine. Thus, without depreciating the authority of so many preeminent men, I judge the position we have been discussing to be insufficiently safe from the point of view of the faith.

21. *Response to the first argument.* As for the first argument proposed on behalf of that position at the beginning,[23] it should be said that no

[20]*PL* 32, 1275.

[21]*PL* 44, 924.

[22]*PL* 65, 703. Fulgentius of Ruppe (467–533) was a North African bishop and theologian—indeed, the outstanding theologian of the early sixth century. A onetime civil servant, he decided to become a monk upon reading Augustine's commentary on Psalm 36. The work cited here was at one time attributed to Augustine.

[23]See sec. 6 above.

such thing is to be found in Augustine. Still, some want to infer it from the closing words of *Hypognosticon*, book VI, where, after having said many things about predestination, he adds, "As far as we are able, let us exhort all people to good works; let us not bring hopelessness to anyone; let us pray for one another; let us humble ourselves in the sight of God, saying, 'Thy will be done.' It will be within His power to change the judgment of damnation which we deserve, to prolong the undeserved grace of predestination."[24] But the remark cited in the argument is wrongly inferred from these words, since the author of this work—whoever it was—had many times before this taught the contrary in the same book VI and in the other books. Instead, all he was claiming is that the undeserved grace of predestination, that is, the grace that is the effect of the predestination by which He predestined us from eternity, will be within His power to prolong, that is, to give or, taking into account the force of the word, to offer with an increase, namely, of merits. But he is not claiming that by our prayers we are now able, as our opponents maintain, to have it be the case that, though we were not predestined from eternity, God will bring it about that we have been predestined from eternity. This never entered Augustine's mind.

22. *Response to the second argument.* As for the second argument,[25] it should be replied that this as well as other similar texts of Scripture have to do not with repenting taken in either of the two ways that the proposed argument deals with, but with repenting as the revocation or, better, the nonexecution of a divine decree and volition—not an absolute decree, but rather a decree by which God ordained this or that *under some condition* that He placed within the power of our will as aided by His grace. Thus, the meaning of the passage is this: "I will also repent . . . ," that is to say, "I will not inflict the punishment that I resolved to inflict if they did not repent."

23. *Response to the third argument.* As for the third argument,[26] the inference should be denied. For in order that creation or any other of God's effects be said without qualification to be brought about freely by God when it comes to exist in time, it is sufficient that it be brought about by a will that *in and from eternity* was freely determined to produce such-and-such an effect at such-and-such a point of time—even if, by reason

[24]*PL* 45, 1664. As Molina intimates, the authorship of this work is uncertain, though in earlier times it was often attributed to Augustine.

[25]See sec. 7 above.

[26]See sec. 8 above. The inference in question is that if the contrary position were true, then God would have created the world by necessity rather than freely.

of the immutability of God, to whom any shadow of alteration is repugnant, the effect is produced necessarily *at that time* because of a free and eternal decree that is really produced in the divine mind. And this is what St. Thomas taught in *De Veritate,* q. 6, art. 3, in the response, cited above, to the last objection;[27] nor does the proof that is added in the argument establish anything different. Therefore, it should be conceded that when the time arrived at which God from eternity decided to create the world, God created it both freely and necessarily, though in different respects. For He is said to create the world *freely* insofar as He creates it by His free eternal will; whereas He is said to create it *necessarily* because of the necessity of immutability which belongs to His will thus freely determined from eternity.

24. *Response to the fourth argument.* As for the fourth argument,[28] given that the antecedent is conceded, namely, that future contingents are really able not to be, we should deny the consequence by which it was inferred that they are really able not to be known by God. For all that follows is that they would have been able not be known and not to have been going to be known, if, as is possible, they had not been going to be. For from eternity God would have discerned this with certainty, and in that event He would from eternity have known *this* about the contingent thing in question instead of what He now knows about it. But because He discerned and foreknew with absolute certainty that what in fact will occur was going to be, He is not able to bring it about that from eternity He knew the contrary. Nor, given that God discerned and foreknew this thing with such great certainty, is its opposite able to occur in the composed sense, even though in the divided sense its opposite is without qualification able to occur in the same way as if nothing had been foreknown by God—and this notwithstanding God's foreknowledge of the thing, a foreknowledge that would not have existed if, because of human free choice, the thing were not going to exist.

25. *Response to the fifth argument.* As for the fifth argument,[29] given that the antecedent is conceded, the inference should also be conceded with respect to the indivisible now of eternity taken *absolutely,* but not with respect to the now of eternity insofar as it corresponds to some

---

[27] See sec. 13 above.

[28] See sec. 9 above.

[29] See sec. 10 above. The antecedent is that at the point of time at which a human being wills something, he or she is able not to will it.

determinate point of time which was preceded always, for an infinite stretch of time, by the determination of the divine will and knowledge to the one part of the contradiction. For once the determination of the will and knowledge has been made, it involves a contradiction for God to bring it about that from eternity He willed or knew the opposite—as has been shown.

DISPUTATION 52

Whether in God There Is Knowledge of Future Contingents.
Also, the Way in Which Freedom of Choice and the
Contingency of Things Accord with This Knowledge

1. Even though the things that are going to be said in this disputation could have easily been gathered from what has already been said,
nonetheless, the present disputation must also be inserted in order that
certain arguments might be refuted and in order that the compatibility
of freedom of choice and the contingency of things with divine foreknowledge might be grasped more clearly.

2. *First argument.* On behalf of the position that denies that there is
knowledge of future contingents in God, St. Thomas in this place argues
that from a necessary cause there issues forth a necessary effect. But
God's knowledge is a cause of the future things that are known through
it, because, as was shown in article 8,[1] God is a cause of things through
His knowledge; what's more, that knowledge is necessary. Therefore,
everything that is known by it as future is going to happen necessarily,
and hence no knowledge of anything contingent can be found in God.

3. *Second argument.* Second, if a conditional is true and its antecedent
is absolutely necessary, then its consequent is likewise absolutely necessary; otherwise, in a valid consequence the antecedent could be true and
the consequent false—which is in no way to be admitted. But the conditional 'If God knew that this was going to be, then it will so happen' is
true, or else God's knowledge would be false; and the antecedent is
absolutely necessary, both because it is eternal and because it is past-
tense and there is no power over the past. Therefore, the consequent

---

[1] *Summa Theologiae* I, q. 14, a. 8. Molina's brief commentary in the *Concordia* on this
article is found in Rabeneck, pp. 3–4.

will be absolutely necessary as well, and hence no future thing fore-known by God will be contingent.[2]

4. *Third argument.* Third, whatever is known by God is necessary, since, of course, it is even the case that everything that is known by human beings necessarily obtains, and God's knowledge is more certain than human knowledge. But no future contingent will obtain necessarily. Therefore, no future contingent can be known by God.

5. *Fourth argument.* Fourth, we ourselves can argue as follows: No future thing foreknown by God is able not to occur. Therefore, nothing foreknown by God is a future contingent. The consequence is obvious, since a future contingent is nothing other than a thing that is indifferently able to occur and able not to occur. The antecedent, on the other hand, is proved by the fact that if something that is foreknown by God as going to occur were not to occur, then God would be actually mistaken; therefore, if, while that knowledge remains, the thing were *able* not to occur, then God would be *able* to be actually mistaken—which, however, is impious and can in no way be true.[3]

6. *Fifth argument.* Fifth, the things signified by future contingent propositions are no less necessary if God's knowledge of them is determinately true than if the future-tense propositions that signify those same things are themselves determinately true. But from the assumption that future contingent propositions are determinately true, Aristotle (*De Interpretatione* I, last chapter)[4] concludes that it follows that the

[2]This argument is, potentially at least, very powerful. One standard response, now usually identified as Ockhamistic, consists in an attempt to show that the antecedent—'God knew that this was going to be'—is not necessary. See n. 57 below for a passage in which St. Thomas tries to undermine such a response. St. Thomas's own response consists in trying to show that the necessity in question is simply the necessity of the present and hence does not threaten free choice. Molina, in contrast, responds in effect that this 'absolute' necessity is not closed under entailment. (See secs. 32–34 below.) That is to say, even if the consequence is valid and the antecedent is absolutely necessary, it does not follow that the consequent is absolutely necessary as well. As Molina sees it, this is confirmed by the fact that if the consequent were, contrary to fact, made false, then the antecedent would never have been true. I discuss this response at length in Section 4.5 of the Introduction.

[3]This conclusion is "impious" because according to traditional Christian belief, omniscience is not a contingent characteristic of God's. Rather, it is part of God's *nature* to be omniscient, so that He is not even *able* to be mistaken about anything.

[4]*De Interpretatione*, chap. 9, 18b 26. (See Disputation 48, n. 23.) In his response to this argument (sec. 37 below), Molina appears to equate a singular future-tense proposition's being *determinately* true with its being now such that its present-tense counterpart can no

things signified are necessarily going to happen and hence that our deliberations are in vain. Therefore, if God's knowledge of these same things is determinately true, then it follows that everything happens necessarily and nothing contingently, that our deliberations are in vain, and that our freedom of choice is completely destroyed.

7. *Sixth argument.* Sixth, foreknowledge of future things destroys freedom of choice. Therefore, freedom of choice and God's foreknowledge regarding future contingents can in no way be compatible with each other, and thus one of them will necessarily have to be denied. The consequence is obvious, while the antecedent is proved from the fact that given foreknowledge of future things, the following is a necessary and perfectly valid consequence: 'From eternity God foreknew that Peter was going to sin tomorrow; therefore, Peter is going to sin tomorrow.' For it is based on the certitude of the divine knowledge, which no falsehood can in any way be adjoined to, and thus this consequence is as necessary as it is certain that God cannot be mistaken in that knowledge. But whoever does not have the power to negate the antecedent of a necessary consequence does not have the power to negate the consequent either;[5] otherwise, someone would be able to bring it about that in a valid consequence the antecedent is true and the consequent false— which is altogether inconsistent with the nature of a valid consequence. Since, therefore, it is not within Peter's power to bring it about that from eternity God did not foreknow that sin of his which is going to exist tomorrow, and since this is not within God's power either, because there is no power over the past, it follows that it likewise does not lie within Peter's power to bring it about that he is not going to sin tomorrow; and from this it follows that given the foreknowledge that God in fact has, no freedom of choice remains in Peter.

---

longer be prevented (at least by created causes) from being true in the future. In his commentary on the *De Interpretatione* (see n. 27 below), he seems to imply that a future contingent proposition can nonetheless be true now, though only *indeterminately* true, that is, true, but not unpreventably so. So Molina does not appear to deny the law of bivalence for future contingent propositions; indeed, much of what he says about God's foreknowledge clearly presupposes that bivalence holds for such propositions.

[5]"To negate" something simply means here to make it false (though not necessarily to make it false *after it has been true*). The principle enunciated here is something like the following: For any (metaphysically contingent) propositions p and q and any agent S, if (i) p entails q and (ii) S does not have the power to make p false, then S does not have the power to make q false. Molina rejects this argument, maintaining in effect that S can have the power to make q false without having the power to make p false *as long as* it is also true that if S were indeed going to make q false, then p would never have been true. (See sec. 38 below.) In essence, this is the same response that Molina makes to the second argument. I discuss this point in Section 4.5 of the Introduction.

8. That there is foreknowledge of future contingents in God is absolutely obvious from the Sacred Writings, so much so that the contrary position is not only irrational, as Augustine maintains in *De Civitate Dei* V, chap. 9,[6] but is also a manifest error from the point of view of the faith.

Psalm 138:3–4,[7] "You have understood my thoughts from afar; my path and my portion You have scrutinized. And all my ways You have foreseen. . . . You have known all things, the newest as well as the old." In Wisdom 8:8 this is said of the divine wisdom: "She knows the signs and the wonders before they come to be, and the unfolding of the times and of the ages." Ecclesiasticus 23:28–29,[8] "The eyes of the Lord are brighter than the sun, observing all the ways of man and the depths of the abyss, and looking into the hearts of men in their secret paths. For all things were known to the Lord God before they were created." And at 39:24–25,[9] "The works of all flesh are before Him, and nothing whatever is hidden from His eyes. From age to age He watches, and nothing is surprising in His sight"—as though, that is to say, something might happen which He had not foreseen beforehand. Isaiah 41:23, "Announce what is going to happen in the future, and we will know that you are gods." And at 48:5, "I revealed things to you beforehand; before they happened I announced them to you, so that you would not say, 'My idols did these things, and my carved images and metal images decreed them.'" John 14:29, "And I have told you this now, before it happens, so that when it has happened, you might believe." Moreover, according to Hebrews 4:13 God knows all contingent things when they come to be and are already actual: "No creature is hidden from His sight. All things are exposed and open to His eyes." But He does not *begin* to know these things when they are actual—since that would be for Him to change from not knowing to knowing, and a shadow of alteration would plainly befall God. Therefore, He knows future contingents *before* they exist. Last, if there is no foreknowledge of future contingents in God, then prophecy perishes and the greater part of Sacred Scripture is ruined—which is manifestly inconsistent with the Catholic faith. Thus, in *Adversus Marcionem* II Tertullian justifiably says, "God's foreknowledge has as many witnesses as He has made prophets."[10]

---

[6]*PL* 41, 149.

[7]Throughout Molina uses the Vulgate rather than the Hebrew numbers for the Psalms. Thus, the present reference is to (Hebrew) Psalm 139. (The allusion should actually be to verses 3–5.)

[8]The Vulgate 23:28–29 corresponds to 23:19–20 in more modern editions.

[9]The Vulgate 39:24–25 corresponds to 39:19–20 in more modern editions.

[10]*PL* 2, 290.

9.   Unless we want to wander about precariously in reconciling our freedom of choice and the contingency of things with divine foreknowledge, it is necessary for us to distinguish *three* types of knowledge in God. One type is purely *natural* knowledge, and accordingly could not have been any different in God. Through this type of knowledge He knew all the things to which the divine power extended either immediately or by the mediation of secondary causes, including not only the natures of individuals and the necessary states of affairs composed of them but also the contingent states of affairs—through this knowledge He knew, to be sure, not that the latter were or were not going to obtain determinately, but rather that they were indifferently able to obtain and able not to obtain, a feature that belongs to them necessarily and thus also falls under God's natural knowledge.[11]

The second type is purely *free* knowledge, by which, *after* the free act of His will, God knew *absolutely* and *determinately, without any condition or hypothesis,* which ones from among all the contingent states of affairs were *in fact* going to obtain and, likewise, which ones were not going to obtain.

Finally, the third type is *middle* knowledge, by which, in virtue of the most profound and inscrutable comprehension of each faculty of free choice, He saw in His own essence what each such faculty would do with its innate freedom were it to be placed in this or in that or, indeed, in infinitely many orders of things—even though it would really be able, if it so willed, to do the opposite, as is clear from what was said in Disputations 49 and 50.[12]

10.   Perhaps someone will ask if such middle knowledge should be called free or if it should be called natural.

To this question it must be replied, first, that such knowledge should in no way be called *free,* both because it is prior to any free act of God's will and also because it was not within God's power to know through this type of knowledge anything other than what He in fact knew. Second, it should likewise not be said that this knowledge is *natural* in the sense of being so innate to God that He could not have known the opposite of that which He knows through it.[13] For if created free choice were going

---

[11]Molina holds, then, that God knows a state of affairs *p* through purely *natural* knowledge only if *p* is metaphysically necessary.

[12]See esp. Disputation 49, sec. 11, and Disputation 50, sec. 15.

[13]The following, then, are the marks of middle knowledge: (i) what God knows through it He knows *before* (in our way of conceiving it) any free act of His will; (ii) God has *no control* over what He knows through it; and (iii) whatever God knows through it is such that it is metaphysically possible that He should have known its contrary (though, of course, given [ii], God does not have and never has had the power to *bring it about* that He knows the contrary). See Sections 2.8 and 4.2–4.3 of the Introduction.

to do the opposite, as indeed it can, then God would have known *that very thing* through this same type of knowledge, and not what He in fact knows. Therefore, it is no more natural for God to know through this sort of knowledge one part of a contradiction that depends on created free choice than it is for Him to know the opposite part.

Therefore, it should be said (i) that *middle* knowledge partly has the character of *natural* knowledge, since it was prior to the free act of the divine will and since God did not have the power to know anything else, and (ii) that it partly has the character of *free* knowledge, since the fact that it is knowledge of the one part rather than of the other derives from the fact that free choice, on the hypothesis that it should be created in one or another order of things, would do the one thing rather than the other, even though it would indifferently be able to do either of them.

And this last point is surely demanded by the freedom of the created will, a freedom that, even after divine foreknowledge has been posited, is no less *de fide* than are that same foreknowledge and predestination, as was shown at length in Disputation 23.[14] This same point is very plainly echoed by the testimony of the saints that we will soon refer to.[15] And it is reechoed in the common opinion of theologians, which we in part related in the preceding disputation and which we will discuss in a little while.[16]

Now lest this doctrine confound you at first glance, bear in mind that all of the following theses very clearly agree with and cohere with one another:

Nothing is within the power of a creature that is not also within God's power.[17]

By His omnipotence God is able to influence our free choice in whatever way He wants to, except toward sin—for that would involve a contradiction, as was shown in Disputation 31.[18]

Whatever God does by the mediation of secondary causes He is able to

---

[14]Rabeneck, pp. 134–154 (see Disputation 50, n. 12). A doctrine that is *de fide* (literally, of the faith) is one explicitly affirmed by the Church in a solemn manner (for example, in a creed or conciliar decree).

[15]See secs. 21–29 below.

[16]See sec. 20 below and Disputation 51, sec. 18.

[17]This thesis should apparently be interpreted as follows: Whatever effect is within a creature's power to bring about is also within God's power to bring about, *either* by Himself alone *or* by the mediation of secondary causes. The thesis requires further commentary, however, since it is still not clear how to apply it to sinful actions. A further problem arises if the proponent of middle knowledge claims that creatures have the power to make true what God knows through His middle knowledge. But, as far as I know, Molina never makes such a claim, and I for one see no reason why he should make such a claim. (For more on this, see Sections 4.5 and 5.7 of the Introduction.)

[18]Rabeneck, pp. 193–197.

bring about by Himself alone, unless it is implied in the effect that it comes to be from a secondary cause.[19]

God is able to permit sins, but not able to command them or to incite or incline anyone to them.

Likewise, the fact that a being endowed with free choice would, were it placed in a given order of things and circumstances, turn itself toward one or the other part does not stem from God's foreknowledge; to the contrary, God foreknows it because the being endowed with free choice would freely do that very thing. Nor does this fact stem from God's willing that the thing in question be done by that being. Rather, it stems from the fact that the being would freely will to do that thing. From this it follows with absolute clarity that the knowledge through which God, before He decides to create a being endowed with free choice, foresees what that being would do *on the hypothesis* that it should be placed in a particular order of things—this knowledge depends on the fact that the being would in its freedom do this or that, and not the other way around. On the other hand, the knowledge by which God knows *absolutely, without any hypothesis,* what is *in fact* going to happen because of created free choice is always *free* knowledge in God, and such knowledge depends on the free determination of His will, a determination by which He decides to create such-and-such a faculty of free choice in such-and-such an order of things.

11. Perhaps someone will ask whether this middle knowledge is to be countenanced in any of the blessed in heaven, at least in the most holy soul of Christ—so that just as God qua God, by discerning His own essence, sees what would freely come to be through created free choice on the hypothesis that free choice should be created in such-and-such an order of things, so too this most holy soul, by intuiting the divine essence by means of its beatific knowledge, sees what would come to be through free choice, especially the free choice of a human being who has already been produced by God.[20]

It should be replied that knowledge of this sort is in no way to be countenanced even in the very soul of Christ. The reason is that Christ's soul does not *comprehend* the divine essence. But this sort of knowledge

[19]So, for instance, God cannot bring it about by Himself alone that the water is heated by the fire, or that Michael freely raises his arm.

[20]The beatific knowledge had by the blessed in heaven is a special (supernatural) intuition of the divine essence. Medieval theologians commonly attribute this same knowledge to Christ as a human being even during his life on earth. Since Molina has already claimed that God's middle knowledge is based on His discernment of His own essence, the present question provides an opportunity for him to distinguish two different ways of intuiting the divine essence and to develop a bit further the notion of *comprehension.* See also Disputation 53, pt. 1, sec. 20.

concerning created things is attributed to God by Jerome, Augustine, and the other Fathers because He is God and for this reason comprehends each created faculty of choice in a certain absolutely profound manner. For in order to see which part a free being will turn itself toward, it is not sufficient that there be a comprehension of the being or even that there be a comprehension that is greater than is the thing comprehended. Rather, what is required is an *absolutely profound and absolutely preeminent comprehension,* such as is found only in God with respect to creatures.

This is why we likewise do not concede that through His natural or middle knowledge (which we deny of Him in this regard) God sees, before the determination of His will, which part *He Himself* is going to choose.[21] For in God the intellect does not surpass the *divine* essence and will in depth and excellence in the way that it does far surpass *created* essences and wills. Therefore, just as human beings and angels do not know, before the determination of their own wills, which part they are going to turn themselves toward, since their intellects do not surpass their essence and will by an infinite degree, so too neither does God know, before He determines His own will, which part it is going to be turned toward.

Nor do I understand very well how complete freedom would be preserved in God if, before the act of His will, He foreknew which part it was going to be turned toward. For if such knowledge existed, then He would in no way be able to choose the opposite part; thus, if He foreknew before that determination which part His will was going to be turned toward, then I do not see at what point He had the freedom to choose the opposite part.

12.   Now in order that you might understand this point better, notice that it is one thing for a suppositum, because of its preeminence over another suppositum, to know through middle knowledge what is going to be chosen by that *other* suppositum by virtue of its freedom; it is a far different thing for *one and the same* suppositum to foreknow through middle knowledge what *it itself* is freely going to choose.[22] For the fact that (i) the

---

[21] It is important to remember that Molina is using the term 'before' nontemporally, so that what he says here in no way implies that there is some *time* at which God does not yet know what He Himself is going to choose to do.

[22] For present purposes it is enough to take a suppositum to be an ultimate subject of properties. The medievals distinguished between the notions of *suppositum* on the one hand and *substance* (or *individual nature*) on the other mainly to accommodate the mystery of the Incarnation (one suppositum having two natures) and the mystery of the Holy Trinity (three supposita in one nature). (For more on this distinction, see my "Human Nature, Potency and the Incarnation," *Faith and Philosophy* 3 [1986]: 27–53.) Molina uses 'suppositum' here rather than 'substance' because one of the examples he uses below involves Christ and thus invokes the distinction between suppositum and nature.

first suppositum, comprehending the other with an infinite excess, knows through its middle knowledge, not freely but quasi-naturally, what that other suppositum will embrace in its freedom on the hypothesis that it should be placed in such-and-such an order of things, and the fact that (ii) it would likewise know whichever contrary part that very same suppositum was going to choose if perchance it was freely going to turn itself toward a contrary part, as it is really able to—clearly, none of this implies anything astonishing or thus anything prejudicial to the other suppositum's freedom. But I do not see how one and the same suppositum's knowing, *not freely but quasi-naturally*, what *it itself* will choose before it actually chooses it can be compatible with that same suppositum's freedom. For in the prior moment at which it knew this fact *quasi-naturally and not freely*, it did not have the power to know the contrary; in fact, since it knew the relevant part of the contradiction quasi-naturally and not freely, it follows that as long as there is preexisting knowledge of this sort, then it involves a contradiction to will or to have known the contrary. For in that case either God would be mistaken or there would be something such that, after having known it, He would never have known it—which involves a contradiction. This will be made clearer by the things that are going to be said in Part 1 of the next disputation.[23]

And you should not object against me that Christ is the same suppositum and that through his beatific knowledge he foreknew with certainty which part his own will was freely going to turn itself toward—and this without any prejudice to his freedom. You should not, I repeat, raise this objection against me. For the knowledge in question was communicated to his most holy soul not by himself as a human being but by the whole Trinity; and surely, Christ's freedom is no more impeded by the fact that what Christ as a human being would freely choose with his own will was made manifest to the human nature by the divine nature than Peter's freedom not to sin was impeded by the fact that Christ revealed his future sin to him. For as far as the matter at hand is concerned, there is no difference between (i) one *nature's* knowing, because of its depth and perfection, something about another nature and revealing it to that nature and (ii) one *suppositum's* likewise foreknowing something about another suppositum and revealing it to that suppositum.[24] What's more, in the absence of an utterly compelling

---

[23]See Disputation 53, pt. 1, secs. 15–20.
[24]So foreknowledge of what Christ would freely decide by means of his own human will, a foreknowledge proper to him by virtue of his having a divine nature, is revealed to him as a *human* knower by his divine nature and thus becomes such that he knows it with his human cognitive faculties. Molina's claim is that this is exactly analogous to God's revealing to Peter something about Peter's future behavior.

reason we should not extend to other things what, justifiably in light of God's infinite preeminence over the created faculty of choice, we are necessarily forced to assert in order to safeguard the freedom of that choice, a freedom that we experience and that is no less certain on the basis of Sacred Scripture than is divine foreknowledge. But in the present case there is no such reason.

13.   At this juncture it should be observed that it is one thing to claim that God does not know through the knowledge that precedes the free act of His will which part His own will or choice is freely going to determine itself to, even though He does know through that same knowledge which part each created faculty of choice would determine itself to on the hypothesis that it should be placed in such-and-such an order of things or circumstances from among the infinitely many such orders in which it can be placed; it is a far different thing to claim that God does not know which part His own free will would have determined itself to on any hypothesis that did not obtain and yet could have obtained, so that He does not know, say, whether, if Adam had not sinned, He would have willed the incarnation of the Word in a human nature not susceptible to suffering.

I have never made this second claim, either in this disputation or anywhere else; quite the opposite, it is the contrary claim that is implied by the thrust of my doctrine. For even though (i) God does not know through the knowledge that *precedes* the free determination of His will which determinations of His will would have existed on hypotheses of the sort in question, and even though (ii) there is thus in God no *middle* knowledge concerning those determinations of His own will as there is concerning the determination of any created faculty of free choice given any hypothesis involving it, still He does know these determinations through the *free* knowledge that *follows upon* the free act of His will. For that free act regarding the things that are able to be done by God—an act in itself infinite, unlimited, and lacking any shadow of alteration—freely determined itself to one part of a contradiction with respect to all possible objects at once, not only (i) by freely establishing those things that He decided to bring about or to permit and by freely deciding not to bring about or permit the rest, but also (ii) by freely deciding which things He *would have* willed on any hypothesis that *could have* obtained and did not obtain. Indeed, the act in question reflects an absolutely complete and unlimited deliberation, made on the basis of both the purely *natural* knowledge and also that knowledge, in the *middle* between free knowledge and purely natural knowledge, which existed in God's intellect before (in our way of conceiving it, with a basis in reality) the act of His will. And it would be absurd and repugnant to God's absolute perfection for Him to leave undeliberated anything having to do with any part of a contradiction from among all those things that He was then freely able to deliberate about—especially since in God there is no room for deliberating afterward about something that He had left undeliberated, and since it is inconsistent with His supreme and unlimited perfection that He should never be able to deliberate about it.

Therefore, through His free knowledge, which follows upon the act of His will, He knows in that free determination of His will what He would have willed in any circumstances and under any hypothesis that could have obtained and did not obtain.

It is, instead, the first of the above claims that I am asserting, namely, that God does not know, just by virtue of the knowledge that *precedes* the act of His will, which part *His own* will is going to determine itself to with regard to any object able to be created by Him, even though by virtue of that same knowledge He *does* know, on the hypothesis that His will should choose to determine itself to one or another order of things and circumstances, what each *created* faculty of choice would in its freedom will or do within that order. Now the reason for this is that while the divine intellect and knowledge surpass in perfection by an infinite distance each *created* faculty of choice which they contain eminently in themselves and which for this reason they comprehend in a certain infinitely more eminent way than that in which it is knowable, they do not likewise surpass the *divine* will in perfection or comprehend it in a more eminent way than that in which it is knowable in itself. Yet, as has been said, it is *this* sort of comprehension that is required in order to know regarding free choice, before it determines itself, which part it is going to determine itself to in its freedom under any given hypothesis.

It does not follow from this, however, that the knowledge in question does not comprehend the divine will, since for comprehension it is sufficient to know all the things that this will is able to determine itself to and that it is able to will or to reject; but God *does* know all these things regarding His own will through that knowledge, taken precisely as such, *before* He is thought of as eliciting an act of will.

Likewise, from the fact that through this knowledge, taken precisely as such, God does not know the determination of His own will, it does not follow that this knowledge is imperfect. For just as (i) this knowledge is not judged to be imperfect by reason of the fact that it is thought of as not yet having the status of free knowledge, a status it acquires after the determination of the divine will, and just as (ii) the will itself and God Himself are not judged to be imperfect by reason of the fact that the act of the divine will is thought of as not yet being in them, or even by reason of the fact that the procession of the Holy Spirit is thought of as not yet being in them—for there is no instant at which the one is found in God without the other, but rather these are the conceptions of *our* intellect in God, with a foundation in reality—so, too, neither can the knowledge we are discussing be judged imperfect on such grounds.[25] For, of course, it is not the case that there are many knowledges in God; rather, there is one absolutely simple knowledge that always has the added character of a *free* knowledge by which God knows the free determinations of His own will.

Nor is the following consequence valid: 'Through that knowledge, taken precisely as such, God does not know the free determinations of His own will (or, God does not know the free determination of His own will before He freely determines it); therefore, God does not know those same determinations of His own will.' For, as has been said, He knows them by the very fact that He elicits the act of His will and freely determines it—and this determination is *simultaneous in reality* with that knowledge, though *later in our way of conceiving it*, with a basis in reality. In the same way, we say of our own will that within the instant at which it elicits a free act and determines itself to one part of a contradiction, (i) *earlier in nature* it is free and indifferent as to whether it will determine itself to one or the other part and (ii) *later in nature* it is determined and elicits a determinate act.[26]

14. There are those who contend that in future contingents, it is always the case that the one part is determinately true from eternity before it obtains and the other part determinately false, and that for this reason the one part is *by its nature* knowable as determinately future and the other part as determinately not future; and they maintain that since whatever is *by its nature* knowable is such that God knows it *naturally, before* any free act of His will, it follows that God knows before any free act of His will not only (i) what will come to be on any hypothesis because

---

[25] According to Roman Catholic teaching about the Trinity, the Son proceeds from the Father and the Holy Spirit proceeds from the Father and the Son. Whereas the former procession involves only the divine act of knowing or understanding, the latter procession involves the act of the divine will as well, though in this case the object of the divine will is a *necessary* one (that is, one that God necessarily wills) and not a contingent one. So we can consider God as having a certain sort of knowledge while not yet having an act of willing with regard to any object, whether necessary or contingent. But, Molina insists here, the fact that we can consider God in this incomplete or imperfect way does not justify the imputation of any imperfection to God Himself. For there is never an instant at which God's act of willing does not exist. Likewise, there is no instant at which God does not know the free determinations of His own will. Molina's point is simply that such knowledge must be thought of as conceptually posterior to God's act of willing and thus must not be thought of as being middle knowledge.

[26] See Disputation 51, n. 9.

of created free choice, but also (ii) what God Himself is freely going to will later in nature (or, later in our way of conceiving it, with a basis in reality). For the latter is likewise determinately true before it is decided upon by God.

15. The claim that future contingents are by their nature determinately true, however, conflicts with the teaching of Aristotle and the common opinion of the Doctors, as well as with the very nature of contingent things, each of which is of its nature, by the very fact that it is contingent, indifferent as to whether it obtains or does not obtain, as we showed in commenting on *De Interpretatione* I, last chapter.[27] So this foundation of theirs completely breaks down, and it goes beyond the nature of those future contingents that depend on created choice that God should know them; and God's knowing them, as we have explained, stems from His infinite and unlimited perfection, by which He comprehends each created faculty of choice in a certain absolutely profound and eminent way. Thus, since (i) this foundation of *ours* has no place in God as far as the free determination of *His own* will is concerned, a will that can in no way be surpassed in perfection, and since (ii), as we said a little while ago, we should not extend to other things that which, in relation to created free choice, we are forced by necessity to countenance in God because of His absolutely eminent comprehension exceeding the perfection of the object, clearly it should not be claimed that God knows before the determination of His own will which part that will is going to determine itself to, but it should rather be claimed that in that prior instant the divine intellect only shows Him all the *other* things at once, including those things that would come to be because of any creatable faculty of choice on any hypothesis and within any order of things—so that, given an absolutely comprehensive deliberation on the part of the intellect, the will by its choice establishes and arranges all things, and, consistently with the freedom of created choice, provides for all things, and predestines those whom it wants to or, if you will, mercifully decides to guide them to everlasting happiness.

16. Perhaps someone will object as follows: In order to know something it is sufficient that there be a relation of proportionality between the faculty and the object, in the sense, namely, that there be as much ability to know in the faculty as there is being or knowability in the object;

---

[27]Molina's complete commentary on Aristotle's *De Interpretatione* (written in 1563 and 1564) is found in manuscript form at Evora, cod. 118-1-6. A brief question on future contingents from this commentary is found in Stegmüller, pp. 1–9. See n. 4 above on Molina's use of the term 'determinately true.'

therefore, whoever comprehends a given will is going to discern in it which part it is going to determine itself to by its freedom; accordingly, God will foreknow which part His own will is freely going to determine itself to, and, in particular, the soul of Christ will by its beatific knowledge foreknow which part its own human will and the wills of other human beings are freely going to determine themselves to, since through this knowledge it comprehends those wills in a deeper way than that in which they are knowable by their very nature.

17. To this argument it should be replied that the antecedent is true of those things that are knowable in the object by their very nature or because of their being,[28] but it is not true of those things that are known in a way exceeding their nature solely because of the eminence and unlimited perfection of the knower—things such as the determination of a free choice before it exists and, in general, future contingents before they exist. For in order to know these things it is not sufficient that the knowing faculty be equalized with the source of the contingency of those things, or that there be a comprehension of this source;[29] instead, what is required is an *absolutely profound and preeminent comprehension* of this source, a comprehension such as is found in God alone with respect to the free choice of all His creatures. Therefore, since this sort of middle knowledge is not to be countenanced in the blessed in heaven, we claimed in question 12, article 8 and elsewhere that the blessed in heaven are unable to know with certainty those future contingents that depend on created free choice *simply* on the basis of the vision of the divine essence and on the basis of that determination of the divine will which has to do with placing each person's free choice in a given order of things.[30] And so we conjectured that the revelation of these things to the blessed in heaven is accomplished by means of a displaying of the knowledge that God has of them, or in some other way.

[28] Here Molina accepts the assumption made in the objection that *entitas* (translated here as 'being') is a property that a thing (whether substance or accident or essential part, that is, matter or form) may possess to a greater or lesser degree than other things. Moreover, a thing's degree of *entitas* corresponds to its degree of *intrinsic knowability*. God, as the First Being, is the most knowable intrinsically, whereas creatures have greater or lesser knowability and being to the extent that they bear a greater or lesser resemblance to God.

[29] The *equalization* (Latin: *adequatio*) referred to here is that alluded to in the objection, namely, a correspondence between the knowing faculty's intellective ability and the intrinsic knowability of the object known.

[30] See *Commentaria*, pp. 121b–140b. Molina's point here is that by their beatific knowledge the blessed in heaven know only that God has decided to allow given creatures to exercise free choice in such-and-such circumstances. In order for them to know beyond this just how these creatures will use their free choice, they need a further and special revelation from God.

18. With these matters thus explicated, in view of the fact that, as has been said repeatedly, among all the things created (i) some are from God immediately, (ii) others come to be through the mediation of just those secondary causes that act by a necessity of nature without any dependence on created free choice, and (iii) still others emanate from created free choice or are able to undergo alteration because of it, God was, to begin with, a cause, whether particular or universal, of all things of the first and second types solely through His purely natural knowledge (the first kind explained above) complemented by the free determination of His will, a determination by which that knowledge was directed toward the production of those effects in the way in question, as was explained and proven in article 8.[31] For that knowledge alone has the character of an art by which God knew the mode and manner of fashioning those things in the way in question and of providing for each of them in such a way that they might be fitted to their ends. But since an art is not operative unless determined by the will of the artist, who commits to execution what the art prescribes, it follows that, given the addition of the divine volition by which God freely willed that those things should exist, God's natural knowledge was a remote (in our way of conceiving it) cause of those things, whereas the free determination of the divine will was a proximate and sufficient cause. But even though human and angelic free choice are things of the first type, still, because God created them both in order that, placed in the hand of their own counsel, they would be able either to attain both their natural end and also, with God's help, their supernatural end, or to turn themselves away from both ends by their own choice, it clearly follows that in order for God (i) to be a cause, sometimes only a universal cause but sometimes a particular cause as well, of things of the third type, which depend on free choice, and in order for Him (ii) to be able to exercise the appropriate providence over free choice with regard to both sorts of ends, sometimes by disciplining a human being through various events, sometimes by tolerating and permitting his failures, sometimes by calling him and aiding him and moving him toward the good, and finally, in order for Him (iii) to be able to predestine certain human beings or angels and to ordain all things to their proper ends, besides His purely *natural* knowledge (the first kind explained above), it was also necessary for Him to have that *middle* knowledge through which, on the hypothesis that He should will to bring about this or that order of things, He foresaw with certainty all that would come to be because of angelic and human free choice in each one of those orders of things. Therefore, God is a cause—

[31]Rabeneck, pp. 3–4.

sometimes universal, sometimes particular—of things of the third type; specifically, He is a cause *remotely* (in our way of conceiving it) through the two types of knowledge just explained, while He is a cause *proximately* through the determination of His will, a determination by which, while deciding to place human beings and angels in that order of things in which He placed them, He simultaneously decided to cooperate with their free choice in this or that way. But you should not infer that He is in any way a cause of sins; for as far as their fault and defectiveness are concerned, sins are traced back to created free choice *alone* as to their cause. This was shown in Disputation 31.[32]

On the other hand, the *free* knowledge by which God, after the determination of His will, knew *absolutely* and *without any hypothesis* which effects of each of these three types were going to occur, is *in no way* a cause of things. For that knowledge comes *after* the free determination of God's will, a determination by which the *whole* notion of a cause and principle of immediate operation is satisfied on God's part.

19.   From these remarks it can easily be seen that even though God acquires no knowledge *from things* but instead knows and comprehends everything He knows in His own essence and in the free determination of His own will, nonetheless it is not because He knows that something is going to be that that thing is going to be. Just the opposite, it is because the thing will come to be from its causes that He knows that it is going to be.

For since things of the *first* type will come to be solely from God's free will as from their immediate and total cause, it follows that it is through *free* knowledge, which is *posterior to* the determination of the will in God, that God knows in the very determination of His will, as in the cause of their coming to be, that those things will come to be. But it is not the case, conversely, that those things will come to be because He knows that they will come to be, since the fact that they will come to be by virtue of the free determination of the divine will is *prior* (in our way of conceiving it, with a basis in reality) to God's knowing this fact on the basis of that very same determination.

Again, since it is partly because of God's free will, by which He decided to create secondary causes immediately and to concur with them as a universal cause, and partly because of the necessary action of those secondary causes themselves that things of the *second* type will come to be in such a way that no other cause is powerful enough to impede effects of this sort, it surely follows that (given the preexistence of the

[32]Rabeneck, pp. 193–197.

natural knowledge by which God foresees that things of this type will necessarily come to be on the hypothesis that He should will to create their causes) in the determination of His will, by which He decided to create these things, God foreknew absolutely and without any hypothesis, through the *free* knowledge that *followed upon* this determination, that these effects were going to exist. And He foreknew this because these things would come to be from these causes; and it was not the case, conversely, that they would come to be from these causes because God knew that they would come to be.

Finally, since (i), given the cooperation of other secondary causes as well as God's cooperation (partly as a universal cause, partly as a particular cause), things of the *third* type will, by virtue of created free choice or with dependence on it, come to be in such a way that they are able not to be, while (ii) through His natural knowledge and through that knowledge that lies between purely natural knowledge and free knowledge God foresaw that these things were going to be because of free choice on the hypothesis that He should will to create human beings and angels in the order of things in which He in fact placed them, it follows that in the free determination of the will by which He decided so to create them, He knew through His *free* knowledge, a knowledge that *follows upon* that determination, that those things were going to be. For it was because of freedom of choice that they were going to come to be in that way, but it was not the case, conversely, that they will come to be or have come to be because He foreknew that they would come to be.

20.   This last point we have made is in fact affirmed as well by all those Doctors whom we cited in the preceding disputation.[33] For as long as they assert that when free choice by its innate freedom indifferently chooses this or its opposite, then God will bring it about that from eternity He foreknew nothing else, they are obviously teaching not that things will come to be because God foreknows that they will, but rather just the opposite. The rest of the Scholastic Doctors seem to share this view—though, to tell the truth, in article 8 above, response to the first objection, St. Thomas seems to intimate the contrary position when he expounds and tries to read the contrary sense into the text from Origen which is going to be cited shortly, a text in which Origen is clearly advocating the same position.[34]

---

[33]See Disputation 51, sec. 3.
[34]St. Thomas, *Summa Theologiae* I, q. 14, a. 8, ad 1. See sec. 22 below for the passage from Origen. St. Thomas's comment is as follows: "As for the first argument, the response is that Origen was thinking of the sort of knowledge which does not fall under the concept of a cause unless it is accompanied by an act of will, as has been said. But his claim that God

21. The common opinion of the holy Fathers clearly affirms the same thing.

In *Expositiones Quaestionum a Gentibus Christianis Propositarum*, q. 58, while discussing Judas's betrayal and God's foreknowledge, Justin Martyr says, "Foreknowledge is not a cause of that which is going to be, but rather that which is going to be is a cause of foreknowledge. For that which is going to be does not ensue upon foreknowledge, but rather foreknowledge ensues upon that which is going to be. So it follows that Christ is not a cause of the betrayal, but rather the betrayal is a cause of the Lord's foreknowledge."[35] He says that the same thing holds for foreknowledge of the sin of the angels and of the first parents. So he is speaking not only about the foreknowledge that Christ has as a human being, since this foreknowledge did not exist before the sins of the angels and the first parents, but also about the foreknowledge that God has as God. He is not, however, using the term 'cause' to stand for a *real* cause; for the things are not a cause of Christ's foreknowledge, since neither the uncreated foreknowledge that he has insofar as he is God nor the created foreknowledge of future contingents with which he was endowed as a human being devolve from the things themselves.[36] Instead, he is talking about the *explanation* of why this foreknowledge exists, since the relation of reason which the divine knowledge bears to the things that it knew were going to exist depends on the fact that those things would come to be from their causes, as has been explained.

22. In book 7 of his commentary on the epistle to the Romans, while commenting on Romans 8 [8:30], "Whom He foreknew and predestined," Origen likewise says, "It is not because God knows that something is going to be that that thing is going to be, but rather it is because it is going to be that it is known by God before it comes to be. For even if we imagine for the sake of argument that God does not foreknow anything, it was without a doubt going to happen that, say, Judas became a traitor, and this in just the way the prophets foretold it would happen. There-

---

foreknows things *because* they are future should be understood in terms of a cause of logical inference and not a cause of existing. For it follows that if something is future, then God foreknows it; but the future things are not the cause of God's knowledge."

[35]*PG* 6, 1300C.

[36]Molina here is careful to dissociate himself from the view that God finds out about created things by looking at them rather than by looking into Himself, as it were. (Ironically, the model of divine knowledge repudiated here is at least suggested by Aquinas's claim that God knows what is future to us in a way analogous to that in which someone perched at the top of a hill might see all the travelers on the road.) God knows that such-and-such will happen because it will so happen, but, Molina insists, it does not follow that God acquires such knowledge from the things themselves or that the things themselves act as efficient causes of God's knowledge of them.

fore, it was not because the prophets foretold it that Judas became a traitor, but rather it was because he was going to be a traitor that the prophets foretold the things that he was going to do by his wicked designs, even though Judas most certainly had it within his power to be like Peter and John if he had so willed; but he chose the desire for money over the glory of apostolic companionship, and the prophets, foreseeing this choice of his, handed it down in their books. Moreover, in order that you might understand that the cause of each person's salvation is to be found not in God's foreknowledge but in that person's intentions and actions, notice that Paul tormented his body and subjected it to servitude because he feared that, after having preached to others, he himself might perhaps become reprobate."[37]

23.   In *Dialogus adversus Manichaeos* Damascene says, "From this it is clear that foreknowledge was not in the least a cause of the devil's becoming evil. For a physician, when he foresees a future illness, does not cause that illness. To the contrary, the real cause of the illness consists in a perverse and immoderate way of life. For its part, the physician's foreknowledge is a sign of his erudition, whereas the cause of the foreknowledge is the fact that things were going to turn out that way."[38]

24.   In homily 60 on Matthew, while commenting on Matthew 18:7, "Woe to the world because of scandals," Chrysostom says, "It is not because he foretold the future scandals that they will occur; rather, it is because they will occur in their entirety that he foretold them. For they would not occur if worthless and pestiferous human beings did not will to contrive them; but if they had not been going to occur, then neither would he have foretold that they would occur. They were going to occur, however, since there were many deeply sick people who did not will not to act maliciously, and he foretold that this would happen. 'But if these people had been cured,' someone will object, 'and if there were no one who would create scandals, then wouldn't his words be convicted of falsity?' Certainly, if everyone had willed to be cured and to be made well, then he would not have said, 'It is inevitable that scandals will come.' But because he foresaw that these people would willingly become incurable, he foretold that the scandals would come in their entirety."[39]

---

[37]*PG* 14, 1126C–D.
[38]*PG* 94, 1544B.
[39]*PG* 58, 574f.

25.   While commenting on Isaiah 16:13, "This is the word the Lord spoke against Moab," Jerome says, "God's foreknowledge is not a cause of the desolation, but rather the future desolation is foreknown to God's majesty."[40] And at the beginning of Jeremiah 26 [26:3], he says, "It is not because God knows some future thing that that thing is going to be; rather, it is because it is going to be that God knows it, since He is one who foreknows future things."[41] Likewise, in commenting on Ezekiel 2:4, "And you will say to them, etc.," he says, "It is not the case that because He knows that those things are going to occur, it is necessary for us to do what He foreknows; rather, He knew as future what we are going to do by our own will. For He is God."[42] Again, in *Dialogus adversus Pelagianos* III: "It is not the case that Adam sinned because God had known that this would happen; rather, God, because He is God, foreknew what Adam was going to do by his own will."[43]

26.   In *De Civitate Dei* V, chap. 10, Augustine says, "For it is not the case that a human being sins because God foreknew that he would sin. Indeed, there is no doubt that he sins, when he sins; for He whose foreknowledge cannot be mistaken did not foreknow fate or fortune or anything else—rather, he foreknew that he would sin. If he wills not to sin, then he does not sin at all. But if he is going to will not to sin, then God likewise foreknew this."[44] And in *De Praedestinatione et Gratia,* chap. 15, the author of that work says, "If it is claimed that Pharaoh was not at that time able to change because God had foreknown that he was not going to change, the reply will be that God's foreknowledge does not force a human being to be such as God foreknew he would be, but rather it foreknows that he is going to be such as he will be, even though God does not make him be that way."[45]

27.   In book 9 of his commentary on John, chap. 10, Cyril says, "It is because some people were willingly going to act in this way that the prescient Holy Spirit foretold that these things would happen."[46]

28.   In sermon 16, Leo I says, "The Lord does not incite the wicked hands of madmen against Himself, but He does allow it. Nor by foreknowing what is going to happen does He force it to happen."[47]

[40]*PL* 24, 173C.
[41]*PL* 24, 844B.
[42]*PL* 25, 33B.
[43]*PL* 23, 575C.
[44]*PL* 41, 153.
[45]*PL* 45, 1675.
[46]*PG* 74, 132B.
[47]*PL* 54, 369C.

29.   From what has been said in this disputation and in the preceding disputations it is sufficiently clear, I believe, how our freedom of choice and the contingency of things cohere with divine foreknowledge.

For (i) the things that issue forth from our choice or depend on it are not going to happen because they are foreknown by God as going to happen, but, to the contrary, they are foreknown by God as going to happen in this or that way because they are so going to happen by virtue of our freedom of choice—though if they were going to happen in a contrary way, as they are able to, then from eternity they would be foreknown as going to happen in that contrary way instead of in the way they are in fact foreknown as going to happen—and, indeed, (ii) the knowledge by which God knew *absolutely* that such-and-such things would come to be is not a cause of the things, but rather, once the order of things that we see has been posited by the free determination of the divine will, then (as Origen and the other Fathers observe) the effects will issue forth from their causes—naturally from natural causes, freely and contingently with respect to both parts from free causes—just as if God had no foreknowledge of future events. From this it clearly follows that no prejudice at all is done to freedom of choice or to the contingency of things by God's foreknowledge, a foreknowledge through which, because of the infinite and wholly unlimited perfection and acumen of His intellect, He sees with certainty what the free causes placed in any order of things will do, even though they could really, if they so willed, do the contrary; rather, even though that knowledge exists, freedom of choice and the contingency of things with respect to both parts remain intact, just as if there were no foreknowledge. In addition to Boethius in *De Consolatione* V, last prose, and many others, Augustine teaches the same thing excellently while arguing with Evodius in *De Libero Arbitrio* III, chap. 4.[48] For when Evodius asks Augustine how God's foreknowledge and human free choice fit together, given that what God foreknows as future must by all means necessarily occur, Augustine responds: " 'Why does it seem to you that our free choice conflicts with God's foreknowledge? Is it because it is foreknowledge, or because it is *God's* foreknowledge?' *Evodius:* 'Mainly because it is God's foreknowledge.' *Augustine:* 'What, then, if *you* foreknew that someone was going to sin, wouldn't it be necessary that he sin?' *Evodius:* 'Indeed it would be necessary that he sin. For I would have no foreknowledge unless I foreknew things that are certain.' *Augustine:* 'Then it is not because it is *God's* foreknowledge that the things He foreknows will necessarily come to be, but it is only because it is foreknowledge, which

---

[48]*PL* 32, 1276.

would surely not exist at all if He did not foreknow things that are certain.' *Evodius:* 'I agree. But what's the point of these remarks?' Then *Augustine:* 'It's that, unless I am mistaken, you would not directly force someone to sin whom you foreknew was going to sin; nor would your foreknowledge force him to sin, even though he was without a doubt going to sin; for otherwise you would not really foreknow it as future. And so, just as the two things are not opposed to each other, with the result that by your foreknowledge you knew what the other was freely going to do, so too God foresees those who are going to sin of their own will without compelling anyone to sin. Why, then, should He not be a just judge of those things that He foresees but does not force anyone to do? For just as you do not by your memory force past things to have been done, so neither does God by His foreknowledge force future things to be done. And just as you remember things that you have done even though it is not the case that *you* have done all the things that you remember, so too God foreknows all the things of which He is the author even though it is not the case that *He* is the author of all the things that He foreknows. Rather, He is a just judge of things that He is not the evil author of. From this you should now see with what justice God punishes sins, since He did not bring about the things He foreknew were going to be. For if, because He foresees sins, He ought not to condemn sinners, then neither should He give rewards to those who act righteously, since He likewise foresaw just as well that they would act righteously. In fact, we should say that it is by virtue of His foreknowledge that no future thing is hidden from Him, and that it is by virtue of His justice that sin, because it is committed willingly, does not go unpunished by His judgment, since His foreknowledge does not force it to be committed.'" These are Augustine's words.

30.　What's more, on the basis of what has been said so far we should caution that although theologians are absolutely correct in claiming that even if it is known that Peter will sin tomorrow, Peter is able in the divided sense, though not in the composed sense, not to sin, still with regard to these two senses there are two grievous errors that have to be avoided.

The first error, which has to do with the divided sense, we have already impugned in the preceding disputation,[49] namely, we should not believe that the explanation for Peter's being able in the divided sense not to sin is that whatever he does freely in the future is such that God will likewise freely bring it about in the future that from eternity He

[49]See Disputation 51, secs. 1, 2, and 14–17.

knew none other than that same thing. For this is to destroy the certitude and determinateness of the divine knowledge regarding future contingents before they come to be, something that is obviously incompatible with the excellence of the divine knowledge and is such that utter absurdities follow from it, as was shown above in the same place. For this reason it must be acknowledged that the firm foundation was already in place from eternity: "The Lord knew His own" [2 Tim. 2:19].

The second error has to do with the composed sense, namely, we should not claim that because the divine foreknowledge already exists beforehand, Peter is in reality not able not to sin, as if because of the preexisting divine knowledge he has lost something of his freedom and power not to sin in reality should he so will. For I would not hesitate to call this sort of interpretation an error from the point of view of the faith. Indeed, even though that knowledge did exist beforehand, it was just as truly within his power not to sin as it would have been had that knowledge not existed, and he was just as truly able to refrain from the act in light of which he was foreknown to be a future sinner as he would have been had that knowledge not existed, as has been explained; thus this interpretation is not the one that the theologians have in mind. Rather, they are claiming, absolutely correctly, that given the divine knowledge, Peter is not able in the composed sense not to sin, because these two things, namely, Peter's being such that he is *not* going to sin and God's knowing that he *is* going to sin, cannot both obtain together. But if, as is now truly possible, he were not going to sin, then that knowledge would not have existed in God, and so that knowledge, which would not have existed if, as is possible, Peter were not going to sin, does not in any way prevent Peter's now being able in the divided sense not to sin, in just the way he would have been able not to sin had such knowledge not existed beforehand.

31. *Response to the first argument.* As for the first argument proposed at the beginning,[50] first of all, regarding the major premise, it should be said that this premise is true if it is understood as having to do with a cause that is both (i) a *total* cause, *absolutely speaking* (and not total merely within some order of causes—namely, universal causes—as was explained in Disputation 26),[51] and (ii) a *necessary* cause that not only *exists* necessarily but also *acts* necessarily; for from such a cause there issues

[50]See sec. 2 above. The major premise is that from a necessary cause there issues forth a necessary effect.

[51]See Rabeneck, pp. 164–170. According to Molina, God is a total universal (or general) cause of any effect that is produced by secondary causes. His point here is that in order for the first premise to be true with respect to God's causal activity in a particular case, God must be acting not as a universal cause but as a total particular cause, determining by Himself the exact nature of the effect.

forth a necessary effect. As far as the first part of the minor is con-cerned,[52] however, if it has to do with God's *free* knowledge, through which future contingents are known by Him *absolutely* and *without any hypothesis*, then it should be denied that that knowledge is a cause of future contingents, as is sufficiently clear from what has been said in this article and in article 8.[53] On the other hand, if the premise has to do with God's *natural* knowledge and with that other *middle* knowledge, through which, before any free act of His own, He knows future contingents not as *absolutely* future, but as future *on the hypothesis* that He should will to create this or that order of things in which these or those creatures are endowed with free choice, then it will have to be conceded that God's knowledge is a cause of future contingents. It is not a *total* cause, how-ever, since the faculty of choice itself is part of the whole cause of those future contingents that depend on created free choice—a part by virtue of which it is not only the case that there are or are not future con-tingents, but also the case that there are these rather than those. Now as far as the last part of the minor is concerned,[54] we should say the following: Even though, after knowledge of this sort has once been conceived to exist, it is a knowledge that is necessary as regards both the part that is *natural* in God and the part that *would be different* in God if, as is possible, created free choice were by its innate freedom going to turn itself to the opposite part, still such knowledge does not produce future contingents necessarily, but rather produces them in a way that depends on both the free determination of the divine will and the free election of created choice, an election by which it embraces this rather than that part of a contradiction. But the effects acquire contingency from this sort of free determination of the parts of the one total cause, despite the necessity of the foresaid knowledge—as St. Thomas taught in this place in the response to the first objection.[55]

32. *Response to the second argument.* For the response to the second argument[56] it should be noted that a proposition that is merely con-

---

[52]The first part of the minor premise is this: 'But God's knowledge is a cause of the future things known through it.'

[53]Molina refers here to the whole of the *Concordia* up to this very place, "this article" being article 13 of question 14 of *Summa Theologiae* I. His brief commentary on article 8 appears in Rabeneck, pp. 3–4.

[54]The last part of the minor premise is that God's knowledge is necessary.

[55]St. Thomas says: "As for the first argument, it should be said that even if a highest cause is necessary, its effect can still be contingent by virtue of a contingent proximate cause. For example, the sprouting of a plant is contingent by virtue of its proximate cause, even though the motion of the sun, which is a first cause, is necessary. And, similarly, the things known by God are contingent by virtue of the proximate causes, even though God's knowledge, which is a first cause, is necessary."

[56]See sec. 3 above.

tingent if we consider the natures of the terms and the causes or principle from which the joining of the predicate with the subject emanated, at
times becomes *absolutely necessary* because of some condition—not, to be
sure, a condition that is *imagined* to be in it or that, though it is able to be
in it and able not to be in it, is nonetheless *hypothesized* to be in it, but
rather a condition that is *already actually* in it in such a way that its being
removed involves a contradiction. For although the first two types of
conditions only make for a necessity that is *relative* and *hypothetical*—in
the way in which it is necessary that a horse have wings *if* it is flying, or in
the way in which everything that exists is such that, *on the hypothesis* that it
exists, it is necessary that it exist—nonetheless, the third type of condition makes for an *absolute* necessity distinct from any relative or purely
hypothetical necessity. Thus, in this sense, even though it was absolutely
contingent that Adam existed (for he was freely produced by God), still
by the very fact that he has really existed, his having existed is now at the
present time necessary in such a way that his not having existed involves
a contradiction; for the fact that he existed can no longer be negated or
prevented in any way. In the same way, even though it was likewise
contingent that God foreknows that the Antichrist is going to sin at such-
and-such a point in time (since if, as will be possible, he were not going to
sin, then God would not have foreknown that he is going to), nevertheless, by the very fact that from eternity He did foresee this sin as future, it
now involves a contradiction for Him not to have foreknown it, both
because there is no power over the past and also because no change can
befall God. St. Thomas should be interpreted as talking about this sort of
absolute necessity in this place in the response to the second objection,
when he says that this and similar true propositions about the past are
absolutely necessary.[57]

---

[57]St. Thomas's exact words are: "As for the second argument, it should be said that some
claim that the antecedent 'God knew that this contingent thing was going to be' is not
necessary but contingent; for even though it is past-tense, it nonetheless connotes a
relation to a future thing. But this does not take away its necessity; for that which had a
relation to a future thing is necessarily such that it had it, even though the future thing
sometimes does not follow.

"Now others claim that the antecedent in question is contingent because it is composed
of something necessary and something contingent, in the same way that the dictum 'that
Socrates is a white man' is contingent. But this does not help, either; for when one says,
'God knew that something is a future contingent,' the contingent thing is posited here only
as the object of the verb and not as the principal part of the proposition; hence, its
contingency or necessity is irrelevant to the question of whether the proposition is necessary or contingent, true or false. For it can be just as true that I have said that a man is a
donkey as that I have said that Socrates is running or that God exists; and the same thing
holds for the modes 'necessary' and 'contingent'.

"So it has to be said that the antecedent is absolutely necessary."

33. Second, and this is also clearly enough implied by what has been said, one should notice what is peculiar to God's knowledge of those contingent things that depend on created choice, namely, that by virtue of the acumen and absolute perfection of His intellect God foreknew what was going to happen because it was going to happen that way on account of the faculty of choice itself by virtue of its innate freedom, and if, as is possible, the opposite were going to happen, then God would have foreknown *it* instead. Thus, what was in itself uncertain He knew with certainty, a certainty that stemmed not from the object, but from the acumen and absolute perfection of His intellect, though with dependence on the fact that things were going to happen that way because of the faculty of choice itself.

34. With these points established, we should deny the major premise[58] for any case in which (i) the antecedent is absolutely necessary *only* with the necessity just explained, and (ii) the knowledge in question (a) has been formed with dependence on the fact that the thing was going to happen freely or contingently, and (b) would have been formed in the contrary way if, as is possible, the thing were going to happen in the contrary way, and (c) has its certainty not from the object but solely from the acumen and immense perfection of the knower. For in such a case, even if (i) the conditional is necessary (because in the composed sense these two things cannot both obtain, namely, that God foreknows something to be future and that the thing does not turn out that way), and even if (ii) the antecedent is necessary in the sense in question (because it is past-tense and because no shadow of alteration can befall God), nonetheless the consequent can be purely contingent. In response to the proof of the major, where the inference is drawn that "otherwise in a valid consequence the antecedent could be true and the consequent false," it should be denied that this follows. For if, as is possible, the opposite of the consequent were going to obtain, then the antecedent would never have obtained beforehand—an antecedent that was conceived in the way it was by the acumen and perfection of the divine intellect because the thing was going to turn out that way, even though it could have turned out otherwise. Therefore, it would never be the case that the antecedent is true and the consequent false. From this it follows that if the truth of the antecedent is posited (as is in fact the case), then the consequent is necessary only with a necessity of the *consequence*, by which it is validly inferred from that antecedent, and *not* with a necessity

---

[58]The major premise is that if a conditional is true and its antecedent is absolutely necessary, then its consequent is likewise absolutely necessary.

of the *consequent,* since the condition in question does not render the consequent absolutely necessary in the way that it *does* render the antecedent absolutely necessary. The consequent is not affected by it in any way, but is instead unqualifiedly able to obtain and able not to obtain; if, however, it were not going to obtain, as is possible, then the antecedent would never have obtained beforehand, and, accordingly, the condition in question, which has its source solely in the divine acumen and perfection, would not be found in the antecedent.

35. *Response to the third argument.* As for the third argument,[59] the major premise should be conceded if it has to do with the necessity of the *consequence,* since the following consequence is necessary: 'God knows that this or that is going to be; therefore, it is going to be.' But if it has to do with the necessity of the *consequent,* as if to say that it is necessarily true that the thing known by God to be future is necessary or certain in itself, then the major premise should be denied. Now as far as the proof is concerned,[60] the inference should be denied if it is understood as having to do with the necessity of the consequent, in which case it would have the following sense: 'Everything that is known by human beings is necessary with a necessity of the consequent, or is at least certain in itself (taking the term "knowledge" in the broader sense, so as also to include that certain cognition of contingent propositions that is verified by sense experience); therefore, everything that is known by God as future will also be necessary with a necessity of the consequent, or will at least be certain in itself—especially since God's knowledge is much more certain than ours.' Now the reason this inference should be denied is that our knowledge gets no certitude from the perspicacity and depth of the knower over and beyond the things known, as it would if we perceived things with more certainty than the things have in themselves and of their nature. For this reason, the certitude of our knowledge depends on the necessity or certitude of the objects in their own right, nor can there be more certainty in *our* knowledge than is found in the objects themselves. On the other hand, because of the acumen and depth of the knower, who sees with certainty what is going to happen in an object that in its own right is uncertain, the *divine* knowledge has more certitude in itself than there is certitude in the objects. And this is the reason we posit knowledge of future contingents only in God and not in human beings, as was said in question 1 of the First Part.[61] So the fact that God's

[59]See sec. 4 above. The major premise is that whatever is known by God is necessary.

[60]The proof is: "since, of course, it is even the case that everything which is known by human beings necessarily obtains, and God's knowledge is more certain than human knowledge."

[61]*Commentaria,* pp. 2b–36a. Also, see Disputation 51, n. 18.

knowledge is more certain than human knowledge works to the advantage of our position. For from this fact it obviously follows that even if *we* cannot have knowledge except of an object that is already certain in itself, there is no corresponding reason *God* cannot have knowledge except of an object of this sort. For future contingents of the kind in question are objects that are uncertain in themselves, and yet because of the depth and eminence of His intellect God knows them with absolute certainty and hence has an absolutely unique knowledge of them which exceeds their nature. This is why the kingly Prophet, who by means of the gift of prophecy had received a revelation of some of them, said as he addressed God in Psalm 50:8, "The uncertain and hidden things of Your wisdom You have made manifest to me."[62] He said "uncertain" in order to express the essence and nature of the things revealed, and he added "of Your wisdom" because of the utterly certain and altogether infallible cognition of those things by virtue of the depth, eminence, and infinite perfection of the divine intellect. I realize that the Hebrew text does not have these two adjectives, but only one that means "hidden and concealed," and so, given the Hebrew text, "uncertain" has to be understood here as "uncertain *to us,* whether or not they are also uncertain *in themselves.*" Notwithstanding, "in themselves" is the true teaching that I have proposed in this matter. And this same teaching is not insignificantly corroborated by the fact that the Septuagint translators rendered the above text in this way and by the fact that the Vulgate edition goes along with them.[63]

[62]This reference is to Hebrew Psalm 51:8. Some modern translations render this verse in a way that makes it useless for Molina's purposes here. For instance, the New American Bible renders the relevant part of the verse as follows: "and in my inmost being you teach me wisdom."

[63]The Vulgate is the Latin translation of the Scriptures first made by St. Jerome in the fourth century. Molina is using the Clementine edition published at Rome in 1592. The Septuagint is a translation of the Hebrew Scriptures into Greek made in Egypt in the third and second centuries B.C. A popular legend had it that the translation was completed in seventy-two days by seventy-two translators.

Molina is obviously concerned here with the charge that this passage from Psalm 51 undercuts his view that a future contingent is uncertain in itself (rather than simply to us) and thus corroborates the Bañezian claim that future contingents are certain to God only because God predetermines them. We find him again addressing this issue in the Appendix to the *Concordia,* sec. 36 (Rabeneck, pp. 366–367), where he has this to say:

"From this you can see that the kingly prophet did not contradict me when he called uncertain that which was known by the divine wisdom. Rather, he was expressing our position succinctly when, talking of those things that depended on human freedom in the future, he said, 'The uncertain and hidden things of Your wisdom You have made manifest to me.' For when he said 'uncertain,' he was expressing what the object is in itself and of itself; whereas when he added 'of Your wisdom,' he meant the depth and unlimited perfection of the divine intellect—perfection of such a degree that with respect to something uncertain it could have divine knowledge, the distinguishing feature of which is certitude. But since the knowledge by which God, after the decree of His will, already knew

36. *Response to the fourth argument.* As for the fourth argument,[64] if the antecedent 'No future thing foreknown by God is able not to occur' is taken in the *composed* sense, then, even though the antecedent may be conceded, the consequence should be denied. And in response to the proof,[65] it should be said that in order for something to be a future contingent absolutely speaking, it is sufficient that it be in the divided sense able to be and able not to be, since if it were not going to be (as is really possible, God's foreknowledge notwithstanding), then that divine foreknowledge with which its nonoccurrence is incompatible would not have existed beforehand. On the other hand, if that same antecedent is taken in the *divided* sense, then it should be denied. Next, in response to the proof that goes 'If something that is foreknown by God as being such that it will occur were not going to occur, then God would really be mistaken; therefore, if, while that knowledge remained, the thing were *able* not to occur, then God would really be *able* to be mistaken,' it should be said, first of all, that if both the antecedent and the consequent are taken in the composed sense, then the proof should be conceded, for this antecedent and consequent are of no use in proving that other antecedent[66] *in the divided sense,* and we are *not* claiming that, given the knowledge, the thing is able not to occur *in the composed sense.* But since we are claiming (i) that the foreknowledge that actually exists does not in any way prevent the thing from being able to turn out otherwise, and so (ii) that despite the knowledge it is able in the divided sense not to occur (for if it were not going to occur, as is really possible, then such fore-knowledge would never have existed beforehand), it follows that, with the antecedent of the proof having been conceded, then the conse-quence should be denied, since the thing's being such that it will occur in just the way it is foreknown coheres straightforwardly with its being really able not to occur; for if, as is really possible, it were not going to occur in that way, then God would never have foreknown that it was going to occur. Therefore, the divine foreknowledge in question is

---

absolutely and without any hypotheses what was going to occur, came after all the causing of things on God's part was completed (a causing that is completed by such a decree), this knowledge is clearly not a cause of things. And the certitude of this knowledge depends on both the decree of the divine will and the certitude of middle knowledge."

[64]See sec. 5 above.

[65]The proof is that a future contingent is nothing other than a thing that is indifferently able to occur and able not to occur.

[66]The "other" antecedent is that no future thing foreknown by God is able not to occur. Molina has already claimed that this antecedent is false if taken in the divided sense, but he now claims that this is the only sense that is of use to the argument. At best, the proof establishes only the composed sense, which is equivalent to (A) 'It is impossible that something foreknown by God never occur.' Molina, of course, can accept (A) with equa-nimity.

indeed incompatible with the thing's turning out otherwise, but it is perfectly compatible with the thing's merely *being able* to turn out otherwise. Still, if it were going to turn out otherwise, then that foreknowledge would not have existed. For it is a foreknowledge that imposes *no necessity or certitude of the consequent* on future things, but rather leaves them as uncertain in themselves and in relation to their causes as they would be if there were no such foreknowledge.

37. *Response to the fifth argument.* As for the fifth argument,[67] the major premise should be denied. The reason is the same as that which we gave in response to the third argument. For since our knowledge and cognition do not have more certitude than there is certitude in the object considered in its own right, it follows that if we were to have certain knowledge of future contingents and if propositions about those same things were determinately true, then that would be because the things in themselves were certainly and determinately going to be—something that could be the case for no other reason than that the things in themselves were necessary with a necessity of the consequent.[68] However, as has been repeatedly explained, because of the acumen and perfection of the knower, God's knowledge of future contingents, which have no certitude *from themselves or from their causes*, is absolutely certain. Thus, from the fact that future contingents are known by *God* with certainty it does not follow that they are going to occur necessarily in reality—in the way that this *would* follow if *our* cognition of those things were certain or if the propositions *we* form about those things were determinately true.

38. *Response to the sixth argument.* As for the sixth argument,[69] the antecedent should be denied. As for the proof, the major may be conceded, that is, we may concede that the following consequence is necessary and perfectly valid: 'From eternity God foreknew that Peter was going to sin tomorrow; therefore, Peter is going to sin tomorrow.' But the minor should be denied if it has the following sense: 'Whoever does not have the power to negate the antecedent of a valid consequence does not have the power to negate (that is, not to posit) a consequent that it

---

[67] See sec. 6 above. The major premise is that things signified by future contingent propositions are no less necessary if God's knowledge of them is determinately true than if the future-tense propositions that signify those same things are themselves determinately true.

[68] As was pointed out in n. 4 above, Molina here seems to equate a proposition's being *determinately* true with its being now unpreventable by any secondary causes.

[69] See sec. 7 above. The antecedent is that foreknowledge of future things destroys freedom of choice.

follows from the antecedent must be posited.' (It is only as taken in this sense that the minor premise is of any use to the argument, since for Peter not to sin tomorrow in the way foreknown by God is not for Peter to *negate* anything, but is rather for him *not to posit* the sin that it necessarily follows from the antecedent must be posited.) This premise should be denied, because if the consequent were not going to be posited, as it possibly will not be, then God would never have foreknown that Peter was going to sin, and thus the antecedent would not have obtained. Therefore, even though it is no longer within the power of either Peter or God Himself to bring it about that there was no such foreknowledge in God, it *is* nonetheless within Peter's power at present to do something (that is, not sin) which is such that if, as he is able to, he were to do it, then that antecedent would never have obtained. Therefore, it does not follow from Peter's power not to sin that in a valid consequence there can be a true antecedent and a false consequent, since if he were not going to sin, as is possible, then the antecedent in question would never have obtained at all.

39. I think it is sufficiently clear from what we have said thus far that (i) our freedom of choice and the contingency of things is perfectly compatible with divine foreknowledge, and that (ii) such foreknowledge in no way prevents it from being the case that with the help of God, who will always furnish as much help as each person needs, it is within our power to avoid all mortal sins, to recover from them after a lapse, and in the end either to attain or to lose eternal life, and that (iii) if we do not attain eternal life, then we ourselves are to blame in just the way we would be if there were in God no foreknowledge of future things.

Now, God foreknows those things that are relevant to our salvation or damnation in the same way that He foreknows those things that are relevant to other future contingent effects; nor do the former acquire any more necessity from the divine foreknowledge than the latter. Surely, a farmer would be considered crazy if, worried about God's fore-knowledge, he became remiss in sowing his seed and if for this reason, lured by the idea that God foreknows everything from eternity and that things are going to occur just as He foreknew they would, he did not plant his seed or was going to plant less than he otherwise would have. For since the foreknowledge neither helps nor hinders him, he shall reap as he has sown. (The more seed he has planted, the more he will reap; but if he has planted nothing, then he will harvest nothing—a situation he ought afterward to attribute not to God's foreknowledge but to his own stupidity and negligence.) So, too, we should regard as much more insane someone who, worried about God's foreknowledge and lured by a similar line of reasoning, became more remiss and lax in acting righteously, in restraining his drives, in overcoming temptation, and in doing those things that are required in order to attain a greater reward of beatitude; nor should he afterward blame God's foreknowledge and predestination, but rather he should blame himself—especially since, whereas the farmer's labor might be wasted because of adverse weather or chance events, this man by contrast can be deprived of the fruits of his labor by no cause other than his own will. Indeed, he will find that the more strongly he binds himself in obedience to God, the more prepared and prompt God always is to bestow more gifts.

The example that has been used concerning the farmer could also have been adapted to the sick man who, relying on the fact that God foreknows the future, decides not to avail himself of the cure for his illness; and to the soldier who, lured by the same idea, goes into battle unprotected by any weapons; and to infinitely many other cases.

Therefore, with not a worry at all about the divine foreknowledge, let us, in accord with the advice of St. Peter [2 Pet. 1:10], busy ourselves so that by good works we might do what we are called to do. For just as the devil, who has understood far better than we have that God foreknows all things, caring not a bit about the divine foreknowledge, leaves no stone unturned and carefully roams about and circles the earth, seeking whom he might devour,[70] so too let us, freed from every care about the divine foreknowledge, diligently work out our salvation, relying on God's help; for in this way it will come to pass that without any doubt we will attain eternal happiness. And in this regard it should be sufficient for each of us to keep in mind that God is God, that is, infinite wisdom, goodness, etc., in order that in these matters, which are beyond the understanding of many, we might commit ourselves firmly to God's goodness and providence and busy ourselves to the extent of our power with those things that it is our responsibility, with God's help, to look after most diligently.

[70]The wording here parallels 1 Pet. 5:8.

DISPUTATION 53

On Predeterminations, and Where the Certitude
of God's Knowledge of Future Contingents Comes From

In Order That This Disputation Might Be More Perspicuous,
and Lest It Engender Annoyance because of Its Length,
It Will Be Divided into Four Parts.

Part I
The Position of Others on Both the Topics
Mentioned in the Title

1. There are those who, in order to propound and defend, with respect to all the nonevil acts of free choice, divine predeterminations of a sort that completely destroy freedom of choice with respect to those acts, argue against and try with all their might to resist the middle knowledge that we established in the preceding and other earlier disputations and that we deduced from their own principles and corroborated with the testimony of the Scriptures, the holy Fathers, and even the Scholastics (though they do not call such knowledge by that name).[1]

2. For they maintain[2] that all things in general (with the exception of sinful acts) are such that it depends solely on the free predetermination of the divine will whether they are with certainty going to be or are with certainty not going to be.

---

[1] Disputation 53 initially appeared in the second edition of the *Concordia* (1595) as a response to criticisms of the first edition version of Part IV, and most especially as a response to the criticisms set forth by Francisco Zumel in his *In Primam Divae Thomae Partem Commentaria* (Salamanca, 1590). (See Disputation 47, n. 10.) In several of the notes below I cite those parts of Zumel's text which parallel Molina's characterizations of the position of "those who disagree with us." These references are due to Rabeneck.

[2] Zumel, *Commentaria*, q. 14, a. 1, disp. unica, concl. 1 and 2, pp. 36off.

[196]

And so they claim, further, that just as, with respect to all the things that emanate immediately from Him alone as well as with respect to those things that afterward issue forth from the first things merely by a necessity of nature, God has nothing but (i) purely *natural* knowledge, which precedes the free act of the divine will, and (ii) purely *free* knowledge, which follows upon that same act, so too the same thing holds for those future contingents whose proximate source of contingency is created free choice, as long as they are not moral evils.

Now the things that are produced immediately by God alone or that afterward issue forth from just those first things by a necessity of nature are, before the free act of the divine will, only known purely *naturally* as *merely possible*, whereas after the divine predetermination or free act of the divine will by which God decides to produce just those first things or to cooperate with them by His general concurrence in the production of the other things that emanate from them thereafter, they are *freely* known with certainty as *future* in that very predetermination or free act of will; so, too, they claim, all the things that depend on created free choice, both angelic and human, and that are not morally evil—whether God cooperates in their production with special and supernatural assistance—or only with general assistance—are known by purely *natural* knowledge alone *prior to* the divine predetermination or free act of the divine will by which He decides to create free choice, to situate it within such-and-such an order of things and circumstances, to assist it naturally or supernaturally in such-and-such a way, and to cooperate with it. But they are *not* known in *any* way, even under a hypothesis, through that middle knowledge posited by us, a knowledge that, they contend, could not have existed in God. Rather, by the very fact that He predetermined all the things just enumerated, in and from this predetermination alone He knew with certainty through His *free* knowledge that they were going to be, since this volition or predetermination of God's so to cooperate with created free choice is a divine volition that is *efficacious* in such a way that each of those future contingents follows upon it, and the concurrence, whether natural or supernatural, by which He decides for His part so to cooperate in time is an *efficacious concurrence*, and hence, given the existence of such a divine predetermination, the effect is not able in the *composed* sense not to follow—though they add that in the *divided* sense it is able not to follow.

So these authors[3] not only divide God's *supernatural* aids into those that are intrinsically and by their nature efficacious for moving a created

---

[3] Ibid., q. 23, a. 3, disp. 7, concl. 1, p. 669, and disp. 8, pp. 674ff. This paragraph contains a response to comments made by Molina against Bañez in Disputation 50, sec. 13.

faculty of choice and those that by their nature are inefficacious for this, but they also divide in the same way God's *natural* aids and concurrences with regard to the nonevil acts of free choice. And so they maintain that when God's efficacious assistance or concurrence is present, then the consent and nonevil effect of free choice to which God is moving the faculty of choice follows with certainty, whereas when it is absent, then the effect is with certainty not going to follow, even if an assistance or concurrence that is intrinsically inefficacious is present. Indeed, they claim that what follows is an act of free choice that is only as intense as was the efficacious assistance or concurrence by which the faculty of choice was moved by God to such an act, so that all the certitude that the act is going to occur here and now, as well as all the certitude that it will be just so intense or just so languid, stems from the character of the concurrence by which God moves the faculty of choice and cooperates with it.

Accordingly, they go on to assert[4] that all the certitude of the divine knowledge regarding whether or not these future contingents are going to be depends solely on the predetermination by which God decides to cooperate in this or that way with free choice and to move it to nonevil acts. For if He decides to move it by an assistance that is intrinsically efficacious, then it will certainly and inevitably consent and elicit the act, since a divine volition of this sort is efficacious for the occurrence of such an act and hence cannot be frustrated. If, on the other hand, He decides not to move free choice in this way, then, even if He should decide to move it by an assistance that is not intrinsically efficacious, it will certainly and inevitably *not* consent or elicit the act, since *this* sort of volition is inefficacious with respect to the act's occurring thereafter. So given just God's *natural* knowledge, by which He knew all the things that were possible by virtue of created choice, by the very fact that God predetermined or decided from eternity to cooperate in this or that way in time and to move or determine the faculty of choice efficaciously (that is, with an assistance or concurrence that is of its very self efficacious), He knew certainly and infallibly, in and from that very predetermination, which nonevil acts of free choice were going to occur—and He knew this *without any sort of middle knowledge* by which He might foresee what would happen on the hypothesis that He should decide to move and assist free choice in that way. For by the very fact that He decides to move it in that way and to determine it to an act, free choice is in the composed sense not able not to elicit such an act; and the fact that the motion and concurrence that God will furnish in time are efficacious *does not in any*

[4]Ibid., q. 14, a. 13, disp. 7, pp. 450ff.

way depend on free choice, as though it were within the power of free choice to render this concurrence efficacious or inefficacious by freely consenting to it or not consenting to it.[5]

3. Consequently, in addition to what has been said thus far, they claim further that before (in our way of conceiving it) God's eternal predestination there is in God an election of some persons for eternal happiness through an absolute and efficacious volition, *prior to* any foreknowledge of the circumstances and future use of free choice, even under a future hypothesis; and likewise there is a rejection of other persons by a similarly absolute volition.[6] Now they maintain that the predestination of an adult is accomplished in a predetermination or volition to confer efficacious aids, aids by means of which the created faculty of choice is determined in such a way that it performs its works with certainty (the certitude arising antecedently from the character of the aids) and perseveres in those of its works through which it attains eternal life. Thus, they trace *all* the certitude that there will be such good use of free choice, and hence all the certitude that these good works will occur and be persevered in until death, back to the efficaciousness of the aids and, consequently, back to God's predetermination or, if you will, God's eternal, absolute, and efficacious volition to confer these aids in time. And *this* is the source, they maintain, of *all* the certitude and infallibility of the free knowledge by which God knows, after that predetermination, that those good works are going to occur and that there is going to be a good use of free choice; and this certitude does *not* in

[5] Molina's view is that one and the same instance of divine concurrence (whether natural or supernatural) with respect to an agent *S*'s freely performing a morally good action *A* is by its nature capable of being efficacious and also capable of being inefficacious. More precisely, such concurrence is *rendered* efficacious or inefficacious *extrinsically*, by *S*'s own choice as to whether or not to perform *A*. Thus, this sort of divine aid is not *intrinsically* efficacious or *intrinsically* inefficacious, but is compatible both with *S*'s freely performing *A* and with *S*'s freely refraining from performing *A*. It follows that God cannot know what *S* will do simply on the basis of His predetermination to grant the concurrence in question to *S*. He must also know what *S* would freely do were such concurrence to be granted—and this, of course, is where middle knowledge enters the picture. In sec. 3 below the same point is applied to predestination and reprobation in general and not just to individual actions. See Sections 2.8–2.9 of the Introduction.

[6] Election is related to predestination as the intending of an end is related to the choosing of means to that end. So in election God wills for certain individuals the glory of beatitude and in predestination He wills for them the means to this glory, namely, grace.

On Molina's view election and predestination are both willed in light of God's middle knowledge. This position, however, is optional for one who posits middle knowledge. Suarez, for instance, seems to have held with the Thomists that God elects individuals prior to (in our way of conceiving it) and independently of any knowledge of their use of free choice. Middle knowledge enters the picture only when God, in predestining the elect, chooses means that He knows through His middle knowledge will be efficacious.

addition have its source in any kind of middle knowledge by which, because of the depth of His intellect, God might, *before that predetermination,* see what would be done by the faculty of choice assisted by the aids in question—as though (i) despite God's deciding for His part to help out in this way, the opposite might be able to occur because of created choice and as though (ii) if this were going to happen, then God would have foreknown it. For because they deny that free choice is in the composed sense able to do the opposite when it is assisted by these aids or while that eternal predetermination of God's is in effect, they consequently deny that there is such a thing as a middle knowledge by which God might have been able to know *indifferently* that the one thing or the other was going to occur, solely because of the freedom of created choice, on the hypothesis that He for His part should will to assist it in the way in question.

4. In accord with these same principles, they also teach[7] that every nonevil act or effect of free choice is individually provided for by God in such a way that it will certainly and inevitably occur in the particular way in which it occurs solely because of the order of divine providence or predetermination; and they are irritated by those who affirm the contrary. For these authors contend that (i) *no* act of this sort—even if it is purely natural, and indifferent in itself with respect to being morally good, and extremely easy to perform—is able to occur without an intrinsically efficacious concurrence on God's part, a concurrence by which the faculty of choice is premoved and determined to perform the act, and that (ii) when this concurrence and premotion of God's are present, the faculty of choice is not able in the composed sense not to consent or not to perform the act.[8] And this is why they claim that since God from eternity provides for each such act or effect of free choice by resolving beforehand to contribute this sort of efficacious premotion and determination of free choice, each of these acts is certain and inevitable because of such a predetermination or, if you will, because of the order of divine providence.

---

[7]Zumel, *Commentaria,* q. 22, a. 4, disp. unica, concl. 2 and 3, pp. 607–608.

[8]According to the Thomists, divine concurrence is an action of God's *directly upon* the created agent (directly upon the creature's will in the case of free actions). This action of God's is said to move the created agent prior to and as a necessary condition of that agent's then moving (that is, acting) in its characteristic way to bring about the effect in question. Hence the term 'premotion'. In contrast, Molina holds that divine concurrence is an action of God's *along with* (rather than *upon*) the created agent to bring about the effect. That is, the effect produced, rather than the agent, is the direct or immediate terminus of God's action, just as it is the direct or immediate terminus of the created agent's action. For Molina's own discussion of the differences between his understanding of concurrence and St. Thomas's, see Disputation 26 (Rabeneck, pp. 164–170).

5. The same authors[9] pose the question of whether God knows that those contingent things would have existed which never will exist but which Scripture tells us would have existed on some condition that neither has obtained nor will obtain; such things these authors accordingly call *conditioned* future contingents. Numbered among them are the things we made mention of in Disputation 49,[10] namely, (i) the repentance of the Tyronians and Sidonians, on the condition that the wonders worked in Chorozain and Bethsaida had been worked in their presence; (ii) the descent of Saul into Keilah and David's being given over into the hands of Saul, on the condition that David not flee from that place; and (iii) the future lapse of certain of the righteous into mortal sin, on the condition that God had not mercifully taken them by premature death from this iniquitous world.

6. Now, having rejected as dangerous the position of those who deny that God knows that these things would have existed on a condition or hypothesis, these authors rightly defend the contrary position. They add, however, that since these things were never going to exist, God knows them only as *possible,* in just the way He also knows the other things that are able to exist and yet never will. For they refuse to countenance a middle ground between what is *absolutely future* and what is *merely possible*—and they do this in order to avoid middle knowledge. And yet in the matter under discussion, unless they want to fall into the dangerous position of those others who reject and clearly want to resist the words of Christ in Matthew 11, they have to countenance such a middle ground, that is, a *conditional future* that comes closer to the absolute future than it would if it were not *future* on the given condition, but were instead *merely possible* on that condition.[11] For since (i) the repentance of the Tyronians and Sidonians and the repentance of the inhabitants of Chorozain and Bethsaida were both equally *possible,* and since (ii) on the hypothesis that the *same* wonders should be performed in both regions, Christ asserted that the repentance of the Tyronians and Sidonians *would have* occurred, even though the repentance of the

[9]Zumel, *Commentaria,* q. 14, a. 13, disp. 8, concl. 2 and 3, pp. 455ff.

[10]See Disputation 49, sec. 9.

[11]Matt. 11:20–24. The text goes as follows (New American Bible translation): "He began to reproach the towns where most of his miracles had been worked, with their failure to reform: 'It will go ill with you, Chorozain! And just as ill with you, Bethsaida! If the miracles worked in you had taken place in Tyre and Sidon, they would have reformed in sackcloth and ashes long ago. I assure you, it will go easier for Tyre and Sidon than for you on the day of judgment. As for you, Capernaum, "Are you to be exalted to the skies? You shall go down to the realm of death!" If the miracles worked in you had taken place in Sodom, it would be standing today. I assure you, it will go easier for Sodom than for you on the day of judgment.'"

inhabitants of Chorozain and Bethsaida did *not* occur *on that very same hypothesis,* but instead merely remained in the realm of something *possible,* it clearly follows that they have to countenance the middle ground that we are pointing to between what is *future absolutely* and what is *merely possible.* For it was because there was going to be less hardness of heart and culpability of choice among the Tyronians and Sidonians, given that hypothesis, than there was guilt and hardness of heart among the inhabitants of Chorozain and Bethsaida that Christ on that score preferred the Tyronians and Sidonians to the inhabitants of Chorozain and Bethsaida, and said that it was going to be easier for the former than for the latter on the day of judgment. I claimed that such a middle ground has to be countenanced unless they want to fall into the dangerous position that they reject, since the proponents of that dangerous position were most assuredly not denying that God knows conditioned future things of this sort as things that are *possible,* but rather only that He knows them as things midway between those that are *absolutely future* and those that are *merely possible* because of the faculty of choice. That is, they were denying not that He knows them as *absolutely* future but that He knows them as *conditionally* future, that is, future on a hypothesis that will never obtain.

7.   Notice at this point that since the authors with whom we disagree trace all the certitude that contingent things will occur back to efficacious concurrence or assistance and thus back to God's predetermination to confer it, whereas, on the other hand, the wonders that were worked at Chorozain and Bethsaida were not by themselves alone an intrinsically efficacious assistance, given that the inhabitants of those places were not converted by them, it follows that these authors believe and (if you ponder their words) are claiming that (i) on the hypothesis in question, taken by itself, the inhabitants of Tyre and Sidon would *not* have been converted either, but rather that (ii) they would have been converted only if God had simultaneously predetermined to confer *efficacious* assistance on them, assistance such that had He likewise predetermined to confer it on the inhabitants of Chorozain and Bethsaida, then they too would have been converted. Hence, you see that in order to avoid middle knowledge and to provide a ground for intrinsically efficacious concurrences or aids, as well as predeterminations of the sort just explicated, they weaken and distort these words of Christ's in Matthew 11. For if, on the hypothesis that *those very wonders* should have been worked in Tyre and Sidon, the Tyronians and Sidonians would not have been converted unless God had, *in addition,* predetermined to confer on them some *other* assistance, intrinsically efficacious, which was not in fact conferred on them and with which the people of Chorozain

and Bethsaida would have been converted had it likewise been predetermined for them—if this is so, then, I ask, what is it that Christ is reproaching the people of Chorozain and Bethsaida for, given that (i) the Tyronians and Sidonians need no less assistance than those people need in order to be converted, and given that (ii), according to the position of these doctors, both groups, taken in themselves, are equally likely to be converted or not to be converted, and given that (iii) their being converted or not being converted depends no more on the free choice of the one group than on that of the other? In fact, however, the correct interpretation of Christ's words is the one we proposed in Disputation 40, where we showed that the assistance of grace is not efficacious or inefficacious *by its very nature*, but rather that its being efficacious or inefficacious depends on whether or not the faculty of choice that is moved and stirred by it wills to consent to and cooperate with it—as the Council of Trent clearly taught.[12]

8. Now even though both things are necessary for our conversion, namely, that (i) God stir and move our faculty of choice by the assistance of supervening grace and that (ii) the faculty of choice consent and cooperate, still, since God is always generously ready to stir and move us by the assistance of grace if we do not stand in His way, and since miracles worked in our presence have the greatest power to move us to consent (as we showed in the same place), it follows that Christ, who is prepared to help everyone through the assistance of prevenient and cooperating grace, justifiably reproached the inhabitants of Chorozain and Bethsaida.[13] For although so many signs and wonders had been worked in their presence, they willed for their part not to give their consent to repentance and conversion, a repentance and conversion to which the Tyronians and Sidonians would have given their consent, had those very same signs been worked in their presence.

9. After having read our works, the authors with whom we disagree[14] now propose yet a second way in which God knows infallibly and

[12]Disputation 40 is found in Rabeneck, pp. 244–257. The passage cited from Trent appears in session 6, *Decretum de iustificatione*, found in H. Denzinger and A. Schönmetzer, *Enchiridion Symbolorum*, 32d ed. (Freiburg, 1963), 1520–1583 (new numbering), pp. 368–381 (hereafter cited as Denzinger).

[13]*Prevenient* grace and *cooperating* grace are two types of *actual* (as opposed to *habitual*) grace. *Prevenient* grace is a supernatural influence on the will, disposing it toward consent to a good action, whereas *cooperating* grace is God's supernatural concurrence with the action. As one might expect, the differences between the Bañezian and Molinist accounts of God's general concurrence surface again in their accounts of cooperating grace.

[14]Zumel, *Commentaria*, q. 14, a. 13, disp. 8, concl. 5, pp. 458–459; q. 14, a. 1, disp. unica, concl. 2, p. 361, and concl. 5, p. 364.

with certainty which contingent things are going to exist and which are not—a way different from that, explicated above, according to which God individually predetermines the acts of created free choice through an efficacious concurrence or assistance. They propose this second way, even though they do not use it in the development of their theory, but instead adhere solely to the first way, which they had heretofore taught exclusively and in accordance with which they had propounded the rest of their teaching.

10. They claim that (i) by the comprehension of His essence, in which, as in a primary object, He comprehends all the other things in a way that is most eminent and far more excellent than that in which they exist in themselves (just as we ourselves were claiming), God knows all the things that are in fact going to exist because of created choice on the hypothesis that He should decide to create it in such-and-such an order of things and circumstances, intending that it should do these particular things and permitting it to do those particular things, and yet that (ii) God *does not determine* the will itself in particular, but rather leaves it free to refrain from acting or to turn itself toward one or the other part. They add, however, that God knows this through *natural* knowledge in His essence and in the ideas, which *naturally* represent to God, not only in possible existence but in future existence as well, all the things that are going to exist because of created free choice. For, they say, since (i) on the hypothesis that the faculty of choice should be created and situated in this or that order of things and circumstances, one part of each contradictory pair of future contingents that are within its power is going to obtain, and since (ii) the idea by which that part is naturally represented to the divine intellect does not begin to exist in God in time, one has to acknowledge that such an idea exists in God from eternity, before the free act of His will. For all things, including future contingents in their future existence, exist eminently in the essence itself insofar as the essence is *prior to* (in our way of conceiving it) that act.[15]

11. Even though all these points have, with a few changes, been plucked from our own doctrine, still, they are far removed from it, as their authors rightly affirm. Indeed, to the extent that these points deviate from our doctrine, they seem designed to circumvent our middle

---

[15] Sometimes the cause of an effect is both *nonunivocal* (that is, different in species from the effect) and of a *metaphysically higher* species than the effect. In such a case, before its production the effect is said to exist *eminently* (that is, in a higher way) in its cause. Thus, creatures are said to exist eminently in the divine essence before God's free act of willing them into existence.

knowledge and thereby to do away completely with the freedom of choice that these authors appeared to be affirming when they (i) abandoned predeterminations via an efficacious concurrence on God's part which would determine each act individually, and hence (ii) left the faculty of choice free to turn itself toward whichever part it might choose.

12.   This new doctrine, first of all, seems to allege that one part of a contradiction concerning those future contingents dependent on our free choice is determinately true before the future contingents exist, and thus that this part is *naturally* represented as determinately future in an idea or, if you will, in the divine essence—a claim that we rejected in the preceding disputation as contrary to the teaching of Aristotle and to the common position of the Doctors, and as incompatible with the very nature of future contingents, which are, as such, indifferent, so that each of them might exist or might not exist, as we showed in our commentary on the *De Interpretatione*, book 1, last chapter.[16] Nor is it possible to understand how it might be the case both that (i) one part of a contradiction is determinately going to obtain because of free choice itself and also that (ii) the faculty of choice is free to posit in reality either part indifferently.

13.   Next, one might argue as follows: Take the divine idea that, because choice by its freedom is going to turn itself toward the one part of the contradiction, represents this part as future by virtue of the created faculty of choice on the hypothesis that it should be created in such an order of things and circumstances. Now either (i) that idea would represent the opposite part if the faculty of choice, as it is able to, were by that same freedom going to turn itself toward the opposite part or (ii) it would not represent the opposite part, but is instead an idea that represents the first part *altogether naturally,* just as it would if it were in no way able to represent the opposite part and if the faculty of choice were thus determined to that first part.

If you posit the first alternative,[17] then, since the nature of a divine idea is the same as the nature of the divine knowledge that corresponds to that idea, you are actually countenancing the middle knowledge which you shrink from and so often repudiate and without which our freedom of choice cannot be preserved intact. For just as that idea is able

---

[16]See Disputation 52, n. 27.
[17]The first alternative is that the idea in question would have represented the opposite part of the contradiction if the will were going to turn itself to that part.

to represent the contrary and would *in fact* have represented it if, as is possible, the contrary were going to obtain because of created choice, so too through the knowledge that corresponds to that idea and that precedes the free act of His will God would have known the contrary, even though that knowledge is still *natural* in God as opposed to *free*—granting, however, that it is *nonnatural* when contrasted with the knowledge that is so innate in God that what is known through it is such that its contrary is neither able to obtain nor able to be known by God through that knowledge.

Suppose, on the other hand, that you posit the second alternative, namely, that the idea of, say, Peter's consent to fornication represents this consent *naturally* to God as future, as though it were altogether innate to God to represent it in such a way that the representation in question is not at all able not to exist, with the result that Peter's choice is determined to that consent and that the consent is not able not to occur in the future. In what sense, I ask, are you preserving Peter's freedom not to sin? What's more, exactly the same point applies to the rest of his free actions.

14. Beyond this, the opinion under discussion is unsatisfactory in that it posits in God ideas that represent things in their future existence *before* the free act of the divine will. For an idea represents the thing of which it is an idea only in *possible* existence; and it represents the way in which such a thing can come to be and its very coming to be or existence only as *possible* and as a way in which the thing is *able*, in an exercised act, to be posited in existence. Now, things follow with their actual existence from the artist's knowledge as *determined by* the same artist's freely willing that the thing be committed to execution in accord with the idea and knowledge; and so none of the things in question is known as future except in the free volition of the artist, though before the artist's free volition they are known as *future on the hypothesis* that the artist should will to commit them to execution. But when things depend on *two* free artists, in the way that the things that come to be from the created choice of angels and human beings depend both (i) on God, who creates the faculty of choice in this or that order of things and decides to cooperate with it in this or that way, and at the same time (ii) on the influence of created choice, then surely in order for the things to be known as *future on a hypothesis*, it is necessary that the free determination of *both* wills be posited. But God knows the determination of a created faculty of choice before it exists because of the infinite and unlimited perfection of His intellect and because of the preeminent comprehension by which He comprehends that faculty in His essence in a way far deeper than that in

which it exists in itself; and thus on the hypothesis that He should will to situate it in such-and-such an order of things and circumstances, He knows which part it will in its freedom turn itself toward. I should also caution that since the being and the existence of the things in question are altogether the same whether the things are apprehended as possible or as actually existing, it is not required, in order to comprehend a thing, that everything falling within its power be known in *future* existence. For if that were so, then God—not just if He had decided not to create anything, but even now—would not comprehend Himself, since He is not able to know in future existence everything that falls under His omnipotence. So in order to comprehend a thing it is sufficient that everything that it is able to produce, along with the existence of each of those things, be known in *possible* existence, as has been said elsewhere in the commentary on the First Part.[18]

15. The same authors[19] propose yet a third way in which God, even before the free act of His will, knows with certainty which contingent things are going to exist. For, they claim, since at that prior moment God comprehends His own essence, power, and will through the knowledge that precedes His act of will, He surely knows at that prior moment what His will is going to determine itself to, and thus He knows which contingent things are actually going to exist and which ones would exist on the hypothesis that He should decide to determine His will in some other way. But this is to know not only *actual* future contingents but also *conditioned* future contingents, such as the repentance of the Tyronians and Sidonians, and the descent of Saul into Keilah and David's being given over into the hands of Saul.

16. They argue for this proposal as follows: The divine will is, as it were, guided to such an extent by the divine intellect and by the eternal natures[20] belonging to God's infinite wisdom that all things, even as far as their future existence is concerned, are contained in and shine forth in the ideas of God, the supreme artist. So even though things that are contingently future do not have the stability to be actually future before the free decree of the divine will and cannot be known as actually future

[18]See *Commentaria*, q. 12, a. 7 and 8, pp. 120b–140b. Also, see sec. 20 below. Molina's point above is that since many pairs of contingent states of affairs which are within God's power to effect are by their very nature incompossible with one another, He cannot know all such states of affairs as future. But it hardly follows from this that God does not comprehend all such states of affairs or all the individuals involved in them.

[19]Zumel, *Commentaria*, q. 14, a. 13, disp. 8, concl. 6, pp. 459ff.; q. 14, a. 1, disp. unica, concl. 2, p. 362.

[20]The Latin term here is *rationes aeternae*. See Disputation 49, secs. 5 and 6, and n. 4.

except by being related to such a decree, nonetheless, to the extent that (i) at that prior moment they are contained in and shine forth in the ideal natures and that (ii) such a decree, which occurs *later* in our way of conceiving it, is comprehended and seen as future, surely at that prior moment it is known which contingent things are actually going to exist by virtue of that same decree or, if you will, free determination of the divine will. For if the determination of the will were not known in that prior moment, and if it thus were not known which contingent things would actually come to exist by virtue of such a determination, then at that prior moment God's knowledge would not be comprehensive, absolutely universal and absolutely perfect, since there would be something hidden at that moment from God's knowledge which He would later come to know. But no such thing may be affirmed of the divine knowledge in that prior moment.

17. In the first place, those who talk this way cannot, by appealing to the decree of the divine will and to the fact that future contingents depend on that decree, deny that God has middle knowledge of future contingents, unless they want to deny that there is freedom of choice in God with respect to His decree. For clearly there could not have been in God any sort of knowledge through which He knew, *before* the decree of His will, what that decree would determine itself to and hence which contingent things were going to exist because of that decree. For that decree was able to determine itself to other things or to decide to create nothing at all; but if that had been going to happen, as was possible, then the knowledge in question would not have existed in God. It follows that even if the knowledge of the determination of His decree as well as of the future things that depend on it was *natural* in God, as opposed to *free*, in that it preceded the act of His will, still it was not so innate in God that it was not able not to have existed; and so the knowledge in question is *middle* knowledge, which the authors whom we disagree with deny exists in God before the free act of His will. And notice that since this knowledge not only precedes any act of the divine will, but is also a cognition by which the will is, as it were, illuminated and guided in its willing, it follows that as long as an object is being shown to God through this knowledge—whether it is an object to which His will can be moved only naturally or an object or objects to which it can be moved freely—the knowledge in question can in no way be *free*, but must instead be altogether *natural*, as opposed to *free*.[21]

---

[21]As was pointed out in Disputation 52, n. 25, God wills some things *necessarily* or *naturally* (for example, love of self, the generation of the Son, the spiration of the Holy

18. Second, this position is unsatisfactory in that it claims that in a divine idea there is a representation of future contingents in their future existence. For, as was said above, both the nature of those things and their existence are represented and known through an idea only as *possible* and only with respect to the way in which the things are *able to be* posited in existence—and *not* as future, since this depends on the determination of the artist's will, a determination that is *posterior* to the idea and to the representation via the idea.[22] Nor can the determination of the divine will be represented in an idea, both because (i) there are ideas only of creatures and not of the divine will or its determination, and also because (ii) the divine will is in itself indifferent and free to determine itself to whichever part it chooses, and, accordingly, before that determination there neither is nor can be anything in God that shows which part His will is going to determine itself to. And since there is no nature superior to God that might contain Him in an absolutely eminent way, as He Himself contains every *created* faculty of choice in an absolutely eminent way, it is most certainly not the case that just as, because of the infinite excess of His cognition over and beyond the being and perfection of any created faculty of choice and because of the absolutely eminent way in which He comprehends it, He knows which part a created faculty of choice is going to turn itself toward by its freedom, so too He or some other being knows, before the determination of His will, which part He is going to turn Himself toward. Nor is this required in order for Him to be said to *comprehend* Himself in that prior moment, since in order for Him to comprehend Himself it is sufficient that He see all the things to which His power, His intellect, and His will can extend, and thus it is sufficient that He see in His will all the parts to which it is able to determine itself with respect to any given object. For He does not cease to comprehend Himself by virtue of the fact that there are many determinations He does not now know Himself to have had with respect to various objects, determinations such that He *could have* had them and would have known them if He had had them—for He knows that all those determinations were *possible* and were *future on the condition* that He should have willed to determine Himself to them. And, in the same way, He does not cease to comprehend Himself in that prior moment by

---

Spirit), and other things *freely* (for example, the existence of creatures). Molina's point here is that God's *knowledge* of the possible objects of His will must in either sort of case precede the act of His will if it is to guide that act. So the knowledge in question cannot, contrary to the claims of Molina's opponents, be a *free* knowledge of the divine decree or of future contingents.

[22]See sec. 14 above. Here have I translated the Latin *entitas* as 'nature' rather than 'being'. (See Disputation 52, n. 28.) The reason is that here it is contrasted with existence and hence signifies the content, as it were, of a kind-concept.

virtue of the fact that before His determination He does not know which part He is going to determine Himself to. For He sees all the things to which He can determine Himself and He sees that all those things are within the range of His power or choice, a power and choice that are known as free and as not in the least determined at that moment to one part with respect to every creatable object.

19.   Further, as we were saying in the preceding disputation,[23] I do not see how it can be the case both that (i) God knows, before the determination of His will, which part it is going to determine itself to and yet that (ii) afterward it determines itself to that part freely and not necessarily. For such a cognition would be infallible and certain, because it is God's, and it would be *natural* as opposed to *free*, as was shown above; for it would precede any free act on the part of the divine will, and it would be a cognitive act by which the divine will is, as it were, illuminated and guided in its first volition, and thus an act that cannot be free or commanded by the will, but is instead necessary. But I do not understand how it could possibly be the case that one and the same suppositum first knows, by means of this sort of certain and natural cognition, the future determination of its own will, and yet later determines itself to that part freely and not necessarily. And thus I do not understand how it would not be the case that all things happen by a necessity of nature, given that they emanate from and depend on such a cognition and such a determination of the will.

20.   In response to the argument for the contrary opinion,[24] it should be said that in order for the divine will to be guided, as it were, by the divine intellect and by the ideal natures in its willing, it is not necessary either that the ideas represent things in their future existence or that the cognition had by the divine intellect know them in their future existence. Rather, it is sufficient that the ideas represent the things and that the cognition knows them in their *possible* existence and as regards the way in which they are *able to be* produced. Hence, it should be denied that there is any other way in which future things shine forth or are represented in the divine ideas, or any other way in which they are known in that prior moment by the divine knowledge.

Now, as for what is added concerning the comprehension of the decree in question at that prior moment and concerning the comprehensiveness, universality, and perfection of the divine knowledge at that

[23]See Disputation 52, secs. 11ff.
[24]See sec. 14 above.

same prior moment, the following should be said: In order that something be comprehended it is not necessary that it be known as *future*—
for otherwise God would not comprehend things that will never exist—
but rather it is sufficient that all the *possible* modes of the thing be known;
and this is what God knows concerning His own free decree at that prior
moment. For in knowing each of its future or nonfuture modes in that
same now of eternity, He knows all the power, nature, and perfection of
the thing in question, as well as all the modes in which He can determine
it, just as later (in our way of conceiving it, with a basis in reality) He will
have decided to determine or not to determine those modes. This is
sufficient for the comprehension of the thing, especially in view of the
status it has when it is considered as *prior to* (in our way of conceiving it)
the decree's issuing forth within God. For just as it is not at all absurd for
God, as viewed in that prior moment (in our way of conceiving it) to be
understood as not yet having that decree or act of will—not only insofar
as that act has the character of a *free* act, but even insofar as it has the
character of the *natural* act by which God loves Himself[25]—so too for
even stronger reasons it is not at all absurd for His knowledge to be
understood as not yet having at that moment the character of a free
knowledge or cognition concerning which part the decree *will* freely
determine itself to, but only as having the character of a knowledge or
cognition concerning which parts it is freely *able to* determine itself to.
This is so especially because the fact that the decree in question will
determine itself to this or that part adds to the decree only a *relation of
reason,* as will become clear from what is going to be said in the course of
this First Part—a relation that is also such that it is known in that prior
moment as something possible and future, not as absolutely future but
rather as future *if* the will should decide to determine itself to the part in
question.[26]

Notice at this point that, in the matter we are now discussing, "priority
in our way of conceiving it, with a basis in reality" is not priority in the
sense that there actually is an instant of either nature or time in which
the one thing exists and the other does not, as Scotus holds and as will be
shown to be false in the course of this First Part.[27] Rather, this priority is
posited only in view of the fact that because of the dependence that an
act of will has on the intellect's knowledge, and not vice versa, the one
thing is conceived by us as presupposed when the other thing is still not
yet conceived. And yet the two are always conjoined in reality—indeed,

[25]See n. 21 above, and Disputation 52, n. 25.
[26]*Commentaria,* q. 14, a. 15, pp. 236b–238a.
[27]Ibid., q. 23, a. 4 and 5, disp. 1, memb. 8, pp. 314a–315b.

the acts of the divine intellect and will and the rest of the attributes mutually include one another, as will be explained in the material on the most Holy Trinity.[28] Therefore, just as, despite the fact that the attributes are conceived by us separately from one another, it is by no means the case that *in reality* the one lacks the perfection of the other, so too in the case at hand, despite the fact that the divine knowledge, to the extent that it is a prerequisite for the act of the will, is conceived of by us as not yet having adjoined to it a knowledge of the determination of that same act, it does not follow that there is in reality a moment when it exists without that knowledge—as though there were in reality a moment at which God's knowledge is *natural* without simultaneously having the added character of being *free* knowledge.

21.   In order that our argument might be fully satisfactory it must be added that the divine knowledge is not rendered more universal or more perfect by the fact that something future is known through it; otherwise, a certain perfection or universality of knowledge would be lacking in God by reason of the fact that (i) many things are not going to exist which are such that He could have decided that they should exist, and that (ii) if He had so decided, He would now know that they are going to exist, even though He does not in fact now know that they are going to exist. Therefore, since God knows these nonfuture things as possible and as future *on the condition* that He should have willed that they exist, it is neither a distinct perfection nor a greater perfection in God for Him to know something as future than it is for Him to know it as possible and as future on the condition that He should will or should have willed to create it. Hence, it follows that there is no less perfection and universality in God's knowledge if He knows a thing as absolutely future than if He instead knows it as possible and as future on a condition. Moreover, God's natural knowledge always has the free knowledge adjoined to it in reality, as has been said, even though the one type of knowledge is able to be *conceived by us* as existing before the other and without the other.

Part 2
The Foregoing Position Is Attacked

1.   The authors of the position set forth in the preceding part neither can reject nor seem to reject middle knowledge in God with respect to the morally *evil* acts of the created faculty of choice.

---

[28] Ibid., qq. 27–44, pp. 359a–514b.

2. For, first of all, with respect to such acts they do *not* posit an *efficacious* concurrence on God's part. Rather, they correctly attribute the fact that these acts result to the proper determination and influence of free choice itself, a determination and influence by which free choice in its freedom channels God's general concurrence to these acts, the general concurrence being in itself indifferent as to whether these acts or others, far different from them, should follow; and for this reason these authors agree with us in attributing sins, even taken materially,[1] not to God, who contributes His general concurrence, but rather to the faculty of choice itself as their proper and particular cause. This is clear from the things we reported in the preceding part and in Disputation 27.[2] Indeed, for morally evil acts they do not posit a divine general concurrence *on the cause*, that is, a concurrence by which God moves the cause and applies it to its operation, but instead they posit only a general concurrence *along with the cause* directly *on the effect*, as was reported in Disputation 27.[3]

3. Second, as we saw in the preceding part, with respect to those same acts they do not posit *divine predeterminations*, since God does not determine the created faculty of choice to those acts, but instead the faculty of choice determines itself to them in its own freedom and wickedness.[4]

4. Third, in the preceding disputation we supported middle knowledge with passages from the holy Fathers, where they teach that our acts of choice were not going to occur because God foreknew that they would occur, but that, to the contrary, it was because they were going to occur through freedom of choice that God foreknew them; now the authors with whom we disagree interpret this testimony as having to do with *sinful* acts, which *alone* they judge it to be true of, since God does not predetermine such acts, nor does He move or determine the faculty of choice to them.[5] But it is different with *nonevil* free acts, which, they claim, occur because they are predetermined by God and which are such that it is because of that predetermination *alone* that it is certain they will occur—and *not* because of any sort of middle knowledge, through which such things might, by virtue of the depth of the divine intellect and without any other predetermination, be foreknown as certainly future

---

[1] See Disputation 50, n. 18, for a brief discussion of the material element of sins.
[2] See Disputation 53, pt. 1, sec. 2; also, see Disputation 27, secs. 2–3 (Rabeneck, p. 171).
[3] Rabeneck, p. 171. Also, see Disputation 47, n. 22, and Disputation 53, pt. 1, n. 8.
[4] Zumel, *Commentaria*, q. 22, a. 4, disp. unica, concl. 4, p. 610.
[5] Ibid., q. 14, a. 1, disp. unica, concl. 6, p. 365.

on the hypothesis that the faculty of choice should be created and should be placed in a given order of things and circumstances.

5. Thus, (i) the knowledge by which God foresaw which *sins* were going to occur through which created faculty of choice is *certain* knowledge; and (ii) these authors cannot attribute the certitude of this knowledge to the predetermination of the divine will or to a determination by which the divine will directs the created faculty of choice toward evil acts, as is clear from the things that have been recounted from their theory; and (iii) there is nothing else that this certainty can be traced to other than the certainty of middle knowledge, a knowledge through which (a) because of the depth of His intellect and His absolutely eminent comprehension of the created faculty of choice, God knew with certainty in His essence something that in itself was uncertain and contingent vis-à-vis both parts, namely, which part the faculty of choice was by its freedom going to turn itself toward on the hypothesis that it should be situated in this or that order of things and circumstances, and through which (b) He would have known the contrary if the faculty of choice, as it is able to, was going to withhold its consent to the sin or was going to elicit its dissent. Since all this is so, it surely follows that these authors appear to countenance middle knowledge with respect to sinful acts— and this is attested to by many of the claims they make when they discuss sinful acts.

6. Perhaps, however, they, like those with whom we took issue in Disputation 50,[6] want to trace the certitude of the knowledge by which God knows which sins will occur back to the certainty and inevitability that a created will, by the very fact that it is not efficaciously determined by the divine will to act well, is going to sin with regard to the material element of any given virtue—as though in predetermining which nonevil acts created free choice is going to be determined to by an intrinsically efficacious concurrence or assistance, God sees with certainty (where the certainty stems from the object itself) *both* which *nonevil* acts are going to occur *and also* which *sins* are going to occur, whether by commission or omission, and with what degree of intensity or lassitude they will be elicited, and at what point in time, and with what other circumstances. It is as though the will were by that very fact unable to avoid the sins, but were instead, given that predetermination with respect to just the nonevil acts, determined in itself to perpetrate all these other things by commission or omission in a way contrary to right reason

[6]See Disputation 50, secs. 10ff.

and to the law of God. Again, it is as though it were the condition and intrinsic nature of each created faculty of choice, whether angelic or human, that at whatever moment of time and in whatever order of things and under whatever circumstances it might be situated—even if it is in the state of sanctifying grace, as were the angels and the first parents before their sin[7]—it will in that situation perpetrate all these things by commission or omission in opposition to right reason and the law of God, and it will perpetrate the things that it is then able to perpetrate by omission or commission with as much intensity as it can, *unless* God impedes it and draws it back thence toward nonevil acts through a determination via efficacious concurrence. It would thus have to be said that (i) every created faculty of choice is led spontaneously, to be sure, but by a necessity of nature into all the sins that it is able to commit and that (ii) it fails to fall into them only to the extent that it is subsequently drawn back and inhibited from committing sins by an assistance that is efficacious for eliciting nonevil acts. Indeed, all these points are necessary for preserving the certitude of God's knowledge of future sins on the theory in question. For if (i) free choice is not, through an innate propensity, carried by a necessity of nature into every kind of sin that it is able to perpetrate by commission or omission at any given instant and under any given circumstances, but if instead (ii) it has the power to refrain from a given sin, or to elicit the sinful act with more lassitude or more intensity, or to change any of the other circumstances, then clearly, given this theory alone, God will not know infallibly and with certainty which sins are going to occur, or what sort of sins they will be, or how grave they will be. This is abundantly self-evident. Look at the objections we raised against this view in Disputation 50.[8]

If, on the one hand, (i) God knows with certainty all the future *nonevil* acts of the created faculty of choice by reason of the fact that in the order of things which He decided to create He predetermined by His own free will alone to confer a concurrence, intrinsically efficacious for those acts, in the absence of which the faculty of choice is not able to elicit them and in the presence of which it is not able *not* to elicit them, while, on the other hand, (ii) He knows all future *sins* with certainty because by the very fact that He decided not to confer more or different efficacious concurrences for nonevil acts, the faculty of choice itself is certainly and

---

[7]Molina stresses here that the theory under discussion in this section is a *global* theory meant to apply to *all* evil acts, even those evil acts that, like the sin of the first parents, are original or primordial and hence in no way influenced by a strong inclination toward evil of the sort endemic to human nature after the Fall. I should also mention that I have here rendered the Latin *gratia gratum faciens* as 'sanctifying grace'.

[8]See Disputation 50, secs. 10 and 13–14.

inevitably going to fall into those sins in just the way they will occur and with just the circumstances with which they will occur in the course of time, so that, given that predetermination to nonevil acts, it is not within the power of the faculty of choice to avoid those sins—given all this, I do not understand how freedom of choice, whether with respect to good acts or bad acts or even indifferent acts, can endure intact, or how a fatalistic necessity with regard to all these things can be avoided, or, again, how the other very serious absurdities that we deduced from this theory in Disputation 50 would not follow from it; and consequently, I do not see why the theory we are arguing against should not be called a manifest error from the point of view of the faith.[9] To be sure, spontaneity and voluntariness of the sort that the Lutherans recognize in our faculty of choice and that is found in brute animals remains intact, since (i) the faculty of choice will consent to nonevil acts *without coercion* and cooperate with a concurrence that is intrinsically efficacious for *agreeably* moving it to elicit such acts, and since (ii) it falls into sins *by its own innate propensity* in the absence of a concurrence, efficacious for nonevil acts, by which it might be restrained and inhibited from sinning. Nevertheless, I do not understand how in that case it remains within its power *not* to consent to and *not* to cooperate with the concurrence that is efficacious for a nonevil act—a condition that is required for there to be any sort of freedom or moral good or merit. Nor do I understand how, in the absence of a concurrence that is efficacious for a nonevil act, the faculty of choice is able to refrain from sinning—a condition that is required for there to be any sort of freedom to sin and even for there to be such a thing as sin itself. And hence the claim that there is sin in such a case involves a contradiction.

In fact, I do not understand why our sins would not have to be attributed to God as the author of nature who has conferred upon the created faculty of choice a propensity toward those sins. For just as (i) the acts and effects of those agents that act by a necessity of nature are attributed to God because of the propensities and powers that He confers upon them, and just as (ii) for this reason the works of nature are called by philosophers the works of intelligence and hence of God, so too our sinful acts would have to be attributed to God as the author of nature

[9]Here and elsewhere Molina uses terms such as 'error', 'erroneous', 'dangerous', and 'unsafe' as semitechnical terms of theological censure. Such terms as used in official Church proclamations are intended to indicate reservations about theological opinions that are not straightforwardly heretical but that nonetheless lean too far in that direction. But the precise meaning and ordering of such terms (as well as of their positive mirror images) is itself the subject of theological inquiry. For an interesting treatment of some of the issues involved, especially as they redound upon the post-Tridentine period, see John Cahill, O.P., *The Development of the Theological Censures After the Council of Trent (1563–1709)* (Fribourg, Switzerland, 1955).

who instills in the created faculty of choice this propensity toward committing sins.

Now to say that it is *in the divided sense* that the faculty of choice retains the power not to elicit a nonevil act and not to sin, since (i) if God had not predetermined to confer efficacious concurrence, then the faculty of choice would not elicit a nonevil act, and since (ii) if He were to confer a concurrence that is efficacious for a nonevil act, then the faculty of choice would not sin—to say this is clearly not to establish that there is freedom in the *created* faculty of choice, but only to establish that there is freedom in *God* to move or not to move the faculty of choice toward a nonevil act, and to restrain it or not to restrain it from sinning, just as, when a beast of burden is being led in one direction or another by a halter, the freedom is not in the *beast,* but is instead in the *human being* who is leading the beast in the one direction or the other, as was said in Disputation 50 and elsewhere.[10]

7. Now, if someone claims that all the sins that are going to occur because of any created faculty of choice are known by God with certainty within that free determination of His will by which He decides to *permit* them, since in the composed sense it is impossible that God should have decided to permit a given sin and yet that the sin not occur—if, I say, someone makes *this* claim, he should pay attention to the fact that the permission of sin, as will be explained later in this work,[11] *presupposes* that (i) the sin will occur because of the created faculty of choice on the condition that it be placed in such-and-such an order of things and circumstances, and that (ii) God foresees that the sin will occur unless the faculty of choice is assisted by stronger or different aids, and that (iii) God is able to prevent it. Now, *willing to permit* such a sin is nothing other than *not willing,* given all the presuppositions in question, *to confer* those other aids by which the sin would be prevented, and, likewise, the permission itself is nothing other than *not conferring* in time the aids by which the sin would be prevented. For one is said to permit that which is such that, even though he sees that it will otherwise occur and that he is able to prevent it, nonetheless he does not prevent it, but instead allows it to happen. Therefore, since willing to permit a sin *presupposes* foreknowing that through the faculty of choice the sin will freely occur unless it is prevented by other aids, it is because of that *foreknowledge* that it is impossible in the composed sense that God should will to permit it and yet that it not occur.[12]

---

[10]See Disputation 50, sec. 9.

[11]*Commentaria,* q. 19, a. 12, pp. 271a–272a; and q. 23, a. 3, pp. 291a–294a.

[12]This line of reasoning amounts to an elaboration of the argument found in Disputation 49, sec. 14.

8. But as regards the source of the certitude of the foreknowledge that precedes God's freely willing to permit a sin, we must still ask, in turn, whether this certitude stems from the fact that the faculty of choice is of itself inclined toward sinning in such a way that (i) unless it is inhibited and held back from sinning by an efficacious assistance through which it is drawn toward a nonevil act, it will be led by a necessity of nature toward the sin, and in such a way that (ii) it is thus *because of the very nature of the object* that God knows with certainty that the sin will occur—as the theory that we have heretofore been taking issue with was maintaining, to the quite obvious destruction of the freedom of the created faculty of choice. Or is it not rather that this certitude stems from the fact that, because of the depth of His intellect and because of His absolutely eminent penetration of the created faculty of choice, (i) God knows, in a way *surpassing the nature of the object,* that the sin will occur because of freedom of choice and (ii) He would know the contrary if, as is possible, *it* were going to occur because of that same freedom of choice—which latter explanation amounts to positing middle knowledge in God with respect to those future contingents that depend on the created faculty of choice.

9. So the authors with whom we disagree do not join with the Lutherans and other heretics in positing predeterminations or divine motions and determinations by which, via efficacious concurrence, God moves and determines the created faculty of choice toward *sinful* acts, with the result that it is in these determinations that He is able to know with certainty which sins are going to occur because of created faculties of choice. Nor, likewise, do they seem to trace the certitude of that same foreknowledge back to the certitude and inevitability that a created will is going to sin unless God holds it back and inhibits it from sinning by a concurrence that is efficacious for nonevil acts—as though the will were so inclined toward sins that it is led into them by a necessity of nature unless it is held back from elsewhere. For this position would be an error from the point of view of the faith. And there is nothing else that this certitude can be traced back to other than the certitude of middle knowledge, a knowledge by which God, because of the depth of His intellect and His absolutely eminent comprehension of the created faculty of choice, knew with certainty in His essence which sins each created faculty of choice was by its freedom going to fall into on the hypothesis that it should be placed in such-and-such an order of things and circumstances—even though (i) on that same hypothesis it would really be able *not* to fall into them, and (ii) if this were going to happen, God would have foreknown *it* and not that other thing. Since all this is so, we should, it

seems clear, affirm that these authors do not deny middle knowledge in God with respect to future sins, especially in view of the fact that when they chance into a discussion of sins, they speak in a manner well suited to middle knowledge and propound views that cannot survive without middle knowledge, as was noted to some extent above—even though, to be truthful, they sometimes seem to suggest the view that we argued against in Disputation 50, and they take refuge in the permission of sins and claim that this alone, without any previous middle knowledge, is the reason God's knowledge regarding future sins is certain.[13]

10.   Meanwhile, however, let me point out that if they countenance middle knowledge with respect to *sins*, then it is unjust of them to attack it in general. What's more, as long as they talk about *conditioned* future contingents and correctly concede that God has certain knowledge of them, it is unjust of them, in order to salvage the certitude of all the things they enumerate, to resort to divine predeterminations that would have existed if the conditions in question had obtained—as though it were *in those predeterminations* that the things are foreknown with certainty as future on such conditions. For Saul's descending into Keilah to capture and kill David, if David should remain in Keilah, was a mortal sin on Saul's part; likewise, the handing over of an innocent David, from whom they had received only good treatment, would seem to be a mortal sin on the part of the people of Keilah; and last, the sins into which the just would have fallen had they not been taken prematurely by death were also mortal sins. Thus, God could not have predetermined any of these things, nor could He have efficaciously moved and determined the created faculty of choice toward them in such a way that He might be able to know them with certainty as future in and by such predeterminations. Rather, what He had was the certitude of middle knowledge regarding sins, on the hypothesis that the relevant conditions should be fulfilled.

11.   Again, in the preceding part it was shown that in the case of the repentance of the Tyronians and Sidonians, Christ's words are manifestly weakened and distorted by an appeal, not to the certitude of middle knowledge, but rather to the predetermination via intrinsically efficacious assistance that would have existed if the wonders that were worked in Chorozain and Bethsaida had been worked in Tyre and Sidon.[14] So it follows that in general God's certitude that all the condi-

---

[13]See Disputation 50, secs. 10ff.
[14]See Disputation 53, pt. 1, sec. 7.

tioned contingent things would have occurred is the certitude of middle knowledge, and *not* the certitude of a predetermination by which the created faculty of choice would have been determined by God to those things via efficacious concurrence had such-and-such conditions obtained.

12. But now let us turn our attention to the *nonevil* acts of free choice. Surely, if, without God's predetermination and intrinsically efficacious concurrence, a created faculty of choice is able to exercise all the *sinful* acts it in fact exercises, even though some of them might involve great difficulty—as, among many other examples, advancing on the enemy and scaling the walls when the war is unjust and there is much danger and strong natural fear—then I do not understand why, in the absence of that same efficacious assistance and predetermination and in the presence of only a general concurrence directly upon the acts and effects (the sort of concurrence by which God concurs with sinful acts, according to the theory of those with whom we disagree), the faculty of choice would not be able to elicit indifferent acts or even morally good acts that are not difficult but rather delightful and pleasurable, for example, willing to go to sleep or to eat when one is able to do so without sinning and when both things are pleasurable; having sexual intercourse with one's wife; willing to go for a walk or to play for the sake of reviving of one's spirits; and doing many other similar things. For it would be ridiculous to deny this, especially since (i) God does not restrict or limit the innate freedom of secondary causes when what is going to be done is not evil but is instead good, and since (ii) God's concurrences should not be multiplied or increased without necessity, especially with respect to acts and effects that are purely natural. What's more, it is truly remarkable if, when men are warring among themselves, those for whom the war is unjust are fighting *without* God's predetermination and efficacious concurrence, whereas those who are not fighting illicitly *need* God's predetermination and efficacious concurrence in order to resist and fight. Therefore, if the created faculty of choice is able to exercise acts of this sort without God's intrinsically efficacious concurrence and predetermination, and if it is able to alter these acts with regard to many of their circumstances (for example, to begin or end them now rather than earlier or later, to elicit them more intensely or more languidly, to walk in one or another direction and do it more quickly or more slowly, and so on for the other circumstances), then clearly the fact that it is *with certainty* that God foreknows these acts as absolutely future and foreknows that they will occur with these rather than with some other circumstances cannot be traced back to the certitude of any predeter-

mination or of any determination of the faculty of choice by God's intrinsically efficacious concurrence. Rather, this fact has to be traced back to the certitude of the middle knowledge through which (i) God, because of the depth of His intellect, knew with certainty which part and which circumstances the created faculty of choice would by its freedom turn itself toward on the hypothesis that He should will to create it and place it in that order of things and circumstances in which He has in fact placed it, and through which (ii) He would have known not this, but something far different, if because of that same freedom of choice something different had been going to occur on that same hypothesis.

13. We can confirm this particular point as follows: In Disputation 33 we showed that numerically one and the same act in the *natural* order, elicited here and now, is indifferently able to be *morally* good or *morally* evil with the alteration of just a single circumstance that does not change the identity of that act within the natural order.[15] For instance, numerically the same act of consent, here and now, to intercourse with this woman is indifferently able to be either an act of conjugal chastity, if a marriage contract has at some time preceded it, or an act of fornication and of sin, if such a contract has not preceded it. We also showed that when that act is produced in the *natural* order by the influence of the secondary cause and of God, then a formal notion in the *moral* order, whether it is of a virtue or of a vice, results without any additional influence on the part of God or of the secondary cause. Therefore, if, when a marriage contract *has not* preceded it, that act, since it is an act of sin, is produced without an efficacious concurrence by which God might premove and determine the faculty of choice, but is rather produced only with His *general* influence on the act, an influence that is indifferent as to whether that act or its contrary should follow, then surely that act

[15]See Disputation 33, sec. 5 (Rabeneck, p. 205). Molina's point here is intuitively plausible, though difficult to state in a simple and uncontroversial manner. He assumes that an action (or, in technical terminology, the 'substance' of an action) is distinct from at least some of the action's circumstances, so that the *very same* action that in fact occurred in, say, circumstances C might have occurred in circumstances C^* (where C is distinct from C^*). The example he uses is an apt one, since we can easily imagine that the two situations depicted are exactly the same in every respect (including the agent's intentions, deliberations, and other psychological acts and states) except for a certain historical circumstance, namely, the making of a marriage contract. According to Molina, the *very same* act of consent to sexual intercourse could occur in either of the two situations. Thus it would be awkward to claim that the act requires a divine predetermination of the sort under dispute in the one case and not in the other. Yet this is just what Molina's opponents are forced to claim, given that the act is virtuous in the one case and vicious in the other. For they treat good and bad acts asymmetrically. It goes without saying, of course, that this distinction between the 'substance' of an act and its circumstances has to be fleshed out more clearly and carefully. See Section 3.3 of the Introduction.

will be produced without God's efficacious concurrence when a marriage contract *has* preceded it and when the consent is an act of conjugal chastity. Thus, it is not because of any predetermination or any efficacious concurrence that God foreknows with certainty that this good act is going to occur. Rather, He knows this with the certitude of middle knowledge, a certitude that arises from the depth and eminence of the knower, who sees with certainty that which in itself is uncertain.

14.   It is surely surprising that predeterminations and intrinsically efficacious concurrences are extended by these authors to *all* nonevil acts, even *natural* ones. For there are those who posit them just for *supernatural* acts—not, indeed, for the acts performed by angels or by human beings in the state of innocence, but only for those acts performed by human beings with a fallen nature; and they incorrectly assert that this is the grace of Christ.[16]

15.   Again, if the authors with whom we disagree countenance middle knowledge with respect to sinful acts, in accordance with what was said above, then surely, since many other things that have been and will be done by human choice, from the beginning of the world right up to its consummation, depend on sinful acts, God did not know these other things as absolutely future with certainty, unless it was with the certitude of middle knowledge, by which He foresaw that, on the hypothesis that such-and-such sins would be committed by the created faculty of choice, such-and-such other things would occur that otherwise would not have occurred.

The minor premise, namely, that many things that are done by human choice depend on sinful acts and would not have occurred unless sinful acts had preceded them, is proved as follows: The fact that Eve was tempted and seduced depended on the sin of the angels; for if the angels had not sinned, then there would have been no demons to tempt and seduce Eve. Likewise, the fact that Adam fell into the sin that infected and corrupted the human race depended on the temptation and sin of Eve. Now that original justice had been lost, the sin of Adam led, in turn, to a tremendous difference with regard to both sins and

---

[16]From Molina's point of view, the reason this assertion is incorrect is that predeterminations of the sort in question, executed causally by intrinsically efficacious concurrences, would obliterate genuine human freedom. He would, of course, agree that the grace of Christ empowers us and incites us to perform good actions with supernatural effects (for example, actions that contribute to our meriting eternal life). But he would insist that the operation of this grace must be understood in such a way as to be compatible with genuine human freedom.

good works in the whole human race; further, since (i) the generations of human beings were to have a far different history, and since (ii) the human beings who were to exist were not the same ones who would have existed in the state of innocence (as will be explained in its proper place),[17] and since (iii) there was to be a marked change in the circumstances regarding place of habitation, length of life, and much else, it turned out that far different things, both for good and for evil, would be done by different human beings after the fall of the human race and right up to the end of the world than would have been done otherwise. Likewise, many things depended on the sins of Adam's descendants. For instance, the death of Christ, the redemption of the human race, and all the things that followed therefrom depended on the sins of the Jews; the crowns of the martyrs depended on the sins of tyrants; acts of adultery, sacrilege, and incest, as well as other acts of fornication, led to the procreation of all those who were generated by such acts of fornication, and thus led to the doing of all those things, both good and evil, that were going to be done by the free choice of those so procreated; again, unjust wars and other homicides led to its being the case that all those things were never done that would have been done by the faculty of choice of those so killed, and the same goes for all the things that would have been done by the faculty of choice of those who would have been procreated by the people who were killed in this way; and so on for the many other things that were dependent on the sins of human beings, both as regards their existence or nonexistence and as regards numerous variations in their circumstances. For because of battles, unjust litigations, inordinate diversions, and other heinous deeds it often happens that (i) due to the lack of a dowry many women do not marry at all or do not marry those with whom they would otherwise have contracted marriage, and that (ii) many people migrate from one place to another, with the result that there is a considerable variation in the generations of human beings. In addition, many other things vary because of these and other similar circumstances. Thus it follows that many of the *good* things that were going to occur because of the human faculty of choice from the beginning of the world up to its consummation would not have been known with certainty by God as absolutely future except because of middle knowledge, a knowledge through which He knew that the *sins* on which those things depended were going to occur, on the hypothesis that the order of things which was in fact produced at the beginning should be produced by Him.

---

[17]See *De Opere Sex Dierum*, disp. 30ff., in *Commentaria*, pp. 706b–710b.

16. But let us reflect in general on the sort of predeterminations that the authors with whom we disagree posit via an efficacious concurrence by which God moves, applies, and determines the faculty of choice to all its nonevil acts. And to prepare for the first argument, I claim that in order for an act to have the character of a sin it is not sufficient that it be spontaneous in the way in which the acts of brute animals are spontaneous, but rather it is necessary that the act be free with the freedom of either *contrariety* or *contradiction,* as they call it, so that when the faculty of choice consents to the act, it has the power not to consent to it, given all the circumstances obtaining at that time; otherwise, if, given those circumstances, the faculty of choice were not able not to consent, then it would not sin by consenting at that time, since no one sins in, or is deserving of punishment for, anything that he is unable to avoid. Now if it was at a previous time within the person's power to remove an accompanying circumstance by reason of which it is not now within his power not to consent (as when someone has freely gotten drunk, knowing that when drunk he is wont to kill others), then that person sinned, to be sure, when he got drunk, not only because he deprived himself of the use of reason by his intemperance, but also because he committed the sin of homicide by exposing himself to the danger of unjustifiably killing others—and this whether or not a homicide actually ensued afterward; but he did *not* commit a sin when, already inebriated, he perpetrated the killing, since at that time it was no longer within his power not to kill. And the freedom just explicated, which, as the light of reason teaches, is absolutely required in order for there to be any sin at all, is what Augustine called *voluntariness* and what he accordingly held to be necessary in order for there to be a sin, so that if something was not voluntary, then straightaway, without any argument, he would claim that it was not a sin.[18]

17. Given this, I construct the following line of argument: Just as, in order for an act to be a *sin* it is not sufficient that it be spontaneous, but is instead necessary that it be free in such a way that, when the faculty of choice consents to it, it has the power not to consent to it, given all the surrounding circumstances obtaining at that time, so too in order for there to be *merit* or for an act to be *morally* good—indeed, even in order for there to be a free act that is indifferent to moral good and evil—it is necessary that when the act is elicited by the faculty of choice, it be within

[18]Perhaps it is worth noting here that Aquinas uses the term 'voluntary' somewhat more inclusively, so that it is applicable, in at least an extended sense, to many of the acts of brute animals. See *Summa Theologiae* I–II, q. 6, a. 1 and 2.

the faculty's power not to elicit it, given all the circumstances obtaining at that time. This, of course, is the freedom which is called the *freedom of contradiction*, and which is the very least that has to be present for an act to be called free, even if the act is only indifferent with regard to moral good and evil; and this is the freedom in the absence of which, as all Catholics confess, there can be no such thing as the morally good or the meritorious. Indeed, it is by reason of this sort of freedom that (i) we are in control of our acts, and that (ii) if our acts are meritorious, we are, in return for them, deserving of the everlasting reward, praise, and honor with which the eternal Father, by the act of His will and the judgment of His intellect, will unceasingly honor, for all eternity in the presence of all His saints, those who have served Christ in this life; for He is greatly pleased with and approves of their having freely discharged those obligations that it was within their power not to discharge. Indeed, this is the freedom in light of which our faculty of choice is called free, as was explained in Disputation 2; for when our acts lack this sort of freedom, then even if they are spontaneous, they are nonetheless called *natural* and *not free,* as Catholics all concur.[19]

Now after so long and so extensively elaborated and corroborated a major premise, let us add the following minor premise: But if God has predetermined all nonevil acts of the created faculty of choice in such a way that He has decided to move and determine the faculty of choice to those acts by an intrinsically efficacious concurrence, in the absence of which the faculty of choice is not able to elicit those acts and in the presence of which it is not able not to elicit them, then the freedom of choice just explicated is manifestly destroyed with respect to those acts.

Therefore, this opinion is dangerous from the point of view of the faith—indeed, I would call it a manifest error.

The minor premise is proved as follows: At the instant at which the faculty of choice elicits those acts, it is not able not to elicit them; otherwise, the concurrence by which the will is moved to them would not be intrinsically efficacious, but, instead, its being or not being efficacious would depend on whether or not the faculty of choice at that moment willed to consent to and to cooperate with the concurrence—and thus the sort of predetermination that these authors are trying to introduce

---

[19]An agent S has freedom of *contradiction* with respect to an object A at a time t if S is at t able to will A and able not to will A. But to have freedom of *contrariety* with respect to A at t, S must in addition be able to will *not-A*, that is, the contrary of A. So freedom of contrariety entails freedom of contradiction, but not vice versa. What's more, freedom of contrariety implies a power to resist the object in question positively (by willing its opposite), and not just a power to resist it negatively (by refraining from willing it or its opposite). This distinction is the same as that between freedom with respect to the *exercise* of an act and freedom with respect to the *species* of an act. See Disputation 47, n. 12.

would perish, and along with it the certitude, based on such a predetermination, with which God knows that contingent things of the kind in
question are absolutely future. Nor would any alternative basis for this
certitude remain besides the certitude of a middle knowledge that precedes the other, absolute, knowledge and through which God, because
of the eminence and depth of His intellect, foresaw which part the
created faculty of choice would in its freedom turn itself toward on the
hypothesis that He should will for His part to situate it in such an order
of things, circumstances, and aids—even though it could have done the
opposite, and even though, if it had been going to turn itself toward the
opposite part, then God would have known *this* and not the other thing.

18.   Nor in this case—unlike when we were talking before about the
man who killed while he was drunk—is there any room for an appeal to
some circumstance that was able not to obtain because of the created
faculty of choice and by reason of which the faculty was rendered unable
not to elicit the act in question. For (i) the movement caused by God's
efficacious concurrence, a movement by reason of which the faculty of
choice is, on the theory of these authors, rendered incapable of not
cooperating and not consenting, does not, on the theory of these same
authors, depend on the *created* faculty of choice, but instead depends
only on the free will of *God*, who willed to confer it, and also (ii) merit and
freedom would not be present at the time when the nonevil or meritorious act of choice is elicited, but instead *would have been present* at the
time when the circumstance in question was posited by the created
faculty of choice, which was at that time able not to posit that circumstance.

19.   In the case under discussion there is likewise no room for recourse to the *divided sense,* the sense in which these authors claim that the
faculty of choice is able not to elicit the act, and which they claim to be
sufficient for the act's being free and meritorious. For in the case under
discussion they cannot understand the divided sense otherwise than as
follows: 'If from eternity God had not decided to move the faculty of
choice by an intrinsically efficacious concurrence, and if, at the time
when the act is elicited, He were not to move the faculty of choice by that
same efficacious concurrence, than at that time the faculty of choice
would be able not to elicit the act.' But then it would *be able not to elicit* the
act only insofar as, according to their own theory, it would *not be able to
elicit* it, since they had claimed that in the absence of efficacious concurrence it is not able to elicit the act. And so they never allow for an event
or an instant in which, given all the surrounding circumstances obtain-

ing at the time in question, the faculty of choice has the power indifferently to elicit the act or not to elicit it; but *this* is what is required if the act is to be free and meritorious, as has been explained.

Nor does a divided and composed sense of this sort preserve freedom in the *created* faculty of choice itself in such a way that it has the power indifferently to elicit or not to elicit the act, but instead it only preserves freedom in *God*, a freedom by which He is indifferently (i) able to confer on the faculty of choice an efficacious concurrence by virtue of which it is going to elicit the act in such a way that it does not retain the power not to elicit it, and also (ii) able *not* to confer that same efficacious concurrence on the faculty of choice, in which case it is not going to elicit the act, because it does not retain the power to elicit it. But if this were sufficient for freedom of choice, then there would truly be freedom of choice in brute animals, since God is equally able to confer or not to confer efficacious concurrence on them with respect to their spontaneous acts. And when He does confer it on them and they do elicit the act, then, similarly, in the divided sense, if He were not to confer it on them, they would be able not to elicit such an act; and when He does not confer it on them and they do not elicit the act, then, similarly, in the divided sense they would be able to elicit the act if He were to confer an efficacious concurrence on them with respect to eliciting the act.

Now in order for there to be room for a divided and composed sense that does not destroy freedom of choice, it is necessary that the faculty of choice itself be really able *by itself* to elicit or not to elicit the act, even when there exists something which the one part of the contradiction does not cohere with and hence which that part is incompossible with in the composed sense. For clearly the something in question preexists because, by virtue of freedom of choice, the part of the contradiction that it does not cohere with is not going to obtain; yet if this part of the contradiction were going to obtain, as is possible despite that thing, then that thing would never have existed—as was explained in the preceding disputation with regard to God's knowledge of the contingent things that depend on our faculty of choice.[20]

20. When the authors with whom we disagree, pressed by arguments, clearly see that, given their predeterminations, freedom of choice is scarcely defensible, they are wont in the matter under dispute to flee toward the less secure "anchor of ignorance," claiming that, instead of

---

[20]The "something" in question alluded to in this paragraph is, of course, God's foreknowledge of those future contingents that will in fact obtain. This particular foreknowledge would not have existed if it had not been the case that just those future contingents were going to obtain.

rejecting predeterminations, it is better to join Cajetan in confessing that we are ignorant of the way in which freedom of choice fits together with foreknowledge, providence, predestination, and reprobation.[21] Yet, on the one hand, predeterminations of the sort they conjure up have a basis neither in Sacred Scripture or Tradition nor in the councils or the holy Fathers; to the contrary, such predeterminations manifestly subvert freedom of choice, are incompatible with the Scriptures and the defined teachings of the Church, and are advocated by very few Scholastics. (Indeed, thirty years ago they were unknown by that name among the Scholastics.) On the other hand, if we speak straightforwardly about foreknowledge, providence, predestination, and reprobation without such predeterminations, then freedom of choice coheres extremely well with these things. It follows that there is absolutely no reason we Catholics should take refuge in ignorance in such a public way, with no small disgrace on our part and with a lessening of the reputation of the dogmas of the faith in the eyes of unbelievers, especially since neither the holy Fathers, nor St. Thomas, nor any others among the leading Scholastics flee to such a refuge.

21.   Further, the authors with whom we disagree, in order that they might persist in their predeterminations, contemptuously call the freedom explicated above, which is clearly *de fide* (as was shown at length in Disputation 23), "I know not what freedom."[22] I leave it to others to judge how safely and with how much reverence for what the faith teaches this was said.

22.   Also, it matters little to them that on the basis of the certitude of middle knowledge we have so plainly reconciled this same freedom with foreknowledge, providence, predestination, and reprobation.[23] In fact, they insist that middle knowledge should be rejected precisely because all these things come into harmony so plainly and easily on the basis of it, whereas the holy Fathers labored greatly in reconciling them with one another and always thought of the exact reconciliation of freedom of choice with these four things and with divine grace as one of the most difficult of tasks. But, surely, since truth agrees with truth, whereas truth will not easily harmonize with falsehood, the fact that these four things cohere so easily and perspicuously with freedom of choice on the basis of middle foreknowledge is a manifest sign that we have propounded a

[21]Zumel, *Commentaria,* q. 19, a. 8, disp. 1, p. 559b.
[22]Ibid., q. 14, a. 1, disp. unica, concl. 2, p. 360b.
[23]Ibid., p. 362b.

comprehensive and legitimate way of reconciling all of them. Now if, in this way of ours of reconciling all these things, we deviated even a little from the dogmas of the faith, or from the intent of the holy Fathers or the Catholic Doctors, or from their undoubted opinions, then our way of reconciling these things could indeed be justifiably viewed with suspicion. But the fact is that having studied their works closely and having been enlightened by so many disputations and by the outstanding writings and discoveries of others, we have laid out just a little more clearly the foundation on which all these things cohere with one another and on which all the difficulties are easily resolved. And thirty years ago in private and public disputations, and twenty years ago in our commentaries on the First Part, we proposed this foundation under the name of *natural* knowledge, since it is not *free* knowledge in God and since it precedes every free act of the divine will. Most recently, however, in this our *Concordia,* we have propounded the same foundation more exactly than ever before under the name of *middle* knowledge. Surely, no one can justifiably blame me for this, especially because (i) even though (and I am mindful of this) the holy Fathers did not use the distinction between *free* and *natural* knowledge in God in those very terms, and even though, likewise, they did not distinguish a *middle* knowledge between *free* and *purely natural* knowledge, still by unanimous consent they taught that those future contingents that depend on our faculty of choice are not going to exist because God foreknows that they are going to exist, but rather that God, because He is God, that is, because of the depth of His intellect surpassing their nature, knew that they were going to exist because they were so going to exist through freedom of choice, as we asserted in the preceding disputation, and also because (ii) these same Fathers taught by unanimous consent that on this same foundation our freedom of choice coheres with divine foreknowledge, if you consult the passages cited in the preceding disputation as well as in Disputation 23 and elsewhere.[24] And this, plainly, is nothing other than to affirm middle knowledge—at least in fact, if not in our very words.

23.   Nor is the response of the authors with whom we disagree satisfactory, namely, that these passages should be interpreted as having to do just with the *sinful* acts of the created faculty of choice, and not with its *nonevil* acts.[25]

For, first of all, if they have to countenance middle knowledge in God

---

[24]See Disputation 52, secs. 21–29. Also, see Disputation 23, pt. 4 (Rabeneck, pp. 140–154).
[25]See sec. 4 above.

with respect to the *sinful* acts of the created faculty of choice, given that
they do not want to claim that it is led into sins by a necessity of nature,
and given that, as was said above, they do not want to subvert freedom of
choice completely, then why do they not extend this middle knowledge,
which they already countenance in God, so that it might be had with
respect to *all* the acts that are produced freely by the faculty of choice in
such a way that it has the power not to produce them? For, as was shown
by argument a short while ago, there is no other way that this freedom
can be preserved in the faculty of choice.

Next, when the holy Fathers speak in this way, not only (i) are they
talking *in general* about future contingents (as the authors with whom we
disagree concede), even when they use examples involving sins because
the train of argument requires it and because their point is more easily
understood and explained in the case of sins than in the case of other
acts, but also (ii) they sometimes talk specifically about good and meritorious acts.

For example, in the passage referred to in the preceding disputation
Justin Martyr is plainly speaking of future contingents *in general*.[26] He is
doing the same thing in the passages alluded to in Disputation 23, where
he expressly talks about *good acts* as well.[27] And in *Responsiones ad Christianos de Quibusdam Quaestionibus Necessariis*, response to question 8, he
says, among other things, "Thus, the cause of our virtue and vice is not
God, but rather our own intention and will," as we related in the same
place.[28] Whence you see that, to the extent that acts of virtue freely
depend on our faculty of choice, Justin Martyr attributes them to that
faculty itself as to a free cause that was able to produce them and able not
to produce them—and *not* to the divine foreknowledge by which they
were foreknown as going to occur.

Likewise, in the passage cited in the preceding disputation Origen is
clearly speaking of future contingents as comprising evil acts and also
good and meritorious acts.[29] And near the end he says, "In order that
you might understand that the cause of each person's salvation is to be
found not in God's foreknowledge but in that person's intentions and
actions, notice that Paul . . ."[30] Clearly, intention or choice is not a cause
of salvation except through good acts, among which are numbered
tormenting the body and subjecting it to servitude, which Origen men-

---

[26]See Disputation 52, sec. 21.
[27]See Disputation 23, pt. 4, sec. 2 (Rabeneck, pp. 140–141). The references to Justin
Martyr's works include *PG* 6, 456B–C, 714B, 798B–D, and 1257B–C.
[28]*PG* 6, 1257C. This passage is cited in Rabeneck, p. 141.
[29]See Disputation 52, sec. 22.
[30]Ibid.

tions in this place because of Paul. Likewise, Origen is speaking *in general* in the other passages quoted in Disputation 23, and he proposes as many examples of virtues as of vices that are within the power of the faculty of choice.[31]

Although the passage from Damascene cited in the preceding disputation deals only with the sin of the devil, it is quite clear from the other passages we cited from this Father in Disputation 23 that he would say the same thing about the good acts of the faculty of choice.[32]

Though the passage from Chrysostom has to do with sins, it is nonetheless evident from this same passage and from those others we quoted from this Father in Disputation 23, part 4, that he would say the same thing about virtuous acts, not to mention indifferent ones.[33]

In the second and third of the passages cited in the preceding disputation, Jerome is without a doubt speaking *in general,* and it is clear from the other passages of his cited in Disputation 23, part 4, that he thought the same thing about virtuous acts.[34]

In the passage referred to in the preceding disputation, Cyril of Alexandria is also speaking *in general,* and it is manifest from the passages we quoted from this Father in the above-cited part 4 that he held the same view with regard to both virtuous and vicious acts.[35]

Furthermore, it is clear from the passages cited in the preceding disputation that Augustine held one and the same view with respect to both virtuous and vicious acts.[36] For he speaks in the same way about the foreknowledge of an act of consenting to a sin and about the foreknowledge of an act of dissenting that is a good act. And in that splendid passage from *De Libero Arbitrio* III, chap. 4, where he reconciles freedom of choice with foreknowledge on the same foundation as we do, he clearly reconciles them in one and the same way when the act that is

---

[31]See Disputation 23, pt. 4, sec. 6 (Rabeneck, p. 143). The references to Origen include *PG* 11, 118B–C, 250A, 860B, and 1033A; and *PG* 13, 196B.

[32]See Disputation 52, sec. 23. Also, see Disputation 23, pt. 4, sec. 12 (Rabeneck, pp. 145–146).

[33]See Disputation 52, sec. 24. Also, see Disputation 23, pt. 4, sec. 14 (Rabeneck, pp. 147–148), where the references to Chrysostom include *PG* 48, 984; *PG* 49, 377; *PG* 53, 158–159 and 169–170; *PG* 55, 133, 345, and 436; *PG* 57, 362; *PG* 58, 573ff.; *PG* 59, 73–75 and 257f.; *PG* 61, 117; *PG* 62, 209, 586, and 647; and *PG* 63, 99f.

[34]See Disputation 52, sec. 25. Also, see Disputation 23, pt. 4, sec. 30 (Rabeneck, p. 153), where the references to Jerome include *PL* 22, 383, 393, 511, and 1158; *PL* 23, 428D, 429A, 505D, and 581B; *PL* 24, 796C–D; *PL* 25, 37A and 138B; and *PL* 26, 157A, 157C, and 642D.

[35]See Disputation 52, sec. 27. Also, see Disputation 53, pt. 4, sec. 30 (Rabeneck, p. 153), where the references to Cyril include *PG* 68, 145D; *PG* 73, 553C and 632A; *PG* 74, 129B; *PG* 76, 620D–621C and 937C–940B.

[36]See Disputation 52, sec. 26.

foreknown is going to be good and when it is going to be evil.[37] Hence, in the end he concludes, "For if, because He foresees sins, He ought not to condemn sinners, then neither should He give rewards to those who act righteously, since He likewise foresaw just as well that they would act righteously." The same thing is also clear from the other passages from this Father that we have referred to many times, in the above-cited part 4 as well as in other places.[38]

The same thing is clear from the rest of the passages (if each is pondered carefully) taken from the other Fathers, passages with which we extensively confirmed in the above-cited part 4 that there is freedom of choice with regard to both good and evil.

24.   Now let us return to that from which we digressed and propose a second argument for rejecting predeterminations of the sort that they conjure up: If (i) before predestination there was an election of some for beatitude through an absolute and efficacious volition on God's part, prior to any foreknowledge of the circumstances and use of free choice, even under a future hypothesis, and if likewise (ii) there was a rejection of others by a similarly efficacious volition, and if, further, (iii) the predestination of adults was fixed in a predetermination to confer on them the efficacious assistance by which their faculties of choice would be so determined that they would with certainty (where the certitude stems from the character of the assistance) perform and persevere in those works by which predestinate adults attain eternal life, whereas (iv) the others on whom God did not decide to confer similar assistance have by that very fact remained outside the number of the predestinate, then it would follow, first of all, that a predestinate adult's faculty of choice does not retain the power to turn away from beatitude or, likewise, from any of the particular means through which it will arrive at beatitude. This, I have no doubt, is an error from the point of view of the faith.

25.   For in that case a predestinate person's freedom of choice with regard to the means to beatitude is destroyed, and as a result the notion of the proper merits through which one progresses toward that beatitude and arrives at it is also destroyed—which is clearly heretical.

Now the inference is proved as follows: If, with respect to each of the particular means through which someone is going to attain eternal life

[37]See Disputation 52, sec. 29.

[38]See Disputation 23, pt. 4, sec. 17 (Rabeneck, pp. 150–151), where the references to Augustine include *PL* 32, 595–599, 1239ff., 1269–1275, 1295, and 1307; *PL* 33, 677 and 971; *PL* 34, 176; *PL* 35, 1777f. and 1842; *PL* 37, 1938; *PL* 38, 902–903; *PL* 39, 2162 and 2211; *PL* 40, 685 and 814; *PL* 42, 121, 538, 541, and 1152.

(either as a proximate or a remote disposition to grace or as a meriting of eternal life or of an increase in grace),[39] you claim that such a predestinate person's faculty of choice really does have the power either not to consent to that means or to impede it by previous sin or destroy it by subsequent sin, with the result that the person does not attain eternal life via that means, then it follows that the assistance that God prepared for him and decided to confer on him was not *intrinsically* efficacious for the existence and perseverance of that means until death, contrary to what you were maintaining and asserting; instead, its being efficacious for both these things depends on the faculty of choice's willing or not willing to consent to it and, similarly, on its willing or not willing to fall into sin. In addition, it follows that it is not certain, just on the basis of God's predetermination to confer this assistance on His part, that those means will exist; instead, that those means should exist with certainty depends as well on the middle foreknowledge through which, because of the depth of His intellect, He foresaw what would occur because of the freedom of such a faculty of choice on the hypothesis that He should decide to furnish this assistance—even though the contrary could have occurred, and even though if the contrary had been going to occur, then God would have foreknown *it* and not that other thing. You, on the other hand, maintain and affirm just the opposite with your predeterminations. Therefore, either you are going to claim that the certitude of the means of predestination does not arise solely from the predetermination and from the character of the assistance, but instead depends on the certitude of middle knowledge, or else you are going to say that the predestinate person is not free in such a way that he is able to turn away from beatitude and from the means by which he will attain beatitude. Nor, as we showed quite clearly in the preceding argument, is there any room in this matter for an appeal to the divided sense, namely, by claiming that it is sufficient for this sort of freedom that the person would have been able to turn away in the event that God had not decided to confer such assistance on him.

26. Next, from this same account of predestination and predeterminations it would follow that it is not within the power of those adults who have *not* been predestined to attain beatitude or to perform any of

[39]On the Catholic view, God predestines some for eternal life and wills to provide these persons (as well as the reprobate) with the means necessary to attain eternal life within the economy of salvation that He has contingently established. These "means" include the various forms of supernatural assistance which God bestows on us and which empower us, prompt us, and otherwise help us to perform meritorious acts. According to Molina, the certainty of predestination entails God's foreknowing with certainty, via His middle knowledge, just how the predestinate will freely respond to this assistance in the relevant circumstances.

those good acts that are necessary for beatitude and that they are not in fact going to perform; nor, indeed, is it even within·their power to perform any *nonevil* or *indifferent* act that they are not in fact going to perform. Thus it would follow further that with respect to the sins they will commit they do not have the freedom of contrariety, but only the freedom of contradiction. That is, they have the freedom not to consent to those acts, but not the freedom to dissent from them and to resist them.[40] Now, is there anyone who doubts that these claims contain an error from the point of view of the faith?

27.   The inference is proved as follows: According to the position of those with whom we disagree, no one who is not numbered among the predestinate is able, without God's efficacious assistance, to perform an act required for beatitude which he is not in fact going to perform; nor, likewise, is he able, without God's intrinsically efficacious concurrence, to perform any other nonevil act that, again, he is not in fact going to perform. But, given this account of predestination and predeterminations, God decided not to confer such assistance or concurrence on any of these people with respect to such acts. Therefore, it does not remain within the power or choice of any of them to exercise any such acts that they are not in fact going to exercise, and hence neither does it remain within their power to attain beatitude, because without such acts they neither are going to nor are able to attain it. Now, since dissenting from and resisting a sin is not only a *nonevil* act of will but a morally *good* act as well, it clearly follows that when they consented to the sins, they did not, according to the theory of these same authors, retain the power to dissent from them; for without God's efficacious concurrence they were not able to dissent, even though if they had had that concurrence, then they would in fact have dissented and not sinned—otherwise, the concurrence would not be efficacious. Therefore, all the things that have been said follow clearly from the account of predestination and predeterminations that these authors try to propound and defend.

28.   Indeed, it likewise follows that God has not left it within the choice and power of *predestinate* people to exercise more nonevil or meritorious acts than those that they will in fact exercise, or to exercise different such acts; likewise, it follows that He has not given them the freedom of contrariety to dissent from and resist the sins into which they will fall, but has given them only the freedom of contradiction, since

---

[40]See n. 19 above for a brief characterization of the distinction between the freedom of contradiction and the freedom of contrariety.

with respect to all those acts He decided not to confer on them intrinsically efficacious concurrence, a concurrence in the absence of which they are not able to elicit those acts and in the presence of which they are not able not to elicit them. In fact, given this position, there is quite clearly room for the error of those monks who used to claim that no one should be reproached for not doing good, but that instead all should petition God to confer on them the efficacious grace or assistance by means of which they might act well. This error was discussed in Disputation 1.[41]

Nor will the authors with whom we disagree appease us if they respond that (i) it is the fault of the nonpredestinate that they do not dispose themselves to receive God's efficacious concurrence, with which they would be able to exercise the acts whereby they might attain beatitude and would be empowered to dissent from and resist the sins into which they will fall, and that (ii) God is always prepared to assist them efficaciously if they do not stand in His way. These authors will not, I repeat, appease us if they say this. For, first of all, according to their theory, God, *without having any foreknowledge or idea of the circumstances or future use of free choice,* decided or predetermined from eternity to bestow intrinsically efficacious concurrence with respect to these particular acts on some people but not in like manner on others; therefore, on their theory this was not left to depend on the created faculty of choice or on the free disposition of that faculty with respect to both parts—unless these authors want to contradict themselves. Second, a disposition of the sort in question cannot be understood except as involving some act or cooperation on the part of free choice. But on their theory the faculty of choice cannot have this sort of cooperation without God's antecedent efficacious assistance or concurrence, a concurrence in the presence of which the cooperation is not able not to be elicited and in the absence of which it is not able to be elicited. Third, whatever this disposition might be in the final analysis—even if it is a disposition not to consent to a sin by not eliciting any act whatsoever, but by instead refraining from acting and being related negatively to acting[42]—clearly, if God's conferring or not conferring efficacious concurrence depends on such a disposition, then just as without middle knowledge there cannot be any certitude about whether that disposition is or is not going to exist through created

---

[41]See Disputation 1, sec. 15 (Rabeneck, p. 11).

[42]Here Molina is arguing that even if the disposition in question involves no *positive* act of free choice (that is, the sort of act which would *obviously* require a divine predetermination on his opponents' view), but instead involves only a *refraining* from acting, still, if this refraining is free, then God must have middle knowledge in order to foreknow it with certainty.

choice, so too the question of whether such efficacious concurrence is going to be conferred and whether God has predetermined to confer it was *also* dependent on the certitude of the middle knowledge that preceded that predetermination and without which there would have been no such predetermination. And so these authors stumble into the middle knowledge that they deny in God and that they assiduously flee from; and they are forced to concede that predestination and reprobation have not been accomplished without prior middle knowledge of what they designate as a *disposition for* God's efficacious concurrence.

29. In fact, if the method of predestining some adults and not others was the one that has been gleaned from the theory of these authors with their predeterminations, then I do not see in what sense it is true that God wills all human beings to be saved if they themselves do not prevent it, or in what sense it is true and not fictitious that all human beings without exception have been created by God for eternal life. Nor do I see how God could justifiably reproach the nonpredestinate for not living in a pious and holy manner and for not attaining eternal life; indeed, I do not see how it is true that God has placed human beings in the hand of their own counsel, so that they might direct their actions as they will. To the contrary, given this method of predestination and predeterminations, the freedom of the created faculty of choice perishes, and the justice and goodness of God with respect to the reprobate are greatly obfuscated and obscured. Thus, this theory is neither pious nor in any way safe from the point of view of the faith.

30. We might also propose this third argument: The assistance through which we are helped by God toward justification is not efficacious intrinsically and by its nature; rather, its being efficacious depends on the free consent of the faculty of choice, a consent that the will is able not to give despite that assistance—indeed, when it consents, it is able to *dissent,* as the Council of Trent (sess. 6, chap. 5, and canon 4) clearly teaches[43] and as we have proved quite extensively in other places and especially in Disputation 40 and in the Appendix (response to the third objection).[44] Likewise, when it consents to the assistance of grace, it is able in its freedom to cooperate and consent more intensely or more languidly, and with greater or lesser effort, and hence it is able to elicit a more intense or more languid act, as was shown in Disputation 39.[45]

[43]See Denzinger, 1525, p. 370, and 1554, p. 378.
[44]See Disputation 40, sec. 12 (Rabeneck, pp. 248–249). Also, see the Appendix to the *Concordia,* sec. 55ff. (Rabeneck, pp. 644ff.).
[45]See Disputation 39, sec. 4 (Rabeneck, p. 242).

Thus, both of the following things should be conceded all the more concerning the concurrence by which God concurs with the nonevil natural acts of free choice, namely, (i) that this concurrence is not intrinsically efficacious, but rather, despite the concurrence, the faculty of choice, when it consents to and elicits those acts, is able not to consent to and not to elicit them, so that its innate freedom is not taken away from it by God's concurrence and assistance; and, likewise, (ii) that when the faculty of choice elicits acts, it is able to enter into them with more or less effort, and hence is able in its freedom to produce more intense or more languid acts, just as all the Doctors hold concerning the natural acts of free choice. Thus are destroyed predeterminations of the sort that the authors of the contrary position try to introduce via God's intrinsically efficacious concurrence with respect to all the nonevil acts of free choice; in fact, such predeterminations are extremely dangerous from the point of view of the faith. And destroyed along with these predeterminations is that certitude, which would be based solely on these predeterminations, of God's foreknowledge of the future contingents that depend on free choice; and we must of necessity have recourse to the certitude of the middle knowledge by which God, because of the depth of His intellect and because of His absolutely eminent penetration of the created faculty of choice, knew, with a certainty surpassing the nature of the object, which part it would turn itself toward, and with what degree of intensity, on the hypothesis that it should be assisted by such-and-such aids in such-and-such an order of things and circumstances.

31.   This argument is, in my judgment, effectively confirmed for the case of human beings by the definitions cited from the Council of Trent, since the authors in question neither deny nor are able to deny that in those places the council teaches that our faculty of choice, when moved and stirred by prevenient grace, is able to elicit the consent by which it consents to that grace in such a way that when it elicits it, it is able not to elicit it—indeed, it is even able to dissent from it at that moment if it so wills; they, on the other hand, maintain that this consent is prior to the conversion, and they claim that the conversion requires, over and beyond prevenient grace, the distinct efficacious assistance of cooperating grace, by which the conversion is completed.[46]

On this basis I propose the following argument: This prior consent is a nonevil act of free choice, since it is not evil to consent in this way to

---

[46] In Disputation 53, pt. 4, secs. 11–12, Molina discusses more fully what is involved in the conversion of a sinner to faith or repentance.

prevenient grace. Therefore, there is a nonevil act of free choice which was elicited without efficacious concurrence in such a way that when it was elicited, it was able not to be elicited—indeed, the contrary dissent was able to be elicited. Therefore, God did not foreknow this act with certainty merely on the basis of a predetermination by which He predetermined it via His efficacious concurrence, but rather He foreknew it with certainty by virtue of the fact that because of the depth of His intellect He saw, through His middle knowledge, which part the faculty of choice would turn itself toward on the hypothesis that He should premove and stir it in this way by prevenient grace; and so these authors are mistaken in claiming that the entire certitude of God's foreknowledge with respect to all the nonevil acts of free choice in general has its source *solely* in the predetermination of those acts via efficacious concurrence, and not in any middle knowledge.

And when these authors wish to defend (i) the claim that it is the fault of those who are reprobate that they are not converted and do not attain eternal life, or (ii) the claim that God does not desert anyone in such a way that He is not always prepared on His part to confer sufficient assistance on him, and that it is the sinner's own fault that he does not accept that assistance, or (iii) other claims similar to these, they oftentimes are wont to appeal to something that *precedes* the efficacious assistance, something that depends indifferently on the created faculty of choice for its existence or nonexistence. So remember that you should insist at that point that the existence or nonexistence of the thing in question does not depend on any *predetermination*, and that there is no certitude, *except from God's middle knowledge*, about which part this thing is going to be channeled to by the created faculty of choice. At the same time, you should also remember that the authors with whom we disagree trace *all* the certitude of *every* nonevil act of free choice *in general, with absolutely no exceptions*, to the certitude of predeterminations via a concurrence on God's part that is intrinsically efficacious with respect to those acts. So you should carefully observe whether they always speak in a way consistent with this theory, or whether they do not instead make covert exceptions when it is necessary to defend these other claims.

Part 3
The Extent to Which Predeterminations Should Be Countenanced

1. Now that we have ruled out the predeterminations favored by the authors with whom we disagree, we have to make clear which predeterminations on God's part are required in order for all created things to

exist, and also in order for them to be universally subject to His divine providence.

Now, in order to do this better, we should note that among created things there are some whose proximate source of contingency is *God's faculty of choice alone.*[1] These include both (i) the things that are produced immediately by God alone and do not depend on any other source of contingency, as was the case with all the things that were produced by God in the first establishment of things, and also (ii) the things that thereafter have emanated from those first things just by a necessity of nature, without any dependence on any other source of contingency.

2. If the discussion has to do with all future contingents of *this* sort, before they exist in reality, then we agree that they all depend *just* on the predetermination by which God through an absolute volition decided from eternity to produce some of them directly and not to withhold that concurrence of His which was necessary in order for the rest of them to be derived thereafter from those first things. We also agree that all the certitude of the knowledge by which God knew, before they existed, that these things were going to exist depends *just* on that predetermination. Further, we agree that with respect to future contingents of this sort just *two* types of knowledge have to be distinguished in God, namely, (i) *free* knowledge, by which, *after* that free predetermination of His, He knew those things as *absolutely* future, and (ii) *purely natural* knowledge, by which, *before* that determination, He knew them as *possible* by virtue of His omnipotence and, in addition, knew them as future *on the hypothesis* that He should will to produce some of them and, once they were so produced, will not to withhold the concurrence required for them to act. Clearly, no one can deny that there is in God this type of conditional knowledge with regard to future contingents of the sort in question. Nor, likewise, can one deny that this knowledge is purely natural, since on the hypothesis in question it is altogether necessary that those things exist. We do, however, differ from the authors with whom we disagree on this point: We claim that God's general concurrence with the things He produced directly, in order that the other things might be derived from them, is *not* an influence of God's *on the cause,* so that the cause might act after having first been moved and applied to its act by that influence, but is instead an influence *along with the cause directly on the effect*—as was explained in Disputations 25 and following.[2]

---

[1] See Disputation 47, sec. 4.

[2] See Rabeneck, pp. 159ff. According to the Thomists, God 'premoves' the secondary cause and 'applies' it (or its power) to its proper operation in a way analogous to that in

3. The reward for this labor is that we may now distinguish for the sake of clarity a sort of *middle* genus of things between the foregoing things and the things we will be speaking of in a moment, that is, a middle genus comprising those things that (i) are indeed produced directly by God, even though a human or angelic intellect or will may concur in the production of some of them, not as a free faculty but only insofar as it is operating by a necessity of nature, and yet that (ii) depend on some other source of contingency besides God for their subject or for something else.[3] The following are examples: the raising up of Lazarus; the granting of sight to the man born blind; the calling of Paul while he was traveling to Damascus (not just the *external* calling, but also the *internal* calling via an antecedent illumination and movement of the will *prior to* Paul's eliciting any free act of assent); and other similar occurrences in the internal calling of others to faith or repentance.[4] For even though the actual existence of Lazarus, along with the rest of the things that accrued to him up to the instant at which he was raised by Christ, had, in addition to God, other sources for their existing contingently in such-and-such a way—and the same holds for the man born blind and for Paul, the former up to the moment at which he received sight, the latter up to the moment at which he was called to faith and repentance—nonetheless, the raising up of Lazarus, the receiving of sight by the man born blind and the calling of Paul had, presupposing all those other things, no source for their existence other than the free will of God, by which alone they were produced. For this reason, if we are speaking of *just* these things, before they existed, presupposing those other things, then the same claim should be made as was made about the sort of future contingents explicated in the first place above, namely, that they depend *only* on that free predetermination of God's by which He decided from eternity to bring them about in this way in time. Similarly, it should be said that the certitude of the knowledge through which God on *that* basis knew these things as absolutely future also depends solely on that same predetermination; but there is a difference to the extent that these

which a craftsman moves and applies tools to their characteristic operation. (See Disputation 53, pt. 1, n. 7.) St. Thomas himself also uses the interestingly different example of the cook applying the fire to the food to be cooked.

The relevant texts in St. Thomas's works include *Summa Theologiae* I, q. 105, a. 5; *Summa Contra Gentiles* III, chaps. 67 and 70; and *De Potentia Dei*, q. 3, a. 7. Molina discusses the issues involved at some length in Disputations 25–28 (Rabeneck, pp. 159–185).

[3] The things in question here are miraculous occurrences that are brought about by God alone but take place within a historical context that is itself at least in part the result of the free choices of created agents. Compare Disputation 53, pt. 2, sec. 15, where Molina speculates about how *sinful* free choices have affected the subsequent history of the world. See Section 2.7 of the Introduction.

[4] The story of the raising of Lazarus from the dead is found in John 11, and the story of the man born blind is found in John 9. Paul's conversion is recounted in Acts 9.

things *presuppose* for their existence those other things that depend in many ways on the created will; for with regard to the certitude of the knowledge through which God knew the things in question on *this latter* basis as absolutely future, we should say the same thing as we will presently say concerning the certitude of His knowledge of things of the third type.[5]

4. The third genus comprises those things whose *proximate source of contingency* is created free choice, regardless of whether they depend on it proximately or remotely for their *existence*.[6]

Now, in view of the fact that once we have explicated divine predeterminations with respect to the human actions of *our* faculty of choice in the state of *fallen nature*, we can easily understand both (i) the predeterminations required for the actions of *angels* and of human beings in the state of *innocence*, whose freedom was greater than ours, and also (ii) the extent to which the things that depend *mediately* on the created faculty of choice are dependent on divine predeterminations, we will be discussing divine predeterminations just with regard to *our* human actions.

5. As we said in the Appendix, response to the second objection (and this is relevant to the present discussion), we are able to distinguish three types of human actions.[7] The first type includes indifferent actions or actions that, even if they are morally good, nonetheless involve so little difficulty that they can be performed with just God's *general* concurrence. The second type consists of those actions that are supernatural or that involve so much difficulty that they require God's *particular* assistance.[8] The third type includes those actions that are sinful. In the

---

[5]So there are two ways of considering the certitude of God's foreknowledge of the fact that Lazarus was going to be raised from the dead. On the one hand, God is the sole cause of the precise effect in question (the raising of Lazarus), and so the certitude of His foreknowledge of it stems solely from His predetermination to raise Lazarus up. On the other hand, God has predetermined to raise Lazarus up within a historical context whose causal ancestry involves many human free choices, and so God needs middle knowledge in order to know with certainty that just those circumstances will obtain and hence in order to know with certainty that Lazarus will be raised up *in just those circumstances*. The proximate source of the contingency of Lazarus's being raised up is God's will alone, whereas the proximate source of the contingency of many of the circumstances surrounding the resuscitation of Lazarus is human free choice.

[6]See Disputation 47, sec. 11, for Molina's careful distinction between the proximate source of a contingent effect's *existence* and the proximate source of a contingent effect's *contingency*.

[7]See Appendix, response to the second objection, in Rabeneck, pp. 625–642, esp. pp. 631–636.

[8]God's concurrence is called *general* when it does not by itself determine the exact nature of the effect. God's *particular* assistance consists of prevenient and cooperating graces. See Disputation 53, pt. 1, n. 13.

Appendix we used as examples of all three types acts of speaking commanded by free choice, and we will continue to use this sort of example here as well.

6. Now we must assume that in an account of divine predeterminations it cannot be denied that prior to any free act of the divine will, and hence prior to any predetermination, there existed in the divine intellect a *nonfree* knowledge through which God knew not only (i) all the things that were able to exist because of His omnipotence (either directly through Him alone or via the mediation of secondary causes), but also (ii) all the things that would come to be through any created faculty of choice and, in general, through any other agent, on any hypothesis or given any predetermination on His part. For no one can deny that this knowledge exists in God, even though there could be disagreement about whether this sort of knowledge of all objects, a knowledge conditioned on predeterminations, is *purely natural* to God (as it is, we claimed above, when it is a knowledge of created things of the first type), or whether, with respect to those things that depend mediately or immediately on the created faculty of choice, it has in God the character, not of *natural* knowledge, but instead of a *middle* knowledge that was able not to exist if the faculty of choice by its freedom had been going to do the opposite on the hypothesis in question. In fact, the authors with whom we disagree seem to imply that this knowledge is *purely natural* with respect to *all* the things whose predeterminations they posit in God; for they claim that God's predetermination and concurrence direct the faculty of choice to those things and that the faculty of choice is not able in the composed sense to do the opposite. This seems to be the type of knowledge they posit in God with respect to *conditioned* future contingents, according to the points that were cited from their position in Part 1;[9] but they do not explain clearly what they think about sinful acts (with regard to which they reject divine predeterminations), though in the two preceding parts we explained by way of conjecture what they *appear* to think about such acts.

7. With this point thus established, it follows that with respect to a human action of the first type—for example, an indifferent act of speaking which will occur tomorrow on Peter's part or the same act now rendered morally good by its relation to wholesome diversion in accordance with the virtues of affability and congeniality—it is necessary that such an act be preceded from eternity by the following predetermina-

[9]See Disputation 53, pt. 1, sec. 2.

tions on God's part: (i) a volition to create the whole order of things all the way up to Peter, and to concur with each secondary cause, whether free or natural, which existed in the series extending from the beginning of the world all the way up to the begetting of Peter; (ii) a volition to create Peter's soul and to infuse it into his body, and to cooperate together with all the causes that directly concur to generate Peter; and thus (iii) a volition to confer on Peter, in part by Himself directly and in part via the mediation of secondary causes, free choice and the rest of the powers required for speaking as well as for other things; likewise, (iv) a volition to concur in the production of all those things that were required up until Peter would arrive at the instant of the speaking with all the circumstances then obtaining; finally, (v) a volition not to deny Peter His general concurrence for speaking in that manner, should Peter in his freedom will thus to speak, but always to assist him by means of that concurrence in such a way that if Peter should will to speak or to exercise some other operation, He would aid him in the same way, and thus (vi) a volition to confer that concurrence on him because He saw that in his freedom Peter would speak.

Now according to our position, this concurrence is not a motion of God's *on* the faculty of choice by which He moves, applies, and determines it either to precisely *that* act of speaking or even to *some* act of speaking or other; instead, it is an influence *along with* the faculty of choice, an influence that depends for its existence on the influence and cooperation of that faculty itself, in the way that, as was explained in Disputation 40, a habit's influence on and cooperation with a faculty for acting depends on the cooperation of that faculty.[10] But in the proposed case, just as this general concurrence depends for its existence on the influence and cooperation of the faculty of choice, so too, reciprocally, the influence of the faculty of choice depends for its existence on the general concurrence, as was explained at length in both regards in Disputation 25.[11] Likewise, this general concurrence is intrinsically indifferent as to whether it is followed by a volition to speak or a volition not to speak, or by any other act of the faculty of choice; and it is by the faculty of choice itself, as a particular cause, that this general concurrence is channeled to a specific type of act.[12]

Look at the divine predeterminations that this indifferent or morally good act of speaking of Peter's which will occur tomorrow depends upon. Clearly, despite these predeterminations and God's general con-

---

[10]See Disputation 40, sec. 5 (Rabeneck, pp. 244–245).

[11]See Disputation 25, sec. 14 (Rabeneck, pp. 162–163).

[12]Literally, God's general concurrence is thereby directed to a species (Latin: *species*) of act.

currence, Peter remains free, and at the designated instant he can will to speak or will not to speak; in the same way, he can will to speak zealously or, by misusing his will and the general concurrence and the other gifts of God, he can will to speak for an evil purpose or perversely; or he can will to apply himself toward performing some other, far different, act. All this must be conceded, unless, by a patent error from the point of view of the faith, we want to deprive Peter of his freedom of choice and deprive his act of its moral goodness and merit, assuming that it was performed in the state of grace.

But because this zealous act of speaking is included in the end for which God predetermined to give Peter free choice as well as His general concurrence and all the other gifts listed above, it is clear that God, foreseeing that the act in question would occur by Peter's freedom on the hypothesis that He should will to predetermine all those things, intended *this particular* act and, in accord with His well-pleased will,[13] willed it to exist by means of (i) the predetermination itself, and thus by means of (ii) His providence with respect to that effect, a providence carried out via the predetermination, and, likewise, by means of (iii) the gifts themselves—always with a dependence on Peter's free cooperation, which God foresaw to be forthcoming.

---

[13] According to St. Thomas (*De Veritate*, q. 23, a. 3 and 4), talk of God's well-pleased will (literally, *voluntas beneplaciti*, the will of one well pleased) is proper and literal talk of what God wills. The well-pleased will is divided into God's *antecedent* will or volition and God's *consequent* will or volition. St. Thomas characterizes this distinction as follows:

"That which God has ordained for creatures, to the extent that it is from Himself, is said to be willed by Him through a sort of *primary* intention or *antecedent* volition. But when a creature is kept from this end because of its own defectiveness, God still brings to fulfillment in it the goodness of which it is capable—and this through a sort of *secondary* intention or *consequent* volition.

"Therefore, since God has made all human beings for beatitude, He is said to will the salvation of all through His antecedent will. But because there are those who resist their salvation, those whom, because of their own defectiveness, the order of His wisdom does not allow to attain salvation, in them He brings to fulfillment in a different way that which pertains to His goodness, namely, by condemning them through His justice—so that while they are falling short of the primary order of His will, they are slipping into the secondary order, and while they are failing to fulfill God's will, God's will is being fulfilled in them." (*De Veritate*, q. 23, a. 3, corpus.)

St. Thomas hastens to add that God in no way—either antecedently or consequently—wills or intends sins by His well-pleased will. Instead, He merely *permits* them.

God's well-pleased will is contrasted with His *signified* will. Talk of the latter is, according to St. Thomas, figurative (and *not* literal) talk of God's will. Such talk is based on certain correlations between willing and acting commonly found among human beings. For instance, just as what we prohibit is a *sign* of what we will the opposite of, so too with God. The five signs of God's will are *prohibition, precept, counsel, operation,* and *permission*. As noted above, what God permits is not something that He literally wills. Still, we often *figuratively* assign to a person's will what he merely permits. And so too we often say "It is God's will" when speaking of tragic events, whether the tragedy is moral or merely physical.

Further, God's intending and willing in the way just noted, by means of His predeterminations and providence, *all* our good acts *in particular*, even the supernatural ones, and indeed *every nonevil* effect of secondary causes—this is what the Fathers call God's "predestining" and "predetermining" those effects. Thus in the epistolatory decree to Peter of Antioch, Leo IX says, "I believe that God predestined only good things, but that He foreknew both good and evil things."[14] And Augustine (or whoever else the author of this work is) says in *De Articulis Sibi Falso Impositis,* article 10, "We must detest and abominate the opinion that holds that God is the author of every evil volition or bad action—God, whose predestination is nowhere outside the bounds of goodness, nowhere outside the bounds of justice. For all the ways of the Lord are mercy and truth (Ps. 24:10). For the holy Divinity knew not to provide for but to condemn acts of adultery on the part of married women and the seductions of virgins; He knew not to arrange them, but to punish them. Thus God's predestination did not incite or induce or set in motion the lapses of those who go to ruin or the malice of the iniquitous or the excessive desires of sinners; rather, He plainly predestined that judgment of His by which He is going to repay each in accord with what he has done, whether good or evil."[15]

8.   As far as human actions of the second type are concerned, let us take as our example an action that is *supernatural* and *extremely difficult*, namely, a confession of faith under torture all the way up to the end of one's life, a confession that makes the person in question a martyr; and let us assume that this confession is elicited from an unbeliever, who is justified through it.

Clearly, for an action of this sort it is not only necessary that there should exist all the divine predeterminations spoken of above with reference to the aforementioned indifferent or morally good action, but it is also required that there be a predetermination to call, assist, and comfort the man at the time in question by means of the extraordinary aids of prevenient and cooperating grace, without which the man's faculty of choice would be unable to persevere. Still, these and the aforementioned predeterminations and aids leave him able, at the instant at which he is converted, not only not to be converted but even to dissent from the faith and to repudiate it; and they leave him able afterward, as long as his torments last, all the way up to the end of his life, to succumb and to repudiate the faith. Nor, in accord with what was

---

[14]*PL* 143, 772C.
[15]*PL* 51, 182f. The scriptural reference is to Hebrew Psalm 25.

said in the preceding part and in other places, do we doubt that this opinion is *de fide*;[16] otherwise, such a conversion to the faith and such perseverance in confessing it would not be meritorious—indeed, they would not even constitute a morally good act, since there can be neither merit nor moral goodness in any act unless there is freedom, whether of contrariety or of contradiction, with respect to the opposite.

But since God foresaw that, because of the man's freedom, this confession and perseverance right up to the end of life would occur on the hypothesis that He should will to predetermine and assist him in this way, clearly, He *specifically* intended that the confession and perseverance should exist because of those aids and because of that predetermination or order of His providence, a providence that is fulfilled by that predetermination with respect to the effect in question; and through the volition of His well-pleased will He willed this act, greatly pleased that it was going to occur in that way because of His gifts together with the free volition of the faculty of choice. And it is for this reason that He is said to have predestined and predetermined this action, as was said above concerning morally good actions.

What has been said about this sort of supernatural and extremely difficult operation of our faculty of choice should also be taken to apply to the other operations for which God's particular assistance is required; for the predetermination to confer such assistance in no way deprives the faculty of choice of its freedom not to elicit the action in question or even of its freedom to dissent from it—as the Council of Trent taught in session 6, chapter 5, canon 4.[17]

9.   Finally, as regards *sinful* human actions, included among which was Peter's threefold denial,[18] the authors with whom we disagree correctly claim that such actions have not been predetermined by God; still, one should not give the explanation of this point that *they* give, namely, that God does not apply or direct the faculty of choice to such actions by His efficacious concurrence—as though He *does* direct it to *good* actions by His efficacious concurrence. Instead, one should say that even though God decided to confer on the sinner the faculty of free choice along with His general concurrence and the other things necessary for eliciting these acts, He did not *intend* them, but rather resolved to confer all these things for a far different end, whereas it is the sinner himself who in his freedom misuses all these things in order to exercise the acts in question.

---

[16]See Disputation 53, pt. 2, sec. 12ff. For a brief characterization of what makes a doctrine *de fide*, see Disputation 52, n. 14.

[17]See Denzinger, 1554, p. 378.

[18]For the gospel accounts of Peter's denial of Christ, see Matt. 27:69–75, Mark 15:66–72, Luke 22:54–62, John 18:15–18 and 25–27.

Now, even though it should be said that God has not predestined or predetermined evil actions, it should nonetheless be affirmed that certain predeterminations on God's part were necessary in order for those actions to be able to exist in reality through the created faculty of choice. Thus, if we are speaking of Peter's threefold denial, all those predeterminations were necessary which we claimed above to be necessary for eliciting an *indifferent* act at the very moment at which Peter denied Christ—including God's predetermination to grant (or not to deny) Peter His general concurrence. Furthermore, it was likewise necessary for there to be a predetermination to permit Peter, for the sake of the excellent end that God Himself intended by this permission, to perform the evil action that He foresaw would occur under those circumstances because of Peter's free choice—that is, a predetermination not to alter the circumstances or to confer on Peter other aids in the presence of which he would not lapse into that denial because of the same freedom of choice.[19]

10. Notice, we have laid out all the predeterminations required for *all positive future contingents in general.*[20] Now briefly consider the entire source of the difference between us and the authors with whom we disagree. They claim that God's eternal predeterminations, along with the concurrences by means of which He decided through those predeterminations to concur in time with each created faculty of choice in order to produce all the *nonevil* acts, direct the faculty of choice to those acts in such a way that it does not retain the power not to elicit them; for they insist that each such concurrence is intrinsically efficacious, and that its efficacy does not in any way depend on the faculty of choice. Thus, as a result, they insist that all the certitude of the divine foreknowledge by which God knew all those acts as absolutely future depends *only* on the predeterminations by virtue of which those acts are going to be elicited

[19]An interesting question lurking in the background here is whether, necessarily, each sin is such that God could have prevented it simply by increasing the intensity of His prevenient and cooperating aids, so that the person in question would *freely* refrain from sinning. According to the negative response, there are (or could be) true counterfactual conditionals expressed by sentences of the following form: 'Person *S* would still have freely sinned at time *T* no matter how much supernatural assistance God had given him at *T*.'

[20]By a *positive* future contingent Molina means an affirmative future contingent proposition expressed by a sentence of the form 'It will be the case that *S* is *P*,' where *S* and *P* are place holders for the subject-term and predicate-term, respectively. Such propositions, as affirmative, entail the future existence of the things referred to by the subject-terms. By contrast, a *negative* future contingent proposition, for example, one expressed by a sentence of the form 'It is not the case that it will be the case that *S* is *P*,' is true if the thing purportedly referred to by the subject-term will never exist. It should be clear that a complete set of predeterminations with respect to positive future contingents would also fix the truth-value of every negative future contingent.

by the created faculty of choice not only infallibly but also inevitably.[21] Thus again, they consequently deny that any middle knowledge is to be countenanced in God with regard to those acts—and, indeed, given their principles, middle knowledge certainly *should* be denied, since, as was said above, the knowledge by which, before any free act of God's will, these things would be foreknown by Him as future on the hypothesis of those predeterminations would be *altogether natural* in God.[22] And for this reason they claim that the knowledge by which God knew *conditioned* future contingents, for example, that there would have been repentance among the Tyronians and Sidonians on the hypothesis that the wonders performed in Chorozain and Bethsaida should have been performed among them, is *purely natural* in relation to the predetermination that *would have* existed in that case. We, on the other hand, believe that it is an error from the point of view of the faith to posit divine predeterminations and concurrences of a sort that do not leave it within the power of the faculty of choice, at the instant when it elicits a nonevil act, not to elicit it or even to dissent from it if it so chooses; and as a result we claim that all the certitude of the divine knowledge by which God foreknew both the good and the evil acts of the created faculty of choice as absolutely future does *not* have its source *just* in the predeterminations to confer aids and concurrences, since the faculty of choice is able to turn itself toward the contrary part despite those predeterminations. Rather, it has its source in the middle knowledge by which (i), before any act of His will, God knew which part the faculty of choice in its freedom would turn itself toward on the hypothesis that He should will to grant it those aids and concurrences, and by which (ii) He would have known the contrary, if the faculty of choice were through that same freedom going to turn itself toward the contrary part. And it is through this same knowledge, we claim, that God knew with certainty all those future things that the authors of the opposed position call "conditioned."

We claim that the certitude of this middle knowledge has *its* source, in turn, in the depth and unlimited perfection of the divine intellect, a perfection by which God knows with certainty what is in itself uncertain, and this because of an absolutely eminent comprehension, in His divine essence, of every faculty of choice that He is able to create by His omnipotence.

11. Last, observe that middle knowledge is indeed in God before any free act of His will, and that it is a knowledge of *all* effects in general, not

---

[21]The term 'infallibly' here should be understood as having epistemic import and as characterizing God's knowledge, whereas the term 'inevitably' should be understood as having metaphysical import and as characterizing the things of which God has knowledge.

[22]See sec. 6 above.

only (i) of those effects that are in fact going to exist because of the faculties of choice that He has decided to create within the order of things and circumstances that He chose to establish, but also (ii) of those effects that would have been going to exist (whether because of these very same faculties of choice or because of the infinitely many others that He could have created) if any of the circumstances had been altered within the order of things He chose to establish or if any other order of things had existed from among the infinity upon infinity of orders of things that He could have created; and yet notice that this middle knowledge is a knowledge of all those effects in such a way that it is a knowledge of none of them *except on the hypothesis* of a predetermination of the divine will to choose to establish this or that order of things and to provide for and assist the order of things in question (or its means and circumstances) in this or that way. But since it is through such a pre-determination that the notion of divine providence with respect to each of these effects is satisfied, it most assuredly follows that through His middle knowledge, prior to any act of His will, God foresaw nothing except *on the hypothesis* and *under the condition* that He should will to provide for the effect in question in this or that way. Thus it is not the case that middle knowledge of this sort destroys or impedes divine providence; to the contrary, it is an illumination and cognition that is a precondition in God, on the part of His *intellect*, for an absolutely perfect and exact providence. For through this knowledge and cognition, be-fore He establishes anything by His will, and thus before He provides for anything having to do with the created faculty of choice in keeping with the free nature of that faculty, He foresees what is going to occur because of it—*not absolutely*, but rather *on the hypothesis and condition* that He should provide for it in this or that way. Thus, at that prior instant, before God predetermines or establishes anything by His will, the notion of providence is not yet satisfied in God with respect to either the created faculty of choice or anything else, since at that instant there is still lacking something that is required on the part of His *will* for the notion of providence. So, too, nothing is at that instant known as *absolutely* and *simply* future, but only as future *under the condition* that God should will to determine and provide for things in this or that way.

12. Consider now the difference between us and the authors with whom we disagree on the matter of God's providence regarding those things that depend immediately on the created faculty of choice.[23] They rightly insist that God has providence over each particular *nonevil* act of

[23]For a general discussion of the doctrine of providence, see Sections 1.2–1.3 of the Introduction.

created free choice, and that He intends those acts, and that they are the effects of that same providence; however, they think that He intends them and is a cause of them by His providence in virtue of the fact that (i) He decided from eternity to move and determine the created faculty of choice to those acts by an assistance or concurrence that is intrinsically efficacious, and by virtue of the fact that (ii) in time He in fact moves the faculty of choice by that very same efficacious assistance in such a way that it does not remain within the power of the faculty, placed under that predetermination and concurrence, not to exercise those acts. As a result, they go on to assert that those acts are certain and infallible *solely* because of the order of divine providence.

13. We, on the other hand, having no doubt that this sort of predetermination and intrinsically efficacious concurrence completely destroys freedom of choice with respect to those acts and thus involves an error from the point of view of the faith, claim, first of all, that through His wisdom God provides for each thing in accordance with its nature and, for this reason, provides for free beings with respect to their free effects, whether these effects are natural or supernatural, in a way that always preserves their freedom of choice, that is, by leaving it within their power, at the very moment at which they produce those effects and despite all the circumstances obtaining at that moment, not to produce those effects and, indeed, if they so will, to produce contrary effects—so that they are the masters of their own actions, and they are fit for virtue and vice, praise and blame, reward and punishment.

14. Second, we claim that God intends those acts and that they are *particular effects* of His providence;[24] for all the causes by which they are individually produced and by virtue of which God through His middle knowledge foresaw that they would be produced on the hypothesis that He should will to arrange the universe in such-and-such a way or to provide for the things in it in such-and-such a way—all these causes are, of course, the means and effects of His providence, conferred by that same eternal predetermination and providence of His in order to produce these and other similar acts. Yet, clearly, among these causes and means is included and numbered the faculty of choice itself, conferred by God on angels and human beings through that same providence of His for those acts, but with the power *not* to produce them—even

[24] It is important to remember that Molina is speaking here just of the *nonevil* acts of created free choice. God does not intend evil acts; rather, He permits them while intending the good to which He can turn them despite their nature.

though there preexisted in God a knowledge by which He saw that the faculty of choice *would in fact* produce them on the hypothesis that He should will to place it in this order of things and aids and circumstances. Therefore, the created faculty of choice is counted among the means through which God by His providence intends those acts and by virtue of which He is a cause of those things *in particular* when they actually come to be—the created faculty of choice, which really has the power not to produce them, if it so chooses. It surely follows that those acts would be neither certain nor infallible *solely* because of the means of divine providence *if you were to rule out middle knowledge,* a knowledge by which God, because of the depth of His intellect and in a way surpassing the nature of the object, foresaw that, because of freedom of choice, those acts would come to be from those same means and from the order of divine providence.

15. Third, we claim that since (as has been explained thus far) these same acts depend simultaneously both on freedom of choice and on God, who by His eternal predetermination or providence wills to bestow the faculty of choice as well as all the other means that are required for or even facilitate those acts, it clearly follows that whereas God foresaw through His middle knowledge that those acts would occur because of freedom of choice on the hypothesis that He should will to predetermine and provide for things in the way appropriate to produce the acts, by the very fact that He later (in our way of conceiving it, with a basis in reality) did so predetermine and provide for them, He thereby willed by an absolute volition that they should be as He foresaw they would be, well pleased that those acts should be dependent *both* on His own predetermination and providence itself and *also* on freedom of choice—as on *two* causes that were necessary for the existence of those acts in such a way that if the latter of the two was absent by its own freedom, then the acts would not occur.

16. Fourth, we claim that since (i) it is not only our *good* acts that depend, in the way explained above, on our faculty of choice, but also our *evil* acts that depend on that same freedom of choice, whereas (ii) God does not provide for all human beings and angels equally or in the same way, with regard to either supernatural or natural gifts, but rather decides to distribute the gifts of His mercy as He pleases, though no one is ever deprived of what is necessary, it clearly follows that for an absolutely perfect providence on God's part there had to be (as we were saying in the preceding disputation) a *middle knowledge* through which God, foreseeing what would occur through *any* creature's faculty of

choice on *any* hypothesis and in *any* turn of events among things, was able, from eternity and without any shadow of alteration in the course of time itself, to predestine what he pleased on the part of those creatures whom He should decide to create, while preserving their freedom; and He was able to provide for all free creatures with respect to each event in accordance with His wisdom and the pleasure of His will, deciding (i) to prepare the way for their acts by various means and aids, (ii) to discipline them in various ways, (iii) to permit and tolerate their failures and sins, (iv) to call them to faith and repentance, (v) to confirm them, now called and justified, in goodness, and (vi) to do many other things with respect to them.

17. Finally, we claim that all *good* things, whether produced by causes acting from a necessity of nature or by free causes, depend on divine predetermination (of the sort we have just explicated) and providence in such a way that each is *specifically intended* by God through His predetermination and providence, whereas the *evil* acts of the created faculty of choice are subject as well to divine predetermination and providence to the extent that the causes from which they emanate and the general concurrence on God's part required to elicit them are granted through divine predetermination and providence—though not in order that *these particular acts* should emanate from them, but rather in order that *other, far different, acts* might come to be, and in order that the innate freedom of the things endowed with a faculty of choice might be preserved for their maximum benefit; in addition, evil acts are subject to that same divine predetermination and providence to the extent that they cannot exist in particular unless God by His providence *permits them in particular* for the sake of some greater good. It clearly follows that all things without exception are *individually* subject to God's providence and will, which intends certain of them *as particulars* and permits the rest *as particulars*. Thus, the leaf hanging from the tree does not fall, nor does either of the two sparrows sold for a farthing fall to the ground, nor does anything else whatever happen without God's providence and will either *intending* it *as a particular* or *permitting* it *as a particular*.[25] This is the greatest consolation of the righteous, who place all their hope in God and rest comfortably in the shadow of the wings of His providence, desiring that in both prosperity and adversity God's will with regard to them might always be fulfilled.[26]

---

[25]See Matt. 10:29.
[26]The image of the believer being under the shadow of God's wings is found in the following Psalms (Hebrew numbering): 17:8, 36:8, 57:2, and 63:7.

18. From what has been said you can easily see just how false the frequent charge made against me is, namely, that because I posit in God a middle knowledge by which He foresaw what the created faculty of choice would do on the hypothesis that it should be placed in this or that order of things and circumstances and aids, I am thereby claiming that there is *only general, and not particular,* providence with respect to those things that depend on the created faculty of choice. Nor do those who make this charge against me pay attention to the fact that included in the very being endowed with free choice and in the order of things and circumstances and aids are all the means of divine providence through which God *intends in particular* all the good things that He foresees are going to exist because of the freedom of such a created faculty of choice. But since I am not concerned with what anyone reports about me—for what I myself have said can easily be ascertained by anyone who reads the first edition of our *Concordia* or this second edition—I will purposely disregard the many opinions that are falsely referred to as mine; in addition, there are many other opinions that I find it unnecessary to apologize for.[27]

Part 4
Some Objections Are Answered

1. *First objection.* The authors of the contrary position argue, first, as follows:[1] "If God had decided not to create anything at all, then there would be only *natural* knowledge in God, knowledge through which He would comprehend Himself and in Himself all possible beings, both natural and free. But His decision to create things results only in there being *free* knowledge in God, knowledge through which He knows which things are going to exist because of that free decision. Therefore, there is in God no distinct third genus of knowledge, namely, middle knowledge.

2. "This is confirmed by the fact that either (i) God's knowledge is thought of in relation to *possible* things, *before* they are brought into existence by an act of the divine will, and viewed in this way it is *natural* in God; or (ii) it is thought of in relation to the things that are going to exist

---

[27]This somewhat plaintive plea for the reader's sympathy is reflective of Molina's difficulties with those who accused him of holding unorthodox views. Such charges deeply troubled him, since he was convinced not only that his own views were orthodox but that his opponents' views were erroneous from the point of view of the faith.

[1]Zumel, *Commentaria,* q. 14, a. 1, disp. unica, concl. 2, p. 361.

in various intervals of time *after* the free determination of the divine will, and in that case it is *free* knowledge. Thus, there is no third kind of knowledge in God."

3. *Response.* As far as the argument is concerned, the major premise should be denied. For besides the purely natural knowledge by which all those things would be known as merely possible beings, there would also be middle knowledge, by which (i) God would know, with respect to any contradictory pair of future contingents dependent on the created faculty of choice, which part is going to be true—not *absolutely,* but rather *on the hypothesis* that He should will to establish this or that order of things—and by which (ii) He would know the contradictory if the contradictory were going to be true because of the created faculty of choice on that same hypothesis. This has already been demonstrated, and our opponents themselves are constrained to acknowledge the same point with regard to the *sins* that would occur on the hypothesis in question because of the created faculty of choice—unless either (i) they want to assert that God is ignorant of the sins that would occur on that hypothesis, or (ii) they want to claim that, given that hypothesis, the faculty of choice would commit those sins by a necessity of nature—a claim that was attacked at length in Part 2.[2] Notice that even if God had decided not to create anything, there would still have existed in Him *free* knowledge through which He would have known that none of those things that He could have created was going to exist; for just as He would have freely decided not to create, so too He would freely know that nothing that He could have decided to create but did not decide to create was going to exist. Our opponents, though, are talking about free knowledge of *positive* things.[3]

4. As for the confirmation, it should be replied that there is a third way of thinking of God's knowledge, namely, in relation to things that are future, not *absolutely* but rather *on the hypothesis* that God Himself should will to create this or that order of things; for what is future in this way *on a hypothesis* occupies a sort of middle ground between what is

[2] See Disputation 53, pt. 2, secs. 1–11.
[3] Molina's point here presupposes that necessarily, for any contradictory pair of future contingent propositions, exactly one is true and exactly one is false. So even if God had decided not to create anything, He would still have known a full complement of future contingent propositions and hence would still have had *free* knowledge. In such a case, however, each of the future contingent propositions He knew would be negative and hence such that it does not entail the existence of any creature at any time. See Disputation 53, pt. 3, n. 20, for more on the distinction between positive and negative future contingents.

merely possible and what is *absolutely future*, as was explained in Part 1.[4] But God's knowledge, thus viewed in relation to things that would occur on the hypothesis in question because of created free choice, is *middle* knowledge. For even though it is not *free* in God, still God would have known the contradictory if, as could have been the case on the very same hypothesis, the contradictory were going to be true.

5. *Second objection.* They argue, second, as follows:[5] "If God's predetermination to confer intrinsically efficacious concurrence for a good act of the will and also the intrinsically efficacious concurrence itself were such that they should not be posited, this would be because, by efficaciously determining the will to one act, they destroy the will's freedom with respect to the opposite, and thus the will would elicit that act necessarily rather than freely, with the result that the moral goodness and merit of the act would perish. From the fact that the will is determined to one act when it acts, however, it does not follow that it is not acting freely. Therefore, it is unreasonable to reject on these grounds either the divine predetermination to confer intrinsically efficacious concurrence or the intrinsically efficacious concurrence itself. The minor premise is proved by the fact that, even in the opinion of those who do not countenance predeterminations or efficacious concurrences of the sort in question, when the will acts freely, it has *already* determined itself to one part of a contradiction—indeed, it acts *because* it has determined itself. Yet this does not prevent it from acting freely. Therefore, from the fact that the will has been determined to one act when it acts, it does not follow that it is not acting freely."

6. *Response.* In response to the major premise of this argument, it should be said that the reason these predeterminations and intrinsically efficacious concurrences ought not to be countenanced is that those who posit them claim that (i) when they are absent, the will is not able to elicit the good act in question, and that (ii) when they are present, the will is not able not to elicit the act, and further that (iii) their presence or absence does not depend on the *will* that is supposed to elicit the act, but depends instead solely on *God's* freely predetermining or not predetermining the act from eternity. Given these conditions, the will itself *never* retains the power to determine or not to determine itself indifferently, or to determine itself to one or the other part; yet such power is abso-

---

[4]See Disputation 53, pt. 1, sec. 6.
[5]Zumel, *Commentaria*, q. 23, a. 3, disp. 8, p. 676a; and q. 19, a. 8, disp. 1, notabile 2, p. 560a–b.

lutely necessary for there to be true freedom. Now, the claim that, given these conditions, this power would never exist in the will is obvious, since at an instant when that concurrence is not present, the will is not able to determine itself to elicit the act, nor is it then within the will's power to do anything such that were the will to do it, then that concurrence would be present. For in that case the concurrence and predetermination would depend not only on *God's* free will but also on what the *created* will was in its freedom going to do or not going to do, as foreknown by God through middle knowledge. On the other hand, at an instant when that efficacious concurrence is present, the will is not able not to be determined to elicit the act; for if at such an instant the will had the power not to determine itself, then it would be able to render such a concurrence inefficacious, and thus it would depend on the will whether the concurrence was efficacious or inefficacious.

So given that the major premise of the proposed argument has been conceded, if that premise has to do with the kind of determination I have just explained, that is, the kind that destroys the will's freedom with respect to the act and along with it the moral goodness and merit of the act, then the minor premise should be denied, as long as it likewise has to do with the same kind of determination to one act.

Now, as far as the proof is concerned, it should be denied that when the will acts freely, it has determined itself *naturally prior to* its acting.[6] Quite the opposite, it is in fact *by* acting freely that it determines itself to its act, and *earlier in nature* at the same moment it was *indifferent* as to whether it was going to determine itself to act or not to act, or to act with respect to this object rather than that one, or to will it rather than reject it—and this *prior to* its determinately acting or determinately not acting, and *prior to* its determinately eliciting a volition with respect to this or that object or a volition with respect to its opposite, as was shown in Disputation 24.[7] Indeed, the will acts freely or determines itself freely to an act by virtue of the fact that (i) earlier in nature it is indifferent as to whether it is going to determine itself or not determine itself in a given way, and thus that (ii) when it determines itself, it is able not to determine itself. But *after* the will is thought of as already determined to one object at a given moment, then a contradiction is involved in its not

---

[6]Molina denies here that the determination of the will is prior, even in some non-temporal sense, to the will's free act. As he goes on to explain, he does believe that the very instant at which an act of will occurs can be divided into a "naturally" prior and posterior. But even so, the determination of the will, which occurs naturally posterior to the will's being indifferent with respect to both parts, is just identical with the act of the will. So there is no room on Molina's view for any (divine or human) *pre*determination of the will.

[7]Rabeneck, pp. 155–158.

having determined itself at that moment, and thus it is no longer free not to determine itself in that way—and this, as was explained in the disputation just cited, is what Aristotle and Boethius meant by the familiar formula, "What is, when it is, is not able not to be."[8]

7. *Third objection.* Third, they argue as follows:[9] "Even though, when an efficacious willing of an end exists, the will is not able in the composed sense not to will the means necessary for that end, still this does not destroy the freedom and moral goodness, or even the merit, of the willing of such a means. For instance, when an efficacious willing of eternal happiness exists in a wayfarer,[10] and when there occurs on his part an act of obedience to some precept that obliges under pain of moral guilt, then even though he is not able in the composed sense not to will that act of obedience (since it is a means absolutely necessary for attaining beatitude), nonetheless this does not prevent that act of willing from being free, morally good, and meritorious. Therefore, the fact that when there is a divine predetermination to confer efficacious concurrence on someone with respect to some good act, such a person is in the composed sense not able not to elicit that act—this fact will in no way prevent such an act from being free and morally good, or even meritorious, if it is elicited by someone who is in the state of grace."

8. *Response.* As for this argument, given that the antecedent has been conceded, the consequence should be denied. For in the *first* case each of those acts that cannot in the composed sense exist at the same time is within the power of the wayfarer's free will, so that when he wills his occurrent act of obedience to such a precept, he is able not to will it and thereby able at the same time to refrain from efficaciously willing the end; and thus he retains true freedom or indifference with respect to both parts, as far as obedience to such a precept is concerned. In the *second* case, however, if a predetermination and intrinsically efficacious divine concurrence of the type in question are admitted, then he does not retain the freedom to elicit or not to elicit that good act, as was shown in the preceding argument and quite often in the ones before that.

---

[8]See Disputation 24, sec. 4 (Rabeneck, p. 155). The passage from Aristotle is found in *De Interpretatione,* chap. 9 (19b 23), and the passage from Boethius is found in *De Consolatione Philosophiae* V, prose 6 (*PL* 63, 861C).

[9]Zumel, *Commentaria,* q. 19, a. 8, disp. 1, ad 3, p. 564a–b.

[10]The Latin term *viator* (literally, traveler) is used to designate a human being who is still in this life as opposed to the afterlife. Hence, such a person is a wayfarer, a pilgrim, someone still 'on the way' (*in via*) to a heavenly homeland. Below Molina discusses Christ's condition as a wayfarer, that is, in the time between his conception and his death and resurrection.

9. *Fourth objection.* Fourth, they argue like this:[11] "If an exceptionally prudent general or head of a household were able to provide for his army or his household by prearranging each and every thing and particular means for the attainment of victory or for the just governance of the household, then he would certainly do so, and therein his great providence and wisdom would shine forth; if, on the other hand, he does not do this, it is because he is unable to. But God can very easily provide for all things in this way, and freedom is not on this account taken away from the created faculty of choice. Therefore, He provides for things by predetermining all of them individually."

10. *Response.* This argument should be accepted as a whole if it is meant to assert only that in God there is providence with regard to all things individually. Nor in that case does the argument impugn our position, since we posit in God a providence with regard to each individual thing; the good things He intends individually and the evil things He permits individually, as was shown in the preceding part.[12] If, however, the argument is meant to assert that God provides for individual things and means in such a way that He intends each of them by a predetermination via intrinsically efficacious concurrence, then, given that the major premise and the first part of the minor have been conceded, the last part of the minor should be denied, namely, that this kind of predetermination does not take away freedom from the created faculty of choice; for the contrary has already been proven. Next, the consequence itself should be denied, since the cases are altogether dissimilar. For victory and the just governance of a household so that no rebellion afflicts it—these are the goals of the *general* and of the *head of the household,* goals that they intend and that they would always bring about if they were able to. By contrast, however, the natural and supernatural ends in the service of which God provides for free creatures are not *God's* ends, but rather the ends of the *very creatures themselves,* proffered to them in such a way that God leaves it within their power to attain those ends or not to attain them—so that the means to those ends might thus result in merit, praise, and honor for them and so that the ends themselves might result in a reward. And for this reason it was expedient for God to provide for those creatures not by means of efficacious concurrences, but instead by means of concurrences that are such that it is up to those very creatures endowed with free choice to render them efficacious or inefficacious with respect to the works in question.

[11] Zumel, *Commentaria,* q. 22, a. 4, disp. unica, concl. 3, p. 608b.
[12] See Disputation 53, pt. 3, secs. 13–18.

11. *Fifth objection.* Fifth, they argue as follows:[13] "Many things that come to exist could not have existed without being individually predetermined by God's efficacious will. Therefore, a predetermination on God's part has to be acknowledged. The consequence is manifest, while the antecedent is obvious from all those things that occur beyond the common course of the universe, for example, the miraculous calling and conversion of Paul in the very act of persecuting Christ and the Church; the things that befell Joseph when he was looked upon with hatred, when he was tossed naked into the well and sold by his brothers, when he was afterward thrown into jail though innocent, and in the end raised to such great glory—along with the other things that happened to him, especially since in all of them he prefigured Christ.[14] Clearly, none of these things could have occurred without God's special design or without the predetermination of His efficacious will. Another example was the astonishing feat of the two brothers Perez and Zerah, who during their delivery at birth acted in such a way that the one put his hand out first, at which moment the midwife tied a scarlet thread to it and said, 'This one will be born first'; but when the first brother had drawn back his hand, the other one came out.[15] We can say the same thing about Esau and Jacob, when the younger was chosen in preference to the elder, and when, not because of their works but because of the one who was doing the calling, it was said, 'For the elder will serve the younger.'[16] And the same thing holds for many other similar occurrences."

12. *Response.* As far as this argument is concerned, the antecedent should be conceded not only for those things that are accomplished by God *miraculously* beyond the common course of the universe, but also for those things that are done *directly by God alone*—at least in the measure to which they have God alone as the source of their contingency, as was explained at the beginning of the preceding part.[17] For with respect to things of this sort we countenance predeterminations via God's efficacious will and via an efficacious concurrence on God's part for producing them, as was said in the same place. Thus, if the consequent has to do only with the predetermination of things of this sort, then the consequence should also be conceded; but if it *also* has to do with the same

---

[13]Zumel, *Commentaria*, q. 22, a. 4, disp. unica, concl. 2, p. 607b.

[14]The story of Paul's conversion is recounted at Acts 9:1–19, 22:3–16, and 26:2–18. The story of Joseph occupies the last fourteen chapters of the Book of Genesis (37–50).

[15]Gen. 38:27–30.

[16]The relevant biblical passages are Gen. 25:23 and Rom. 9:10–13, where St. Paul remarks that the election of Jacob over Esau was God's doing alone and thus not the result of Jacob's merits.

[17]See Disputation 53, pt. 3, secs. 1–4.

kind of predetermination of the things that depend on the created
faculty of choice or of those other things to the extent that they depend
for their subject or for something else on the created faculty of choice (in
the sense explained in the preceding part), then the consequence should
be denied.[18] As for the examples by which the antecedent is supported,
it should be said with regard to the first one that (i) the miraculous
calling of Paul, both external and internal, was indeed predetermined by
God via His efficacious will and concurrence, and yet that (ii) Paul's
consent to this same calling and thus Paul's conversion, to the extent that
it depended on his free consent, were *not* predetermined in that way, as
will be obvious from the response to the next objection. As for the
second example, it should be said that Joseph's dreams, as well as the
other aids by which God specially assisted the occurrence of many of the
things that happened to Joseph, were indeed predetermined by God in
the manner in question; however, his brothers' hatred and persecution
of him, his being thrown into the well, his being sold, the false testimony
of Potiphar's wife, and her tempting him into adultery—these things,
since they were mortal sins, were not predetermined by God in the way
in question, as those with whom we disagree themselves admit. Rather,
since God foresaw that because of the wickedness of the brothers and of
Potiphar's wife these things would occur on the hypothesis that He
should for His part will to establish that whole order of things and
circumstances, He decided only to *permit* them. Again, the remaining,
nonevil things that happened to Joseph, to the extent that they depended on the created faculty of choice, were predetermined by God
not in the manner claimed by the authors with whom we disagree, but
rather in the manner we explicated in the preceding part. As for the
third example, the things that happened miraculously in that instance
were predetermined by God in the way in question. Likewise, the internal movement by which the midwife seems to have been induced by God
to tie the scarlet thread on the one who put his hand out first, seems to
have been predetermined by God.[19] Concerning the fourth example,
the eternal preference or election by which Jacob was chosen over Esau
came from God's free will alone. But even though the election was not
based on foreseen works, still it was not made without foreknowledge of
the works that were going to occur through the faculty of choice of both

[18] Ibid. To use Molina's example, God's internal calling of Paul presupposed the existence of Paul as the metaphysical subject of the change that God was bringing about in
him; yet Paul's existence depended on a multitude of previous free human choices.
[19] By an "internal movement" (Latin: *motio interna*) Molina means a movement of the will
by God.

men, given the relevant order of things, circumstances, and aids.[20] Now, among the things that occurred in the carrying out of that election, some were predetermined by God in the manner claimed by the authors with whom we disagree, and the rest were predetermined in the manner we explicated in the preceding part—just as was said above about the other examples.

13. *Sixth objection.* They argue, sixth, as follows:[21] "The conversions of Paul, of Mary Magdalene, and of the thief hanging on the cross were all accomplished through God's intrinsically efficacious concurrence or assistance, and they were predetermined by God from eternity to occur by means of such assistance; and the free choice of Paul, Magdalene, and the thief consented to predeterminations of this sort. Therefore, predeterminations via God's intrinsically efficacious concurrence have to be countenanced, and at the same time it must be admitted that this concurrence is in no way prejudicial to our freedom of choice."

14. *Response.* As far as this argument is concerned, it should be denied that the conversions in question were accomplished through an assistance on God's part that was intrinsically efficacious in such a way that the faculties of choice of Paul, Magdalene, and the thief, having once been overtaken and moved and stirred by that most powerful assistance, did not have the power not to consent despite such assistance. This denial is in keeping with what the Council of Trent decreed, without any exceptions, about the assistance of grace in the conversion of sinners.[22] Thus, it was up to the free will of Paul, Magdalene, and the thief whether or not it was going to follow from that assistance that their faculties of choice would be moved to consent to or to cooperate with that same assistance in order to bring about contrition and conversion,

---

[20]Though Molina affirms the orthodox belief that God's election of Jacob over Esau is not based on or caused by Jacob's good works or merits, he nonetheless insists that God chose Jacob only with full (middle) knowledge of how Jacob would freely respond under the hypothesis that he should be chosen and given the various graces in question. Molina is trying to avoid the position according to which God first chose Jacob over Esau and only afterward (in our way of conceiving it) predetermined Jacob's positive response to that election. On Molina's own account, by contrast, God chose Jacob as one who would respond freely in such-and-such a way to such-and-such graces. This is the key to Molina's understanding of the doctrines of predestination and reprobation. See esp. *Concordia,* q. 23, a. 4 and 5, disp. 1, pt. 11 (Rabeneck, pp. 539–563).

[21]Zumel, *Commentaria,* q. 14, a. 1, disp. unica, concl. 3, p. 363a–b; and q. 23, a. 3, disp. 8, prop. 3, p. 679b.

[22]Council of Trent, sess. 6, chap. 5 and canon 4 (in Denzinger, 1525, p. 370, and 1554, p. 378).

and thus whether or not that assistance was going to be efficacious for this purpose. For they had it within their power to render the assistance inefficacious by not consenting to it and by not cooperating with it, if they should so choose.

Now, in order that you might understand this better, notice that nothing less than the clear vision of God necessitates the will with regard to the exercise of an act;[23] rather, the will always remains free instead to exercise or not to exercise the act, though the greater the good perceived in the object and the more the will is drawn to it and the less resistance it offers to it, the more easily and more frequently the will by its own freedom is wont to determine itself to a desire or act regarding such an object—always, however, with the freedom to refrain from the act, since there is nothing that necessitates it as far as the exercise of the act is concerned. And this is the freedom that suffices for merit, as long as the act is morally good in itself and is elicited by someone in the state of grace. Now, when a human being is addicted to the things of this world, then the greater the temporal good proffered to him and the less the difficulty involved in obtaining it, the more easily and frequently he is wont to elicit a volition for it *without any hesitation*. Thus, no prudent person doubts that if he were offered many thousands in gold, to be had for free, or if he were offered a kingdom or control of the world, he would immediately elicit a volition; and yet he would elicit it *freely* as far as its exercise is concerned, so that if his striving after the object in question involved at least a venial sin, he would truly sin—which would not be true if he were unable to refrain from the act. In exactly the same way, a sinner can be internally illuminated by God with so great a light to acknowledge his own wicked deeds and the penalties they impose on him and ultimately the goodness of God and the ingratitude shown Him, and the sinner's will (including its sentient part) can be imbued with so great a rapture and delight and so stirred toward contrition and love that we must unreservedly believe that he would unhesitatingly elicit his consent; and yet he would always have the freedom to refrain from doing this if he so willed—even though he would rarely or never withhold his consent in the face of so great an illumination and such powerful assistance, especially if there was at the same time some *external* sign inducing him to the same act, as, for example, the heavenly light's surrounding Paul, and his falling to the ground, and Christ's appearing to him and saying, "Saul, Saul, why do you persecute me? It is hard for

---

[23]That is, no human being can reject God if he or she has a clear and immediate cognition of God. Molina later alludes to the fact that the blessed in heaven, given their beatific vision of God, are not free to reject God or to sin against Him.

you to kick against the goad" [Acts 9:4–5]. Now, the conversions of Paul, Magdalene, and the thief on the cross were, it appears, of just this type. We should not, however, use the example of these three people as a measure of those other conversions that occur daily in the Church through ordinary assistance and with far greater difficulty on the part of the people who are converted. What's more, assuming equal assistance on God's part, the conversions of Paul, Magdalene, and the thief could have been more or less intense, if their faculties of choice had cooperated more or less intensely with God's assistance. This is what Christ seems to have been praising in Magdalene when he said, "Many sins are forgiven her, because she has loved much" [Luke 7:47]. Also, notice that, as we showed in Part I–II, question 10, no particular object is necessarily desired in this life, as regards the species of the act, with such a pervasive necessity that it cannot sometimes (even if rarely) be rejected through a negative volition because of some evil that is able to be conjoined to it.[24] Therefore, despite the assistance in question, it was within the power of Paul, Magdalene, and the thief to will not to be converted—and this because of the great difficulty involved in keeping themselves free from mortal sin throughout their entire lives, as they had to resolve to do in order for there to be genuine contrition, even if a mortal sin would very rarely or never occur in the face of assistance of such a quality and quantity. So it follows that even in these conversions the decree of the Council of Trent has a place, when it states that a human being's faculty of choice, though moved and stirred by God toward justification through the assistance of His grace, is able to dissent if it so chooses.[25]

15. *Seventh objection.* They argue, seventh, as follows:[26] "Each of the meritorious acts of the Most Blessed Virgin and of the others who were *confirmed* in grace—especially those acts by which they fulfilled precepts and those acts that they were obliged to elicit under pain of mortal guilt or loss of grace—each of those acts was predetermined by God through an intrinsically efficacious concurrence or assistance.[27] Nor did this

---

[24]Molina's commentary on Part I–II of Aquinas's *Summa Theologiae*, a commentary that dates from 1568–70, is found in manuscript form in the National Library at Lisbon, Fundo Geral cod. 2804.

[25]Council of Trent, sess. 6, canon 4 (in Denzinger, 1554, p. 378).

[26]Zumel, *Commentaria*, q. 14, a. 1, disp. unica, concl. 3, p. 363b; q. 19, a. 8, disp. 1, concl. 4, p. 562b; and q. 23, a. 3, disp. 8, prop. 1, p. 676a.

[27]A person S is confirmed in grace at a time *t* if and only if (i) S is in the state of grace at *t* and (ii) S will always be in the state of grace (and hence will never fall into *mortal* sin) after *t*. According to Catholic doctrine, the Blessed Virgin was not only confirmed in grace from the time of her conception but, in addition, avoided even *venial* sin throughout her life.

detract from the freedom of those acts, since even though these people were not able in the *composed sense* not to elicit the acts (because it involves a contradiction for someone to be confirmed in grace and yet not to elicit an act that he is obliged to elicit under pain of mortal guilt), still, in order for them to be said to have elicited the acts freely and in order for them to be able to gain merit by those acts, it is sufficient that they were able in the *divided sense* not to elicit them. Therefore, predeterminations via God's intrinsically efficacious concurrence have to be countenanced. Nor is freedom of choice impaired by the fact that, as long as such a predetermination is in force, the predetermined act is not able in the *composed sense* not to be elicited; for it is sufficient that the act be able in the *divided sense* not to be elicited."

16. *Response.* As far as this argument is concerned, even though it should be conceded that the acts in question were predetermined in the sense we explicated in the preceding part, it should nonetheless be denied that they were predetermined through an intrinsically efficacious assistance, as the argument claims. For despite God's concurrence and the assistance of grace, it was always within the power of the Blessed Virgin and of the others confirmed in grace not to elicit those acts, and it was always within their power to render such assistance or concurrence fruitless—even at the moment at which they elicited the acts and even under the influence of the assistance by which they elicited them; otherwise, they would not have gained merit by means of the acts elicited at that moment or under the influence of that assistance. Nor should the Blessed Virgin and the others confirmed in grace be denied the honor, among other things, of the just man who "could have sinned and yet did not sin, who could have done evil deeds and yet did not" [Ecclus. 31:10].

Now, confirmation in grace involves God's deciding to confer on someone, during the entire course of his life, grace and assistance by which He foresaw that the person in question would never fall by his freedom into mortal sin, even though he was able so to fall despite that grace and assistance. It also involves God's making it manifest that He has decided to protect the person in this way. Likewise, for the Blessed Virgin to be preserved from *every* sin, even venial sin, is nothing other than for God to bestow on her and to have decided from eternity to bestow on her, during the entire course of her life, grace and gifts and aids by which He foresaw that she would not fall by her freedom even into venial sin—though, despite those same aids and gifts, she could fall by that same freedom if she so willed. And so God's certitude that a person confirmed in grace will not sin mortally or thus fall out of grace for the whole course of his life from the point at which he is said to be confirmed in grace—this certitude is traced back to the certitude of the divine foreknowledge by which He foresaw that this would happen, given the grace and aids in question, because of the freedom of choice of the person so confirmed; and it is *not* traced back to an intrinsic efficacy on the part of the divine assistance—as though it were not the case that the person in question was able to fall into mortal sin despite that assistance, and as though the question of whether or not that assistance would be efficacious for that effect did not depend on the innate freedom of the person so confirmed in grace to will or to refuse to cooperate with or consent to that assistance. Therefore, the fact that St. Peter, from the day of Pentecost onward, fell under the concept of a human being confirmed in grace depended both on the fact that (i) God willed to confer on him the plenitude of grace and assistance which He had decided from eternity to confer on him from that time onward, and also on the fact that (ii) God foresaw that St. Peter, given the grace and assistance in question, would not in his freedom lapse into mortal sin for the rest of his life. But it was not because God foreknew this second fact that it was going to obtain; to the contrary, it was foreknown because it was going to obtain by virtue of the freedom of St. Peter as fortified by those gifts. Clearly, therefore, the fact that one confirmed in grace is not able in the composed sense not to fulfill the precepts that bind under pain of mortal guilt does not take away any freedom at all from the one confirmed in grace; thus, such a person is able not to fulfill those precepts if he so chooses. For if one of those precepts were such that he was not going to fulfill it, as indeed is possible despite the divine foreknowledge in question, then such foreknowledge would never have existed in God; and thus St. Peter did not fall under the concept of one confirmed in grace simply by virtue of the fact that God had decided from eternity to confer on him that plenitude of grace and those aids.

17. *Eighth objection.* Last, they argue as follows:[28] "The acts of Christ the Lord were predetermined by God through intrinsically efficacious assistance, especially that act by which he fulfilled the Father's command concerning the redemption of the human race by his own death. For Christ, since he was at the same time God, was in no way able to sin, and hence was not able not to elicit the act by which he was to fulfill that command. And yet he elicited that act freely; otherwise, he would not have merited anything by it, and, consequently, he would not have redeemed the human race by it—which is heretical. Therefore, the necessity in the *composed sense* of eliciting some act—whether because the

[28]See n. 26 above.

act is predetermined via efficacious concurrence, or because through it a command is fulfilled and it is elicited by someone who, since he is at the same time God and man, is in no way able to sin—this necessity does not absolutely destroy either the act's freedom or its merit. For it is enough that the act should be free in the *divided sense,* as it was in the case of Christ. It follows from this that predeterminations via intrinsically efficacious assistance should not be ruled out on the grounds that they take away freedom from the acts, since it is sufficient for freedom that a predetermined act be able in the *divided sense* not to be elicited, as has to be affirmed of that act of Christ's."

18. *Response.* This argument forces us to explain, outside its proper place, (i) in what sense it involved a contradiction for Christ to sin while he was a wayfarer, and (ii) how it was that he had during that same time the freedom to fail to perform an act whose omission would have been blameworthy in Christ, and thus (iii) how he gained merit both by fulfilling the rest of the commands, according to John 15:10, ". . . just as I too have observed the commandments of my Father, and I remain in His love," and also by fulfilling in particular the command of the Father having to do with the death he had to undergo for the redemption of the human race, according to John 10:18, where he says of his death, "This commandment I have received from my Father," and according to John 14:31, where he says of his passion and death, "I do as my Father has commanded me; arise, let us go," and according to Philippians 2:8, "He humbled himself, becoming obedient unto death, even to the death of the cross," and according to Hebrews 5:8, "Though he was the Son of God, he learned obedience from the things that he suffered."

19. Now, in order that this might be understood better, it should be noted that what is owed to the human nature assumed by the Word by reason of the assumption or grace of union is far different from what belongs to it because of the mere assumption, excluding all the other gifts that are owed to it by reason of the grace of union.[29] For the Word *as Word* has no causal effect at all on the assumed human nature, but instead merely terminates the dependence of that nature without any

---

[29]Molina is here trying to establish some conceptual space between what follows as a matter of *metaphysical necessity* from the fact that a human nature is assumed by a divine person and what follows as a matter of what might be called *natural propriety* from such an assumption. He will argue below that some gifts that follow from the grace of union by a quasi-natural necessity or propriety can be and are miraculously withheld from Christ before his death, and this allows Christ to have genuine freedom to obey or disobey, through the operations of his human nature, the commands of his Father.

causality at all; whereas the hypostatic union has as its efficient cause the *whole Trinity* as one God, through a causal influence on the humanity by which the humanity's very own *esse* is supernaturally conferred on it—though with a dependence on the suppositum of the Word, which is why the humanity is united to the divine Word.[30] Thus, clearly, the assumed nature has no powers, *just* by virtue of this union, over and beyond those it would have if, left to itself, it were to subsist on its own or in its own proper suppositum.

20. For in the sacrament of the altar, at the moment of time at which the transubstantiation of the bread into the Body of Christ takes place, the accidents that were in the substance of the bread come to exist in themselves through the supernatural influence of the whole Trinity—not in the sense that the accidents acquire a new *esse*, but rather in the sense that the very same *esse* now becomes independent of a subject, in a way surpassing the nature of the accidents, through a new causal influence in the genus of efficient causality, an influence by which (i) the accidents are actualized in themselves and (ii) the material causality of the subject, a causality otherwise necessary for the accidents to exist, is replaced and compensated for. In the same way, since an individual human nature is intrinsically such that it subsists in itself and is a suppositum if left to itself, so that it requires nothing else to support and sustain it, clearly it surpasses its nature that it should, through a new influence on it by the whole Trinity, be made dependent on the distinct suppositum of the Word, to which it is united in the sense of existing in it and being sustained by it; nonetheless, it becomes dependent in this manner not because the Trinity confers a different *esse* on it by means of that influence, but rather because it confers the very same *esse*, which is now made weaker in itself, as it were, so that it requires a distinct suppositum by which it might be sustained in a far more felicitous and dignified way than it would be if it subsisted in itself or in its own proper suppositum.[31]

[30] In every other case an individual human nature is itself a suppositum or ultimate subject of characteristics. In the case of Christ, however, the Word (that is, the Second Person of the Blessed Trinity) is the suppositum for the assumed human nature. St. Thomas elucidates this point by claiming that the assumed nature lacks its own proper substantival *esse* or being. Molina's somewhat different elucidation makes use of the distinction between a thing's *esse* being dependent on something distinct from it and that same *esse*'s being independent of any other thing. For more on the metaphysics of the Incarnation, along with references to pertinent medieval texts, see my "Logic, Ontology and Ockham's Christology," *New Scholasticism* 57 (1983): 293–330, and "Human Nature, Potency and the Incarnation," *Faith and Philosophy* 3 (1986): 27–53.

[31] Molina assumes that each entity has its own *esse* or being and that this being is neither *intrinsically* independent nor *intrinsically* dependent, but can instead be made either inde-

21. From this it will now be easy to see that (i) the human nature, to be sure, acquires the grace of union as a result of its assumption by the divine Word, that is, it has the Word as its suppositum, but that (ii) just as the human nature by that very fact imparts to the Word the being of this man who is at the same time truly God, so in turn it receives from the Word an infinite dignity by reason of which the works performed through it are of infinite merit and glory. But even though the human nature acquires this grace of union through the assumption, and even though this grace is the source and origin of the fact that the human nature is owed all the gifts that befit a man who is at the same time the only begotten of the Father, still, if we prescind from the gifts, the nature does not have greater powers than it would have were it left to itself to subsist in itself or in its own proper suppositum. Therefore, just as, despite the assumption, it would be able to die were it left to its own nature, as it died in Christ, and just as it would be able to suffer the rest of the tribulations and miseries that other mortals suffer, so too it would be able to have the natural movements of sensuality, as well as the intense emotions and the rebellions against reason that others experience (more or less, depending on the sort of temperament with which it had been endowed); and it would also have natural freedom of choice, by which it would be able to resist and to consent, just as if it subsisted in itself or in its own proper suppositum. Thus, just as (i) the human nature in Christ stands in need of the light of glory in order to see the divine essence and in order for its soul to be beatified, and just as (ii) the human nature also needs the glory of the body, or the gifts that flow from the glory of the soul over into the body from the moment of the resurrection onward, in order to be immortal and impassible and in order to have the rest of the characteristics that belong to glorified bodies, so too in order for the intense emotions and movements against reason not to have risen up against reason in its sentient part while it was still a wayfarer, that nature needed a plenitude of habitual grace and virtues, and it needed gifts such as original justice in its sentient part—gifts by which that sentient part might be restrained and kept within the bounds of duty.[32] And the same holds for the other gifts required for other functions and ends.

---

pendent or dependent by divine fiat. In the Eucharist the sensible accidents of the bread and wine first have *dependent* being of the sort characteristic of accidents and then by a special act of God miraculously come to have *independent* being, since after the consecration of the bread and wine there is no longer any subject or suppositum for them to inhere in. In the Incarnation an individual human nature, which would have had *independent* being if left to itself, comes to have that very same being as *dependent* instead.

[32]The "glory of the soul" is the immediate effect of the soul's beatific vision of God. Molina's claim here is that neither this glory nor the resultant glory of the body follows by

22. Finally, observe that even though by reason of the grace of union all those things were owed to Christ or to his humanity that he had *after* the Resurrection, nonetheless, since (i) the Incarnation was by the same token arranged by God in order that Christ might by his merits and death redeem the human race, and in order that by his most holy and perfect life he might furnish mortals with an especially shining example, an example by which they would be instructed in every kind of virtue and perfection, and by which they would be strongly stimulated and impelled toward imitating him, and since (ii) it was more glorious for Christ to gain the glory and exaltation of the body by his own proper merits than for him to have had this glory immediately from the very beginning, it follows that even though from the moment of his conception, when the Holy Spirit fashioned that most sacred body in the womb of the Virgin, he acquired an absolutely perfect constitution, and even though his soul saw the divine essence, and even though the whole of Christ, body and soul, was filled with those habits and gifts that did not conflict with the purposes of the Incarnation explained above or with his status of being simultaneously a wayfarer and a comprehender of the divine essence, nonetheless he did not receive the glory of the body until the Resurrection. Nor was it just this bodily glory that God miraculously prevented from arising out of the glory of the soul; but at the same time the vision of the divine essence, along with the beatific love and enjoyment, was also communicated by God to the human nature in such a way that by preventing (in a manner surpassing the nature of these goods) the effects that ought to have resulted from them by a necessity of nature, He left Christ's will susceptible to anguish and sadness and hence free to fulfill or not to fulfill the precepts that bound him under pain of guilt—just as if the glory of the soul had not existed in Christ. For it was necessary that this be so in order that he might be able to gain merit and redeem the human race by his most innocent life and death, and in order that he might be able to bequeath to mortals with such great honor and glory the especially shining example of his life and to attain the glory and exaltation of the body. In fact, the dual status of wayfarer and comprehender is attributed to Christ from the moment of his conception in the womb of the Virgin up to his expiration on the cross

---

metaphysical necessity merely from the human nature's being assumed by a divine person. All that follows is a strong inclination toward such glory, an inclination that may be impeded in the same way that the natural causal inclinations of ordinary material substances may be impeded. The same holds for other gifts, such as "original justice" of the sort that characterized the first parents before their sin. All such gifts and special graces are, to be sure, "owed" to the assumed nature because of their quasi-natural connection to the grace of union. But some of them may be miraculously impeded and withheld for other reasons—and this is what Molina claims to have happened in the case of Christ.

precisely because the glory of the soul was held back in such a way that Christ's will was free to fulfill or not to fulfill the commandments in question, just as if he had not had that glory, but had instead been a mere wayfarer.

23. We may now formulate a response to the objection in accordance with the points just explicated. If Christ is thought of as having those things that are owed to his nature by reason of the grace of union, then it must be claimed that Christ was in no way able to sin—as Augustine affirms in *De Praedestinatione Sanctorum*, chap. 15, in *Enchiridion*, chap. 40, and frequently in other places, and as the rest of the Fathers generally affirm as well.[33] For it was owed to Christ's humanity that it should in no way be permitted by God to sin, and it was altogether abominable and improper that the Word should sin, even through the assumed nature. Therefore, just as it involves a contradiction for God to lie—not, to be sure, because God lacks the power to form those sounds that, if they were uttered, would constitute a lie, but rather because for God to lie is altogether unseemly and incompatible with His infinite goodness—so, too, it involves a contradiction for Christ to sin, not because Christ as a wayfarer lacks the ability to transgress commands, but rather because it is impossible for God to permit it, and because it is incompatible with the infinite goodness of the divine Word that he should sin, even through his assumed nature, and thus that God should permit it. Therefore, it pertained to divine providence to arrange things in such a way that while Christ's freedom was preserved, a freedom required for merit and for the purposes explained above, he would in no way sin; and this is in fact what happened. Hence, it is also the case, in keeping with what was said in response to the last objection, that Christ was not able in the *composed sense* to sin, since he was the most exalted of those confirmed in grace and goodness, having received far more excellent gifts and supports than even his most holy mother. Now in the *composed sense* it involves a contradiction for someone confirmed in grace and goodness to sin—though not in the *divided sense* and absolutely, since if he were going to sin, as he is able to despite the gifts, then (i) God would not foreknow that he was in his freedom not going to sin, given those gifts, and thus (ii) he would not fall under the concept of one confirmed in grace and goodness, as was explained in the response to the preceding argument.

But suppose that Christ is thought of insofar as he was a wayfarer and insofar as the glory of the soul was suspended for the purposes ex-

[33] *PL* 44, 982, and *PL* 40, 252.

plained above, that is, lest that glory take away Christ's freedom to transgress commands in the way that it takes away the freedom of those other beatified persons who are not at the same time wayfarers;[34] and suppose that he is thought of as having submitted to death with the greatest difficulty and grief, and as having performed other laborious and difficult tasks for the salvation of the human race, as is attested to by Luke 12:50, "There is a baptism by which I have to be baptized, and what straits I am in until it is accomplished," and by Matthew 26:37–39, "He began to grow sorrowful and to be sad [Mark 14:33 has: "He began to be fearful and weary"]. And he said to them 'My soul is sorrowful until death. Stay here and keep watch with me.' And he fell on his face praying, and said, 'My Father, if it be possible, let this cup pass from me; still, not as I will, but as You will.'" And his agony and sadness were so great that, as Luke 22:42 says, his sweat "became like drops of blood, trickling down to the ground." The same thing is corroborated by Hebrews 4:15, "For we do not have a high priest who cannot have compassion on our infirmities, but one who in all things was tempted in a similar way [that is, as if he were one of us] without sin," and by Matthew 27:46, "My God, my God why have you forsaken me?" If, I repeat, Christ is thought of in this manner, then clearly, despite the other authorities that were cited above, Christ really did have the freedom not to do those things that he was obligated by precept to do; and yet he was certain that, even though his nature resisted very strongly, he would in his freedom fulfill all those commands as completely and perfectly as possible, and that he would be helped toward this end by the most powerful gifts and aids.

It follows that Christ's death was not only *spontaneous* but also absolutely *free* with the freedom of contradiction or even of contrariety, and at the same time it was commanded of him—nor does the one point conflict with the other. Indeed, Christ taught both of these points at John 10:17–18 when he said, "This is why the Father loves me, because I lay down my life. No one takes it from me, but rather I lay it down by myself. I have the power to lay it down and I have the power to take it up again. This commandment I have received from my Father."

It also follows that Christ's death was especially laborious and difficult, since his nature was horrified by it and resisted it as much as possible, as is clear from the passages already cited and also from Romans 15:3, "For Christ did not please himself, but as it is written, 'The reproaches of those who reproached you fell upon me.'" And yet, because of the gifts

---

[34] Molina refers here to the blessed in heaven, who are no longer free to reject God, since they lack the power to reject Him.

and the assistance by which Christ was supported, and because of the incredible magnitude and fervor of the love that he extended to God and to his neighbors, he was at the same time absolutely willing—this according to Matthew 26:41, "The spirit is willing, but the flesh is weak," and Psalm 18:6, "He has rejoiced, like a giant, to run the course," that is, the task of the passion and death by which he finished the course.

Finally, it follows that Christ's death and his other works were in every way absolutely perfect and complete, the sort of works that were fitting for a redeemer, both as far as our advantage and example are concerned and as regards his own highest (in both quality and quantity) praise and honor.

24.   Therefore, as far as the form of the argument is concerned, it should be denied that Christ's acts—even that act by which he fulfilled the Father's command regarding the redemption of the human race by his death—were predetermined by God through intrinsically efficacious assistance, as though in the presence of this assistance Christ did not have the power not to elicit those acts despite such assistance; for this would be to take away Christ's freedom at the moment of time at which he elicited those acts, and hence to take away their merit.

As for the proof, it has already been explained that it is not because of the efficacy of the assistance but rather because of those other two things that Christ was not able in the *composed sense* to sin and hence not able in the *composed sense* not to elicit those acts;[35] and this does not deprive Christ of his freedom in the *divided sense* or *absolutely,* with the result that he was able not to elicit those acts at the very moment at which he elicited them.

Now, from what has been said it is sufficiently clear that the rest of the things added in the argument do not prove that divine predeterminations via efficacious assistance have to be countenanced, since assistance of this sort absolutely deprives the faculty of choice of the one on whom it is bestowed of its freedom at the moment at which it elicits the act.

Nor is it the case that a divided sense of the sort intended by those who posit such predeterminations leaves intact the freedom of a faculty of choice which is aided by intrinsically efficacious assistance. Rather, such a divided sense merely places in *God* the freedom to confer or not to confer such assistance, and thus the freedom to bring it about that the

---

[35]The two things referred to here seem to be (i) God's being unable to permit Christ to sin and (ii) its being incompatible with the infinite goodness of the divine Word that he should sin even through the operations of his human nature. But it may be that Molina is counting (i) and (ii) together as one thing and that the second thing is the fact that Christ is confirmed in grace, indeed is the most illustrious of those who are confirmed in grace.

faculty of choice elicits or does not elicit such an act, as was explained above; but this is not so with that divided sense that stands opposed to the composed sense in which Christ, because of the other two grounds, was not able to sin or to desist from eliciting an act to which he was obliged by a commandment, as we have explained.[36]

[36]See n. 35 on the two grounds referred to here. One general comment on Molina's discussion of Christ's freedom to sin: Although I have not treated this topic in the Introduction and am not entirely comfortable with Molina's stated views, I am convinced that what Molina says here is worth taking seriously, both philosophically (because of its implications for the analysis of freedom) and theologically (because it addresses in a creative and yet straightforward fashion one of the thorniest problems of traditional Christology). I hope to discuss Molina's treatment of this problem in more depth elsewhere.

BIBLIOGRAPHY

Works from the Patristic Era Cited by Molina in Part IV

Ambrose, Saint. *De Excessu Fratris Sui Satyri*, book 1.
——. *Enarratio in 12 Psalmos Davidicos*, Psalms 40 and 45.
——. *Epistola 38*.
Augustine of Hippo, Saint. *De Civitate Dei*, book 5, chaps. 9 and 10.
——. *De Correptione et Gratia*, chap. 7.
——. *De Libero Arbitrio*, book 3, chaps. 3, 4, and 10.
——. *De Praedestinatione Sanctorum*, chap. 14.
——. *Epistolae* 105 and 107.
——. *Hypognosticon*, book 6.
——. *Quaestiones ad Simplicianum*, book 1, q. 2.
Cyprian, Saint. *Ad Quirinum*, book 3, chap. 58.
——. *De Mortalitate*, chap. 23.
Cyril of Alexandria, Saint. *In Iohannem* 13:18.
——. *Thesaurus*, assertion 15.
Fulgentius of Ruppe. *De Fide ad Petrum*, chap. 35.
Jerome, Saint. *Dialogus adversus Pelagianos*, book 3.
——. *In Ezechielem*, book 1.
——. *In Isaiam*, book 5.
——. *In Ieremiam*, book 5.
John Chrysostom, Saint. *In Matthaeum*, homily 59.
John Damascene, Saint. *Dialogus adversus Manichaeos*, no. 37.
Justin Martyr, Saint. *Expositiones Quaestionum a Gentibus Christianis Propositarum*,
    q. 58.
——. *Responsiones ad Christianos de Quibusdam Quaestionibus Necessariis*, q. 8.
Origen. *In Epistolam ad Roman*, book 7.
Pelagius. *Expositiones in XIII Epistolas Sancti Pauli: In Ephesios*, chap. 1.
Pope St. Leo I. *Sermo 67*.
Tertullian. *Adversus Marcionem*, book 2.

Other Works Cited by Molina in Part IV

Aquinas, Saint Thomas. *De Veritate*, q. 2, a. 12; q. 6, a. 3.
——. *Summa Contra Gentiles* I, chap. 67.
——. *Summa Theologiae* I, q. 14, a. 8 and 13.
Aureoli, Peter. *Commentaria in Primum Librum Sententiarum*, dist. 38 and 39.
Auxerre, William of (Altissiodorensis). *Summa Aurea in Quattuor Libros Sententiarum*, book 1, chap. 12.
Bañez, Domingo. *Scholastica Commentaria in Primam Partem Summae Theologicae S. Thomae Aquinatis*, q. 14, a. 13.
Biel, Gabriel. *Epithoma Pariter et Collectorium Circa Quattuor Libros Sententiarum*, book 1, dist. 38.
Boethius. *De Consolatione Philosophiae*, book 5, last prose.
Bonaventure, Saint. *Commentaria in Quattuor Libros Sententiarum*, book 1, dist. 39 and 40.
Cajetan (Tommaso de Vio). *Commentaria in Sancti Thomae Summam Theologiam*, I, q. 14, a. 13.
Capreolus, Johannes. *Libri Defensiorum Theologiae Divi Thomae Aquinatis*, book 1, dist. 36 and 38.
Carthusianus, Dionysius. *Enarratio in Librum Sapientia*, chap. 4.
Cordubensis, Antonius. *Quaestiones Theologicae*, book 1, q. 55.
Deza, Didacus de (Hispalensis). *Novarum Defensionum Doctrinae Angelici Doctoris Beati Thomae de Aquino super Primum Librum Sententiarum.*
Driedo, Johannes. *De Concordia Liberi Arbitrii et Praedestinationis*, chaps. 2 and 3.
Duns Scotus, John. *Commentaria Oxoniensia ad Quattuor Libros Sententiarum*, book 1, dist. 39–41; book 3, dist. 7.
Durandus, William. *In Sententias Theologicas Petri Lombardi Commentariorum Libri Quattuor*, book 1, dist. 38.
Ferrariensis, Francisco Sylvestri. *Commentaria in Quattuor Libros Divi Thomae Contra Gentiles*, book 1, chap. 66 and 67.
Jansen, Cornelius (Gandavensis). *Annotationes in Librum Sapientiae*, chap. 4.
Leo IX, Saint. *Epistola ad Petrum Antiochenum.*
Lyra, Nicholas of (Lyranus). *Postillae Perpetuae, sive Brevia Commentaria in Universa Biblica, In Sapientiam*, chap. 4.
Middleton, Richard of. *Quaestiones Quodlibetales*, quodlibet 3, q. 1.
——. *Super Quattuor Libros Sententiarum Quaestiones*, book 1, dist. 38.
Molina, Luis de. *Commentaria in Primam Divae Thomae Partem.*
——. Unpublished lectures on Aristotle's *Organon*. Manuscript (Library of Evora, cod. 118-1-6).
——. Unpublished lectures on Part I–II of the *Summa Theologiae*. Manuscript (National Library at Lisbon, F.G. 2804).
Natalis, Hervaeus. *In Quattuor Libros Sententiarum Commentaria*, book 1, dist. 36.
Ockham, William of. *Super Quattuor Libros Sententiarum Annotationes*, book 1, dist. 38.
Pigge, Albertus (Pighius). *De Libero Hominis Arbitrio et Divina Gratia*, book 8.
Porrée, Gilbert de la. *Commentaria in Boethii De Trinitate*, book 1, chap. 9.

Prieras, Sylvestro Mazzolini. *Conflatus ex Sancto Thomae,* q. 14, a. 16 and 19.
Rimini, Gregory of. *Lectura in Libros 1 et 2 Sententiarum,* book 1, dist. 38 and 42.
Vega, Andreas à. *Tridentini Decreti de Justificatione Expositio et Defensio Libris XV Distincta,* book 2, chap. 17; book 12, chap. 22.
Zumel, Francisco. *In Primam Divae Thomae Partem Commentaria,* q. 14, a. 1 and 13; q. 19, a. 8; q. 22, a. 4; q. 23, a. 3.

Other Works Cited in Introduction and Notes to Translation

Adams, Marilyn McCord. "Is the Existence of God a 'Hard' Fact?" *Philosophical Review* 76 (1967): 492–503.
Adams, Marilyn McCord, and Norman Kretzmann, trans. *William Ockham: Predestination, God's Foreknowledge and Future Contingents.* 2d ed. Indianapolis, Ind., 1983.
Adams, Robert M. "Alvin Plantinga on the Problem of Evil." In James Tomberlin and Peter Van Inwagen, eds., *Alvin Plantinga* (Dordrecht, Holland, 1985), pp. 225–255.
———. "Middle Knowledge and the Problem of Evil." *American Philosophical Quarterly* 14 (1977): 109–117.
Alluntis, F., O.F.M., and A. B. Wolter, O.F.M., trans. *John Duns Scotus: God and Creatures.* Princeton, N.J., 1975.
Aquinas, Saint Thomas. *De Malo,* q. 14, a. 1–5; q. 16, a. 1–6.
———. *De Potentia,* q. 3, a. 7.
———. *De Veritate,* q. 1, a. 2; q. 2, a. 3 and 14; q. 4, a. 5; q. 5, a. 1–10; q. 19, a. 8.
———. *Summa Contra Gentiles* I, chap. 65; II, chap. 24; III, chaps. 66–70.
———. *Summa Theologiae* I, q. 14, a. 5, 8, 13, and 16; q. 22, a. 1–4; q. 103, a. 1–8; I–II, q. 6, a. 1–2.
Billot, Louis, S.J. *De Deo Uno et Trino.* Rome, 1926.
Bilynskyj, Stephen. "God, Nature and the Concept of Miracle." Ph.D. diss., University of Notre Dame, 1982.
Brodrick, James, S.J. *Robert Bellarmine: Saint and Scholar.* London, 1961.
Burrell, David, C.S.C. "God's Eternity." *Faith and Philosophy* 1 (1984): 389–406.
Cahill, John, O.P. *The Development of the Theological Censures after the Council of Trent (1563–1709).* Fribourg, Switzerland, 1955.
Davis, Stephen. *Logic and the Nature of God.* Grand Rapids, Mich., 1983.
Denzinger, H., and A. Schönmetzer, eds. *Enchiridion Symbolorum.* 32d ed. Freiburg, 1963.
Donagan, Alan. "Thomas Aquinas on Human Action." In Norman Kretzmann, Anthony Kenny, and Jan Pinborg, eds., *The Cambridge History of Later Medieval Philosophy* (New York, 1982), pp. 642–654.
Dummett, Michael. *Truth and Other Enigmas.* Cambridge, Mass., 1978.
Edidin, Aron, and Calvin Normore. "Ockham on Prophecy." *International Journal for the Philosophy of Religion* 13 (1982): 179–189.
Farrelly, Dom M. John, O.S.B. *Predestination, Grace and Free Will.* Westminster, Md., 1964.

Fischer, John Martin. "Freedom and Foreknowledge." *Philosophical Review* 92 (1983): 67–79.
——. "Hard-Type Soft Facts." *Philosophical Review* 95 (1986): 591–601.
——. "Ockhamism." *Philosophical Review* 94 (1985): 81–100.
——. "Responsibility and Control." *Journal of Philosophy* 79 (1982): 24–40.
Flint, Thomas P. "Hasker's 'Refutation' of Middle Knowledge." Unpublished manuscript.
——. "The Problem of Divine Freedom." *American Philosophical Quarterly* 20 (1983): 255–264.
Flint, Thomas P., and Alfred J. Freddoso. "Maximal Power." In Alfred J. Freddoso, ed., *The Existence and Nature of God* (Notre Dame, Ind., 1983), pp. 81–113.
Frankfurt, Harry. "Alternate Possibilities and Moral Responsibility." *Journal of Philosophy* 66 (1969): 829–839.
Freddoso, Alfred J. "Accidental Necessity and Logical Determinism." *Journal of Philosophy* 80 (1983): 257–278.
——. "Accidental Necessity and Power over the Past." *Pacific Philosophical Quarterly* 63 (1982): 54–68.
——. "Human Nature, Potency and the Incarnation." *Faith and Philosophy* 3 (1986): 27–53.
——. "Logic, Ontology and Ockham's Christology." *New Scholasticism* 57 (1983): 293–330.
——. "Medieval Aristotelianism and the Case Against Secondary Causation in Nature." In Thomas V. Morris, ed., *Divine and Human Action: Essays in the Metaphysics of Theism* (Ithaca, 1988).
——. "The Necessity of Nature." *Midwest Studies in Philosophy* 11 (1986): 215–242.
——. "Ockham's Theory of Truth Conditions." In A. J. Freddoso and H. Schuurman, trans., *Ockham's Theory of Propositions: Part II of the Summa Logicae* (Notre Dame, Ind., 1980), pp. 1–76.
Gál, G., O.F.M., and S. Brown, eds. *Guillelmi de Ockham: Opera Theologica*. Vol. 1, *Ordinatio*. St. Bonaventure, N.Y., 1967.
Garrigou-Lagrange, Reginald, O.P. *God: His Existence and Nature*. St. Louis, 1936.
——. *The One God*. St. Louis, 1943.
Geach, Peter T. *Providence and Evil*. Cambridge, England, 1977.
Geach, Peter T., and G.E.M. Anscombe. *Three Philosophers*. Ithaca, 1961.
Harré, Rom, and Edward Madden. *Causal Powers*. Totowa, N.J., 1975.
Hasker, William. "Foreknowledge and Necessity." *Faith and Philosophy* 2 (1985): 121–157.
——. "The Intelligibility of 'God Is Timeless.'" *New Scholasticism* 57 (1983): 170–195.
——. "A Refutation of Middle Knowledge." *Nous* 20 (1986): 545–557.
Hoffman, Joshua, and Gary Rosenkrantz. "Hard Facts and Soft Facts." *Philosophical Review* 93 (1984): 419–434.

James, William. "The Dilemma of Determinism." In *The Will To Believe and Other Essays in Popular Philosophy* (New York, 1897, 1956), pp. 145–183.

Kenny, Anthony. *The God of the Philosophers.* Oxford, 1979.

Kretzmann, Norman. "Medieval Logicians on the Meaning of 'Propositio.'" *Journal of Philosophy* 67 (1970): 767–787.

——, trans. *Aristotle: Boethius' Translation of De Interpretatione (Perierminias), chap. 9.* Translation Clearing House, Philosophy Department, Oklahoma State University, Stillwater, Okla., 1981.

——, trans. *Averroes: Middle Commentary on Aristotle's De Interpretatione, chap. 9.* Translation Clearing House, Philosophy Department, Oklahoma State University, 1980.

——, trans. *Boethius: First Commentary on Aristotle's De Interpretatione (editio prima), chap. 9.* Translation Clearing House, Philosophy Department, Oklahoma State University, 1980.

——, trans. *Boethius: Second Commentary on Aristotle's De Interpretatione, chap. 9.* Translation Clearing House, Philosophy Department, Oklahoma State University, 1980.

——, trans. *Gersonides: Supercommentary on Averroes on Aristotle's De Interpretatione, chap. 9.* Translation Clearing House, Philosophy Department, Oklahoma State University, 1980.

——, trans. *Peter Abelard: Introductiones Dialecticae: Editio Super Aristotelem De Interpretatione, chap. 9.* Translation Clearing House, Philosophy Department, Oklahoma State University, 1981.

——, trans. *Peter de Rivo: A Proof of Aristotle's Opinion That Neither of the Contradictories Regarding a Future Contingent Is Determinately True, Together with the Refutation of Two Arguments to the Contrary That Have Been Formulated by a Certain Person.* Translation Clearing House, Philosophy Department, Oklahoma State University, 1981.

——, trans. *Peter de Rivo: A Quodlibetal Question on Future Contingents.* Translation Clearing House, Philosophy Department, Oklahoma State University, 1981.

——, trans. *Richard Campsall: Certain Noteworthy Sayings of Master Richard Campsall on Contingency and Foreknowledge.* Translation Clearing House, Philosophy Department, Oklahoma State University, 1981.

——, trans. *Thomas Bradwardine: On Future Contingents.* Translation Clearing House, Philosophy Department, Oklahoma State University, 1981.

——, trans. *Walter Burley: Final Commentary on Aristotle's De Interpretatione, chap. 9.* Translation Clearing House, Philosophy Department, Oklahoma State University, 1981.

Lewis, David. *Counterfactuals.* Oxford, 1973.

Lonergan, Bernard, S.J. *Grace and Freedom.* New York, 1971.

Loux, Michael J. "Towards an Aristotelian Theory of Abstract Objects." *Midwest Studies in Philosophy* 11 (1986): 495–512.

Lucas, J. R. *The Freedom of the Will.* Oxford, 1970.

Maritain, Jacques. *God and the Permission of Evil.* Milwaukee, 1966.

Normore, Calvin. "Divine Omniscience, Omnipotence and Future Contingents:

An Overview." In T. Rudavsky, ed., *Divine Omniscience and Omnipotence in Medieval Philosophy* (Dordrecht, Holland, 1985), pp. 3–22.

———. "Future Contingents." In Norman Kretzmann, Anthony Kenny, and Jan Pinborg, eds., *The Cambridge History of Later Medieval Philosophy* (New York, 1982), pp. 358–381.

Pegis, Anton. "Molina and Human Liberty." In Gerard Smith, S.J., ed., *Jesuit Thinkers of the Renaissance* (Milwaukee, 1939), pp. 75–131.

Plantinga, Alvin. *The Nature of Necessity.* Oxford, 1974.

———. "On Ockham's Way Out." *Faith and Philosophy* 3 (1986): 235–269.

———. "Replies to My Colleagues." In James Tomberlin and Peter van Inwagen, eds., *Alvin Plantinga* (Dordrecht, Holland, 1985), pp. 313–396.

Pontifex, Mark. *Freedom and Providence.* New York, 1960.

Rabeneck, Johann, S.J. "De Vita et Scriptis Ludovici Molina." *Archivum Historicum Societatis Iesu* 19 (1950): 75–145.

———, ed. *Luis de Molina, S.J.: Liberi Arbitrii cum Gratiae Donis, Divina Praescientia, Providentia, Praedestinatione et Reprobatione Concordia.* Oña and Madrid, 1953.

Ross, James. "Creation II." In Alfred J. Freddoso, ed., *The Existence and Nature of God* (Notre Dame, Ind., 1983), pp. 115–141.

Smith, Gerard, S.J. *Freedom in Molina.* Chicago, 1966.

Stalnaker, Robert. "A Theory of Conditionals." In Nicholas Rescher, ed., *Studies in Logical Theory* (Oxford, 1968), pp. 98–112.

Stegmüller, Friedrich. "Neue Molinaschriften." *Beiträge zur Geschichte der Philosophie und Theologie des Mittelalters.* Band 32. Münster, 1935.

Stump, Eleonore, and Norman Kretzmann. "Absolute Simplicity." *Faith and Philosophy* 2 (1985): 353–382.

———. "Eternity." *Journal of Philosophy* 79 (1981): 429–458.

Suarez, Francisco, S.J. *De Divina Gratia,* Part Two. *Opera Omnia,* Vol. 7. Venice, 1741.

———. *De Scientia Quam Deus Habet de Futuris Contingentibus.* In *Opera Omnia,* Vol. 10 (Venice, 1741), pp. 163–208.

Swinburne, Richard. *The Coherence of Theism.* Oxford, 1977.

Urbano, Luis, O.P., ed. *Domingo Bañez, O.P.: Scholastica Commentaria in Primam Partem Summae Theologicae S. Thomae Aquinatis.* Madrid, 1934.

Wey, Joseph, C.S.B., ed. *Guillelmi de Ockham: Opera Theologica.* Vol. 9, *Quodlibeta Septem.* St. Bonaventure, N.Y., 1980.

Wolterstorff, Nicholas. "God Everlasting." In Steven M. Cahn and David Shatz, eds., *Contemporary Philosophy of Religion* (Oxford, 1982), pp. 77–98.

INDEX OF NAMES

[281]

INDEX OF SUBJECTS

Library of Congress Cataloging-in-Publication Data

Molina, Luis de, 1535–1600.
  On divine foreknowledge.

  Translation of: Concordia liberi arbitrii cum gratiae donis. Part 4.
  Bibliography: p.
  Includes indexes.
  1. Providence and government of God—Early works to 1800. 2. Predestina-
tion—Early works to 1800. 3. Free will and determinism—Early works to 1800.
I. Freddoso, Alfred J. II.
BT95.M6513 1988   231'.4   88–3887
ISBN 0–8014–2131–4 (alk. paper)